THIS IS OUR CITY

THIS IS OUR CITY

FOUR TEAMS, TWELVE CHAMPIONSHIPS, AND HOW <u>BOSTON</u> BECAME THE MOST DOMINANT SPORTS CITY IN THE WORLD

TONY MASSAROTTI

ABRAMS PRESS, NEW YORK

For Boston

CONTENTS

	PROLOGUE	1
Chapter 1	THE SEEDS OF A DYNASTY	11
Chapter 2	BURYING THE PAST	45
Chapter 3	A CHANGING OF THE GUARD	70
Chapter 4	HIGHER STANDARDS	88
Chapter 5	THE PERFECT NIGHTMARE	103
Chapter 6	GREEN DAYS	124
Chapter 7	THE PUCK STOPS HERE	138
Chapter 8	BROKEN WINDOWS	170
Chapter 9	MARATHON MONDAY	185
Chapter 10	BOSTON RISES	203
Chapter 11	DARKNESS AND DEFEAT	222
Chapter 12	THE EMPIRE STRIKES BACK	239
Chapter 13	THE C'S RISE . . . THEN FALL	260
Chapter 14	SAME OLD BRUINS	276
Chapter 15	COSTLY MISTAKES	296
Chapter 16	OUT WITH A BANG	321
Chapter 17	STARTING OVER	343
	ACKNOWLEDGMENTS	359
	INDEX	363

PROLOGUE

"To me, Boston always has felt like a neighborhood . . . It's one of the things I love most about playing there. . . . I've invested in Boston during my time there, and I feel like Boston has invested in me."

—longtime Boston Red Sox pitcher Tim Wakefield in his memoir, *Knuckler: My Life with Baseball's Most Confounding Pitch*

IN THE MIDDLE OF IT all, in the heart of Boston and amid a crisis that shook the city and the country to its heels, David Americo Ortiz spoke. He spoke for himself. He spoke for his teammates. And he spoke for fans, neighbors, public servants, and city officials during a time Boston boomed with pride, trembled with fear, celebrated its considerable history, and pondered its suddenly uncertain future.

"These jerseys that we're wearing today, it doesn't say 'Red Sox.' It says 'Boston,'" Ortiz noted just beyond the first baseline at Fenway Park, Boston's kitchen, its core. "We want to thank you—Mayor [Tom] Menino, Governor [Deval] Patrick, the whole police department—for the great job that they did this past week."

And then he said this:

"This is our fucking city—and nobody is going to dictate our freedom."

David Ortiz raised his fist.

"Stay strong," he said.

And then, as if both stunned by Ortiz's unexpected vulgarity and in completely unabashed agreement, a capacity crowd at Fenway Park roared to a crescendo, nodding in approval, clapping furiously. *Did Papi just say what I think he said?* Indeed he did. *Well, amen to that.* Just five days after the Marathon bombings of April 15, 2013, which took three lives, wounded nearly three hundred people, and left sixteen others without limbs, Bostonians were also psychologically scarred, significantly wounded. They were unsure. They were frightened.

They were also mad as hell and looking for something—or, perhaps, someone—to rally around, and they found him in Ortiz, nicknamed Big Papi, the titanic teddy bear around whom the Red Sox had been built for the better part of the twenty-first century.

In all, Ortiz addressed Bostonians for less than forty seconds on that brilliant sun-splashed afternoon of Saturday, April 20, 2013, though his words continue to resonate as if he had delivered the Gettysburg Address. At the start of what would become yet another championship during Boston's dynastic beginning to the new millennium, Ortiz was as qualified as anyone—more so, really—to lead Boston back from tragedy, to preach unity and resolve, to commence the healing. As the designated hitter of the Red Sox, Ortiz was a giant, someone more identifiable to Americans than the mayor or the governor. Born under the red, white, and blue flag of the Dominican Republic, Ortiz had come to Boston from the Minnesota Twins and resurrected his baseball career, put an end to the mythical Curse of the Bambino, and led Boston to two championships (and had the Red Sox on the way to a third).

In the process, Boston had become his home. By 2013, Ortiz was in his eleventh season of a Red Sox career during which he had initially struggled for a foothold, eventually endured, and ultimately succeeded. Boston has never been the kind of place to storm in and sweep people off their feet, after all, and the list of those rejected—particularly athletes—was long and distinguished.

Who are you? Where are you from? What do you want here?

But now? Ortiz was not merely welcomed. He had the right to preach, to rage, to lead. His uniform alone spoke volumes. For home games at Fenway Park, the Red Sox customarily wore their traditional white jerseys and pants trimmed in red piping, with button-up tops, black leather belts, red numbers and letters outlined in blue, the words RED SOX emblazoned on their chests in a familiar, unique font. But on April 20, 2013, as Ortiz succinctly pointed out, the jerseys this time featured BOSTON in all-red letters, with no piping and no trim, an understated style designed to issue the simplest of reminders: that the Red Sox were not merely representatives of their city and its values nor solely ambassadors for those from all six New England states—they were neighbors and fellow taxpayers, too, shoulder to shoulder, arm in arm.

Our city.

This is *our* city.

This is *our fucking city.*

Beyond the acceptance by Bostonians, Ortiz was, of course, the perfect man to cross all barriers. He was bilingual, fiercely competitive, wonderfully engaging, genuinely good-hearted, talented and gritty, relentless but patient, and also imperfect. Along with New England Patriots quarterback Tom Brady and coach Bill Belichick during the city's astonishing run of sports championships to start the millennium, Ortiz had become as synonymous with Boston as Paul Revere and the Old North Church. Brady and Belichick had won three championships by then, Ortiz two. The Celtics and Bruins had won one each. Boston had become, in the arena, the Athens or Rome of American sports, the center of the sports universe, the *Hub.* Boston had defeated Los Angeles. Boston had defeated New York. Boston had defeated Philadelphia and Boston had defeated St. Louis. The Boston Marathon bombings were something altogether different, of course, but Boston believed in David Ortiz. Boston trusted him.

And if Boston believed in him, the country did, too. Nearly twelve years after the terrorist attacks of September 11, 2001, Boston had become the primary target this time, the victim. When Ortiz spoke on this occasion, all of America was listening.

"You get goose bumps [listening to the speech]," Boston mayor Marty Walsh would say years later. "At that point, Mayor Tom Menino was sick and we were all in a state of shock, fear—and Big Papi made a statement about our city. He basically put a stake in the ground, and that helped in the healing process. He was speaking for a lot of people. I don't advocate that athletes use that language, but he certainly drove his point home."

Said Tom Manchester, vice president of field marketing for Dunkin' Donuts, the Boston-based coffee empire for whom Ortiz was a spokesperson: "For me personally when he gave that speech, he could have dropped the F-bomb 10 times and it really wouldn't have mattered to me because I was feeling that way and I think he articulated what all of New England was feeling."

Indeed, for all that transpired in Boston and New England in the years to come, Ortiz's words became a rallying cry for the region, a refrain every bit as familiar as "Boston Strong." Ortiz, for however much it matters, claimed he had no recollection of using profanity and insisted it was never part of his plan, which ultimately made the words all that much more meaningful. Somewhere along the line in American sports, after all, athletes became pitchmen and corporations more than they were people, and they had learned to measure their words carefully. NBA icon and Nike merchandising superstar Michael Jordan, for instance, was often criticized for failing to take a stand on social and racial issues, famously remarking once, "Republicans buy sneakers, too." Longtime Baltimore Orioles shortstop, baseball Hall of Famer, and historic ironman Cal Ripken was so wholesome, he was a spokesman for milk. Players like Brady and all-time great New York Yankees shortstop Derek Jeter generally mastered the art of talking and saying nothing, steering clear of all controversy and political lines, from brushfires to full-blown infernos.

Ortiz, meanwhile, was far more authentic, often speaking from his heart and showing his emotions without the slightest bit of reluctance, shame, or regret, frequently to his own detriment. Once, he burst in on then manager Terry Francona's postgame press conference to complain about an official scoring decision, coming off as selfish and childish. Another time, during a game, a frustrated Ortiz took his bat to the phone in the visitors' dugout at Baltimore's Camden Yards, smashing it to pieces. He sometimes jousted with the media. And years before he became teammates with eventual Red Sox left-hander David Price, he publicly engaged the then Tampa Bay Rays pitcher in a verbal jousting competition during which he called the overly sensitive Price "a little bitch."

But always, sometimes to a fault, Ortiz was indisputably real and true to his core, and the fact that he wore his emotions on his sleeve undoubtedly earned him the respect of a Boston fan base that could be impossibly cynical, skeptical, and demanding.

Don't bullshit. Give it to me straight.

We're going to be okay, Ortiz effectively stated. *We'll be back. And we will win again.*

How could Boston doubt him? At the time, after all, Boston had grown very, very accustomed to winning.

* * *

The relationship between sports and society is a fascinating study, though all relationships are not created equal. Sports simply do not mean as much in some places as they do in others, and there are some places where they undoubtedly mean too much. If Boston is either, it is assuredly the latter.

"We care about our teams," said a succinct Wyc Grousbeck, principal owner of the Celtics and a Boston-area native who grew up as a fan of all the major teams in town. "It's our identity as a city."

Said legendary football coach Bill Parcells in February 2021, twenty-five years after the end of his controversial tenure as Patriots coach, "I would tell you that I think Boston is one of the best sports towns in this country. I really do. And I think they have passion for football, baseball, basketball, hockey—all their sports teams are important. That's not true in every city. . . . New York—they've got nine sports teams. It's not the same. . . . I just think they're very passionate about their teams [in Boston]. . . . I think it's a good thing. And it's enjoyable to work in places like that, because you know somebody's interested. . . . It [also] matters to the people that are involved in working there."

Indeed, over the past ten to twenty years, Boston started placing at the top of almost every single list of best sports cities in America. And yet, the same is true if the subject is changed to "best American cities for medicine" or "best American cities for education." Boston Children's Hospital is internationally renowned for caring for the young, and the Dana-Farber Cancer Institute is one of the most globally respected homes for cancer treatment. Boston is home to both Harvard University and the Massachusetts Institute of Technology, educational pillars that have produced some of the most decorated and accomplished minds in the world in an array of professional fields. All of those institutions are merely at the top of very long lists.

And yet, Boston's identity is as much or more about . . . sports.

In the northeastern corner of the United States, of course, the roots run deep. The Pilgrims famously landed at Plymouth Rock in 1620, allowing Boston to serve, in some ways, as a fountainhead for four hundred years of American history. New Englanders, at their core, were farmers, transitioning from one season to the next, from humid, heavy summers to the gray skies and snowdrifts of winter. They were staid, parochial, unbending. There was always a job to do, come hell or high water, green fields or snowplows. The tasks changed, but there was always a task.

Why sports, specifically, mean so much in Boston is largely a matter of opinion, and many theories abound. One of the most popular concerns the volatile New England weather, but that seems like nothing more than a convenient theory. There are, after all, many North American cities that have four seasons and harsh winters. Some of those cities are bigger, some are smaller. Some have college sports and some do not. But whatever the reasons, the combination of Boston's age, size, climate, personality, and tradition makes it indisputably unique. With, of course, one very important caveat.

"Number one, I don't think it is unique. I think that that's an incredible local conceit," said longtime *Boston Globe* reporter and columnist Bob Ryan, a New Jersey native who attended Boston College and built a career in Boston as one of the most respected local and national voices in sports. He continued:

> It's a thing [Bostonians] have been fed and, once having been fed, they love it and they can't get enough of it to hear about themselves. But the fact is that no city with such a colossal disinterest in major college sports on a national scale can possibly claim itself to be the best sports town in America. If you want to put "professional" in parentheses, you can enter the argument. . . . There is no number-one sports town. Everybody's got a *yeah but* somewhere, as far as I'm concerned. So, that's number one. And we're among them. We're in the elite class of major sports towns, but we have this colossal hole in our sporting soul about the college sports thing.
>
> Now, that said, I don't know the reason [why professional sports mean so much in Boston]. I've thought about it. I've only been able to articulate how it plays itself out, but *why*? That's a very good question. I did used to have a theory about why we love baseball . . . and I thought some of it had to do with the change of seasons theory, the springtime and the renewal, and getting [outdoor] in the summer after the cooped-up winter. I think there may have been something to that. But what we got going for us in baseball is very simple: history.

Sure enough, Boston's baseball roots go back to the nineteenth century, when, as Ryan put it, "the first official organized league of any consequence was formed, the National Association, and we were a charter member. And guess who dominated that league until 1876, when the National League was formed? Boston did. So, we've got an unsurpassed—maybe matched but unsurpassed—history on baseball going back to 1871. We've never been without a team, and it's been an important part of the local scene. There's no question about it. So, that explains baseball."

Boston was also one of the earliest members of the NHL and NBA, in that order, the former being critical in distinguishing Boston from other North American cities for a very simple reason: its regionality. Basketball is played indoors and out, in cities and suburbs, in playgrounds and backyards. Hockey, on the other hand, originated and thrived in only pockets of the country, from the Northeast to the Great Lakes to, eventually, the Rocky Mountains. And while that fact is both obvious and well-known, it is important to remember that only four of the famed "Original Six" franchises in the inaugural 1942–43 NHL season were American cities, joining Montreal and Toronto to form what would become the most competitive hockey league in the world: Detroit, Chicago, New York, and, of course, Boston.

Boston was similarly a charter member of the NBA when that league was formed in 1946.

Said Ryan: "We were a charter member of the NHL. We're a charter member of the National League [in baseball]. We're a charter member of the American League. We're a charter member of the NBA. The only one we're not [a charter member in] is football. We had a team and we lost it, the Redskins, and people should know that. And we finally got an AFL team [in the Patriots, who were formed in 1960]. . . . But [in] three of the four major sports, we can pull rank on most anybody. The fourth one, we can't, and that's football.

"But now," Ryan concluded, "what's number one here right now?"

The answer, of course, is the Patriots, whose dynastic run at the start of the millennium rivals the greatest dynasties in all sports from any era.

When the Patriots became elite, in fact, is when Boston began to boom.

* * *

From late 2001 through mid 2022, in the four major professional American team sports and with the Patriots leading the way, teams from Boston won an astounding twelve championships. Quite simply, there has never been anything remotely like it in the history of American team sports, and there may never be again.

Beginning with the New England Patriots' improbable Super Bowl title in February 2002, teams from Boston played in nine Super Bowls, four World Series, three Stanley Cups, and three NBA Finals, an absurd nineteen combined appearances. In corresponding order, the city's championships totaled six, four, one, and one. And yet, as notable as the championships was Boston's incredible consistency in vying for them, a record akin to that of world-renowned golfer Jack Nicklaus, who won a record eighteen major championships in golf, finished second an incredible nineteen times, and placed in the top five of a major championship on a ridiculous fifty-six occasions. From 2002 to 2022, Boston teams reached the league semifinals an incredible thirty-one times, a feat that left the rest of America with no choice but to constantly look over its collective shoulder.

"I can tell you how we look at it, and we look at it through the prism of how it's going to play to the rest of the country," former ESPN senior vice president for programming and onetime *Boston Globe* sports editor Vince Doria said in August 2008. "It's a little big town. Sports are important in Boston, probably more so than anywhere else."

Indeed, for as much as sports can—and do—dominate the American landscape, there are few if any cities that can match the intensity of the Boston fan base, its potency, its passion. Beyond Boston, there are only eight other American cities that possess only one team in each of the four major American team sports of baseball, basketball, football, and hockey: Dallas, Denver, Detroit, Miami, Minneapolis, Philadelphia, Phoenix, and Washington. Others, like New York, Los Angeles, Chicago, and San Francisco–Oakland, have multiple teams in multiple sports, which dilutes the fan base and increases the odds of winning.

During the 1980s, for example, Los Angeles dominated the American sports landscape, winning five NBA championships, one Super Bowl, and two World Series. But the city's hockey team, the Los Angeles Kings, was average at best. The team's other basketball franchise, the Los Angeles Clippers, was a perennial laughingstock, and the city ultimately proved incapable of supporting two professional football franchises, both the Los Angeles Raiders and the Los Angeles Rams leaving the region for other markets—the Raiders moving back to Oakland and the Rams to St. Louis. In Boston, by contrast, the success of the Patriots and Red Sox in particular fueled a competition that lasted twice as long as that of Los Angeles and ultimately inspired the Celtics and Bruins to reach championship levels.

"I like the feeling," said Danny Ainge, a former Celtics player who won championships with the team in the 1980s and served as the team's chief basketball executive from 2003 to 2021. "I like the feeling of the Red Sox being a great team and the Patriots being a great team. I don't know if that's the sports fan in me or the executive side in me, but I think they push me to reach as far. If that's pressure, I like that."

Nonetheless, as important as sports can be to the fabric of a city, there are inevitable side effects and drawbacks. Pressure bursts pipes, as the saying goes, and the burning desire to win clouds judgment. In the new millennium, Boston has hardly been different.

* * *

Steeped in tradition, Boston has always celebrated its values: education, medicine, social responsibility. Athletes are often viewed as fellow residents with equal responsibilities to the community, and the relationships between the players and the fans are, in a word, personal. Former Red Sox pitcher Derek Lowe once remarked that, while standing on the pitcher's mound in most any American baseball stadium, "you look up into the stands and you see colors." But at Fenway Park, where the proximity of the seats often gave players the sense that they were being judged, analyzed, sometimes suffocated—like performers in a cramped theater or defendants in an old English trial—the experience was altogether different.

"You see faces," said Lowe, which meant the opposite was also true.

The fans see yours.

As such, Boston's dominance in professional sports has come with the expected scrutiny and pitfalls, some of which have exposed the city's greatest vulnerabilities and most sensitive wounds. In 2012, after scoring a goal that eliminated the Bruins from the playoffs, Washington Capitals forward Joel Ward was the victim of racist comments by Boston fans on social media, prompting public apologies; five years later, Baltimore Orioles outfielder Adam Jones was the victim of similar taunts at Fenway Park.

In 2007, the Patriots and cutthroat head coach Bill Belichick were penalized by the NFL in a cheating scandal known as Spygate; seven years later the Patriots were reprimanded again by commissioner Roger Goodell in a scandal that came to be known as Deflategate and resulted in the four-game suspension of all-world quarterback Tom Brady. In 2005, native son and Red Sox general manager Theo Epstein submitted his resignation and, on Halloween, left his Fenway Park office in a gorilla costume, all amid a dispute with mentor Larry Lucchino, one of the perceived carpetbaggers tied to new Red Sox ownership. The Epstein-Lucchino feud was Boston politics at its purest, Epstein loyalists rallying around him like the childhood friends who protected renowned criminal Whitey Bulger.

An extreme comparison? Absolutely. But such was the landscape in Boston, where the political and personal worlds usually ended up on two sides—*with us* or *against us*—and where a native son who had delivered Boston its first World Series in nearly a century felt so smothered that he wore a disguise to escape.

And yet, Boston possessed an often paradoxical sense of righteousness that, especially from the outside, was difficult to comprehend. Colleges and universities are expected to place an emphasis on education, not sports, which helps explain why the city's focus is on the professional teams. In the 1990s, when the University of Massachusetts men's basketball team soared to national heights, the program run by coach John Calipari came under great scrutiny. Before long, Calipari was on his way to Memphis, the message apparent.

That's not how we do it here.

But the message to the professional teams?

You'd better win.

Or, more specifically, *You'd better win the right way.*

And in the early 2000s, there were both lofty standards and great expectations to meet.

CHAPTER 1

THE SEEDS OF A DYNASTY

*"I remember how hard it was snowing and I remember the snow piled on
the field and the whole thing. I was right behind the Raiders' bench—not too
many rows up, maybe 12, 14, 16 rows up—and they were all celebrating. The
game was over as far as they were concerned. And then they called the tuck
[rule]. The whole thing turned around, it was a whole big debate for 5, 10
minutes—whatever it was—and then they straightened it all out. . . . The
kick—it was a complete line drive. It never looked like it was more than six
feet above the crossbar. It went straight instead of up. The way I remember
it, it was like a laser. It was like 6, 8, 10 feet above the crossbar at its highest
point, as far as I could tell, and it just made it over. That's what I remember."*

—Celtics owner Wyc Grousbeck, April 2020

IN NEW ENGLAND, FOLLOWING YEARS of what many regarded as
oppression, the final play of Super Bowl XXXVI was the sports equivalent of the
Shot Heard 'Round the World. And in the immediate aftermath, unbeknownst
to all, a new order was soon to be established.

But as New England Patriots kicker Adam Vinatieri positioned himself
for a forty-eight-yard field goal attempt with seven seconds remaining in the
biggest annual event in sports, the weight—and the wait—was suffocating. In
Boston, the breadbasket of New England, pits in stomachs grew to the size of
footballs. Families and friends rose from sofas and seats, paced, joined hands
as if saying grace, even kneeled. Some just closed their eyes and prayed. And
lest anyone tell you otherwise, the large majority of them prepared for the
worst, the seemingly inevitable failure, because that's how sports fans in New

England had been conditioned over a fifteen-year period that felt more like a hundred fifteen.

We'll lose because we always lose, somehow, some way. We'll blow it. We always do.

And then, as if oblivious to it all, a steely Vinatieri swung his leg with confidence and conviction, striking the ball so purely that the flight of the kick was, in a word, picturesque. The ball had loft, was in no danger of being blocked, and was so downright parabolic that it felt as if it could threaten the roof of the Louisiana Superdome, where the game was being held. The kick had power, was in no danger of being short. And the ball had a touch of spin, moving from Vinatieri's right to his left, the kind of coveted high draw chased on practice tees all over the world.

Vinatieri hit the sweet spot. The kick was perfect. And it was, without the slightest hint of doubt, good. Very, very good.

"The way he kicked it, with the height off of the kick, there was no chance for it to be blocked," said Patriots linebacker Tedy Bruschi many years later. "And it was just so straight . . . pretty."

Boston had won twenty-six championships in its history before Vinatieri's kick sealed Super Bowl XXXVI, but, in retrospect, none may have been more important, improbable, and impactful as the Patriots' 20–17 win over the heavily favored St. Louis Rams on February 3, 2002. New England was starving for a winner by then, having last won a championship in 1986, the year Larry Bird (one of Bruschi's childhood heroes) led the Boston Celtics to the most dominating of his three championships, a six-game dismantling of the Houston Rockets. Including the postseason, the 1986 Celtics went 82-18—a rather systematic 67-15 during the regular season and 15-3 in the playoffs—and an incredible 50-1 at home. The championship was the team's third in six seasons, the peak of a Celtics dynasty—or so it seemed—that might extend for years to come.

At the time, after all, the Celtics also had the second pick in the upcoming NBA draft, guaranteeing the team either University of North Carolina center Brad Daugherty or Maryland forward Len Bias, both regarded as elite prospects. Further, the Patriots had just made an unlikely appearance in the Super Bowl and the Red Sox were amid a magical season that would deliver them to the World Series. Even the Bruins, who were unceremoniously dismissed by the Montreal Canadiens in the first round of the playoffs, could take solace in the fact that the Canadiens would go on to win the Stanley Cup.

In 1986, in basketball, baseball, hockey, and football, Boston either won the championship or was defeated by the team that ultimately proved unbeatable, a positive spin with which New Englanders were quite unfamiliar. In the end, of course, 1986 proved to be, simultaneously, one of the most glorious and tragic years in Boston sports history. On June 8, 1986, the Celtics blew out the Rockets to win their sixteenth NBA championship, most in the NBA. Nine days later, after the Cleveland Cavaliers selected Daugherty with the first overall pick in the draft, the Celtics selected Bias, whose combination of size (six foot eight) and athleticism made him "the best athlete available in the draft," according to longtime great Celtics executive and coach Red Auerbach. Two days after that, Bias was dead of a cocaine overdose in one of the great tragedies in American sports history.

By the time the new millennium dawned, the Celtics still had not really recovered. From the time Bird retired during the summer of 1992 through the 2000–2001 NBA season, the Celtics went a woeful 289-417, a .409 winning percentage that ranked twenty-first among the twenty-nine NBA franchises. During the final seasons of that span, they missed the playoffs six years in a row, the longest such span during the existence of what had been the NBA's premier blue-blood franchise.

In 1986, almost overnight, the Celtics went from arguably the greatest single-season team and all-time greatest franchise to the sports world's answer to Schleprock, the *Flintstones* teenager most known for his consistently gloomy attitude and exceptionally poor luck.

Meanwhile, in the aftermath of the Bruins' early playoff exit and the onset of the Celtics' demise, the Red Sox began rumbling through a magical summer that marked the ascension of pitcher Roger Clemens, whose emergence almost single-handedly elevated the team from astonishing mediocrity to championship contender. In 1985, in fact, the Red Sox had finished a perfectly average 81-81, concluding a vanilla six-year period during which they were neither bad enough nor good enough for any decisive judgment or action. And then, seemingly from nowhere, the twenty-three-year-old William Roger Clemens turned into one of the greatest pitchers in baseball history, setting a major-league record for strikeouts in a nine-inning game (twenty, on April 29, 1986) and steamrolling to a 14-0 start that earned him the role as starting pitcher for the American League in the All-Star Game. In the process, on the broad shoulders of Clemens, the 1986 Red Sox suddenly found themselves on a track to do something they had not done since the days of World War I: win the World Series.

At the time, after all, everything about the 1986 baseball season had seemed destined, right from the start. On the very first pitch of the season—for any team, anywhere—Red Sox outfielder Dwight Evans homered against Detroit Tigers right-hander (and future Hall of Famer) Jack Morris. Over the span of the next several months, mostly fueled by Clemens, the Red Sox took command of the American League East and won the division by a comfortable five and a half games, qualifying for their first postseason in more than a decade. And then, after falling behind the California Angels in the best-of-seven AL Championship Series three games to one, the Red Sox were down to their last strike of the season when outfielder Dave Henderson slashed an improbable, breathtaking, season-saving home run, propelling the Red Sox to a Game 5 victory and, ultimately, a place in the World Series.

And make no mistake, in Boston, a World Series championship would have been the defining moment of a year marked with sports drama, from the Super Bowl to the Stanley Cup playoffs to the NBA championship and, tragically, the death of Bias. The Red Sox had not won a World Series since 1918. In the time since, they had made only three World Series appearances—in 1946, 1967, and 1975—losing all three times in a final, decisive seventh game. By the bottom of the tenth inning of Game 6 in 1986, the Red Sox held a 3-2 series advantage over the New York Mets and were leading Game 6 by a 5-3 score with two outs and the bases empty. Red Sox relief pitcher Calvin Schiraldi brought the team to within one strike of the championship—exactly where the Red Sox had been before their incredible comeback against the Angels.

And then, as swiftly as Henderson had saved the 1986 season, the Red Sox blew it in such historic, torturous fashion that the ripple effects seemed to last for decades. The Mets strung together three straight singles. Schiraldi wilted. Veteran Bob Stanley replaced Schiraldi and threw what was officially scored a wild pitch, a tailing pitch that glanced off the glove of catcher Rich Gedman to tie the game at 5. And then Mets outfielder Mookie Wilson hit a slow bouncer to first base that famously dribbled through the legs of hobbled Red Sox first baseman Bill Buckner, delivering the Mets to a Game 6 victory. Two nights later, New York closed out the world championship.

Just like that, at the seeming snap of a finger, New England was left with a figurative crater from which shock waves would emanate for years, forging the belief that no matter how good things got, something bad was lurking just around the corner.

The Patriots, for their part, were the least likely to offer any sort of escape, by then having well established themselves as the runt of Boston's sports litter, easily the least accomplished and, at times, downright pathetic of Boston's four major sports franchises. Established in 1960 as the eighth and final entry of the newly created American Football League, the then Boston Patriots played for the AFL Championship in their fourth season, though they were hardly championship caliber. Under coach Mike Holovak, the Patriots went a mediocre 7-6-1 during the regular season but ultimately won their division, then advanced to the title game with a victory over the Buffalo Bills. Once there, the Patriots were mercilessly pounded by the San Diego Chargers in a 51–10 defeat, fortifying one fact above all else. In 1963, in the AFL, second place sounded good . . . but it was still light-years from a championship.

In retrospect, the loss to the Chargers proved to be something of a birthmark, something with which the Patriots would seemingly always be stained. By the time the Patriots played in their next league championship game—Super Bowl XX on January 26, 1986—the result was virtually identical. After an encouraging 11-5 season and three upset road playoff victories over the New York Jets, Los Angeles Raiders, and Miami Dolphins, the long-shot Patriots were thoroughly destroyed by the Chicago Bears, 46–10, in the Superdome. Within days, *Boston Globe* reporter Ron Borges unveiled a report that detailed a serious drug problem within the team's roster and locker room, reaffirming yet again the belief that the Patriots were a second-rate team with second-rate values and destined to be losers.

From their inception through the 1993 season—the first thirty-four years of their existence—the Patriots went a collective 221-270, a .451 winning percentage that placed them twenty-first among the then twenty-eight franchises that formed what is now the modern NFL. Of the seven teams that ranked behind the Patriots—whose name changed to the New England Patriots when they moved out of Boston and into Foxborough, Massachusetts, in 1971—six were expansion franchises that began playing professional football after the Patriots did. Only one, the St. Louis Cardinals (who eventually moved to Phoenix), had been in existence as long as the Patriots had, which gave Boston an unfortunate label in the football world: The Patriots were doormats, plain and simple.

And yet, by early 1993, New England football fans had hope again, most notably in the presence of Bill Parcells, a two-time Super Bowl–winning coach with the New York Giants who was hired at the end of one of the most tumultuous periods in team history. Over the span of four years, the Patriots were sold twice, first to Remington Products and shaving king Victor Kiam, then to James Orthwein, a descendant of the founders of the Anheuser-Busch brewing company. Orthwein hired Parcells amid a three-year period during which the Patriots went a positively abysmal 9-39, the team compiling individual seasons of 1-15 (in 1990) and 2-14 (in 1992).

Parcells, as it turned out, took the Patriots to another Super Bowl in his fourth season, this one culminating in a 35-21 loss to the Green Bay Packers. By then the Patriots had been sold yet again, this time to local businessman Robert Kraft, whose local roots made him much more endearing to provincial New Englanders. Unfortunately, it also made New England less appealing to Parcells, who deviously choreographed his departure from New England in backroom dealings with the New York Jets even before the Super Bowl was played. As a result, New England's 1996 Super Bowl season ended with more tumult, this time resulting in the departure of a legendary coach.

Still, in his wake, Bill Parcells left the Patriots having made a profound impact on the identity of the franchise, giving essential credibility—and leadership—to an organization that had previously lacked it. Though the Patriots finished a perfectly mediocre 32-32 in Parcells' four seasons there, they twice made the playoffs and reached the Super Bowl in his final season before yet another of Boston's near misses unraveled with dizzying speed.

Said Parcells in an interview with the website the Athletic in 2018: "I regretted leaving the Patriots because there was a pretty good young team. We had a young quarterback [in Drew Bledsoe], we had Curtis Martin, a premier back. I had a lot of speed at receiver, a great tight end [in Ben Coates], a young, up-and-coming defense: Ty Law, Willie McGinest, Tedy Bruschi. . . . That was a long time ago. I don't think back. Temporarily it bothered me. I'd probably do things differently now if I had to do it again."

Indeed, as unsettling as Parcells's breakup with owner Robert Kraft had been, the Patriots were extremely well positioned for success, with a seeming mountain of assets. Among them was a highly regarded assistant coach who had long since caught the attention of the football world in general and, in particular, the eye of Kraft. His name was Bill Belichick.

Another was a kicker whom the Patriots had signed as a free agent prior to the 1996 Super Bowl season. His name was Adam Vinatieri.

* * *

By the time Bill Belichick returned to New England for the start of the 2000 season, the Patriots had deteriorated to the point of mediocrity, going 10-6, 9-7, and 8-8 under the guidance of effusive coach Pete Carroll, a contrast to Parcells in most every way imaginable. Where Parcells was unrelenting, Carroll was magnanimous. Where Parcells bullied, Carroll embraced. Where Parcells thundered, Carroll hummed, whistled, and skipped merrily along, seemingly oblivious to the fact that a football team needed both discipline and a commanding leader, of which Carroll, at the time, was not.

But, at the time, what mattered to Kraft was that Carroll was not Parcells. During his time in New England under Parcells, Belichick had gained the respect of Kraft, with whom he had forged a relationship. And so, three years after Parcells had departed—and taken Belichick with him to the Jets—Kraft negotiated Belichick's exit from New York for three draft picks: in the first, fourth, and seventh rounds of the 2000–2001 NFL drafts, a price that seemed steep but would prove the real-world equivalent of some loose change and pocket lint. (Belichick, in a manner of speaking, would actually cost the Patriots additional first-round picks over the coming years, but that is another story altogether.) Kraft then turned over his football operation to a man who had been one of Parcells's many understudies but who was far more cerebral, tactically superior, and seemingly devoid of all emotion or compassion.

Still, the hiring of Belichick proved to be one of the many proverbial forks in the road that would forever alter the course of the Patriots and, for that matter, all of sports in New England for years to come. What if Carroll had succeeded with the Patriots and built a winner, thereby extending his tenure in New England and ultimately forcing Belichick to land somewhere else? Would Tom Brady have subsequently been drafted by another organization? And what if Kraft had immediately hired Belichick instead of first turning to Carroll, something that Bruschi, among others, seemed to suggest that Belichick himself was anticipating following Parcells's defection after the loss to the Green Bay Packers in Super Bowl XXXI?

During the week leading up to the Super Bowl, in fact, news of the inevitable breakup between Parcells and Kraft already had leaked via respected *Boston Globe* football writer Will McDonough, creating a massive distraction that hovered over the Patriots during preparations for the game. After the

Patriots lost, Parcells bypassed the team's return flight home and traveled alone, concluding a series of events that left a bad taste in the mouths of many, including and especially Kraft and Belichick.

Bill Parcells turned traitor, and much of New England still has never forgiven him for it. Yet, the fact remains that Parcells gave the Patriots something they badly lacked—credibility—and his presence in New England established the framework for what would become the reign of Bill Belichick and the New England Patriots dynasty.

"I was really fortunate for Parcells to lay my football foundation, as I call it, and that type of coaching was hard," says Bruschi.

> Parcells, I never got intimidated by who he was. I just—I was more like, "What do you want?" It was always just something that I would just try to figure out for myself, "What's the coach want? What's he want me to do?" And then, "I'm going to do it" . . . I think it was always clear that if you work hard, you're going to get along with him.
>
> So, [Belichick] was the same way, and I remember him talking to me on the plane after the '96 Super Bowl when Parcells didn't take the plane back, I think because him and Kraft had all of that going on and Will McDonough had reported that Parcells was leaving. And Bill was walking around the plane talking to certain players, like I saw him talk to me and I think Vinatieri was a guy and Lawyer [Milloy] was a guy. He was making his way across the plane talking as if he was going to be the next head coach—almost talking to us like, "You're doing a good job, you're a young player—listen, next year, we're going to be better." And I wondered why he did that, and I didn't know what was going on with him and Kraft about the job or anything. So that sort of still gave me a connection to him that he recognized my progression as a player. So when he came back, I just sort of welcomed it and I knew what he wanted, and having an idea of Parcells, I think I got along with him right away.

Even then, it seemed, Belichick was ahead of the curve.

By now, of course, the manner in which Belichick and the Patriots turned to Tom Brady is folklore, a legend that speaks to that most American of all things: opportunity. After going 5-11 in Belichick's first season, New England lost its season opener in 2001 and was on its way to another defeat in Week 2 against the New York Jets when quarterback Drew Bledsoe scrambled from the pocket, ran to his right, and absorbed a crushing hit from New York Jets linebacker

Mo Lewis. The hit was merely one play in an eventual 10–3 Patriots defeat that left New England at 0-2 and Belichick at 5-13 in his career as New England coach, but it was so figuratively jarring that it knocked the Patriots—and all of the football world—into an entirely different reality.

Though Bledsoe returned to the game, he was ultimately diagnosed with a sheared blood vessel and collapsed lung that would sideline him for weeks, forcing Belichick and the Patriots to turn to a second-year quarterback from Michigan who had never previously started an NFL game.

Of course, sports are littered with countless what-if scenarios. Former New York Yankees first baseman Wally Pipp is famously remembered as the man who was replaced by Lou Gehrig during the 1925 baseball season, a transition that similarly produced one of the great and most dynastic combinations in American sports history—Gehrig, Babe Ruth, and the New York Yankees of the 1920s and 1930s. Having supplanted Pipp, Gehrig subsequently played a then major-league record 2,130 consecutive games during a magnificent seventeen-year career that earned him the nickname the "Iron Horse." He won six World Series and established himself as such an iconic figure in American history that even the disease that ultimately took his life—amyotrophic lateral sclerosis, or ALS—became known as "Lou Gehrig's disease."

In retrospect, the marriage of Belichick and Brady was reasonably comparable, the latter winning six titles (same as Gehrig) and exploiting an opportunity through the misfortune of his predecessor, Bledsoe. (A struggling Pipp is alleged to have been given the day off because of a headache, thereby opening the door for Gehrig.) Belichick himself used the Pipp analogy years later, jabbing receiver Wes Welker as the player's eventual successor, Julian Edelman, excelled during a preseason game in 2009. Said the playful (or not) coach Belichick to the player while both stood on the sideline: "You ever hear of Wally Pipp?" Having been well versed in the story of Brady and Bledsoe as well as the manipulations of his mastermind coach, Welker hardly seemed amused.

But in New England in 2001, nobody could have possibly known what was to come. Brady had been a sixth-round selection of the Patriots in the 2000 draft, Belichick's first with the team, and had shown some quick signs of growth, particularly in the 2001 preseason. But the idea that he would bound from the sideline in a cape and red boots to lead the Patriots to a championship was utterly preposterous, and not a single person considered the short- or long-term fortunes of the Patriots even remotely altered when Belichick had little choice but to name Brady his starter for Week 3 of the 2001 season.

Certainly, people were curious.

OK, let's see what the kid looks like.

But beginning with Brady's first career start on September 30, 2001, everyone from Belichick, Kraft, and Brady to thousands of long-suffering Patriots fans would soon realize that things were different. And that their entire perspective on their teams was about to change forever.

* * *

Precisely twelve days before Drew Bledsoe was felled by the Mo Lewis hit that would alter football history, America was rocked by the attacks of September 11, 2001, when terrorists carried out a highly orchestrated plan in which they hijacked planes and flew them into the twin towers of the World Trade Center and Pentagon. A fourth plane, headed toward Washington, D.C., and perhaps the White House or Capitol, was thwarted by passengers, who upon learning of the other attacks while midair fought back, resulting in a crash landing in a field in Pennsylvania, preserving other lives on the ground. The two planes that struck and toppled the North Tower and South Tower of the World Trade Center had departed from Boston.

In the days and weeks that followed, American sports were brought to a standstill. The Red Sox—who had been rained out of a scheduled game in New York on the night of September 10—and the entire major league had games postponed until the following week, beginning on September 17. The NFL similarly put off its games during the week of the attack, returning to play on September 23, the date of Bledsoe's injury. The focus of the entire world—let alone the United States and Boston—was on the horror of September 11. And when professional sports did resume and America attempted to recommence its day-to-day operations, the Red Sox were the first team to return to the field.

By the time the New England football team returned to the field on September 30, the team's name—the *Patriots*—had become far more meaningful across the country as America celebrated its first responders and heroes, something owner Robert Kraft would memorably cite several months later.

But on September 30, the objective for the 2001 New England Patriots was far smaller, simpler, humbler: to win a football game behind a second-year quarterback who was starting his first NFL game. Tom Brady went a modest and pedestrian 13-of-23 for 168 yards in a 44–13 win over Indianapolis (Peyton Manning threw three interceptions, including two returned for touchdowns), but he was dreadful the following week at Miami, where the Patriots passed for only 86 yards in a 30–10 stomping at the hands of the Miami Dolphins. New England rallied to win four of their next five games, including victories over both the San Diego Chargers and, again, Indianapolis, a two-game stretch during which Brady went a sterling 49-of-74 for 566 yards, five touchdowns, and zero interceptions. After a loss to Denver in Week 7—Brady threw four picks, establishing a career-worst that he matched five other times in his career—the Patriots won in both Week 8 (at Atlanta) and Week 9 (at Buffalo), improving their record to 5-4 and setting their sights on something they had not necessarily envisioned after the 0-2 start under Bledsoe: the playoffs.

To that end, Week 8 was particularly noteworthy, at least with regard to half of the Patriots roster: the defense. In Atlanta, the Patriots encountered a Falcons team that was similarly eyeing the playoffs and was coming off a bye week following a 3-3 start. Atlanta's quarterback at the time was a capable veteran named Chris Chandler, who had posted a 13-1 record as the starter in 1998 and taken the team to the Super Bowl. Chandler's career, in fact, had been marked by streaks of good play, yet he had a long injury history that had mostly prevented him from sustained success.

Unsurprisingly, blessed with much of the defensive talent that Bill Parcells left behind, defensive coordinator Romeo Crennel—whose initials donned him the nickname "RAC" (pronounced "rack")—devised an aggressive game plan intended to take advantage of the Patriots' physicality and toughness while exploiting the Atlanta quarterback who seemed to be made of glass. And it worked to perfection.

"We called him Chris *Chandelier*," mused then Patriots linebacker Ted Johnson of the brittle Chandler. "It was one of those things like, 'Hey, man, if this guy gets hit, he will wilt fast.' So RAC had a game plan—we were going to blitz. We were going to blitz him, and we weren't going to stop. I think we had nine sacks in that game. We brought the pressure. From a defensive standpoint, I think that game really clicked. We had a huge lead. We ended up knocking Chris *Chandelier* out. We did what we were hoping to do. . . . I think that game really clicked for us as a defense."

A week after the 24–10 victory, the Patriots traveled to Buffalo and defeated the division rival Buffalo Bills in a 21–11 contest that featured five more sacks by the Patriots defense and another flummoxed quarterback who had a soft reputation: Rob Johnson. The victories elevated the Patriots to 5-4—possessors of a winning record—entering a Week 10 meeting at home with the highly powered St. Louis Rams, a team that had won the Super Bowl just two years prior and served as the consummate measuring stick.

For the Patriots, the Rams game came at a perfect time to assess their growth, though there was one small matter to deal with: Drew Bledsoe was healthy again. And he had been cleared to play.

* * *

In the long history of Boston sports, there have been many debates that have fueled discussions from barstools in South Boston to South Berwick, Maine, none more heated than the question over who should be starting quarterback of the 2001 Patriots: Brady or Bledsoe? Certainly, the feud between Parcells and Kraft has ignited a similar fire—How *could the owner let him go? How could Parcells turn traitor?*—but this involved two of the city's current players, both generally well liked: a slightly beat-up, worn-down veteran to whom the Patriots had a committed a ten-year, $103 million contract and a young, poised leader out of central casting who was delivering the Patriots something they had long lacked: wins. Much of the region seemed split, most everyone landing in one camp or the other. Those supporting Bledsoe emphasized loyalty, and that was something Boston valued greatly. The Brady camp emphasized winning, and that was something Boston wanted desperately.

In the end, the only voice that truly mattered was Belichick's; he defied the conventional theory that a starter could not lose his job to injury and selected the new guy over the old. It was Brady. And it would be for a long, long time.

Said the coach in the days leading up to the game when asked how he would handle the decision in practice: "I think if we had lost the last seven games, that probably would look a little different than winning five of the last seven. But until I see it, I just don't know. I'm going to play the guy who gives us the best chance to win every week."

Belichick, of course, had lived through a similar decision earlier in his career, with the Cleveland Browns, for whom he served as head coach from 1991 to 1995, a relatively underwhelming five-year sample during which he went 36-44 while posting just one winning season. Nonetheless, in his fourth year, Belichick led the Browns to an 11-5 record and took the team to the second round of the playoffs, having endured a similar quarterback controversy centered around Cleveland native Bernie Kosar (a fan favorite—and the "loyalty" guy) and Vinny Testaverde (the newcomer and better "winning" guy). Belichick chose Testaverde, much to the dismay of the media and fan base, a decision that wounded him greatly in the eyes of fans and media despite the team's relative success. A year later, it was Browns owner Art Modell who turned traitor on Browns fans, the city of Cleveland, and, for that matter, the entire state of Ohio, literally moving the storied team out of Cleveland and into Baltimore after being wooed by promises of a new stadium. Amid the turmoil, the Browns went 5-11 and missed the playoffs, Modell turning traitor on his coach, too, undermining the 1995 season and firing Belichick at the end of the year.

For Belichick, the lessons were cold, harsh, and lasting. The next time he became a head coach, he did so for an owner he believed he could trust. And he was further intent on making decisions that were entirely dispassionate, based on the only thing that should matter: winning.

I'm doing it my way this time, the rest of you be damned.

And so, all of these factors were at work, at least on some level, when the surprising Patriots (then 5-4) played the surging Rams (then 7-1). Behind innovative and arrogant head coach Mike Martz, the Rams were the talk of the NFL in 2001, having just come off a 48–14 dismantling of the Carolina Panthers. St. Louis's only defeat of the season had come in Week 7 by a 34–31 score to the New Orleans Saints, and they were regarded as an unstoppable force. Nicknamed the "Greatest Show on Turf" because of their speed and offensive firepower—particularly on the artificial surface of their home field, a dome—the Rams had a quarterback (Kurt Warner), running back (Marshall Faulk), and receiving corps (Isaac Bruce, Torry Holt, Ricky Proehl, and Az-Zahir Hakim) that were the NFL equivalents of a ringmaster, contortionist, and high-flying acrobats, most of whom played as if shot out of a cannon. The Rams were successful, supremely talented, well choreographed, and wildly entertaining.

Backed by their home crowd and operating on natural grass—the surface played slower than artificial turf and would help mitigate the Rams' blinding speed—the Patriots showed well. Even after Brady threw an interception deep in his own territory on his third pass of the game—the ball deflected off the shoulder pad of running back Kevin Faulk—the Patriots responded. Trailing 7–0 as a result of the interception and ensuing Rams touchdown, the Patriots scored the game's next 10 points on an interception return by cornerback Terrell Buckley and a field goal by Vinatieri. And then, late in the second quarter, the Patriots appeared on their way to a 17–7 advantage when running back Antowain Smith fumbled inside the Rams 5-yard line with just over 2 minutes remaining in the first half, a scrum that produced a St. Louis recovery, a replay challenge by Belichick, and, ultimately, possession for the Rams, who subsequently zipped the length of the field to take a 14–10 lead.

Just like that, the Patriots were stung again. The swing from a potential 17–7 New England lead into a 14–10 deficit proved even more monumental when the Rams scored the first 10 points of the second half to take a 24–10 advantage before the Patriots closed to 24–17 with slightly more than 7:30 remaining when Brady threw a touchdown pass to David Patten.

With half of the fourth quarter still to be played, the Patriots were still within striking distance of the best football team in the world. But they never got the ball back. Supremely confident and poised, the Rams possessed the ball for the final 7:37 of play, running the final fourteen plays of the game. The final three plays were a formality as Warner simply took the snap and dropped to one knee to burn the remaining time on the clock. But on the eleven previous plays that constituted the final, decisive drive, the Rams delivered the ball to the versatile Faulk eight times, including all three critical third-down conversions that kept the ball in the Rams' possession and secured a 24–17 St. Louis victory. (Remember this.)

The Patriots were beaten, but unlike many of the teams that had been trucked by the potent Rams, they were hardly bloodied.

Said Johnson, even years later: "We felt like we went toe to toe with them. We lost by a touchdown. It was a competitive game, and it was the quintessential moral victory game. It was like, 'Yeah, we lost to these guys, but man, we didn't embarrass ourselves.' And we knew if we ever had a chance at those guys again, that we could do it. We had very, highly competitive guys on the team that were pros, that really liked each other, genuinely liked each other."

Indeed, in the immediate aftermath of the game, the accomplished Rams paid the Patriots nothing but respect, while the Patriots growled like a team that had missed an opportunity. Brady, for one, noted that "it's not like the Rams stopped us—if anything, we're just stopping ourselves." Martz praised his own club for overcoming adversity and handling what he deemed a tough, physical opponent. ("He told us we had beaten a Super Bowl–caliber team," Rams tight end Ernie Conwell would reveal weeks later.) Receiver Proehl, citing his team's championship DNA, stressed that the Rams "don't get rattled."

Patriots cornerback Ty Law, like Johnson and many others, saw the entire three-hour affair as a positive. "We can look at this game and learn from it," Law told reporters, "but I also think we can look at this game and say we can play with anybody."

Translation: The Patriots weren't entirely sure of themselves entering the Rams game. But they were sure now. They belonged.

Nonetheless, in sports, championships often come down to math, particularly in the NFL, where the playoff structure rewards the teams who play best during the regular season. Division winners earned, at a minimum, the right to open the playoffs at home, and the two teams with the best records in each conference would be afforded the invaluable luxury of first-round playoff bye, which was essentially a free ticket into the league quarterfinals. That second thing was something that had proven—and would continue to prove—tremendously advantageous in league history, and no one understood the benefit more than the cerebral, plotting Belichick.

Yes, the Patriots were playing good football. Yes, they had competed with the best team in the NFL. Yes, they were indisputably back on track following the entire Bill Parcells debacle. But the math was still the math, and nobody in New England was talking about fantasies like the Super Bowl, no matter what Mike Martz had told his team in the visiting locker room at Foxborough.

"We were still just 5-5," Bruschi stressed. "It wasn't, I mean—we were still an average football team then. . . . I remember coming in the locker room after that [Rams] game and it was a loss, and people sort of were thinking to themselves, 'I still think we played well, and we look like a good football team,' but then you realize you're still 5-5 and you imagine you can't lose too many more games because you won't make the playoffs. So there was that sort of conflict. We see progress, but man, we're nowhere near the playoffs right now."

For certain, the Patriots still had work to do, problems to iron out, edges and corners to sharpen. In the week leading up to the Rams game, Belichick had split the practice time at quarterback between Bledsoe and Brady, reflecting some level of doubt. That changed immediately after the Rams game. The coach endorsed Brady as his starter, alienating Bledsoe, who understandably grumbled behind the scenes to sympathetic ears. But Belichick knew that a simmering quarterback controversy had no place on a good team, so he prevented any uncertainty. If the 2001 Patriots were to continue their growth, if they were to continue improving and ultimately get however far they could go, the team would need every bit of confidence, commitment, and focus they could muster.

Even then, the Patriots would still need something even their supreme control freak of a football coach could not promise—something most every championship team in every sport would need on the way to a title: luck.

With Brady cemented at quarterback, the Patriots went out in Week 11 and defeated the New Orleans Saints 34–17. Then they went to New York and defeated the Jets, then defeated the Cleveland Browns at home in Week 13. Suddenly they were 8-5. Then came a Week 14 meeting at Buffalo that produced a 12–9 Patriots victory highlighted by a play that had onlookers and both coaches scratching their heads in disbelief.

With a little more than 6 minutes remaining in the game, the Bills had taken a 9–6 lead on a field goal by kicker Shayne Graham. After the subsequent kickoff and return, the Patriots gained possession at their own 37-yard line. Brady promptly completed passes of 19, 8, and 25 yards to deliver the Patriots to the Buffalo 11-yard line, where the drive subsequently stalled. Vinatieri promptly converted a 25-yard field goal to tie the score at 9. The Bills and Patriots exchanged brief possessions at the end of the game, but neither team could even get into field goal range, which forced the game to overtime.

Having won the coin toss and needing just a field goal to win the game—overtime rules at the time declared that the first team to score would be declared the winner—the Bills advanced to their own 48-yard line before the Patriots defense held, defensive back Otis Smith breaking up a pass intended for Bill receiver Eric Moulds on third-and-2. The Bills punted into the end zone, granting the Patriots the ball at the New England 20. The Patriots gained 26 yards on the next four plays, moving to their own 46, when Brady delivered a 13-yard strike to receiver David Patten, who was immediately drilled by Bills safety Keion Carpenter.

Patten fumbled. Having taken the full force of the Carpenter hit, Patten fell to the ground, landing perpendicular to the sideline at Buffalo's Ralph Wilson Stadium, his torso out of bounds, his legs in bounds. Under Patten's legs was the football, which was scooped up by Bills defensive back Nate Clements for a Buffalo recovery.

Or so it seemed.

As much as coaches teach players about the importance of turnovers and fumbles in football, fumbles, in particular, can be arbitrary. Certainly, *causing* fumbles is an indisputable skill—as is preventing them—but the *recovery* is much less controllable. Sometimes the ball bounces straight up. Sometimes it bounces sideways. Sometimes it doesn't really bounce at all. And sometimes, as was the case with the five-foot-ten, 190-pound Patten, it ends up under the legs of an unconscious wide receiver lying across the sideline like a fair maiden tied to the railroad tracks. The Bills were initially awarded possession, but Belichick challenged the call, and it was overturned because that unconscious receiver's body was partially out of bounds.

Instead of Buffalo gaining possession at its own 41-yard line, in excellent field position and needing to advance just a short distance to try a game-winning field goal, the Patriots kept the ball. Had Patten's body remained inbounds, the ball would have gone to Buffalo. Had the ball gone anywhere but under Patten's legs, possession would have gone to Buffalo. Instead, the Patriots maintained possession, all but officially credited with a fumble recovery by a man who was not conscious.

"I have never seen a play like that," said Gregg Williams, then the coach of the Bills. "Tough call."

Not for the Patriots it wasn't. It was, in retrospect, a harbinger of things to come.

On the next play after the Patten fumble, Patriots running back Antowain Smith rumbled for 38 yards to the Buffalo 3-yard line. The Patriots called time-out. Needing just a field goal to win the game, Brady took the snap and settled onto a knee in the middle of the field, setting Vinatieri up perfectly for a 23-yard field goal that gave the Patriots a 12–9 victory. The Patriots were now 9-5 and headed to a Week 15 showdown with the Miami Dolphins, on their home field at Foxboro Stadium, with the American Football Conference East Division championship essentially at stake and the right to host a playoff game at home for the first time in the Belichick era.

Again, they had luck on their side. The Patriots defeated the Dolphins 20–13, claiming their fifth straight victory since the loss to the Rams. They were 10-5 and in complete control of their own playoff destiny. With Brady playing efficiently and avoiding mistakes, Belichick generally was able to rely on the strength, talent, and experience of his defense to win games, playing simple, sound, and fundamental football. Most of all, the Patriots were smart. They made few mistakes. All that remained for New England to clinch the division title was a home meeting with the Carolina Panthers, the worst team in football. Unsurprisingly, the Patriots annihilated the Panthers 38–6 and outscored them 28–3 in the second half. In the game, New England rushed for a touchdown (Antowain Smith) and passed for a touchdown (Brady to tight end Jermaine Wiggins), took back a punt (receiver Troy Brown), and scored twice on interceptions returns (Ty Law and Otis Smith). Vinatieri also kicked a field goal. It was the kind of comprehensive victory that could made a coach like Belichick downright giddy, New England excelling in offense, defense, and special teams. The victory was the Patriots' sixth straight and left their final record at 11-5, unbeaten since the loss to the Rams, and positioned them to host a playoff game the following week.

As it turned out, there wouldn't be a football game in New England the following Saturday or Sunday, known in the NFL as wild card weekend, because the Patriots were not required to play.

Slightly more than three hours after the Patriots began their dismantling of the Panthers, the Oakland Raiders kicked off against the New York Jets, the team that had traded Belichick to New England. Having secured the AFC West Division Championship, Oakland was in position to secure the second bye, granting head coach Jon Gruden and his players an invaluable week off and the right to open the playoffs at home.

The Raiders and Jets, who were vying for a wild card spot, played a back-and-forth affair in which the lead changed several times—7-0 Jets, 9-7 Raiders, 14-9 Jets, 16-14 Raiders, 21-19 Jets. And then, with 6:05 remaining, Raiders kicker Brad Daluiso made a 37-yard field goal to give Oakland a 22-21 advantage.

After the teams exchanged short possessions—the Raiders had a chance to run out the clock, but they failed—the Jets took over at their own 36-yard line with 2:12 left. Their quarterback was Vinny Testaverde, the same man Belichick had chosen over native Ohioan Bernie Kosar back in Cleveland. And then, as if repaying a debt, Testaverde completed four passes to advance the Jets to the Oakland 35-yard line, which nonetheless required Jets kicker John Hall to attempt a lengthy 53-yard field goal to win the game. The kick was good, the Jets were 24-22 winners, and John Gruden and the Raiders, despite having been one of the best teams in the AFC for the majority of the season, would have to play on wild card weekend, albeit at home, against the same Jets.

Oakland won the game that time, but instead of playing in Northern California in the divisional round a week later—fully rested—the Raiders would instead have to travel to New England in the middle of winter.

There would be snow. Lots and lots of snow.

* * *

During the first decade of their existence, from 1960 to 1970, the Boston Patriots lived a nomadic existence, playing their home games at, among other places, Fenway Park, Harvard Stadium, and even Alumni Stadium at Boston College. They became the New England Patriots in 1971 when they moved out of Boston and into Foxborough, where they inhabited a cheaply made stadium first known as Schaefer Stadium (after a beer company), then Sullivan Stadium (after the first owners), and then, finally, Foxboro Stadium (after the town). Truth be told, the place was a dump. And thanks to the Patriots' generally wretched history, there was nothing remotely nostalgic about it until the final year of its existence—or, more specifically, its final game. That finale was an absolute doozy, perhaps the most memorable sporting event ever to take place on New England turf—natural, artificial, or, in this case, frozen. And if Adam Vinatieri's kick later in Super Bowl XXXVI was, indeed, the aforementioned Shot Heard 'Round the World, well, January 19, 2002, was the New England sports equivalent of the Boston Tea Party.

Today, in New England, the AFC divisional playoff game between the Patriots and then Oakland Raiders is known by various names, from the generic (the "snow game") to the more formal (the "Snow Bowl"), though it will be remembered mostly for two plays, the first of which facilitated the second. By the time the game began, snow had been falling in Foxborough for roughly four hours and had covered the playing field. Forecasts called for the heaviest snow between 8:00 and 10:00 P.M., coinciding with the majority of the game. The hours before, during, and after produced a succession of indelible images, a virtual snow globe of plays, moments, and memories like scenes from *It's a Wonderful Life*.

"I think the footing is going to be a little bit of an issue and I think catching the ball is going to be a little bit of an issue with the flakes," a relatively chipper Bill Belichick told CBS sideline reporter Armen Keteyian immediately before the start of the game. "I don't think the quarterbacks will have a problem throwing it—at least it didn't look like they did in pregame."

Nonetheless, football coaches are almost universally a collection of control freaks whose first inclination was simple: avoid mistakes. As such, "throwing it," as Belichick suggested, was not a desirable option because of the accompanying problem of "catching it"—at least until a team had no other choice. And that's where the story really begins.

All in all, Tom Brady *threw it* fifty-two times on January 19, 2002, though an astonishing twenty-six of those came on New England's final thirty-five offensive snaps of the game beginning with 12:29 to play in the fourth quarter. At the time, New England trailed by a 13–3 score and had generated very little offense. With his team's season at stake, Belichick then had little choice but to turn Brady loose, asking his quarterback to whip the ball around Gillette Stadium as if he were in a snowball fight.

Beginning on his own 33-yard line, Brady threw nine consecutive passes on a ten-play, 67-yard touchdown drive that would produce New England's first—and only—touchdown of the game. He completed all nine, to four different receivers, including four to tight end Jermaine Wiggins and three to wide receiver David Patten. The final play was New England's only rushing play of the sequence, a 6-yard run that ended with Brady diving into the end zone, scrambling to his feet, then spiking the ball with such force that he slipped and fell on the slick surface. Vinatieri then converted the extra point—no sure thing in the conditions—to make the score 13–10.

What happened after that is now the stuff of lore. The teams exchanged possessions, the Patriots electing to punt away the football with 2:47 to play and three time-outs remaining. The Raiders subsequently ran the ball three times, gaining 7 yards on first down, two on second. Facing a third-and-1 and its own 44-yard line and New England having exhausted its second time-out, Oakland ran again, handing the ball to fullback Zack Crockett, who was stopped for no gain. Gruden elected to punt, commencing a series of plays that easily could have ended New England's season—and at least delayed the birth of a dynasty—but instead opened the way for the one of the most extraordinary eras in American sports.

On the Raiders' subsequent punt, Patriots receiver Troy Brown had a critical 27-yard punt return—and then fumbled. The ball bounced in the direction of Patriots teammate Larry Izzo, who promptly pounced on it. Brady then completed two passes for 12 yards, giving the Patriots a first down at the Oakland 42-yard line with no time-outs and roughly 1:50 to play.

On the next play, Brady dropped back yet again to pass. The Raiders countered with a blitz by cornerback Charles Woodson, one of the best defensive backs in the league (and in league history) and a former teammate of Brady's from the University of Michigan. Brady was about to pass the ball to his left—seemingly unaware of the onrushing Woodson, who was coming from Brady's right—when the quarterback changed his mind at the last instant, pulling the ball back toward his body. But just before Brady was fully able to secure possession, Woodson delivered a crushing blow that knocked the ball free. This time the fumble—the apparent fumble—was recovered by Oakland linebacker Greg Biekert, giving Oakland possession and effectively winning the game for the Raiders. The Patriots, it seemed, had exhausted all of their luck.

Because the game was in the final 2 minutes, referee Walt Coleman and his crew were required, by rule, to review the turnover, which seemed like a formality. On CBS, which broadcast the game on television, longtime NFL analyst and former New York Giants quarterback Phil Simms expressed little doubt that the play was a turnover, noting that Woodson's hit was what jarred the ball loose, adding, "I don't think the recoil of the fake throw is what made it come out of Tom Brady's hand."

Simms was right. The contact from Woodson clearly dislodged the ball, which was still firmly in Brady's hand as he was pulling his arm down and in toward his body. And yet, as replays appeared on the video board at Foxboro Stadium, Patriots fans began roaring—as most any home crowd would—believing that the play should be called an incomplete pass. As the seconds and minutes lapsed, Simms began to waffle. Only a few seasons earlier, prior to the 1999 season, the NFL had instituted an obscure rule for precisely such a play, though almost no one knew it or remembered it. ("The exact term of it—I can't think of it," Simms said on the broadcast.) But Rule 3, Section 21, Article 2, and Note 2 of the NFL rule book specifically stated: "When [an offensive] player is holding the ball to pass it forward, any intentional forward movement of his arm starts a forward pass, even if the player loses possession of the ball as he is attempting to tuck it back toward his body. Also, if the player has tucked the ball into his body and then loses possession, it is a fumble."

Brady, of course, had not tucked the ball back into his body yet. His arm was certainly moving forward. And even though Woodson's hit—and nothing else—clearly knocked the ball free, the rest was irrelevant.

Coleman returned to the field after a replay review. He turned on his microphone and correctly deemed the play an incomplete pass, restoring possession to the Patriots and triggering an enormous roar from the home crowd. Expressive as always, an exasperated Gruden futilely argued his case from the Oakland sideline—"I think the tuck rule is a crock of shit, personally," he told NFL Films host Steve Sabol years later—but his hot breath ultimately vanished into the cold New England air. The teams would play on.

On the next play, Brady completed a 13-yard pass to David Patten to the Oakland 29. Brady then threw two incompletions before a third-down play in which he scrambled forward for 1 yard. And then, with roughly fifty-five seconds left and no time-outs on a snow-covered field that had affected footing to the point where passing, running, catching, and kicking had been all but impossible throughout the game, Patriots kicker Vinatieri and holder Ken Walter jogged onto the field for a 45-yard field goal attempt that seemed all but impossible.

Like a golfer trying to execute a knockdown in hopes of keeping a shot below a tree branch while maximizing distance, Vinatieri punched a low, hard kick that cleared both the defensive line of the Raiders—who can jump high in the snow?—and the crossbar to tie the game at 13–13 with just twenty-seven seconds left.

In this case, there was nothing lucky about it. A native of South Dakota and a kicker at South Dakota State when signed by Bill Parcells and the Patriots as an undrafted free agent, Vinatieri was accustomed to kicking in poor conditions and someone whom Bill Belichick sometimes referred to as the Patriots' "best player." Under the circumstances, the kick seemed impossible, a notion Vinatieri quickly dispelled with a moment that remains both one of the greatest plays in Patriots history and one of the greatest achievements in the history of the league.

The Raiders, of course, never possessed the ball again—at least, not really. After Vinatieri's subsequent kickoff and a 23-yard return by Terry Kirby, the Raiders offense took the field at their own 35-yard line with twenty-two seconds remaining. Though his team still possessed two time-outs, Gruden ordered his offense to snap the ball and take a knee to run out the clock. In such inclement weather, nobody really questioned the decision. At the start of sudden-death overtime, captains for the teams reported to midfield for the coin toss to determine which team would possess the ball first. The Raiders called heads and, of course, the coin landed tails. *Another good break for the Patriots.* And yet, had the Raiders simply stopped the Patriots and forced a punt—Oakland had a 13–3 lead entering the fourth quarter, remember—the outcome might have been different. Instead, the Patriots just continued to assemble speed and mass like a snowball rolling down a hill until the Raiders simply could do nothing at all.

Brady completed his first six passes of overtime before a handoff to running back J. R. Redmond that lost a yard. Brady then completed two more passes—he was eight-for-eight in overtime, a foreshadowing of his entire Patriots career—including a critical clutch pass on fourth down that whizzed to a kneeling Patten, who secured the ball on his left shoulder pad. The Patriots then ran three times, the final play an 8-yard gain by running back Antowain Smith that converted a third-and-5 from the Oakland 17-yard line and placed the ball at the Raiders' 9. Smith gained 2 yards on the next play to move to the 7.

With roughly 8 minutes having expired from the clock, Belichick called Brady to the sideline and gave him very specific instructions. *Do not hand off. Do not throw. Just take the snap and get to the middle of the field.* Brady then sneaked 2 yards to his left, to the Oakland 5-yard line, leaving the Patriots with a third-and-goal. Belichick sent on his field goal unit, accounting for the potential of a bad snap and giving Vinatieri as many as two chances at a game-winning kick. His defense having proven incapable of stopping the Patriots offense in the fourth quarter and overtime—with a little intervention from the NFL rule book, of course—Gruden tried the last thing he could. He called time-out, hoping to "ice" kicker Vinatieri—the cold-blooded ice man from South Dakota—with a trip to the AFC Championship at stake.

Naturally, Vinatieri needed only one chance. The snap was clean. The hold was good. The kicker popped a simple 23-yard field goal smack dab through the middle of the uprights, giving the Patriots a 16–13 victory that remains one of the most memorable and controversial games in NFL history. Patriots center Lonie Paxton, wearing No. 66, promptly dropped on his back in the end zone on the final play in the history of Foxboro Stadium—the stadium had been scheduled for demolition to begin on December 23, anticipating an earlier end to the New England football season—and made a snow angel. An exuberant Belichick hugged Brady, smiled, and pumped his fist. Vinatieri was carried off the field on the shoulders of his teammates as if he were reenacting the final scene from *Rudy*, the inspiring story of a Notre Dame walk-on and practice squad player who defied all odds.

The Patriots were good. They were well coached. They were fundamentally sound and maybe more than a little lucky, too. And they were headed to the AFC Championship Game with greater belief in themselves than ever before, about to launch both the greatest dynasty in American football history and a reign that would place Boston—and all of New England, really—at the center of professional American sports for the next twenty years.

"It starts with the tuck rule," said longtime *Boston Globe* reporter and columnist Bob Ryan. "The entire empire is built on a lucky break of the correct call of a bad rule. That was a fumble—and that will be Jon Gruden's dying words. He'll be on his deathbed. And his last words will be, 'It was a fumble, dammit.' And it was. It wasn't, technically, but it was. So, it starts with that. Then a great kick in the snow. And that night is the beginning of the Patriots era. You've got to start with the tuck rule game—[with the fact] that the whole empire is built on a lucky break of being the happy beneficiaries of the correct call of a bad rule. So, that's my simple summation of that."

Lest anyone interpret that as a criticism, it isn't. In the end, the participants on all the championship teams spoke of hard work, commitment, teamwork, and confidence. They spoke of a range of factors that led them all to the peak of their respective sports, and they all spoke of one other thing, too: luck. It was, after all, a necessary ingredient.

"I think Bill [Belichick] put it right," says Bruschi. "To win championships, you need good coaches, good players and good fortune. So there were a couple moments during that season, major moments where good fortune was something that really helped us out. . . . I think the tuck rule was one of them."

At the time, of course, nobody in New England was worried about the *how* or the *why*. The win was all that mattered. The Patriots were enveloped in a blizzard of good feeling, and they were now headed to Pittsburgh for the AFC Championship Game with the chance to compete for a place in the Super Bowl.

As Bill Belichick would remind his players many times throughout the years to come, the Patriots had a business trip. And there was still work to be done.

* * *

There is an old adage in football that goes like this: "If you have two quarterbacks, you have none." For one day, at least, the New England Patriots proved otherwise.

Relegated to a backup during the simultaneous ascension of Brady and the Patriots, Drew Bledsoe had bitten his tongue, at least publicly. Privately, he felt as if Bill Belichick had turned on him, gone back on his word, violated one of the understood rules of sports that a player could not lose his job to injury. Bledsoe and his contract totaling more than $100 million had now made him the most expensive backup quarterback in the league, and with each passing day it was becoming clearer that the future of the Patriots rested with Brady, which made Bledsoe's departure from New England inevitable.

But in the interim, the Patriots had a season to finish and—as it turned out—Bledsoe would play a significant role, too.

After defeating the Raiders, the Patriots played the 2001 AFC Championship Game in Pittsburgh, home of the mighty Steelers, who had finished the season with a 13-3 record and as the top seed in the AFC. Only the Rams (14-2) had finished with a better record. As such, Pittsburgh had earned the right to host the AFC Championship Game a week after defeating the Baltimore Ravens by a 27-10 score in the divisional playoffs. Las Vegas oddsmakers favored the Steelers by 10 points, a significant number that suggested a relatively easy Pittsburgh victory.

What everyone neglected to realize, of course, was that Bill Belichick had not merely found a special quarterback in Tom Brady. New England also had an exceptional defense and opportunistic special teams, not to mention a backup quarterback who could start for most every other team in football. And they would all factor into another stunning Patriots victory.

In a game generally controlled by the defenses—Pittsburgh and New England had allowed the third- and sixth-fewest points in the league in 2001—the Patriots scored first on a 55-yard punt return by spark plug receiver Troy Brown for a 7-0 New England lead. The Steelers countered with a field goal to make it 7-3 before, late in the second quarter, the Steelers blitzed Brady on third-and-8 at New England's 32-yard line. As Brady completed a 28-yard strike to Brown over the middle of the field that advanced the ball to the Pittsburgh 40-yard line, Steelers defensive back Lee Flowers came from Brady's right and dove toward the quarterback's front left leg, folding Brady's left ankle outward and, ultimately, under the weight of a sprawling Flowers. (Today, the play would be called a penalty.) The quarterback then struggled to his feet and was incapable on placing any real weight on his left side, significantly limiting his mobility and making him incapable of throwing the football.

Forced to call his third and final timeout of the half with 1:40 remaining, Belichick pulled Brady from the game and inserted Bledsoe, who bolted onto the field as if uncaged. On his first play, he completed a 15-yard strike to Patten. On his second, he ran around right end for a 4-yard gain before absorbing a hard hit from Steelers cornerback Chad Scott—not unlike the hit he had absorbed against the Jets earlier in the year that had effectively had ended his season. But Bledsoe this time jumped to his feet none the worse for wear, clapping with enthusiasm as he returned to the huddle of Patriots teammates, who both believed in him and believed in themselves.

We're a different team now. We have the best backup quarterback in football. We're not going to skip a beat.

With slightly more than a minute remaining in the half against one of the best defenses in football—and with no time-outs—Bledsoe had the Patriots at the Pittsburgh 21-yard line. On his third play he threw to Patten again, this time completing a 10-yard pass to his left. And then, on his fourth game snap in months since being replaced by Brady, the strong-armed Bledsoe lined up in the shotgun and took the snap from the Pittsburgh 11-yard line, backpedaled to the 19, and flicked a pass to the back right corner of the end zone—the pass covered roughly 30 yards in all—that a leaping Patten secured for what would prove to be New England's only offensive touchdown of the game, giving the Patriots a shocking 14–3 lead at intermission.

"It's a ball I throw well," Bledsoe would later say of the play call.

Said Patriots offensive coordinator Charlie Weis of Bledsoe's performance on the scoring drive, during which he went three-for-three for 36 yards and a touchdown along with his 4-yard run: "He gets very few reps [in practice]. I'd say he should be proud. That's a pretty hard thing we asked him to do."

Trailing 14–3 and facing a deficit that matched their largest of the season, the Steelers continued to falter. Pittsburgh's first possession of the second half resulted in a fumble, immediately giving the Patriots the ball at the Pittsburgh 35-yard line. And though the Patriots failed to capitalize, Pittsburgh's subsequent possession delivered the Steelers to the New England 16-yard line when, on third-and-5, Stewart was nearly intercepted by Patriots defensive end Willie McGinest. Pittsburgh promptly lined up for a 34-yard goal with hopes of making the score 14–6 when the 2001 Pittsburgh Steelers football season effectively combusted.

After the snap, Patriots defensive lineman Brandon Mitchell burst through the Steelers offensive line and had almost a clean path toward kicker Kris Brown, blocking the kick. The ball bounced backward toward the Patriots' 40-yard line, where the multitalented Troy Brown scooped it up and ran 11 yards before the Pittsburgh kicker grabbed onto his jersey. Before he could be pulled down, Brown flipped the ball backward to teammate Antwan Harris, who rumbled the remaining 49 yards for another improbable touchdown that gave the Patriots a stunning 21–3 lead.

"I just wanted to make sure it was a lateral," said Brown, one of the smartest, most affable and versatile players in Patriots history. "And he did a great job. It worked out great for us."

For the most part, it continued to. Though the Steelers scored touchdowns on their next two possessions to make the score 21–17 entering the fourth quarter, a Vinatieri field goal extended the margin to 24–17 with slightly more than 11 minutes to play. Pittsburgh never again got closer than the New England 48-yard line, quarterback Kordell Stewart throwing interceptions on his team's final two possessions of the game. All in all, Pittsburgh turned the ball over four times, all by quarterback Stewart, while allowing touchdowns on a punt return and blocked field goal. The Patriots did not turn the ball over once, despite playing two quarterbacks.

"To get to that chance to take the field and contribute to that game, it felt really good," Bledsoe told longtime NFL reporter Don Banks many years later. "There was probably a certain level of vindication in that, 'Hey, look, I've been the guy here for a long time and everybody's completely forgotten,' and I was able to come in and play well enough to help us win the game. I enjoyed that. It just felt really good to be back out there playing the game as opposed to just helping game plan and running the scout team in practice. It was a pretty meaningful moment."

Said owner Robert Kraft after the victory: "This is the true meaning of team. We never talk about individuals here."

And so, as a team, the Patriots packed their bags and headed for New Orleans to encounter the last team to have defeated them. The Greatest Show on Turf. The St. Louis Rams.

* * *

Bill Belichick, despite the beliefs of many New England football fans over many years, was not a demigod. He was neither omnipotent nor entirely prescient, even if it often seemed that way. What he was and is, however, was an excellent football coach. More important, he rarely if ever made the same mistake twice.

One week after defeating the Patriots by a 24–17 score in Week 10, the St. Louis Rams lost to the Tampa Bay Buccaneers. By the time the Rams had reached the Super Bowl, that had been the final defeat experienced by either St. Louis or New England as the teams reunited for Super Bowl XXXVI. Like the Patriots, the Rams had won eight straight games entering the Super Bowl, having obliterated quarterback Brett Favre and the Green Bay Packers in the divisional round of the playoffs before claiming a 29–24 victory over the Philadelphia Eagles in the NFC Championship game. All in all, St. Louis had outscored its opponents by a stunning 136 points in its final eight contests, an average of 17 points per game that suggested the Rams were merely toying with the opposition. St. Louis was rolling.

In *The Education of a Coach*—the book he agreed to participate in with renowned author David Halberstam in 2005—Belichick gave great respect to Rams coaches and players, specifically quarterback Kurt Warner and running back Marshall Faulk, the latter having handled the ball on most every play as the Rams closed out the regular season meeting between the teams roughly two months earlier. Belichick, according to Halberstam, was especially critical of himself after the loss. Regarded as a defensive mastermind, Belichick's plan to stop the Rams during the regular season centered on quarterback Warner, who subsequently shredded the New England defense for 401 yards and three touchdowns. The team blitzed a whopping forty-two times and managed to sack Warner only once. The plan just didn't work.

Prior to the rematch, the Patriots altered their approach. In discussions with confidant Ernie Adams—a mysterious longtime friend and colleague of Belichick whom many playfully regarded as the Patriots' director of covert operations—both Belichick and Adams had concluded that Faulk would be the focus of New England's game plan in the Super Bowl. Faulk was a brilliant talent who could both run and catch with speed and elusiveness, but the one thing he lacked was size. And so the Patriots approach against him was simple: hit him on every play.

Wrote Halberstam, "There were going to be times when [the Rams] went to Faulk, and these were going to be the critical moments of the game . . . [The Patriots] were going to hit him every time he had the ball and hit him every time he didn't have the ball. The phrase they used was 'butch the back,' which meant hit him every time, or, as Belichick later said, 'knock the shit out of him.'"

Aside from the emphasis on Faulk, the concept was a simple one that manifests itself in contact sports. One team is often more talented. The other is tougher. The Rams were loaded with talent. For the Patriots to win, Belichick had determined they would have to be the tougher team.

Further, with regard to the Rams, Belichick understood the tendencies of the opposing coach, Mike Martz, whom many, including Belichick, regarded as an offensive innovator. Martz wanted his offense to move the ball swiftly, explosively, potently. The Rams liked to throw and score—and they liked to score fast. In the years to come, one of Belichick's greatest abilities came in reading the opposing sideline, where he often seemed to know what the opposition wanted to do before the opposing coach himself.

Unsurprisingly, the Patriots were huge underdogs in the game, Vegas oddsmakers now favoring the Rams by 14 points, an enormous number for a Super Bowl. (For the sake of perspective, the miracle 1985 Patriots had been 10-point underdogs against the dominant Chicago Bears in Super Bowl XX, only to lose by 36 points.) The Patriots were plucky, tough, extremely well coached, and talented on defense, but the simple truth was that America looked at them as *lucky*, the kind of team that was now in way over its head, a team whose success was the result of good fortune and, frankly, flukes.

THE SEEDS OF A DYNASTY

Truth be told, the evidence against the Patriots was considerable. Patten had been knocked out cold in the Buffalo game during the regular season . . . *and they won*. New England had lucked into a bye in the first round of the playoffs, then played in a snowstorm against the Raiders, at home, where the Patriots got bailed out by the tuck rule . . . *and won*. Against the Steelers, they returned a punt for a touchdown—after a penalty had forced a re-kick—and blocked a field goal for another score, losing their starting quarterback along the way . . . *and won*. On paper, the list of things that had broken in their favor was long and damning.

To New England fans, that list of events was eerily similar, in some ways, to what the Patriots had experienced in early 1986, when they reached the Super Bowl and were demolished by the Bears. But make no mistake: in Super Bowl XXXVI between the Patriots and flashy Rams, there would be nothing lucky or fluky about it.

* * *

Eschewing the standard pregame routine of individual introductions and living up to the words of their owner, the Patriots entered the field of play at the Superdome as a team. Over the next few hours, they so thoroughly battered and flummoxed the Rams offense that St. Louis, at times, seemed to unravel. They hit, grabbed, and disrupted Faulk on every play, employing a similar pattern with the speedy St. Louis receivers. They slowed the overall pace of the game. St. Louis made one field goal in the first quarter and missed another, and the score was just 3–0 in favor of the Rams when, after a 15-yard run by Faulk, St. Louis had a first-and-10 at its own 39-yard line with just under 9 minutes remaining in the first half.

Warner took the snap and dropped back to pass. The Patriots sent an extra rusher—"That's the first time they've blitzed," announcer Pat Summerall would say seconds later—including linebacker Mike Vrabel, who was unblocked from Warner's right side. Affected by the pressure, Warner stepped backward and carelessly floated a pass intended for wide receiver Isaac Bruce that drifted away from the right sideline—where the pass should have been—and landed softly into the hands of Patriots cornerback Ty Law, one of the Patriots' best players and a future Hall of Fame cornerback. Untouched, Law ran 47 yards down the left sideline and raised his right hand in the air before crossing the goal line, propelling the Patriots to a 7–3 lead and making a rather emphatic statement. *We're playing for keeps. And we're for real.*

Seven minutes later and after the teams exchanged punts, the Rams had a first-and-10 from their 25-yard line with two time-outs remaining. Warner completed a 15-yard pass to receiver Ricky Proehl, who eluded defensive back Terrell Buckley and ran up the middle of the field for a 15-yard gain before he encountered defensive back Antwan Harris, who lowered his head and blasted both Proehl and the football, causing a fumble. Buckley recovered. Five plays later and with just thirty-six seconds remaining in the half, Brady threw an 8-yard touchdown pass to Patten and the Patriots had a 14–3 advantage.

His team shaken, Rams coach Martz instructed quarterback Warner to take a knee and kill the remaining thirty-one seconds of the half so that the Rams might collect themselves.

They almost never did.

Late in the third quarter, with Patriots defensive back Otis Smith pressing receiver Torry Holt at the line of scrimmage, the Rams faced another key third down. Warner took a quick drop from center and fired to his right, but the pass zipped well in front of his intended receiver, who had stumbled trying to avoid contact at the snap. The ball went directly to Smith, who returned the interception to the Rams 33-yard line and set up a 37-yard field goal by kicker Adam Vinatieri that split the uprights, dead center, and gave New England a 17–3 advantage with essentially a quarter remaining in the biggest football game of the season.

To that stage of the game, all of New England's points had come off St. Louis turnovers: two interceptions and a fumble. The Patriots offense had not put together a real touchdown drive with Brady at quarterback since the second half of the snow game against Oakland, and yet they were slightly more than sixteen minutes from claiming perhaps the most improbable Super Bowl victory of all time. But as all sports fans knew—particularly ones from Boston who had seen their teams repeatedly crumble in key and final months over the last fifteen years—there was, as the saying goes, still *a long way to go.*

Operating with newfound urgency, the Rams systematically moved down the field. Warner completed six straight passes to move the ball to the New England 3-yard line before a pair of incompletions left the Rams with a fourth-and-goal. Warner took the snap and was prepared to throw a short pass to Faulk—"there were going to be times when [the Rams] went to Faulk, and these were going to be the critical moments of the game," as Halberstam noted—but the gifted running back was not open. Scrambling, Warner was sacked and fumbled, the football bouncing into the hands of New England safety Tebucky Jones, who bolted 97 yards down the left sideline for an apparent 23–3 Patriots lead that all but secured the championship for New England. There was one small problem: a yellow penalty flag that negated the entire sequence. On the play, the assignment of New England defensive lineman Willie McGinest had been to "butch the back," which Belichick's team, as promised, had done for much of the game. But in this instance, McGinest all but enveloped Faulk in a bear hug. It was an indisputable defensive holding penalty that gave St. Louis an automatic first down inside the New England 2-yard line. Two plays later, Warner pushed his way into the end zone for the Rams' first touchdown of the game, making the score 17–10 following a successful extra point by St. Louis kicker Jeff Wilkins.

As much of New England groused, the entire game flipped. In what felt like an instant, a potential 20- or 21-point New England lead was down to 7 points. And there were still more than 9 minutes remaining in the game.

Unsurprisingly, New England's offensive shortcomings began to haunt Belichick. After the Rams kicked off, the Patriots held the ball for just one minute and thirty-six seconds, almost immediately punting the ball back to the Rams. The good news was that St. Louis was all the way back its own 7-yard line. Still, St. Louis advanced to the New England 38-yard line before Warner—on a second-and-9 play—foolishly took a 16-yard sack when he did not find an open receiver to his liking. Despite having no time-outs, the Rams subsequently faced an impossible fourth-and-20 and punted the ball away with less than four minutes on the game clock, giving the Patriots possession with just 3:44 remaining and just one simple task: kill the clock.

They didn't come close. Though the Patriots kept it ticking with two running plays sandwiched around a completed pass, New England did not come close to a first down, Belichick opting to put the game in the hands of his defense as the game hit the two-minute warning. The Rams subsequently regained possession at their own 45-yard line with 1:51 to play, essentially returning to the same spot on the field where Warner had taken his ill-advised sack. And this time the Rams were flawless.

With the Patriots now seemingly back on their heels, the Rams attacked. Warner completed an 18-yard pass to Hakim, an 11-yard pass to Yo Murphy, and then a 26-yard touchdown pass to Proehl. That tied the game at 17 when Wilkins against converted the extra point, erasing the Patriots' lead and a team performance that had been nearly flawless for the first three quarters of play.

The entire St. Louis possession used just twenty-one seconds of the game clock, tied the score, and left the Patriots glassy-eyed. Trailing 17–3 entering the fourth quarter and excluding punts, the quick-strike Rams had run twenty-two plays while the Patriots had run six. St. Louis had gained 142 yards, New England just 10. Most important, the Rams had outscored the Patriots 14-0 to tie the score while the Patriots had failed to manage so much as a first down.

As fans throughout all six New England states recoiled in exasperation, the Patriots had the look and feel of an exhausted, legless prizefighter. They had held the Rams at bay for almost the entire bout. They had been winning on points. But now the fight was square, and they looked ready to be put down.

"And now, with no time-outs, I think that the Patriots, with this field position, you have to just run the clock out," said CBS analyst John Madden, a former Super Bowl–winning coach with the Oakland Raiders. "You have to just play for overtime now. I don't think you want to force anything here. You don't want to do anything stupid because you have no time-outs and you're backed up."

With the Patriots seemingly staggered, much of America agreed with Madden. Belichick, on the other hand, had no intention of wagering his team's fate on the outcome of the overtime coin toss. At the time, after all, NFL over-time rules called for sudden death, meaning that the team winning the toss would have the chance to possess the ball and win the Super Bowl with only a field goal.

Showing extraordinary faith in both his young quarterback and an offense that had been inside the St. Louis 35-yard line only once in the second half—and that was the result of the Smith interception that had placed the ball at the Rams 33-yard line, producing only a field goal—Belichick put Brady in the shotgun at his own 17-yard line with just 1:21 left and—again—no time-outs. Poised as ever, the young quarterback completed a 5-yard pass to running back J. R. Redmond, then an 8-yarder before spiking the ball to stop the clock with forty-one seconds left. Brady then completed another throw to Redmond for 11 yards before the running back extended the ball beyond the sideline as he was tackled, stopping the clock with thirty-three seconds left. Then, in the face of a blitz, Brady did what Warner earlier did not, deliberately avoiding a sack that would have set the Patriots back and kept the game clock ticking.

With the ball now positioned at the New England 41-yard line with 29 seconds to go, the Patriots needed almost 30 yards to give their kicker, Vinatieri, a chance at a field goal. Brady took the snap. Facing only a three-man rush, he stepped up in the pocket and delivered a strike to a leaping Troy Brown, who caught the pass while cutting across the middle of the field and scurried to the sideline, stepping out at the St. Louis 36-yard line with twenty-one seconds left. The play had gained 23 yards and required just eight seconds.

"This is amazing," admitted broadcaster Madden.

On the ensuing first down, Brady completed a 6-yard pass to tight end Jermaine Wiggins that placed the ball at the St. Louis 30-yard line. Calmly, Brady led his team to the line of scrimmage, set the offense, and spiked the ball. It bounced straight up into the air, just above the six-foot-four Brady's head, before he extended his arm and let the ball land softly in his left hand. The referee blew his whistle. There were six seconds remaining on the clock.

On the drive, excluding the three balls he deliberately disposed of, to stop the clock, Brady was five-for-five for 53 yards to move the Patriots from their own 17-yard line to the St. Louis 30—with no time-outs—to position Adam Vinatieri for the game-winning field goal, the aforementioned Shot Heard 'Round the World. The kick was the perfect ending to a perfect game-winning drive, executed by the coach, quarterback, and kicker with astonishing precision.

Less than five months after the attacks of September 11, the Patriots had pulled off one of the great upsets in American sports history, an event that prompted even the typically stoic Belichick to throw up his arms in disbeliev-ing, euphoric fashion. According to Halberstam, while embracing his confidant Adams, an ecstatic Belichick asked his longtime friend, "Can you believe we won the Super Bowl against the Rams with this team?"

After nearly two decades of Boston's repeated failures on the field and in the arena, much of New England was asking itself a similar question. The Patriots, for so long one of the great laughingstocks in professional sports, had won the Super Bowl. They had upset a Rams group that was regarded as the best team in the league. And they had done it with a smart, hardworking, unassuming group of players who demanded to be introduced as a unit and by a coach who preached the group over the individual, the whole being greater than the sum of the parts.

"The fans of New England have been waiting 42 years for this day—and we are world champions," owner Robert Kraft said after accepting the Vince Lombardi championship trophy from then commissioner Paul Tagliabue. "And the Kraft family is happy to be associated with coaches and players who put team first as the way they came out of the tunnel tonight [demonstrated]. And in a way, the fact that our players and coaches—at this time in our country, when people are banding together for a higher cause—can [reflect] this spirit of America, we're proud to be a symbol of that in a small way. Spirituality, faith and democracy are the cornerstones of our country."

And then this: "We are all Patriots," Kraft said, uttering words that still echo throughout NFL history, "and tonight, the Patriots are world champions."

Indeed, there was no doubt.

And as it turned out, at the time, Robert Kraft had no idea how right he would continue to be.

CHAPTER 2

BURYING THE PAST

"When we were living in Arizona, my kids were playing youth baseball and they were really good players. I had tickets to the Diamondbacks right behind the dugout and when the Diamondbacks won the World Series [in 2001], we were at the games. But when we moved here [to Boston] in '03, they became Red Sox fans in like two weeks because that's what everybody wanted to talk about."

—former Celtics executive Danny Ainge, April 2020

LATE IN 2001, JUST BEFORE the attacks of September 11, the Boston Red Sox were amid the kind of late-season spin that even the most hardened, scarred, and cynical Red Sox fan would have deemed embarrassing. The team had lost thirteen of fourteen games and, following a rainout at New York on Monday, September 10, was preparing for a Tuesday series opener at Tampa Bay when terrorists hijacked planes and flew them into the World Trade Center and Pentagon that morning. Manager Jimy Williams had been fired only weeks earlier. And replacement Joe Kerrigan, who had undermined Williams while serving as the former manager's pitching coach, had lost complete control of a roster that was filled with, at the time, talented malcontents.

During the final days of the season, after Major League Baseball had resumed and while on a team bus in Baltimore, Kerrigan rose from his seat and asked outfielder Manny Ramirez to turn down his boom box, something that was consistent with club policy. Ramirez ignored Kerrigan and disrespectfully sent his manager back to the front of the bus.

The message to the acting manager of the team according to at least one onlooker?

Go fuck yourself.

In retrospect, had the 2001 Red Sox never returned to the field following the attacks of September 11, nobody would have missed them. Nonetheless, the Red Sox as a whole were held in a trust at that point—and in more ways than one. Owned by Thomas A. Yawkey and his wife, Jean, for fifty-nine years, the team moved into a trust overseen by John Harrington beginning in 1992. As a trustee of the JRY Corporation—the initials stood for Jean R. Yawkey—Harrington effectively ran the Red Sox until December 2001, when he agreed to sell the Red Sox to a new ownership group headed by hedge fund billionaire John Henry, a part owner of the then Florida Marlins who wanted his own team.

The Red Sox hadn't won a World Series in eighty-three years when Henry took over in spring training, and the standard for success was obvious.

"Win a World Series? That's not my choice—it's my role, it's my obligation to New England. That's what I've been charged with," Henry said at his introductory press conference. "When you bid on the Red Sox, the challenge you're undertaking is nothing short of winning the World Series."

Provincial as ever, many Bostonians bristled. At the time, many wanted the Sox turned over to local businessman and concessionaire Joe O'Donnell, who had assembled his own group to buy the club. In the end, the preferred choice of commissioner Bud Selig and Major League Baseball was the group led by Henry, which had many Bostonians grumbling that their treasured franchise had been handed over to, for lack of a better description, a *cahpet-baggah.*

Henry, along with fellow owner Tom Werner and new team executive Larry Lucchino, was an outsider. New England was wary of them all. Along with Werner and Lucchino, Henry held individual meetings with a wide range of Red Sox media members, all designed with the idea of making a positive first impression. Henry and his partners privately asked reporters an array of questions about the state and place of the Red Sox, including a most obvious one: *How do we get people to trust us?*

The answers seemed obvious. *You win. And you stay.*

In retrospect, of course, even those replies proved insufficient.

Nonetheless, as the Red Sox began an enormous transition that December, no one could have known how cataclysmic—and beneficial—the change would prove. Almost instantaneously, the Red Sox evolved for the better. During the ownership's first spring training, the team promptly fired both general manager Dan Duquette and Kerrigan, the interim manager whom Ramirez had effectively castrated on the team bus in Baltimore. (Kerrigan had even attempted to visit Ramirez during the off-season and was denied entrance onto Ramirez's property.) The new owners subsequently hired former bench coach Grady Little—an ally of deposed manager Williams—much to the delight of their players, who openly cheered when Little's hiring was announced during a clubhouse meeting behind closed doors in spring training. The Red Sox subsequently rumbled to a fabulous start to the season, going 40-17 and building a three-and-a-half-game lead in the competitive AL East.

Just like that, as if they had performed an exorcism, the Red Sox went from a demoralizing symbol of despair to one of boundless hope, evidence of just how quickly fortunes could change. Though they only went a game over .500 for their final 105 games, they managed to win 93 games, a successful season by most any measure except the one that applied in Boston. The Red Sox, after all, had not won a World Series since 1918, and so anything less than a championship was ultimately deemed a failure, independent of whether the team was undergoing a transition, independent of whether the Red Sox were growing into something bigger and better.

With all of that in mind, the new owners of the Red Sox entered their first full off-season. But before the Red Sox could start remaking the roster, they needed to identify the person with whom they would entrust the entire baseball operation, the next general manager of the team at a time when the game was starting to become far more analytical, the figure who would make the critical decisions that would determine whether the Red Sox would win a World Series championship for the first time since World War I.

In that search, the Red Sox dramatically failed in the pursuit of their preferred candidate. But as is often said in the sports world, sometimes the best moves are the ones you never make.

* * *

In 2002, Billy Beane was the darling of baseball, a handsome, revolutionary executive who was spitting in the face of conventional wisdom—and succeeding. As the chief baseball decision-maker of the Oakland A's, Beane had built a wildly successful operation despite possessing one of the lowest payrolls in baseball. He himself was at the start of a revolution—a commitment to baseball analytics that treated players like commodities on the stock market and conventional wisdom like the gum stuck on the bottom of one's shoe. In late 2002, Beane was coming off a season in which his A's won 103 games, tied with the Yankees for most in baseball. And Beane had done so despite a player payroll that ranked twenty-eighth among the thirty major-league teams at just over $40 million, a mere fraction of the totals spent by baseball's biggest market teams, like the Yankees, whose payroll exceeded $125 million.

In placing emphasis on undervalued players and skill sets—on-base percentage was a perceived staple of the Beane system—Beane and Oakland had turned baseball on its head, establishing a new method that had owners drooling at the prospect of paying as much as 70 percent less per victory.

As such, *cost per win* became a new way for baseball owners to measure the success of a franchise and executive, though Beane's methods were known by another term that became as controversial as it did familiar: "Moneyball."

Unsurprisingly, Henry and his partners made Beane the focus of their search, with team president and organizational bulldog Larry Lucchino leading the way behind the scenes. While Oakland denied the initial request by the Red Sox to pry Beane away, the Red Sox remained steadfast, continuing with the charade of a search while they waited for Beane to express his desire for the job. Though he was in the midst of an eight-year run, from 1999 to 2006, during which the A's would win more games than any major-league franchise other than the Yankees and Atlanta Braves, Oakland would win just one playoff series in six tries and never so much as a single game in the American League Championship Series.

As Beane himself would say in *Moneyball: The Art of Winning*, the book authored by Michael Lewis that simultaneously celebrated the A's and gave baseball's new revolution its name: "My shit doesn't work in the playoffs."

Just the same, the Red Sox offered a different kind of opportunity: He could give them creative ways to find undervalued talent at lower costs; they could give him money—for himself and for his roster. On paper, the match seemed ideal.

And so, after much dallying, Billy Beane finally went to owner Steve Schott and expressed a desire to interview with the Red Sox. Unsurprisingly, word got out that Oakland had relented. But even before the news broke in the *New York Times*, Red Sox officials began to receive a flurry of phone calls, with one reporter asking Lucchino if there was truth to the rumor that the Red Sox were about to interview Beane.

Despite being someone who often joked that there were "no secrets in baseball," Lucchino bristled during the call, abruptly telling the reporter that he was not about to address "fucking rumors" that the door had opened for Beane's arrival in Boston.

Of course, Lucchino already knew that the Red Sox were about to interview Beane, whom they subsequently offered a whopping annual salary of $12.5 million to become their chief baseball decision-maker.

After asking the A's for permission to speak with the Red Sox, all Billy Beane had to do was say yes. Instead, shockingly, he said no.

Whatever the reasons for Beane's ultimate hairpin decision—he was close with his daughter on the West Coast, and the Red Sox were a high-pressure environment in contrast with nothing-really-to-lose Oakland—Beane ultimately stayed out West and, to his credit, never took a job in another market. The A's still have not won a World Series under Beane and were a mere 1-8 in nine playoff series from 1999 to 2021 despite winning the sixth-most games in all of baseball during that twenty-three-year period. The five teams ahead of the A's all won at least one championship.

Among the teams in front of Oakland, as it turned out, would be the Red Sox, who, like Beane might have done, went against conventional wisdom in naming their next general manager. The Red Sox chose a native Bostonian who grew up in Brookline, Massachusetts, within roughly a mile of Fenway Park, though his hiring was nonetheless met with great skepticism. After flirting with an accomplished, veteran executive like Beane who had become the talk of the entire baseball world, the Red Sox spun on their heels and hired a promising young executive who was still a month shy of his twenty-ninth birthday.

His name, of course, was Theo Epstein.

* * *

The idea, from the very beginning, was for Theo Epstein to turn the Red Sox into "a scouting and player development machine," the exact words that Epstein used upon being hired as the general manager of the Red Sox. A protégé of Lucchino, Epstein was young, smart, handsome, and open-minded—and willing to admit what he did not know. The Red Sox flanked him with a longtime baseball scout, executive and traditionalist named Bill Lajoie, whose reputation as an old-school *baseball man* was both well-known and well-respected. Together, Epstein and Lajoie made a fascinating, fabulous team, a blend of youth and energy, eagerness and experience, old and new, that has been the formula of many championship rosters in many sports.

And it worked almost immediately. In their first season with Epstein as GM, the Red Sox won ninety-five games and finished second behind the New

York Yankees in the AL East, good enough to qualify for the postseason. During his first off-season, Epstein had struck gold on a rich market for mid-range offensive players by acquiring, through various means, third baseman Bill Mueller, second baseman Todd Walker, first baseman Kevin Millar, and designated hitter David Ortiz. He had added those players to an inherited group that already included shortstop Nomar Garciaparra, outfielders Manny Ramirez, Johnny Damon, and Trot Nixon, and catcher Jason Varitek, giving the Red Sox a lineup, 1 through 9, that rivaled the very best in the game.

That season, largely on the strength of their relentless, thundering offense, the Red Sox led the major leagues in runs scored and set an all-time record for slugging percentage by a team in a single season. And while Epstein had failures—designated hitter Jeremy Giambi, who proved a bust, actually started ahead of eventual franchise cornerstone Ortiz for two months—the biggest issue for the team was the state of its patchwork relief corps, an area in which Epstein tried to employ untraditional methods that failed spectacularly.

At that point in baseball, thanks largely to the success of Oakland A's manager Tony La Russa two decades earlier, most major-league teams had adopted a bullpen built around the concept of a *closer*—the prototype of which had become New York Yankees right-hander Mariano Rivera. A dominant, unflappable reliever who helped backbone the Yankees to four World Series championships over five seasons and a stunning five World Series appearances in six years, Rivera was routinely asked to pitch the final inning—or sometimes two—of any reasonably close Yankees victory, no questions asked. He anchored a bullpen structure that allowed other pitchers to similarly settle into known, established roles, creating an assembly-line type of system that effectively eliminated any decision-making.

In New York, Rivera got the ninth, last call, no questions asked. Jeff Nelson or Mike Stanton split the seventh and eighth. The roles were clearly defined, and the results were inarguable.

And yet, among new thinkers and younger executives, many—including Epstein—wondered whether Rivera was, in some ways, wasted. What if the more important outs of the game came in the seventh inning? Or the eighth? Wouldn't it make more sense to use him then? And if that was true, could relief pitchers adapt to a system where any of them could be used at any time, specifically in matchups earlier in the game that might allow a proactive manager to employ their individual strengths more specifically? And so, the famed "closer-by-committee" approach was born. And it failed immediately.

On Opening Day 2003, in fact, the Red Sox had a 4–1 lead entering the bottom of the ninth inning against the then Tampa Bay Devil Rays, one of the worst teams in baseball. Without an identified closer, manager Grady Little opted for veteran Alan Embree, a talented, hard-throwing left-hander who had failed in previous attempts at closing with other organizations. Embree allowed a single, home run, and single to the only three batters he faced, making the score 4–3 and placing the tying run on base. Little promptly summoned right-hander Chad Fox, another talented pitcher who had similarly struggled during his career in difficult or "high-leverage" situations.

Fox retired the first two batters he faced on a strikeout and groundout—and then, despite being *this close* to securing the victory, issued a walk and home run that gave Tampa a stunning 6–4 win, sprouting the seeds of doubt that already existed in the Boston bullpen. Within weeks, Epstein smartly reversed course and acquired a succession of relievers—right-handers Byung-Hyun Kim and Scott Williamson were chief among them and each had experience as a closer—but the damage was largely done.

In retrospect, had the 2003 Red Sox had a younger, more progressive manager and a different collection of relievers, the closer-by-committee experiment might have worked. (In 2018, for instance, the Red Sox used the framework of a similar approach in the postseason and steamrolled to a world title.) But in 2003, whether the result of human limitations or because the concept was ahead of its time, neither the Red Sox nor baseball as a whole was ready for it. Baseball players were creatures of habit, after all, and they were indisputably human. They liked the comfort that came along with routines. Most of them pitched worse than normal under pressure. And because the ninth inning came with an indisputable sense of finality, the position of closer came with inherent pressures and responsibilities that could provide a significant mental obstacle that only certain players could handle.

And in the end, despite repeated efforts, Theo Epstein couldn't really find one.

By the time the Red Sox reached the postseason, the instability of the bullpen was still haunting manager Grady Little and his team, though the Sox were able to win because their prolific offense repeatedly and routinely erased bullpen failures. In the first round of the playoffs against the Oakland A's—after newcomer Kim had self-destructed—the Red Sox closed out an opening-round series win by turning to starting pitcher Derek Lowe in the final inning of decisive Game 5, a decision that proved especially dramatic when Lowe struck out pinch-hitter Terrence Long with the bases loaded to preserve a 4–3 Boston victory over both the A's and snake-bitten general manager Billy Beane. The Red Sox victory earned the team a place against the mighty Yankees in the American League Championship Series.

And then, much to the shock of many, the Boston bullpen spontaneously *clicked*, becoming a strength that manager Little was able to rely on throughout the first six games.

Nonetheless, despite the performance of left-hander Embree (who had been returned to a set-up role) as well as right-handers Mike Timlin (in the eighth) and Williamson (in the ninth), the damage to Little's psyche had been done. The Red Sox held a 5–2 lead entering the eighth inning of Game 7, when, against pregame plans, Little sent right-handed Pedro Martinez back out to the mound. Red Sox executives were beside themselves. Throughout the season, after all, the Red Sox had grown accustomed to removing Martinez whenever he approached or eclipsed one hundred pitches, a threshold that had become a tipping point for the pitcher's effectiveness. And finally, after an entire season of tinkering, the bullpen was working as intended. Even so, as if traumatized by an entire season of meltdowns by his relief corps, Little sent Martinez back out to the mound in the most intimidating environment in baseball.

That night, the Red Sox yet again learned an invaluable lesson. In baseball, especially in October, there are no tougher outs than in the eighth and ninth innings at a bloodthirsty Yankee Stadium.

And so, in the seeming blink of an eye, the Yankees tied the score with a flurry of hits against Martinez that left Boston reeling. The Red Sox relief corps, amusingly enough, stabilized things sufficiently to force extra innings. But with Yankees closer Rivera stifling the Sox through ninth, tenth, and eleventh innings, Little had effectively run out of relievers when he asked knuckleballer Tim Wakefield—the best Red Sox pitcher in the series to that point—to extend deep into the night.

Having pitched a scoreless tenth, Wakefield opened the eleventh with a knuckleball to Yankees third baseman Aaron Boone that floated through the upper part of the strike zone, allowing Boone to belt it into the left field seats for a series-clinching home run that sent New York back to the World Series for an incredible sixth time in eight years.

And even though the Yankees ultimately lost to the Florida Marlins—the team John Henry had sacrificed to become the owner of the Red Sox—the wounds in Boston remained deep.

"It's unbelievable," Boone told reporters after the game. "Like Derek [Jeter] told me, the ghosts will show up eventually—and they did."

Little, for his part, was fired shortly thereafter, though that decision came after parting words to a Boston organization that were, in the eyes of many Boston fans despite the recent success of the Patriots, haunted or cursed—or both.

"Just add one more ghost to the list if I'm not there, because there *are* ghosts," Little told *Boston Globe* reporter Gordon Edes. "That's certainly evident when you're a player in that uniform."

Having grown up as a Red Sox fan just a walk from Fenway Park, of course, Theo Epstein knew that as well as anyone.

* * *

If the 2001 Patriots triggered the chain reaction that sent Boston off on the greatest spree in American sports history, let there be no doubt: the 2004 Red Sox delivered the Holy Grail, the championship Boston wanted above all others.

Where the Red Sox of old would have crumbled under the weight of history, the Red Sox of 2003–2004 responded with a vengeance. In the aftermath of the Game 7 defeat to New York and the firing of Little, Epstein—in some ways like Belichick before him—ensured he would not make the same mistake again. Following an extensive interview process, Epstein hired a new, young, and more open-minded manager, Terry Francona, who came to Boston from Oakland. He and assistant general manager Jed Hoyer subsequently traveled to Arizona on what amounted to a recruiting trip for pitcher Curt Schilling, whom the Red Sox subsequently acquired in a trade and signed to a contract extension. And Boston promptly hit the free-agent market to address arguably its greatest need—a closer—to shore up what had been a problematic area throughout the 2003 season.

The Red Sox even came within a whisker of acquiring all-world shortstop Alex Rodriguez, then of the Texas Rangers, in a blockbuster trade that would have sent outfielder Manny Ramirez to Texas and shortstop Nomar Garciaparra to the Chicago White Sox, the latter in return for outfielder Magglio Ordoñez. The maneuverings were part of an explosive off-season during which Epstein and team ownership all but turned over boulders and tore down buildings to take aim at the Yankees, who eventually settled on a countermove of their own.

Weeks after the Red Sox pursuit of Rodriguez had failed, the Yankees settled on a creative solution for their problem at third base, where they had encountered some unexpected misfortune. Following the season, Game 7 hero Boone had ruptured his left Achilles tendon playing a pickup basketball game in January, the kind of mishap that might have normally befallen the Red Sox. Yankees officials were scrambling for a solution when they settled on a creative alternative, then inquired with the Rangers and Rodriguez as to whether the player would be willing to change positions.

Eager to leave a Rangers organization that he deemed hopeless, Rodriguez agreed that he would forgo shortstop, his natural position, and escape to New York. And the Rangers, who were eager to shed Rodriguez and his massive contract, were thrilled at the prospect of acquiring multitalented Yankees second baseman Alfonso Soriano in return. Unlike the talks between the Red Sox and Rangers, the trade between New York and Texas was completed in a relative instant. Just like that, Alex Rodriguez was a member of the Yankees. The Red Sox did all the work and got nothing. The Yankees came up with a quick idea and executed it flawlessly.

Still, the Red Sox, to their credit, remained steadfast. Epstein liked his roster. More important, Red Sox players were more motivated and as headstrong than ever. While team president Larry Lucchino privately thanked reporters who had defended the club on the failed pursuit of Rodriguez, the Red Sox still had more than enough firepower to beat New York. Boston's lineup already was the best in baseball. And the additions of Schilling and closer Keith Foulke gave the Red Sox bookends on a pitching staff that lacked strength at the front and back ends, fortifying areas that had proved fatal in the 2003 American League Championship Series. And even then—without Schilling and Foulke—the Red Sox had a 5–2 lead in the eighth inning of Game 7 at Yankee Stadium, suggesting the gap between the clubs was marginal even before the offseason began.

"They've added some quality guys, and the big one is Schilling," said Yankees shortstop and leader Derek Jeter, a centerpiece of the 2001 Yankees club that lost the World Series to Schilling, Randy Johnson, and the Arizona Diamondbacks. "Obviously, you win with pitching and defense, and they've added a quality guy."

Said Red Sox reliever Alan Embree in the spring of 2004: "Nobody said it would be easy and George [Steinbrenner, the Yankees owner] is going to do everything he can to stop us. I think [the Rodriguez trade to New York] is kind of exciting . . . [because] they're worried about us. They know we have a very good ballclub."

Said backup catcher Doug Mirabelli: "I think there's definitely respect for the Red Sox there, but I don't know if they'd admit that. They know they've got a fight on their hands every time they play us, regardless of who they've got on their team."

Indeed, the 2004 Red Sox would provide a lesson for Boston and all of New England that would prove critical over the next fifteen to twenty years. In the wake of a seemingly devastating defeat, a professional sports team could go one of two ways. The first was to implode under the weight of heartbreaking failure. The second was to come back stronger and more motivated—and approach the next season as if it were unfinished business. The Red Sox, for the first time in nearly a century, chose the latter.

* * *

There is an old adage in baseball that generally goes like this: Do not make any evaluations in April or September; the former because the season is young and teams are still experimenting, the latter because expanded rosters water down the overall talent and similarly dilute the results. More than any other sport, professional baseball is a marathon that requires depth, stamina, mental toughness. A team that wins more than 50 percent of its games is often considered successful; a team that wins 60 percent or more of its game is considered otherworldly.

Nonetheless, much was made of two April 2004 series between the Red Sox and Yankees—at least from Boston's perspective—that took place before the end of the season's first month. From April 16 to 25, the Red Sox and Yankees played seven times: four games in New York (on April 16 to 19), and three times in Boston (from April 23 to 25). When the teams bade farewell to one another after their first encounters of the season, the Red Sox had won six of the seven games, the final three by a combined score of 16–4 to complete a three-game series sweep at Fenway Park. To that point, half of the twelve Red Sox victories had come against the reigning American League champion Yankees, propelling the Red Sox to a subsequent three-game series sweep of the Tampa Bay Rays that left Boston with a sterling record of 15-6.

Frankly, it all seemed a little too easy to be meaningful. And, before long, it would be almost entirely forgotten.

In fact, as much as the start of the season was seen as a statement that the Red Sox had fully healed from the wounds of October 2003, the subsequent months proved costly. Against most everyone other than the Yankees, the Red Sox were an astonishingly mediocre 27-26 over their next fifty-three games. When Boston returned to New York on the final days of June, their division lead over New York had turned into a six-and-a-half-game deficit, placing additional emphasis on a series rivalry that really didn't need more.

Over three days, the Yankees decisively turned the tables, avenging their three-game series loss from April with a devastating three-game victory that swelled their lead in the division to a whopping eight and a half games just one day into July. The final game was a 5–4 Yankees victory that required thirteen innings and featured a stark contrast of shortstops Nomar Garciaparra and Derek Jeter, once regarded as the poster boys for the Red Sox–Yankees rivalries in the late 1990s. While Garciaparra sat on the bench as the result of a scheduled "rest" day while he was recovering from an injury, the already decorated Jeter went headfirst into the Yankee Stadium seats behind third base to grab a slicing popup off the bat of Red Sox outfielder Trot Nixon with the potential winning run on second base of a 3–3 game in the bottom of the twelfth inning. Jeter emerged from the stands with a bloody lip and a sizable contusion on the cheekbone just below his right eye, all while Garciaparra sat in the Boston dugout. The contrast was both striking and impossible to ignore.

Following the game, many Red Sox players sat quietly in their clubhouse at Yankee Stadium, many of them seated at the table that served as the nucleus of the visitor's locker room. One of them was Curt Schilling, whose decision to come to Boston had included a most unusual contract incentive, a $2 million bonus on the option year of his contract if the Red Sox won a World Series during the length of his deal with Boston. Schilling was a winner and had defeated the Yankees while a member of the Diamondbacks in 2001, after all, and he made a point of expressing his respect for Jeter out loud so that most everyone could hear, regardless of the fact that he was not being interviewed by anyone.

"That's why he's got four of those big fucking rings right here," Schilling said, pointing to the knuckles on his hand.

The opposite, of course, was also true.

And that's why Garciaparra and the Red Sox did not.

Frustrated by their own play and the suddenly sizable gap that existed between Boston and New York in the standings, the Red Sox nonetheless continued to play relatively uninspired baseball, at least over the next few weeks.

Boston went 10-8 over its next eighteen games, making the team 37-37 since its 15-6 start. The Red Sox then lost another game to New York in the opener of a three-game weekend series in late July, dropping to nine and a half games behind the Yankees in the AL East standings with a mere sixty-six games remaining in the regular season.

The division, by all accounts, was decided. But the fight, as it turned out, was just beginning.

On Saturday, July 24, in a nationally televised game at Fenway Park, tensions between the clubs finally boiled over. With the Yankees holding a 2–0 lead, Yankees newcomer Alex Rodriguez was hit by a pitch thrown by Red Sox right-hander Bronson Arroyo, a stringy right-hander whose offering struck Rodriguez on the back of his left elbow. As he often did, Red Sox catcher Jason Varitek—never a fan of Rodriguez and his glamour-boy persona—immediately jumped up from his crouch and began moving between Arroyo and Rodriguez with the intention of defending his pitcher, all as Rodriguez began shouting a succession of profanities.

"Fuck you . . . fuck *you* . . . *fuck you!*" Rodriguez said in a matter of seconds, the intensity escalating with each curse.

Varitek reached up with his mitt and shoved Rodriguez in the chest, triggering a wrestling match that quickly escalated into a bench-clearing brawl that resulted in the ejections of both players and left Yankees starting pitcher Tanyon Sturtze—a native of Worcester, Massachusetts, who sprinted from the visiting dugout to join the fight—with a trickle of blood down from his left ear down his jawline. The playoffs were still months away but, again, the message was clear.

It's on.

Whether the result of consequence or circumstance, the Red Sox seemed to awaken. Having gone oh-for-six with two strikeouts against Sturtze over the first two innings of the game, they immediately scored twice in the third inning to trim New York's lead to 3–2. The teams then exchanged rallies as if trading haymakers—the score went from 3–2 New York to 4–3 Boston to 9–4 New York and then 9–8—before the Yankees took a 10–8 lead into the final inning, when manager Joe Torre handed the ball to Rivera, the impenetrable closer whom the Red Sox had been unable to solve the prior October.

And then, with Garciaparra on second base, Red Sox teammates Kevin Millar and Dave Roberts followed with a single and game-winning home run, lifting the Red Sox to an emotional 11–10 victory that all but sent a jolt of electricity through the fabled Fenway Park. The Red Sox won the series finale on

Sunday by a 9–6 score. For almost one hundred years, since the sale of Babe Ruth, New York had bloodied and bullied Boston. In 2004, the Red Sox seemed intent on fighting back.

Yet, despite the popular and convenient narrative that the fight awakened the Red Sox and altered their history, the truth is that it did not. The Red Sox went 6-6 over their next twelve games, immediately lapsing back into the mediocre malaise that had plagued them for much of the season. When the Red Sox played the Yankees, it seemed, their intensity level skyrocketed and they fought furiously with the best team in baseball, but against everyone else they seemed stuck in neutral. That fact, in addition to the team's failings on defense, led general manager Theo Epstein to do something that the fight with the Yankees ultimately failed to accomplish.

It inspired Epstein to grab his team by the collar and give it a good hard shake, serving notice that the season was rapidly approaching its critical stages and that the Red Sox needed to wake up. And wake up they did.

* * *

Theo Epstein was, on the outside, poised, polished, calm, and mature well beyond his years. But on the inside, in some ways, he was still just a young thirty-year-old man who had grown up near Fenway Park, experienced the heartache of being a Red Sox fan, and understood the weight of the Boston uniform. In 2003, with the Red Sox in Cleveland during the playoff race and with a bullpen that was terribly flawed, a reporter stumbled on a solitary Epstein in manager Grady Little's otherwise empty office with the look, to borrow a phrase from *The Secret of My Success*, of "a long-tailed cat in a room full of rocking chairs." He was pacing. The challenge of winning a World Series was daunting to most everyone who ever worked or played for the Red Sox—let alone was invested in them as a fan—and Epstein privately carried that burden as much as anyone, even if he did not necessarily reveal it.

Nervous? You bet he got nervous. And Epstein was never more conflicted than in the moments leading up to the 2004 trading deadline, when he was faced with a most daunting problem: He had to either stand behind one of the greatest and most popular homegrown players in modern Red Sox history or do what he believed was in the team's best interests. He simply could not have both. And so, after much deliberation, he traded Nomar Garciaparra.

The deal, of course, stunned the baseball world, given Garciaparra's status and popularity as one of the game's most talented players—but it shouldn't have been so shocking. After the highly publicized pursuit of Rodriguez the prior winter, the frustrations of new ownership and management with their high-maintenance shortstop had grown apparent. Once news of a meeting between owner John Henry and Rodriguez had leaked in the *Boston Herald* during the fall, Garciaparra called the tabloid from his honeymoon in Hawaii with wife and soccer star Mia Hamm. Typically tight-lipped and uncooperative with the media, Garciaparra was suddenly a fountain of frustration:

"Basically, what I'd like to say is that I know there's always been this speculation that I'm happy there," Garciaparra said. "I've heard it and read it—that I want to go home [to Southern California] and I'm unhappy—and I don't know where that comes from. No words have ever come out of my mouth—publicly or privately—that I don't want to be there. I also believe that my actions have shown I don't want out of there. I go out there and play hard and give it my all, day in and day, not just on the field but off. I have a [charitable] foundation there. I'm coming back in January to my 10th hitting camp, I think. Before we got married, my wife and I purchased a new home [in the Boston area]. If you look at all that, I wouldn't do all that if I wanted to leave."

Though Red Sox officials temporarily bit their tongues—owner John Henry ultimately tore into agent Arn Tellem in particular, calling Garciaparra and his agent "disingenuous" just as the Sox began a hard run at Rodriguez—their feelings were privately well-known. They found Garciaparra to be chronically unhappy—and they were right. For all that Garciaparra spilled to the *Herald*, his actions belied his words. He constantly complained about the media to teammates. And many of Garciaparra's teammates, in turn, felt that he was too easily consumed by the challenges that came along with playing in Boston, much of which manifested itself in the media scrutiny. Garciaparra's absence from their last game at Yankee Stadium crossed a line that had sealed his fate, though it was merely the last straw in a relationship that had been deteriorating badly over a period of months and years. Quite simply, for all that he had accomplished with the Red Sox in nearly eight major league seasons, Nomar Garciaparra couldn't cope with Boston. And the Red Sox felt that his attitude—along with his trick-or-treat defense—was weighing them down.

And so, in a move that would reverberate through Red Sox history, Epstein pulled the trigger. Citing the team's questionable defense as a potential "fatal flaw," he shipped out Garciaparra and outfielder Matt Murton to the Chicago Cubs in a multi-team trade that landed the Red Sox versatile shortstop Orlando Cabrera and first baseman Doug Mientkiewicz, a defensive wizard; in a separate deal, he acquired outfielder and base stealer extraordinaire Dave Roberts from the Los Angeles Dodgers. Though the Red Sox had been spinning their wheels on the field for nearly a half season, Boston was still very much a playoff team with room for improvement, and so Epstein pushed his chips to the center of the table and settled into his chair.

In the first two weeks after the July 31 trading deadline—as if stabilizing from a traumatic half season that included the extra-inning heartbreak in New York, the subsequent fight with the Yankees, and the breakup with Garciaparra—the Red Sox looked very much like the same team they were before the deal, going 8-6. But, in retrospect, they were healing. Beginning with a home game against the divisional rival Toronto Blue Jays on August 16 and devoid of all baggage remaining from 2003 or the early part of 2004, the Red Sox went off on an absolute tear that produced arguably the best baseball in team history. They went a sizzling 20-2 and simply dismantled opponents with a collection of power, pitching, defense, and skill, playing their way back into the division race and putting all of baseball on notice. Overall, Boston finished the season by going 34-12 in its final forty-six games, including a 3-3 record against New York. At times, it seemed as if the Red Sox were capable of winning every game they wanted to—they were dominant at the beginning and again at the end—and possessed the ability to flatten opponents with the flick of a switch.

At times like that, the Red Sox were a terrifying opponent for anyone, including the Yankees. They knew exactly how good they were and exactly how good they could be.

As such, the Sox dismantled the Anaheim Angels in the first round of the playoffs, sweeping the best-of-five series. Boston won Games 1 and 2 in Anaheim by the combined score of 17–6, obliterating an Angels team that had won the 2002 World Series only two years before. The series shifted to Boston for Game 3, where the Red Sox blew a 6–1 lead by allowing five runs in the top of the seventh inning, the final four on a grand slam by Angels outfielder Vladimir Guerrero that tied the game at 6.

Guerrero's homer, at any previous time in modern Red Sox history, might have been the proverbial thread dangling from a sweater that led to a complete unraveling. But not now, not in 2004, not with a collection of Red Sox players who had the willingness to take on history. The game remained tied at 6 entering the bottom of the tenth inning, when the Red Sox sent David Ortiz to the plate with two outs and a runner at first base. Angels manager Mike Scioscia promptly summoned left-hander Jarrod Washburn to face Ortiz, who cracked

Washburn's first pitch over the Green Monster, giving the Red Sox an 8–6 victory and propelling them back into the ALCS.

Prior to the Angels series, Ortiz had largely been a postseason failure in his career, batting a mere .224 with just two home runs in eighty-two plate appearances covering twenty-one postseason games. Though he had performed well in the final stages of the 2003 ALCS against the Yankees—he had six hits in the final three games as the Red Sox came within a whisker of going to the World Series—he was still, at best, a budding force in Boston. Teamed with Manny Ramirez in the middle of the Boston lineup, Ortiz had the best season of his career in 2004, but there was little reason to believe that he would soon become one of the great postseason performers that baseball would ever see.

At the time, after all, Boston was focused squarely on the Yankees, who defeated the Minnesota Twins in the division series to set up a rematch of the 2003 ALCS that went into the extra innings of Game 7. While many had believed that Boston and New York would once again end up back in the ALCS, the rematch nonetheless produced an extraordinary amount of hype. The tension was real. Alex Rodriguez, nicknamed A-Rod, had become *a-lighting-rod*, the latest symbol of the Yankees' willingness to go the extra mile and do, for the good of the organization, what the Red Sox could not. Jeter had sacrificed his body, face-first, to win a game in New York. The teams brawled in Boston, where the Red Sox felled the mighty Mariano Rivera. The trading deadline came and went, the Yankees won the division while the Red Sox secured a wild card berth, and the teams both showed up for the ALCS as if it were a duel scheduled for high noon.

* * *

In 2003–2004, at the top of the baseball world, the Red Sox and New York Yankees were superheavyweights, teams with knockout power, finesse, and skill. After the Yankees defeated the Red Sox in the 2003 ALCS, Red Sox pitcher Derek Lowe famously remarked, "If we played 100 times, I think we'd win 50 and they'd win 50." And he was right. For two years, Boston and New York were bona fide baseball titans, so much the equals that the slightest variable could tilt the balance of power. In 2004, what Malcolm Gladwell might have identified as the "tipping point" was a stolen base by a pinch runner in the ninth inning of Game 4, essentially the precise midpoint of the series.

Nonetheless, in the 2004 ALCS, the early signs for the Red Sox were troubling, right from the start. Curt Schilling—the man Derek Jeter himself had identified as a critical upgrade for Boston—flopped badly in Game 1, largely the result of an injury he suffered late in the series against Anaheim. Though the severity of the injury was not known at the time, a tendon in Schilling's right ankle had ripped through its sheath, causing instability in the joint and, more importantly, weakness in the right foot Schilling used to plant his weight on the mound before driving forward. An impeccable strike thrower with a platinum big-game reputation, Schilling allowed six hits and six runs in three terribly ineffective innings. He had just one strikeout and two walks, the latter as much evidence as anything that he simply was not right.

The Yankees raced to an 8–0 lead and withstood a furious Red Sox rally that trimmed the score to 8–7 in the late innings before winning 10–7, but the health of Schilling was of the utmost importance. Without him, the Red Sox might not have a chance. And Schilling, for his part, said he would not take the mound again if the Red Sox failed to effectively treat the injury.

When Yankees right-hander Jon Lieber masterfully outdueled Pedro Martinez in Game 2 to back a 3–1 Yankees victory, Boston was already on its heels as the series returned to Fenway Park. Following a travel day and then a postponement due to rain, the Yankees subsequently bludgeoned Red Sox right-hander Bronson Arroyo—the weakest link on Boston's pitching staff—in a 19–8 beating that left the Red Sox for dead. The Yankees pounded out twenty-three hits and hit four home runs, two by Hideki Matsui, leaving the Red Sox bloodied and battered. The Red Sox now faced a 3–0 series deficit—something no baseball team in history had overcome in a postseason series of any kind—bringing Red Sox fans back to a familiar dark place.

Here we go again. After all that, we're going to get swept by the Yankees.

Red Sox players, further demonstrating the difference between them and the generations who wore the Boston uniform before them, seemed downright defiant, more intent than ever to prove doubters wrong. During batting practice prior to Game 4, first baseman Kevin Millar warned reporters that the Red Sox and the Yankees had been turning the tables on one another for the better part of two years, a fact that was indisputable. Both the Red Sox and the Yankees were so talented, so mentally tough, that the balance between them could shift in an instant. Momentum could mean a great deal. In the end, Millar proved prescient, thanks to a member of the Red Sox for whom the Yankees had no answer: David Ortiz.

In Game 4, thrust into duty after scheduled starter Tim Wakefield was asked to pitch out of the bullpen during the blowout that was Game 3, Lowe matched Yankees starter Orlando Hernandez through five innings, after which the Red Sox had a 3–2 lead. While Lowe's performance was not spectacular, it was critical for a Red Sox team that had been hammered in the first three games of the series. So much for the fortified pitching staff.

Nonetheless, following Lowe's departure, the Yankees claimed a 4–3 lead when a single by Tony Clark plated catcher Jorge Posada, putting the game in the hands of the mighty Yankees bullpen and brilliant closer Rivera, the man who had played a key role in taking down the Red Sox a year earlier.

And then, in the bottom of the ninth inning, with the Yankees holding a 4–3 edge and needing just three outs to sweep the Red Sox away, the series *tipped*. A brilliant strike thrower like Schilling, Rivera walked leadoff man Millar. Recognizing that outs were of the utmost importance against someone as dominant as Rivera, Red Sox manager Terry Francona dismissed the idea of a sacrifice bunt and summoned base stealer Dave Roberts, whom general manager Epstein had acquired at the trading deadline. That season, Roberts had been a sensational 33-of-34 in stolen base attempts—an incredible 97 percent success rate—when the Red Sox had acquired him precisely for this kind of situation.

And so, with the fate of the 2004 Red Sox tied to his winged feet, Dave Roberts led off first base in what was the purest of scenarios. The Yankees knew Roberts would attempt to steal. Roberts knew the Yankees knew. The question was whether the Yankees could execute the play and whether Roberts simply could outrun the throw of catcher Jorge Posada. There was no deception. It was Roberts's legs against the arms of pitcher Rivera and catcher Posada.

Rivera began his delivery, a pitch that sailed up and away from the left-handed-batting Bill Mueller, a ball that drew Posada out of his crouch and put him in an excellent position to throw. Posada made a smooth transition to his throwing hand and fired a strike to second base. Jeter caught the throw and swiftly dropped the tag. And Dave Roberts was still safe, albeit by a whisker, his hand sliding in under Jeter's glove.

Two pitches later, on a 1-1 offering from Rivera, Mueller recorded his second backbreaking hit of the season against the impenetrable Yankees closer, grounding a single to center field that scored Roberts with the game-tying run. Three innings later, with Manny Ramirez on first base, Ortiz cranked a Paul Quantrill offering into the Yankees bullpen in right field, lifting the Red Sox to a 6–4, twelve-inning victory that extended the series to a fifth game.

In the midst of it all, the Red Sox believed they had devised a strategy to get Schilling back on the mound, thanks to the efforts of team doctor

Bill Morgan and George Theodore, a renowned foot and ankle expert from Massachusetts General Hospital. Though the sheath that housed Schilling's ankle tendon could not be repaired in the short term, the doctors believed they could stabilize the tendon by placing a temporary suture in the pitcher's foot and leg. The suture, like a hemline, would subsequently be locked in place with nowhere to move, allowing Schilling the confidence and strength he needed to drive from the mound.

On the same day Schilling underwent the procedure, Martinez took the mound at Fenway Park for the final time in his brilliant Red Sox career with one goal in mind: to keep the Red Sox alive. For the first time in the series, the Red Sox scored first, plating two runs in the first inning, and took a 2–1 lead into the sixth, when New York scored three times. The Yankees held the lead into the eighth, when Ortiz opened the frame with a solo home run against Tom Gordon, making it 4–3. And then, in a sequence that former Yankees great Yogi might have deemed "déjà vu all over again," Millar walked. Roberts entered the game as a pinch runner. Against reliever Tom Gordon this time, Red Sox outfielder Trot Nixon singled and sent Roberts to third base. Yankees manager Joe Torre then summoned Rivera to face Red Sox catcher Jason Varitek, who hit a sacrifice fly that scored Roberts and tied the game at 4. In ninety-six career postseason appearances during a sterling career that landed him in the Hall of Fame and cemented his place as arguably the greatest relief pitcher of all time, it was the only time Mariano Rivera blew a save in consecutive playoff appearances.

Incredibly, despite two historically prolific lineups and offenses, the Yankees and Red Sox remained locked at 4 over the next five innings. Yankees pitcher Esteban Loaiza, typically a starter, was especially brilliant for New York, holding Boston scoreless for three innings as New York's last line of defense. And then, with two outs in the bottom of the fourteenth, after issuing walks to both Johnny Damon and Manny Ramirez, Loaiza faced Ortiz in a grueling at-bat that lasted ten pitches.

On the tenth and final offering, on a 2-2 count, Ortiz muscled a bloop single into center field that scored Damon with the decisive run, giving the Red Sox a 5–4 win and sending the series back to New York.

The series was still 3-2 in favor of New York, but the Yankees were the ones hearing voices and answering questions. And Curt Schilling was ready to put his mended, makeshift right ankle to the test.

* * *

As much as any player who ever wore a Boston uniform, Curt Schilling was willing to put his money where his mouth was. Unlike many of his peers who joined the Yankees to pursue their elusive first championship—"ring chasing," as it is known—Schilling chose the harder path. Instead of *a* ring, which he already possessed as a centerpiece of the 2001 Arizona Diamondbacks team that ended the Yankees dynasty, Schilling pursued *the* ring, opting to join a Red Sox organization that had not won a championship in nearly a century. The challenge lured him.

"They didn't bring me here to pitch well. They brought me here to put one of those on their mantel," Schilling told the *Boston Herald* after signing with the Red Sox in 2003, referencing the replica of the World Series trophy he had displayed in his home. "If that doesn't happen, to me, this contract would be a failure."

Some of that, of course, was bravado. But much of it was genuine.

And so, on October 19, 2004, after a regular season during which he backboned the Red Sox pitching staff by going 21-6 with a 3.27 ERA in 226 and two-thirds innings covering thirty-two starts, Schilling took the mound at Yankee Stadium in what will forever be known as the "Bloody Sock Game." The tendon in his right ankle sewn in place as if by Dr. Frankenstein, Schilling pitched on the Yankee Stadium mound with a red stain seeping through his right sock, something television cameras focused on throughout the night. (Teammate Kevin Millar was among those who joked that Schilling, who loved the spotlight, colored the sock with a marker.) And he pitched, in a word, brilliantly.

Unlike Game 1 of the series, when he struggled from the start, Schilling retired the first eight Yankees hitters of the game and nine of the first ten, delivering an early message to his teammates, the Yankees, and all of New York, including the capacity crowd at Yankee Stadium: *He's on his game this time.* By the time the Yankees began the bottom of the fourth inning with consecutive singles, the Red Sox already had a 4–0 lead courtesy of a Jason Varitek single and a three-run, opposite-field home run by second baseman Mark Bellhorn against Jon Lieber, the right-hander who had silenced the Red Sox in Game 2.

After Bellhorn's homer, Lieber retired the next eleven Red Sox batters, picking up right where he left off in Game 2. But Schilling was equal to the task, allowing only a solo home run to Yankees center fielder Bernie Williams in the bottom of the seventh, walking off the Yankee Stadium mound at the end of the inning with a 4–1 lead and the Red Sox within six outs of a seventh game.

Roughly a year after taking a three-run lead into the eighth in Game 7, the Red Sox were now faced with a similar task in Game 6. This time, in the baseball cauldron that is the Bronx, the Red Sox withstood the heat—and desperation began to show in a Yankees team that had been bullying the Red Sox only a few days earlier.

With Bronson Arroyo relieving Schilling, the Yankees trimmed the lead to 4–2 on a one-out double by second baseman Miguel Cairo and ensuing single by the typically cool Jeter. Rodriguez then followed with a soft dribbler up the first-base line that Arroyo fielded cleanly, extending his glove to tag the passing Rodriguez. A-Rod swiped at Arroyo's glove with his left hand and knocked the ball free, sending the Yankee Stadium crowd into delirium. The Red Sox were somehow again fumbling away an opportunity, opening the door for another historic Yankees comeback. Except Rodriguez, of course, was immediately called out for interference, committing both a rules violation and something players deemed to be an ethical no-no—a dirty play that drew criticism from all corners of the baseball world.

Said one member of the Red Sox to the media in a private moment during the Red Sox postgame celebration: "You guys need to call him out on that."

If the play, and the reaction, demonstrated the distaste many in baseball had for Rodriguez—most regarded him as a selfish prima donna—it also highlighted the difference between the teams from 2003 to 2004. The Yankees were the ones cracking this time. And thanks to Schilling and Foulke—the latter closed out Game 6 in the ninth inning by striking out first baseman Tony Clark with two runners on base—the Red Sox had the bookends they lacked only a year earlier, when their comeback fell tragically short.

Nonetheless, Game 7 was an entirely different challenge, something the Red Sox had learned a year prior. *The final outs in Yankee Stadium are the toughest in baseball.* Standing in one of the cavernous hallways at Yankee Stadium prior to Game 7, the Red Sox publicist Charles Steinberg noted that the team's best chance to win was to race out to a big, early lead because he feared that winning a close Game 7 in the late innings was an impossible task. As if on cue, the Red Sox subsequently went out and battered a Yankees pitching staff that was now reeling after the two lengthy defeats in Games 4 and 5, not to mention the Schilling masterpiece in Game 6.

In the first inning, after Johnny Damon was thrown out at the plate on a play that could have easily deflated the Red Sox, Ortiz hit Brown's *next pitch* for a two-run home run to immediately give the Red Sox a 2–0 advantage. An inning later, after an ineffective Brown walked two batters to load the bases, the left-handed-hitting Damon greeted reliever Javier Vazquez—again, on the first pitch—with a grand slam into the right-field seats that made the score 6–0. The Yankees trimmed the gap to 6–1 before Damon got another home run, again against Vazquez—this one a two-run job—giving the Red Sox an 8–1 lead. And though the Yankees flurried briefly in the later innings against Pedro Martinez, who worked out of the bullpen, New York never got closer than 8–3 before another home run by Bellhorn and a sacrifice fly by Trot Nixon propelled the Red Sox to a 10–3 win, a series victory, and a place in the World Series against the St. Louis Cardinals.

Sox starter Derek Lowe pitched six sterling innings on a mere two days of rest. The words of Millar—"Don't let us win tonight," he had said before Game 4—and the blueprint of Steinberg had materialized exactly as outlined.

The headline in the *New York Post* on October 21 told the story best: "The Choke's on Us."

Though the Red Sox still had a series to win against the St. Louis Cardinals to claim their first World Series title since 1918, the final stage of the 2004 baseball postseason ultimately proved nothing more than an afterthought. Entering the World Series, though St. Louis had won 105 games during the regular season, the Red Sox believed the Cardinals' pitching staff to be vulnerable against a Boston lineup that had just clobbered the mighty Yankees—and they were right. The St. Louis starters, in particular, were no match for Boston, who scored four runs in the very first inning of Game 1—three on another blow by Ortiz—and rumbled to an 11–9 victory. The Red Sox went on to score in the first inning of all four World Series games and never trailed at any point in the series, so thoroughly dominating the Cardinals that St. Louis couldn't even rightfully justify its place as the second-best team in baseball. That title, after all, belonged to the Yankees, against whom the Red Sox had just completed arguably the greatest series comeback in the history of professional sports.

In the end, after winning four straight against the Yankees, the Red Sox walloped the Cardinals in a four-game series sweep, during which they outscored St. Louis 24–12, including 13–3 over the final three games. Red Sox pitchers finished the series with a collective 2.50 ERA, the Cardinals with a gruesome 6.09. By the time Cardinals shortstop Edgar Renteria grounded out to Foulke for the final out of the 2004 baseball season, the Red Sox had won eight straight games against the two best teams in baseball during the regular season and arguably the two most successful franchises in the history of the sport. Overall, since the middle of August, they had gone an astonishing 45-15 in their final sixty games—a .750 winning percentage that reflected their true dominance. And while there would be other Red Sox teams that could stake their claim as the greatest club in franchise history, the 2004 edition played at such a high level at the most pivotal time—all while bearing the burden of history—that no other club in team history could possibly say it overcame a bigger challenge. The 2004 Red Sox had offense, defense, speed, power, pitching, heart, guts, and a bottomless reservoir of determination, all of which were critical after having blown Game 7 against the Yankees only a year earlier.

On October 30, 2004, despite poor weather—not unusual for New Englanders long accustomed to trick-or-treating in winter coats—crowds estimated as high as three million people lined up along Boston's city streets for the championship parade to celebrate what the Red Sox had accomplished. In the days that followed, many longtime New Englanders visited the final resting places of deceased family members who never witnessed a Red Sox championship, decorating grave sites with Red Sox caps, pennants, and other souvenirs. For the first time in nearly a century, a Red Sox season had ended with neither heartache nor disappointment, and it was as if all of New England, after decades of darkness, had awoken to a sun sparkling off the water of Boston Harbor in the aftermath of a long winter storm.

"We'll never hear the '1918' chants again," said Red Sox knuckleballer Tim Wakefield, who would later finish his career as the team's all-time leader in innings pitched, meaning he would record more outs than any pitcher ever to wear a Red Sox uniform. "It's huge for the franchise. Ever since Mr. Henry and Mr. Werner and Larry took over they've pointed us in the right direction. People that have lived there longer than I have had too many sad days. Now they can rejoice in the city of Boston."

Said catcher Jason Varitek: "I can't explain the great feeling that we have for the whole New England area. They can finally rest."

Added pitcher Lowe, who was credited with the win in the clinching game of all three postseason series: "We're finally winners. . . . This isn't just the 2003 Red Sox. This is eighty-six years here."

Indeed, both the Red Sox and Boston felt healed. And while many had long theorized that the Boston baseball experience would never be the same—that the Red Sox would never again experience something as gratifying as the end of the mythical Curse of the Bambino and that the pursuit of a championship would never again be so gratifying—the opposite happened. For a short time, at least, the Red Sox became bigger than ever.

And Boston became the epicenter of the American sports world—and of all the trimmings and side effects that came along with it.

CHAPTER 3

A CHANGING OF THE GUARD

"I think the Patriots were definitely last [in popularity among the four Boston sports teams]. And it was still that way when Parcells got here. I mean, they got more credibility, but they didn't exactly start winning right away. I got here in '94, and it wasn't till '96 that they got to the Super Bowl. They struggled some. They were not considered Super Bowl–caliber. It's tough to compare it to now, because it's [become] just such a sensation. It was nothing back then. And now it's humongous—the Patriots and the interest in the Patriots from Boston fans."

—former *Boston Globe* sports editor Joe Sullivan, September 2020

FOR THE BETTER PART OF the past fifty to sixty years, the Red Sox, Patriots, Bruins, and Celtics have been akin to siblings, which is to say that the relationship can be complex. As much as parents say they treat all their children the same, some inevitably demand more attention; some require it; some operate just fine on their own. The expectations and needs are almost always different.

In relatively modern Boston sports history, in the sibling rivalry that has taken place inside the walls of Fenway Park and Foxboro Stadium, the old Boston Garden and the newer TD Garden that replaced it in 1995, the first line of demarcation rests in 1967.

Beginning that year, when the Red Sox effectively went from worst to first during what came to be known as the "Impossible Dream," Boston became, first and foremost, a baseball town. The 1967 Red Sox captured the imagination of all of New England, largely thanks to the performance of outfielder Carl Yastrzemski, a blossoming talent who would win both the Triple Crown and American League Most Valuable Player Awards during the summer of '67.

Though the Red Sox ultimately lost the World Series in seven games to the immortal Bob Gibson and the St. Louis Cardinals, 1967 effectively established the Red Sox as contenders for decades and restored the most important things to any sports franchise: credibility. And hope.

Prior to '67, the Red Sox of the 1960s had been something of a laughing-stock, finishing fifteenth among the twenty major-league teams in winning percentage. And minus the great Ted Williams, who retired following the 1960 season, the Red Sox were also anonymous and irrelevant, devoid of any real impact or star quality. But that all changed in '67, when the Red Sox did not merely become dominant on the Boston sports landscape; they became the lifeblood. From 1967 to 2003, the Red Sox were good enough to contend for the championship, but just flawed enough to ultimately fail. It was a perfect storm to generate fan interest. The Red Sox won precisely 3,150 regular-season games, more than any team in baseball but the rival New York Yankees, yet they had not a single championship to show for it. The Red Sox penchant for finishing second—sometimes in spectacularly tragicomic fashion—made them the media's perfect story, poster children for the proverbial never-ending quest. In Boston sports, for the better part of two generations, the one certainty was that the Red Sox would never quite succeed in their eternal chase for a championship.

At least until 2004.

The Patriots, by contrast, were the nouveau riche of New England in the early 2000s, a team whose fortunes turned overnight as if it had accidentally stumbled upon a winning lottery ticket, most notably in the form of quarterback Tom Brady. After the 2001 Patriots won the Super Bowl, the 2002 team labored to a 9-7 finish, losing the AFC East on a tiebreaker to the New York Jets. (All four teams in the AFC finished either 9-7 or 8-8.) By the time the Patriots returned for 2003, relentless head coach Bill Belichick wasted little time recalibrating the standards, cutting strong safety Lawyer Milloy from the roster just before the start of the regular season. The move sent shock waves through the Patriots locker room and established Belichick as the iron fist in the New England organization, making it quite clear that the coach had no intention of going 9-7 again—and that a Super Bowl ring from the 2001 season wasn't enough to keep you safe, even if you were seen by many as a team leader, like Milloy.

The clear and obvious message to the locker room? "Bill meant business," linebacker Ted Johnson would still say many years later.

Though the Patriots were throttled by a Buffalo Bills team that had picked up Milloy in time for Week 1, they did not turtle for long. New England finished September with a 20–17 defeat at Washington that left the Patriots with a 2-2 record, but it would be the last defeat the team suffered for quite some time. Though New England played a number of close games throughout 2003, they won the final twelve games on their schedule, including a memorable 38–34 victory over Peyton Manning and the Indianapolis Colts in Week 13. That game was decided on the final play, when Patriots defensive end Willie McGinest led an effort that stuffed Colts running back Edgerrin James at the New England goal line. The win effectively ensured that New England would have home field throughout the postseason, an enormous edge that became a key ingredient of Patriots championships throughout the Brady-Belichick partnership.

In the postseason, the Patriots then defeated the equally tough Tennessee Titans by a 17–14 score at Foxboro in a night game played as temperatures neared zero degrees; smothered the high-powered Colts by a 24–14 on another wintry day in Foxboro a week later in the AFC Championship game; and toppled the Carolina Panthers in a 32–29 shootout that ended with, fittingly, a field goal by Vinatieri with just four seconds remaining following a short drive during which the customarily cool Brady went four-for-five for 47 yards.

The final sequence, in many ways, exemplified what the Patriots had become and would largely remain for the entirety of Brady's tenure in New England: a team that excelled in situational football, that made the right play at the right time, that followed the leadership of a coach and quarterback who would go on to become the winningest tandem in league history.

"Tom's a winner," Belichick succinctly told reporters after the Carolina victory. "The quarterback's job is to do what he needs to do to help his team win, and that's what Tom does."

And that is generally what he would continue to do for the entirety of his Patriots career.

Nonetheless, for all that the Patriots were accomplishing during the 2003 season—after the Milloy drama, the team went 17-1—the team went relatively unheralded, which is hardly to say that the Patriots were ignored. They weren't. But in the tussle for headlines on the sports pages of Boston's two major dailies, the broadsheet *Boston Globe* and the tabloid *Boston Herald*, the Patriots remained the second-biggest story in town, behind the Red Sox, whose loss to the New York Yankees in the 2003 ALCS was, incredibly, bigger than any Patriots victory, including the Super Bowl—the Patriots' second in three years. Months after the Red Sox defeat, even as the Patriots rolled along on an incredible fifteen-game winning streak, Boston buzzed over the failed Red Sox pursuit of Alex Rodriguez, the accompanying Nomar Garciaparra drama, and the acquisition of Schilling.

Inside the walls at Foxboro Stadium, the Patriots felt like a younger sibling.

And like many victimized by birth order, they did what many children do for attention.

They made noise.

* * *

Joe Sullivan came to Boston from the *Asbury Park Press* in Asbury Park, New Jersey, where he had served as an editor before accepting a position as the senior assistant sports editor at the *Boston Globe* in 1994. He remained in that position for ten years before replacing Don Skwar as executive sports editor of the *Globe* in 2004, then served in that position for fourteen years before retiring in 2018. During Sullivan's time in Boston, the Patriots went from an afterthought to the model for most every organization in professional sports, a stunning transformation for a franchise that was, from birth, the indisputable ugly duckling of Boston sports.

"When I came here in 1994, and up through the early- to mid-2000s, it was, without a doubt, a Red Sox town," Sullivan recalled. "I used to phrase it this way to people when they'd ask me about me it at that time: I think there were diehard fans of all the teams, but the casual sports fan was the person who thought of the Red Sox first—and the Red Sox were the most popular. And I guess I could phrase it this way, too: As the media business changed, one of the first things we thought of at the *Globe* was, 'How can we monetize our Red Sox coverage?' That was the first thing we thought of, not any other. But somewhere in the mid-2000s, you saw it starting to change."

Nonetheless, the transformation hardly took place overnight. And given that reality, the frustration of Patriots officials became palpable.

Despite the countless barroom philosophers who theorized that the popularity of the Red Sox would diminish after the club's first World Series championship in nearly a century, the opposite happened. The Red Sox became *more* popular. Much to the delight of the new ownership group and team president Larry Lucchino, the Red Sox became *trendy*, attracting an entirely new flock of followers from all over. Possessors of one of the most traditional, classic uniforms and logos in sports, the Red Sox began producing novelty items like pink baseball hats, some sporting the traditional red Boston *B* outlined in white, while others formed the letter in, of all things, *sequins*. Overnight, it felt as if the Red Sox turned from a mom-and-pop organization into a cultural phenomenon, Fenway's seats spotted with celebrities from Ben Affleck and Matt Damon to Maria Menounos and Rene Russo. Fenway became to Boston what the Fabulous Forum was to Los Angeles and the Lakers, a clash of cultures that once seemed impossible and was, for many, uncomfortable.

Red Sox owners and administrators, of course, hardly cared. The cash registers were ringing.

The Patriots, for their part, had already spent years fighting for their turf to that point, often to no avail. In the 1990s, Sullivan remembered the team complaining that the *Globe* would staff training camp with interns instead of seasoned reporters, something that happened with regularity. But the *Globe* did it anyway—as did many media outlets, for that matter—which spoke volumes about how Boston operated during the summer months when the Red Sox were the primary show in town.

Said Sullivan: "I think it spoke to how we regarded the importance of Patriots coverage at that point. They just weren't as important as the Red Sox."

By the early 2000s, even the Patriots winning wasn't enough to garner them the publicity and exposure they wanted and deserved—an understandable sentiment given the bizarre reality. In much of America, after all, the NFL reigned as what longtime Oakland Raiders defensive lineman and Charlestown native Howie Long called "America's passion," its football teams serving as rallying points for cities all across the country. Boston remained one of the few places where baseball still held an upper hand, which made the Red Sox an outlier to begin with.

But more importantly, there was this: when the Red Sox took the field during the postseason in late 2004, the Patriots already had won *twice* and were on their way to a third championship. In the simplest, starkest sense, the Patriots were winning championships, while the Red Sox were still finding ways to lose them, which left Patriots officials pounding their heads against the wall and venting to anyone who would listen. For members of the Boston media, it was not uncommon to hear Patriots officials privately explain how they deserved more attention than the Red Sox, who were trying to *buy* championships while the Patriots won them in a league regulated by a salary cap—that the Patriots organization was smarter, better, and more worthy of the media's time.

During the Red Sox run in 2003–2004, the Patriots frustrations grew so great that the team sent director of communications Stacey James to the *Globe* offices for a meeting with Sullivan, whom James presented with evidence that the Red Sox were getting a disproportionate amount of ink.

"He had a binder with him," Sullivan recalled. "And he was actually trying to compare the Red Sox coverage versus Patriots coverage, and how the Patriots were getting shortchanged by the *Globe*—and 'Why were [we] covering the Red Sox to a greater degree than the Patriots?'—and how that was undeserved because of their success."

James was right, of course, but he was missing the point: the Red Sox were a bigger story. Until something changed, the *Globe* and the *Herald* would continue to promote the Red Sox at the front of their sports sections because, simply, that is what people wanted. As good as the Patriots had become, there was simply no way for them to displace the century-long Red Sox quest for a championship. The Patriots were originally a team in the American Football League, and even after the AFL and NFL merged and gave birth to the Super Bowl, the Patriots were still seen as an expansion franchise in the eyes of most New Englanders. At times through the 1970s and 1980s, it felt like the Patriots played in a second-class league compared to teams like the Pittsburgh Steelers and Dallas Cowboys.

Two or three years were not going to change that. What the Patriots needed was to build something longer lasting. And they also needed for the Red Sox storyline to change.

On the outside, the Red Sox and the Patriots played nicely with one another, respected the other's achievements through the early part of the new millennium, celebrated together. But privately Patriots officials wanted to supplant the Red Sox as the crown jewel of Boston's budding sports empire.

"I do remember all the celebrations," Red Sox president Larry Lucchino said during the winter of 2020. "We had an Opening Day with the Patriots and our relationship with the Patriots was always one of rivalry, but come Opening Day we gleefully celebrated their championships and they gleefully participated in our Opening Day to make it even more special."

Said longtime, trusted Lucchino assistant Charles Steinberg, who oversaw many of the productions on Opening Day and other special events: "The Patriots had just won their first Super Bowl when we arrived [in 2002]. And we had imagined and kept hearing people say, 'Wow, just wait till you see what it's like when the Red Sox win.' So we wanted to share the joy. It's a better sports town when all of your sports teams are winning, and it's a better fan base when everybody's still happy about teams winning. We've never ascribed to the competitive theory that we want to win and we want you to lose. We think that a place is better when it is a title town. And so we wanted to celebrate the Patriots on our very first Opening Day. Of course, some of the old timers at Fenway told us, 'Can't happen, won't happen, won't work, can't do it,' which made us want to make it happen even more. And so we did. And then when they won again, well, it was a cool thing. It's cool when Tom Brady walks out on that field at Fenway Park and holds the trophy and throws a ceremonial first pitch."

Cool indeed.

But behind the scenes, as the Boston sports landscape began to shift, that term took on another meeting. As the Red Sox exploded in popularity from 2003 to 2007 under their new ownership, the Patriots' response was, for lack of a better word, similarly *cool*. The Red Sox owners were new, outsiders, perceived as carpetbaggers. The owner of the Patriots, Robert Kraft, had grown up in Boston and turned New England into a winner. And yet the attention was all being directed at the new guys, much to the chagrin of some in the Patriots organization, who felt that their achievements were going overlooked—which, of course, they were.

Fortunately, for the Patriots, the battle over the spotlight did nothing to distract their singularly focused coach, Belichick, who now had a quarterback to build around. And while New England celebrated the Red Sox world championship throughout the 2004–2005 season, the Patriots continued to go about their business of establishing themselves as not only the dominant team in Boston but the most dominant team in North American sports.

And they were having, as it was, arguably the best season in their history.

* * *

What Bill Belichick has always lacked as a coach, indisputably, is the larger-than-life magnetism possessed by many great leaders, on the football field and off. Belichick's mentor, Bill Parcells, for instance, possessed a personality as large as the man himself, an ego that he used as a weapon to leverage his players and establish his control. Parcells was a girthy six foot two, which made him feel bigger, and he was, at his core, a loud, brash Jersey guy with a combative nature. In the prime of his career, especially, he was a type A personality on steroids, someone who could bully people one moment and then reveal a soft, underlying goodness that endeared him to his players, who came to know him by his most famous nickname: the Big Tuna.

"He's the best coach I've ever had," said linebacker Ted Johnson, who was drafted by Parcells and won three championships under Belichick. "His style is so different than Belichick's, but it's a coaching style that resonates with me and that I connect with—a lot of guys did. He's emotionally invested in his players that he sees potential in. You just know when you're being coached by him that—it feels personal. Football's a game of emotion. There's a lot of risk as far as injury and that sort of thing. So it's a job where I think you can perform better when you feel like you have a boss or employer that supports you, that cares about your success. And I would say that's Bill Parcells. I play better for a coach like that, and I think a lot of guys do. Bill Parcells was a guy who, believe it or not, he took time to have interactions, to get to know the players he wanted to see do well.

"When it comes to schemes, when it comes to game plans, he was great at that. Is he on the same level as Bill Belichick? No. As far as scouting the opponents to that degree? Probably not. But he was very good at that. A great tactician, obviously a very high football acumen, but it was the way he related to and connected with his players that, to me, made him the best coach I've ever been around."

Belichick, by contrast, was something of a social misfit, the possessor of a serious, monotonic demeanor that often made him seem perpetually miserable, a quality that, during his time as young assistant, Parcells turned into a humorous but somewhat insulting nickname: "Gloom." During his career as a coach, stories emerged of how Belichick would pass people in the hallways and never make eye contact, never say hello, never acknowledge their existence. During the middle of his tenure, amid a league-produced documentary (*A Football Life*) that chronicled much of his career, Belichick was seen sitting at his desk, eating lunch, while seemingly ignoring Patriots owner Robert Kraft as he tried unsuccessfully to converse with him. And as much as Belichick was described by those closest to him as someone who possessed a dry, acute sense of humor, he rarely showed it in public, particularly at work, where he was usually all business.

But if those were the negatives—or at least the perceived negatives—of Belichick's personality, there were positives that clearly came with them. When it came to football, Belichick was smarter than Parcells, a peerless tactician of both strategy and the finer points of the game. While Parcells could push people's buttons with his personality, Belichick could do it with his smarts. As such, the relationship between the two was complex: Parcells was perhaps threatened by Belichick's intelligence; Belichick seemed resentful of the fact that Parcells offered much criticism, little praise, and even fewer solutions.

More than once, in fact, those who have chronicled Belichick's life and career made it a point to highlight Parcells's attitude toward his assistants, specifically Belichick, who was regarded as something of a prodigy by the media and a head coach-in-waiting. Wrote Halberstam in *The Education of a Coach*: "There was one terrible moment, during a game, when Belichick called a blitz, and Parcells seemed to oppose it. They went ahead with it and the blitz worked—the other team had done what Belichick expected and not what Parcells had—but Parcells was furious, and over the open microphones in the middle of a game, he let go, 'Yeah, you're a genius, everyone knows it, a goddamn genius, but that's why you failed as a head coach—that's why you'll never be a head coach . . . some genius.' It was deeply shocking to everyone who heard it; they were the cruelest words imaginable."

Even as recently as 2009—nearly ten years after Belichick and Parcells had worked with one another and five years after Belichick had won three Super Bowls on his own with the Patriots—the friction between the two was palpable. In an NFL Films and NFL Network documentary that highlighted Belichick's career, cameras accompanied Belichick to a game against the New York Jets at Giants Stadium, where Belichick had made his mark as a defensive coordinator under Parcells during two championship seasons. Belichick walked the crew through the locker room, coaches' room, and meeting room, offering an assessment that spoke volumes about his relationship with Parcells.

"Look, there was a good mutual respect there and he was the boss," Belichick said. "'You know, I would tell him, 'Bill, this is what I think we should do.' And sometimes he would be OK with it, like, 'Yeah that's great.' And there were other times he'd be, 'Well . . .'"

Of course, Parcells was anything but subtle. In the documentary, Parcells is shown berating Belichick on a headset during the game, a scene similar to the one described by Halberstam. And when Belichick resumed speaking, he spoke as if he was less annoyed by Parcells disagreeing with him and more frustrated by what followed.

"You know, I'd say, 'Well, OK, we don't have to do that. What do *you* want to do?'—like, *what's the alternative?*" Belichick continued. And usually his response was something like, 'Well, I'm just telling you what you're doing is screwed-up. This is screwed-up.' How do you want to change it? 'I don't know, but it's just screwed-up and you need to get it fixed.'"

At that point, on camera, Belichick tilted his head and tossed up his hands, an image that, as usual, said far more than his words.

Yet, because of one simple truth, Belichick couldn't do a thing about it. Parcells was, as he noted, his boss. Parcells's word was law. And the combination of Parcells's personality, ego, and power gave him authority over his staff and players, something Belichick understood on the field and off in one word: leverage.

Parcells had it. And Bill Belichick would become a master of it.

After the Patriots won their second Super Bowl, Belichick wasn't about to fall into the same trap the Patriots fell into in 2002, when the team went 9-7 and missed the playoffs. He now had the validation and *leverage* of two Super Bowl titles, not one, and there was nothing fluky about a pattern. Prior to the season, the Patriots struck a trade with the Cincinnati Bengals that delivered running back Corey Dillon to New England, addressing an area that Belichick had previously patched together to win championships. To that point in his career, Dillon had the reputation of being a disruptive malcontent, which Belichick saw as an opportunity to add an elite talent at a moderate cost while giving Dillon the chance to do something he had not been able to do after being drafted by a dreadful Cincinnati Bengals franchise: win. Belichick had Dillon right where he wanted him—happy to be out of Cincinnati and motivated to win—and he saw it as an opportunity to make the 2004 Patriots even better than the 2001 or 2003 editions.

And, as often was the case on the football field, he was right.

"It's really the complete opposite," linebacker Johnson said when asked to contrast Belichick's coaching style with that of Parcells. "You don't feel, as a player, that he has an emotional investment in seeing you do well. People might take that as a criticism but it's plain and simple. He does not make an effort to connect with his players. It's more of a cold business for Belichick. I mean, let's face it—there's more than one way to skin a cat. We all know that. And his way has worked because he has gotten star players, selected players he has identified [as influencers] . . . He does have some connection to certain kinds of players, though I've always seen that as some strategic kind of thing for him. But, he is a phenomenal strategist—there's no one that compare to him as far as game planning, scouting the opponent, and in-game management. He's a phenomenal coach in that regard.

"But I look at coaching as there's two main qualities that make a great coach, and they're very simple: you have to have a high football IQ and understand the game as far as game planning, in-game management, that kind of thing, and also being able to connect [to] and motivate your players. And I would say Bill Belichick is the best at the first thing I described—the strategy part, but he is one of the worst at the second part. Whereas I would say Bill Parcells—his strength was connecting with the players and getting the best out of each individual player [more] than he was the strategist. I mean, it's funny. You talk about how they had success with the Giants [in the late 1980s and early 1990s] and they were completely different coaches stylistically that complemented each other."

By the time 2004 rolled around, Belichick had exactly what Parcells had—two titles as a head coach—albeit from a philosophy that emphasized his strengths, not those of his mentor. Belichick motivated players by preying on their fears and insecurities. He also garnered their attention because he focused on winning, the one common objective they all theoretically possessed.

Having won their final fifteen games of the 2003 season en route to the Super Bowl championship, the Patriots began 2004 by winning another six in a row to bring the number to an astonishing twenty-one, the longest such streak in NFL history at that time. And while the Patriots were upended at Pittsburgh by a 34–20 score in Week 7, they had gone more than a full year without losing a game of any consequence—and they promptly started another streak by throttling the St. Louis Rams with a 40–22 score in Week 8.

By the time the Patriots reached the end of the regular season, their only other hiccup was a 29–28 defeat at Miami in Week 15, an outcome that had little impact on the standings, the NFL playoff seedings, or the events that followed. The Patriots allowed only a touchdown in each of the next two games and finished the season 14–2 while excelling in every aspect of the game.

When the playoffs started, the Patriots toted a 31-4 record in their last thirty-five regular- and postseason games. In 2004 they finished fourth in the league in scoring offense, second in the league in scoring defense, second in turnover differential. They ranked in the top ten of rushing offense and defense, passing offense, and defense, and they excelled in special teams. In the postseason, New England subsequently smothered the top-ranked offense of the Indianapolis Colts by a 20-3 score in the divisional playoffs, then traveled to Pittsburgh, home of the NFL's top-ranked defense, and avenged their regular season defeat by handing the Steelers a 41–27 beating. Belichick had built a team that could surgically win any game of any kind, toppling the Philadelphia

Eagles in the Super Bowl 24–21, a final score that did not accurately reflect how effectively the Patriots had controlled the game.

The final meaningful play of Super Bowl XXXIX was an interception by Patriots safety Rodney Harrison, the man who effectively had replaced Lawyer Milloy a year earlier. With only nine seconds left in the game, Fox broadcaster Joe Buck noted the Patriots were just ticks away from "solidifying their team as an NFL dynasty. . . . In the '60s you think of Green Bay, in the '70s the Steelers, in the '80s the San Francisco 49ers, the Cowboys in the '90s—and the New England Patriots will be the first dynasty of the 21st Century."

All of America agreed.

And yet, in Boston, the Red Sox and their followers were still raging from a championship party that would last through virtually all of the 2005 season. Things were so good for the Boston baseball team that the Red Sox hardly seemed concerned with any threat from, as Lucchino had termed it, the "rivalry" with the Patriots, which had produced an incredible four championships for the city from February 2002 to February 2005.

At the time, little did anyone know that the Red Sox were about to be engulfed in a power struggle.

And that the battle would take place entirely inside the hallowed walls of Fenway Park.

* * *

Despite its place on the American sports landscape, Boston was and is a small city as much as it is a large one. It's a reality that, like everything, comes with a tradeoff: politics. Or, more specifically, *small-town* politics, which is to say that the tiniest rifts can become societal divides pitting one side against the other. And when it comes to the Bruins, Celtics, Patriots, and Red Sox—not necessarily in that order—Boston often burns so hot that any debate can easily deteriorate into an ugly or uncomfortable town meeting, like the one in Hoosiers, where residents pack an auditorium to discuss the fate of basketball coach Norman Dale, played by Gene Hackman, whose teaching methods are not producing immediate results.

In a place like Boston, pride, ego, and stubbornness are often four-letter words. Boston, after all, is not among the top ten largest American cities by population. At the start of 2021, Boston ranked twenty-second among U.S. cities in population, behind places like San Jose, Charlotte, and Indianapolis.

Yet its roots are older and deeper than all of those smaller cities, which can create a conflict between the old and the new in an arena that often feels the size of a small-town chapel. On the playing fields and in the arenas, Boston has always competed with metropolises like New York. Yet, to compare the cultural, racial, and societal issues of the two cities is largely pointless because of the sheer size of the population.

In Boston, conflict can grow intensely personal, particularly in matters of great public importance like the Red Sox. And that personal conflict often manifests itself in something that has similarly marked Boston sports history: grudges.

Intense, deep-rooted grudges.

Observed longtime *Boston Globe* columnist Dan Shaughnessy, who grew up in Groton, forty miles west of Boston, and has covered sports in the city since 1981: "Nobody ever gets over anything around here."

Such is life in a small city deeply proud of its big reputation, which is to say that Boston has something of a Napoleonic complex.

And so, while there was no formal referendum taken during the fall and winter of 2005–2006, the hostilities between Red Sox president Larry Lucchino and protégé Theo Epstein struck nerves so raw that Lucchino and Epstein still declined to speak about them more than fifteen years later—long after Epstein had left the Red Sox organization for the Chicago Cubs and long after Lucchino also had moved on to other ventures. *Theo v. Larry* was the kind of tussle the Boston media drooled over, and, fittingly, the *Boston Globe* and *Boston Herald* ended up on opposite sides, the *Globe* generally backing the older, more accomplished Lucchino while the *Herald* backed the younger, budding Epstein.

It was Boston's old world pitted against Boston's new world, right out there on the street corners, battling it out in the newspaper boxes for the entire country to witness.

In Boston, *my guy against your guy* was hardly anything new, because personal relationships could trump even the most obvious cases of right and wrong—like the law. The most famous example came over a period of decades from the latter part of the twentieth century into the new millennium, when renowned Boston crime boss Whitey Bulger terrorized the city and rose to power, partly thanks to the blind eye of FBI agent John Connolly, who was ultimately prosecuted and sent to prison in 2008. So what facilitated the relationship between Bulger and Connolly? The simplest connection beyond family: They grew up in the same neighborhood, the kind of bond that, in a place like Boston, carried a simple rule.

You watch my back. And I'll watch yours.

The Boston media world was not terribly different, though relationships didn't necessarily mean everything—in some ways they meant even more. In the mid-1990s, during the breakup between Bill Parcells and the Patriots, the rift between Parcells and new Patriots owner Robert Kraft became front-page news, *my guys* and *your guys* fighting it out in the Boston papers in a battle over—what else?—power. In the days and weeks leading up to the Patriots' second Super Bowl appearance in franchise history, *Globe* columnist and longtime NFL writer Will McDonough reported that, upon completion of the season, Parcells was planning to leave the Patriots for the New York Jets, a chief division rival. While the news reverberated throughout the football world given the magnitude of Parcells's persona and accomplishments, New England—the team *and* region—was thrust into a state of civil war.

In the end, the resulting wounds from the Parcells-Kraft affair cut deeply and spoke to the personal issues between Kraft and Parcells, coach and owner, from power and ego to money and politics. But they also spoke to the nature of things in Boston, especially with regard to sports, where the breakups between Boston coaches, teams, and players grew to levels of acrimony that did not exist in other places—where happenings that might have been perceived as neighborhood squabbles in most places routinely turned into all-out feuds like the Hatfields and the McCoys.

* * *

The short story of Theo Epstein and Larry Lucchino goes something like this: Lucchino was the mentor, a graduate of Yale Law School who later worked for Edward Bennett Williams, an accomplished attorney who also had ownership stakes in the Washington Redskins and the Baltimore Orioles. Lucchino subsequently became president of the Orioles, where he identified great potential in Yale student Theo Epstein, then an intern with the team. Lucchino subsequently encouraged Epstein to attend law school on the West Coast while bringing him along to both the San Diego Padres and, eventually, the Red Sox, where he hired the relative youngster to be general manager after the failed pursuit of Billy Beane.

That's when things began to get complicated.

After being hired in 2003—in a move that had Lucchino's fingerprints all over it—Epstein violated what many franchises in baseball deemed as professional etiquette, snagging outfielder Kevin Millar off waivers from the Florida Marlins. While waiver claims were entirely legal, the Marlins had placed Millar on waivers so that the player could pursue a career in Japan, something all major-league teams were aware of. Millar had every intention of playing overseas before realizing he could play for a big-market, storied franchise like the Red Sox instead of the small-time, cash-strapped Marlins. The opportunity so interested Millar that he comically spun on his heels and cited concerns about playing in Japan at a time when America was nearing war with Iraq.

While all parties were eventually satisfied in the transaction—the Red Sox paid the Marlins, who repaid the Chunichi Dragons, who allowed Millar to remain in the major leagues—the entire incident was, of course, good *lawyering*, the kind of last-minute dealing that challenged protocols and exploited loopholes. If someone deemed the action somewhat underhanded, so be it. But there was nothing illegal about it—and nothing that a few wads of cash could not satisfy.

Because he was much older than Epstein, Lucchino had made both allies and enemies over the years, ranging from New York Yankees owner George Steinbrenner to powerful baseball agent Scott Boras—but he was nothing if not relentless and fiercely competitive, sometimes to a fault. Those close to Lucchino frequently advised people not to mistake his abrasive nature as anything other than *passion*, though Lucchino would still cause others to bristle. Those who worked for Lucchino often cited his in-your-face "management style," which was a nice way of saying that Lucchino could be every bit as boorish and egomaniacal as, say, someone like Bill Parcells.

That said, his track record for success was inarguable.

But following a 2005 season in which the Red Sox were eliminated from the playoffs in the first round by the eventual world-champion Chicago White Sox, Lucchino and Epstein found themselves on opposite sides of the negotiating table at a time when Epstein—perceived as the boy wonder who brought Boston its first World Series in a nearly a century—was up for a new contract. Even with that season's first-round playoff loss, Red Sox fans were still relatively euphoric from the world championship only a year earlier, which gave Epstein enormous leverage. He was up for—and deserved—a sizable contract for ending what had been among the greatest championship droughts in American sports history, and yet he was being badgered in negotiations by his own mentor, of whom Epstein was rapidly growing tired.

With roughly a week left before the October 31 end date of Epstein's existing deal, Gordon Edes of the *Boston Globe* became the first to publish rough parameters of the financial gap between Epstein and the team, saying Epstein had rejected a three-year contract averaging $1.2 million annually and triggering a political avalanche that ultimately exposed a crack in the relationship between mentor and apprentice. At the time, the *Globe* was owned by the *New York Times*, which had a sizable ownership stake in the Red Sox. As such, owners John Henry and Tom Werner—and, for that matter, Lucchino—were viewed publicly as having influence over the coverage in the *Globe*, which frustrated newspaper staffers and, naturally, concerned competitors at places like the *Herald*. For both papers, the Red Sox remained an enormously important beat that drove sales, many longtime Boston media members believing that the Red Sox were the most important beat at either publication.

And then there was this: One of the chief *Globe* sports columnists, Dan Shaughnessy, had a long-standing relationship with Lucchino dating back to Baltimore, where Lucchino was a team president and Shaughnessy was then a reporter covering the team. The Lucchino-Shaughnessy relationship was, in some ways, Parcells-McDonough Part II, which produced mistrust on all sides, inside the Red Sox organization and out, from the *Globe* offices on Morrissey Boulevard in Dorchester to the *Herald*'s home at One Herald Square.

Epstein didn't trust Lucchino. Lucchino didn't trust Epstein. And the *Herald* and *Globe* never trusted each other, especially when the *New York Times* owned both the biggest newspaper in Boston and a share of the city's baseball team. Lines intersected everywhere.

"I knew Larry in 1979 when [Edgar Bennett] Williams bought the Orioles because Williams was a Holy Cross guy—he liked me," admitted Shaughnessy, a graduate of Holy Cross and a young reporter at the time. "So I had a relationship with [Lucchino] early, right from the jump. And we were very impressed with him [in Baltimore]. We called him 'the power behind the throne,' and I maintained that. Williams loved me, and Larry had to put up with me because of that. And it was fucking magical for me because I was the young writer and I had access to the owner. But then when my paper went out of business, I came here [to Boston] and lo and behold Larry emerges in 2001 as part of this new group thrown together by Bud [Selig, then the baseball commissioner]. It was great for me. I got access and I was like, 'I *know* Larry.' And I did. I knew Stacy

[Lucchino's wife] and I just I really liked them. I think they're both really smart. I think Larry's really smart. I think Larry's been the adult in the room and was way under credited with all the great things that group did after buying the team, rebuilding Fenway and the hiring [of good people].

"The Larry-Theo [relationship]—Larry created him. It all went back to Baltimore," Shaughnessy continued. "Larry is the one that made him go to law school in San Diego. Then when Larry came here, they basically had to negotiate with San Diego to get Sam [Kennedy, Lucchino's eventual successor as team president] and Theo to come here. I mean, the Padres didn't want to let [Epstein] go and I don't know how it was worked out. So they both show up and a year later, Theo's the GM after the Beane [pursuit]."

Within two years, the Red Sox then won the World Series.

And the *Globe*, for an assortment of reasons, was well positioned.

Once Edes's story hit the streets, Epstein and the *Herald* were suddenly aligned, the paper delivering a scathing attack on Lucchino that put the onus of failed negotiations squarely on the team president, suggesting the Red Sox and the *Globe* were in cahoots, drawing a line right through the middle of Fenway Park. Once again, it was the good old boys represented by the *Globe* while the *Herald* argued for the upstart, a classic Boston battle that once again came with a spectacular, made-for-TV conclusion.

On Sunday, October 30—one day before Epstein's contract was set to expire—Shaughnessy delivered a column in the Sunday *Globe*—the paper's flagship—that defended the stance of Lucchino. In the column, Shaughnessy cited a 2005 trade in which the Red Sox had an agreement with the Colorado Rockies for outfielder Larry Bigbie, a trade that had been negotiated by Sox assistant general manager Josh Byrnes, formerly of the Rockies. At roughly the same time, Epstein had reached a deal with the Arizona Diamondbacks for outfielder José Cruz Jr., whom he preferred over Bigbie. According to Shaughnessy, Epstein "requested that Lucchino fall on the sword and invoke the ownership approval clause to kill the Rockies deal. Accustomed to people hating him, Lucchino took the fall, killing the deal and saving Epstein."

Feeling that Lucchino was undermining him publicly, Epstein boiled. On Monday morning, October 31—the final day of Epstein's existing contract—the *Globe* indicated that the Red Sox and Epstein had settled their differences and were preparing to announce a new, three-year contract for their wonder boy general manager that would pay him an average of $1.5 million per season. The *Herald*, now deeply entrenched in the Epstein camp, suggested that an agreement had not yet been reached. In the end, there was no press conference announcing Epstein's new deal because there wasn't one.

On Halloween night, hours before the contract with his hometown Red Sox was about to expire, Epstein put on a gorilla suit that hid his identity so that he could leave Fenway Park without any interrogation by media members who might have been staking out the ballpark.

Two days later, not unlike the Patriots, the Red Sox held a press conference announcing Epstein's departure in which owner Henry famously said, "I have to ask myself maybe I'm not fit to be the principal owner of the Boston Red Sox." Lucchino did not attend. Epstein spoke of the need to be "all in" to be an effective general manager, an acknowledgment that he did not trust Lucchino. Years later, then-manager Terry Francona's book (written by Shaughnessy), Epstein recapped the entire breakdown succinctly.

"Basically, I thought Larry was trying to mess with me," Epstein admitted. "And Larry thought I was trying to mess with him."

For all of the problems that the meddlesome Boston media helped perpetuate during the struggle, the reality for the Red Sox was far more disturbing. As was the case with Parcells and Kraft, the fractures in the relationship between Lucchino and Epstein were real; the cauldron that was Boston and its media climate only exposed them. The Red Sox subsequently empowered a trio of longtime scout Bill Lajoie along with Epstein assistants Jed Hoyer and Ben Cherington to run the baseball operation, and Lucchino went so far as to say the franchise would "leave a light on" for Epstein if and when the young executive was ready to return.

Epstein, unlike Parcells, made no mention of dinner or groceries after leaving the Red Sox, instead opting for a trip out of the country to see his favorite band, Pearl Jam, perform in South America. For a time, Red Sox business went on without him, though Epstein was constantly staying abreast of all decisions by phone. His relationship with Lucchino improved for a time, then got worse. The wounds in the organization, like the ones suffered by the Patriots, left significant scars.

Meanwhile, Boston's sports teams took their turns on the stage as surely as the New England seasons changed, a constant that New Englanders always could count on. What they did not necessarily expect at that moment was something else that would continue during what would become Boston's twenty-year reign on the American sports landscape.

The winning.

CHAPTER 4

HIGHER STANDARDS

"The Pats won in January of '05, too, right? I remember watching the game
and I had a ton of work to do—I must have been at my parents' house watch-
ing the game—and I was driving back and I was like, 'I've got to go to the
office and get some work done.' And I remember thinking, 'How the fuck are
we going to keep up with these guys? They keep winning Super Bowls. We
just won the World Series and that was so fucking hard.' It was so daunting.
I just remember being impressed and feeling like, 'We've got some more work
to do to win another World Series.' . . . You definitely notice [how the other
Boston teams are performing]. The standards of the city are the standards
of the city. You're always going to be judged relative to the other teams."

—Theo Epstein, winter of 2021

SOMEWHERE BETWEEN WINNING THE 2004 World Series and a feud
with his boss that inspired him to submit his resignation roughly a year later,
a thirty-one-year-old Theo Epstein faced a reality that Red Sox fans similarly
were forced to confront: Life, as always, would have to go on. The party could
only last so long. As historic and meaningful as the 2004 Red Sox championship
was, there would be another baseball season in 2005, then in 2006, then in
2007 . . . and so on. That reality, coupled with the whirlwind that had defined
his first two years as Red Sox general manager, undoubtedly played a role in
Epstein ultimately throwing his hands up in the air, quitting from the team
and job that he had spent his entire life lusting after, effectively extending his
middle finger to his mentor as he walked out the out the door wearing, of all
things, a gorilla suit.

In some ways, it felt like a breakdown—and it was essentially described as such in *Feeding the Monster,* the Seth Mnookin book (authorized by owner John Henry) that provided an inside look at the dealings of the Red Sox.

Wrote Mnookin: "Epstein looked much older than he had on the day in 2002 when he had become, at 28, the youngest general manager in baseball history. His hair had begun to thin, and his face had been shorn of its soft edges. Epstein is a workaholic—he had been in his basement office working early on Saturday, about fifteen hours after the Red Sox had been eliminated—and John Henry, worried about Epstein's stress level and his workload, had recently begun urging him to take some time off."

Little did Henry know that Epstein would heed the owner's advice and, without saying the actual words of media mogul Logan Roy in the HBO series *Succession,* tell everyone involved with the Red Sox to *fuck off.*

In retrospect, though his issues with Lucchino were quite real, Epstein had snapped—an outcome that should have been predictable. In the span of roughly two years Epstein had taken over the baseball operation of the Red Sox and endured some of the most intense on-field competition in baseball history with the dynastic New York Yankees while dealing with the off-field drama of Manny Ramirez, Nomar Garciaparra, and Alex Rodriguez, among countless other brushfires, some of which the media never knew about. He had busted the mythical Curse of the Bambino and delivered Boston its first World Series title in eighty-six years, then been subsequently swept in the first round of the 2005 playoffs. Had anyone taken the time to think, someone other than Henry might have noticed that Epstein was headed for a crash.

Theo was fried. Boston alone could do that to an athlete, manager, coach, or executive, most of whom had decidedly short life spans in the New England market. Until Epstein came along, most everyone had assumed that Boston was a difficult place to survive without winning, but Epstein (among others) was learning that it was simply a very difficult and challenging place to work, win *or* lose. Billy Beane, after all, had his reasons for turning down the Red Sox in the first place, and maybe he was right. Boston wasn't for everybody, even a native son who had grown up within walking distance of Fenway Park, for the simplest of reasons.

The show never ended. It just went on . . . and on . . . and on, one season bleeding into the next, one storyline morphing into another, a new challenge waiting on the other side of an existing one as if it were all just one big obstacle course on *American Ninja Warrior.*

Between the 2004 and 2005 seasons, in fact, the realization hit Epstein so squarely in the face that he sought the advice of someone who had seemingly mastered the art of the grind.

Bill Belichick.

"I had one really funny phone conversation with him that I've told a number of times," Epstein recalled during the winter of 2020–21. "After we won in '04 and I first started to get the sense that things were a little different and our players were out doing commercials, and there seemed to be a little of self-congratulation, and complacency was settling in. I called Belichick because [the Patriots] were so good at turning the page and staying hungry. There was a little bit of small talk and I started to ask the question—and before I could even ask he said, 'Oh you're talking about how to manage things now that you've won.' And I said, 'Yeah.' And he goes—two words: *you're fucked.* That was pretty much the gist of it. And he was right."

Indeed, for the celebration that comes along with winning, one of the side effects is rarely considered: *Then what?* For the Patriots, their first Super Bowl was followed by a relatively mediocre 9-7 season that resulted in the team missing the playoffs in 2002, something to which Belichick did not react kindly. The following season, cutting Lawyer Milloy served notice that *the party was over.* The Patriots subsequently won the next two Super Bowls while going an incredible combined 34-4 in the regular season and playoffs, largely thanks to a disciplined, methodical approach that took nothing for granted and made no game more important than the next one.

Over the years, that kind of focus has earned a rather haughty but well-deserved name: *the Patriot Way.*

In the case of the Red Sox, the challenges were obviously different. The baseball regular season was 162 games long, not 16 like football, which made it impossible to treat every contest like a life-or-death affair. But the on-field management was only part of the equation. From an administrative level, teams and executives similarly had to balance the short term with the long, which necessitated cold maneuvers like the decision to sever ties with a player like Milloy, who was just twenty-nine when Belichick sent him packing. Over the years, there would be economic concerns and issues that would similarly drive decision-making—and balancing the on-field games with the off-field business was something with which all teams struggled. Most ultimately failed at it.

In many ways, the conflict between Epstein and Lucchino was born of that key philosophical difference. In Seth Mnookin's *Feeding the Monster*, the first pages are dedicated to the struggle between business and baseball, the former (Lucchino) calling for splashy, headline-grabbing maneuvers and acquisitions, while the latter (Epstein) preaches the value of long-term team building. If Lucchino was *go, go, go*, Epstein was *no, no, no*, opting for a far more measured approach that would mean taking steps sideways and even backward in the interest of the longer term.

Said Epstein, according to Mnookin: "We sat here in April [2005] and talked about building an über-team. That's dangerous. That's very dangerous. We need to be aware of the potential that the bubble could burst. Yes, it's a pro that, on the business side, we continued to grow. But on the con side is the amount of hype as we turn toward superpower status. Yes, we won 95 games this year, but this approach isn't really sustainable over the long run. Sooner or later we might need to take half a step backward in return for a step forward. . . . I warned about this in April. What if we win 86 games [in 2006]? We're bringing up some young players that are going to better in '07 than they will be [in '06]. And they'll probably be even better than that in '08."

Epstein was right, of course, but the tension in his voice at the time undoubtedly reflected his overall level of stress. Like Lucchino, he was digging in harder. He was pushing even more. Personally and professionally, he wanted to slow down, take a deep breath, reset. It was unrealistic to think that every season would be better than the one before it. But Lucchino was his boss—"Larry runs the Red Sox," owner Henry would famously say many years later—and Lucchino, further, was also hammering away in Epstein's contract negotiations. All of that, of course, precipitated Epstein's departure, a decision that left the Red Sox without their chief baseball executive as they entered the critical team-building stage of the 2006 season.

Unsurprisingly, life went on without him.

Though Epstein remained engaged from a distance with his friends in the team's front office, the Red Sox conducted business without him as he peered through a window. With Lucchino overseeing Lajoie, Cherington, and Hoyer, the Red Sox made a blockbuster deal with the Florida Marlins that delivered pitcher Josh Beckett and third baseman Mike Lowell to the Red Sox for a package of prospects that included multitalented, highly regarded shortstop Hanley Ramirez and pitcher Anibal Sanchez. Though Beckett was still just twenty-five at the time and had a World Series MVP award to his credit, Epstein privately frowned on the move. (Asked whether he would have made the deal at the time, Epstein replied with a subtle "Probably not.") Nonetheless, the Red Sox had the need for a new staff ace given the departure of Pedro Martinez (via free agency) and the injury to Curt Schilling, who was never really the same following his October 2004 heroics.

On January 19, 2006, less than two months after the Beckett deal and less than three months from his resignation, Epstein returned to the Red Sox as general manager and executive vice president in a team-issued and carefully worded statement that insisted the Red Sox had become "closer" as a result of the conflict between mentor and apprentice. Even the *Herald*, which had generally been pro-Epstein, opted for a far more sensational and direct assessment—TANTRUM'S OVER, screamed the front page of the tabloid—which treated the young executive like a petulant child. In the end, the damage done to the Red Sox was considerable, off the field and on, where the new owners and administrators of the organization seemingly lost their shine overnight. And even though Epstein signed Beckett to a three-year contract extension in July, the team played mediocre baseball for much of the season's final weeks and months, barely eclipsing the number of wins Epstein had predicted for them less than a year earlier.

The 2006 Red Sox, in the end, did not win eighty-five games. They won eighty-six.

And after missing the playoffs entirely, team executives ranging from owner Henry to Epstein himself renewed their commitment to winning championships, blending short- and long-term thinking into a time-tested formula that would produce success for the business and baseball branches of the team operation.

Meanwhile, in Foxboro, Bill Belichick was striking a similar balance, albeit from an entirely different direction. The Patriots, too, had stumbled in 2006. And they, like the Red Sox, were intent on reclaiming their place in a 2007 calendar year for Boston that would be one for the ages, arguably the peak of the city's dominance on the American sports landscape.

* * *

The beauty for the Patriots, unlike the Red Sox, was that the power was consolidated, the chain of command simple. Other than owner Robert Kraft, Bill Belichick had no one to answer to but himself when it came to all matters football. Bill picked the players. Bill coached the players. Bill generally decided who stayed and who went, who played and who did not. For the most part, the Patriots generally operated as if Kraft gave Belichick a budget and Belichick decided how to use it. Belichick's process was regimented and reliable. He formed a plan. And he executed it.

And to his credit, at least early in his tenure, he often dealt with his own mistakes by ensuring that they would not happen again.

When Belichick and the Patriots lost to the Denver Broncos in the divisional playoffs that followed the 2005 regular season, the defeat was, incredibly, the first postseason loss of the Brady-Belichick era. Starting in January 2002, New England had gone an incredible 10-0 in postseason games, winning three Super Bowls in four years. Belichick had cast off star players and added others—and the Patriots kept on winning, the kind of outcome that earned Belichick blind loyalty from a rags-to-riches fan base that was of no mind to question his methods. Just like that, a catchphrase was born: *In Bill We Trust.*

As such, when New England finally lost at Denver in January 2006, most everyone chalked it up to the law of averages, the fact that the Patriots' overwhelming success over a five-year span was simply not sustainable. Among the most popular rationalizations for the team's failure in 2005 was that the Patriots simply had played more games than everyone else—and more intense, demanding games at that—and that the team had been a victim of its own success, that the Patriots had merely reached a breaking point. It was all very fair, sound, and rational thinking.

The 2006 season, Patriots fans believed, would be different. And in a manner of speaking, it was.

Having already disposed of Drew Bledsoe and Lawyer Milloy, among others, Belichick faced a crossroads with wide receiver Deion Branch, a favorite target of quarterback Tom Brady and the MVP of the Patriots' most recent Super Bowl victory over the Philadelphia Eagles in February 2005. Branch had led all Patriots receivers with 78 receptions for 998 yards and 5 touchdowns in 2005, his fourth season in the league, and had appeared in all sixteen games for the first time in his career. Entering the final year of his contract at a time when the Patriots were growing thin at the receiver position, Branch had significant negotiating leverage as he approached his first truly significant payday, a fact that would put Belichick's philosophy—the coach's *system*—to the ultimate test.

Predictably, during the off-season, negotiations stalled. Just before the season started, with Branch failing to report to training camp in the absence of a new contract, the team granted him the right to seek a trade. And on September 12, 2006, after the Patriots had defeated the Buffalo Bills by a 19–17 score in Week 1 of the season, the Patriots traded Branch to the Seattle Seahawks, untangling an affair that also included the New York Jets and first-year coach Eric Mangini, a former Belichick assistant whom media members had playfully likened to Fredo Corleone, the turncoat brother in *The Godfather* who was ultimately assassinated under the orders of his younger brother.

And while the feud between Belichick and Mangini would soon reach a fever pitch that dealt major damage to the Patriots in a scandalous affair that came to be known as "Spygate"—more on that later—the Deion Branch affair triggered its own chain reaction inside the Patriots football operation.

Minus Branch—and without receiver David Givens, whom Belichick allowed to depart via free agency—the Patriots entered 2006 without their top receivers from the previous season, while a third, Troy Brown, had aged considerably. Belichick had countered by signing free agent Reche Caldwell and selecting a wide receiver, Chad Jackson, in the second round of the annual NFL draft, and he also believed the team would get more production out of third-year tight end Ben Watson. All three proved to be disappointments to varying degrees—Jackson, in particular, was an out-and-out bust, though expecting anything from him in his first year out of college was, in retrospect, foolish. Ultimately, Belichick had no one but himself to blame for giving Brady such poor targets.

Nonetheless, as the year went along, the Patriots offense gained traction, largely thanks to the persistence and brilliance of Brady, who somehow finished seventh in the league in passing yards, though his overall efficiency slipped. The Patriots finished seventh in the league in scoring while finishing with a 12-4 record, but a pivotal in-season loss to the Indianapolis Colts left them without either a bye or home field advantage in the critical rounds of the playoffs. And while the Patriots defeated the top-seeded San Diego Chargers in a dramatic upset to reach the AFC Championship Game, an unsightly drop by Caldwell and an aging defense contributed mightily to the Patriots blowing a 21–3 lead in an eventual 38–34 Colts victory that propelled Indianapolis to its first Super Bowl title behind quarterback Peyton Manning.

For all the success the Patriots had enjoyed to that point, the 2006 season was regarded as a missed opportunity of the nth degree. In the aftermath, two things happened. First, as if angry and annoyed mostly at himself, Bill Belichick seemingly concluded that he needed to improve his defense if he wanted to effectively contain Manning (in general) and Colts tight end Dallas Clark (in particular) in future meetings. And second, he would have to surround Brady with better options than people like Reche Caldwell and Chad Jackson.

In 2006, like Theo Epstein and the Red Sox, Bill Belichick and the Red Sox were reminded that there was a balance to be struck between the short term and the long term, and that the proper mix could produce extraordinary results.

* * *

Following a third-place finish that relegated them to the status of postseason spectators for the first time since 2002, the Red Sox responded with a vengeance. While expecting contributions from a farm system that had been rebuilt under Epstein, the Sox also grabbed headlines with a series of off-season maneuvers, none more eye-popping than the signing of Japanese pitcher Daisuke Matsuzaka to a six-year contract worth $52 million. In addition to that sum, the Red Sox acquired the rights to negotiate with Matsuzaka by paying a whopping $51.11 million posting fee, a number that obliterated the bids submitted by all other suitors, including the money-wielding New York Yankees. After years of losing out to the richer Yankees on a litany of players, it was as if the Red Sox—emboldened by their 2004 championship and now owned by a billionaire with very deep pockets—walked into a poker game, unzipped their pants, and unfolded their manhood.

We're back. And we mean business.

Along with the Matsuzaka acquisition, the Red Sox spent in excess of another $100 million, most of it on outfielder J. D. Drew and shortstop Julio Lugo, bringing their off-season expenditures to nearly a quarter-*billion* dollars in what amounted to Epstein's first off-season since his resignation. At the same time, the Red Sox had promising young players on the rise in second baseman Dustin Pedroia, outfielder Jacoby Ellsbury, and left-handed starter Jon Lester, all of whom were drafted under Epstein and supported Epstein's vision of the Red Sox becoming the "scouting and player development machine" he envisioned when he took the job.

Theo was happy. Larry was happy. And the Red Sox were loaded.

Armed with a balanced roster, devoid of front-office drama, and rid of the historical burden that had weighed them down since 1918, the 2007 Red Sox played confidently, freely, and efficiently from the start. Having adjusted to Boston and revamped his pitching arsenal during the offseason, Beckett started the year by going 9-0. Left-handed reliever Hideki Okajima—a less heralded Japanese signing during the off-season—proved a key contributor in the bullpen ahead of otherworldly closer Jonathan Papelbon, another product of Epstein's farm system. And with David Ortiz and Manny Ramirez still in the middle of the Boston lineup, the Red Sox started the season 36-15—a whopping .706 winning percentage that translated into a ridiculous 114-win pace—to immediately grab hold of first place in the AL East.

By Red Sox standards, in fact, the 2007 season was remarkably methodical, downright systematic, as if the Red Sox were merely putting things together on an assembly line. The Red Sox never relinquished first place in the division after claiming the position on April 18, leading by as many as eleven and a half games as late as July 5. Boston's lead was so big and so comfortable that the Red Sox effectively began planning for the postseason in August, when manager Terry Francona and pitching coach John Farrell started resting their pitchers with an eye toward having the team at peak efficiency in the postseason.

Nonetheless, given the seemingly interminable grind of the 162-game major-league season, tensions escalated late in the year, largely by default. When the Red Sox slumped some in August and a media member covering the team suggested the team had yet to be tested, Francona snarled, as he was accustomed to doing most every August: "This is the big leagues—every day is a test," he barked. A few weeks later, when the team was struggling in Toronto and the Red Sox's lead had dwindled to a mere three and a half games, Epstein and his manager clashed some, even though a second-place finish would have been sufficient to get the Sox into the postseason.

At the time, after all, baseball's playoff structure drew no real distinction between division winners and wild card teams. The Red Sox and their fans knew as much, though that didn't stop talk shows in need of content to make something of the team's September struggles, particularly when the Sox were swept in a three-game series at Toronto that trimmed their lead in the division to a mere one and a half games.

While the team's overall play did cause some concern for Epstein, Francona privately chalked up his general manager's worries to age and relative immaturity. Epstein, of course, was mature well beyond his years, but the fact remained that he was still just thirty-three years old, unmarried, and without children. When one member of the media suggested that he sometimes overlooked the fact that he was the same age as Epstein, Francona noted that the reporter was married and had started a family.

"Those are big years," the manager said.

At another time and under different circumstances in Red Sox history, all of that might have raised concerns and triggered fears of another Red Sox collapse. But in 2007, with any remnants of a curse having been washed out of the Boston uniform, it was all just part of the typical day-to-day issues in any organization. The difference now was that the Red Sox were *winners*, something that created a confidence and culture throughout the franchise.

Indeed, for all the fears and predictions that Red Sox popularity would dip after the 2004 championship win, the 2007 team set a franchise record for local television ratings and posted one of the biggest such numbers—in any major-league market in the country—since Major League Baseball began tracking them in the early 1980s. Players like Pedroia, Ellsbury, and Lester arrived at Fenway Park as if they were welcomed into a happy home, unlike the countless prospects who had arrived in a relatively toxic Boston environment during the latter years of a championship drought that made players wary, placed impossible pressure on the team, and made some downright paranoid.

In those days, when young players spoke, veteran Red Sox would glare and all but snarl, adding to a culture of mistrust and creating a caste system that defined the Red Sox for decades. As longtime Red Sox reporter Peter Gammons had dubbed them during an era when longtime Red Sox outfielder Jim Rice referred to his teammates as "associates," the Red Sox were "25 players, 25 cabs," an operation that veteran pitcher Curt Schilling neatly described as "fractured."

By 2007, that was all gone—and the Red Sox were unified, bonded, singularly focused.

"That's a great thing to have associated with your organization," Epstein proudly stated during the playoffs. "It establishes a real culture of winning and overcoming obstacles throughout the organization."

Said Francona: "I do think that in games of huge magnitude, our guys don't get overwhelmed. It doesn't assure that you're going to win, but it is a good feeling. You look out there and you see Jason Varitek behind the plate, guys like Beckett and Schilling, they do what they're supposed to do."

Never was that truer than in 2007, when the Red Sox did *exactly* what they were supposed to do. They won.

By the time the regular season ended, the Red Sox were 96-66, winners of the AL East, and possessors of the division lead for the final 166 days of the season and 170 of the 182 in total. When the playoffs began, the Sox dismantled the Angels in a three-game sweep, outscoring their opponents 19–4, leading for twenty-four of the twenty-seven innings in the series. When the Red Sox subsequently opened the ALCS with a 10–3 rout of the Cleveland Indians in which Boston trailed after only the first half inning of the game, the Boston baseball operation had the look of an absolute buzz saw, a machine that would destroy anything and everything in its path.

And then a funny thing happened. The Red Sox fell behind for the first time in months.

Over the next three games, beginning with a 13–6 defeat in eleven innings, the Red Sox bats went cold. Indians pitchers held the Red Sox to just five runs combined in Games 3 and 4 at Jacobs Field, Cleveland victories by the respective scores of 4–2 and 7–3. By the time the Red Sox showed up for Game 5, they faced the very harsh reality of being eliminated, something that rankled the public far more than it did the leaders of the team, many of whom had lived through the 3-0 series deficit to the Yankees only three years earlier. The 2007 club felt it had similar mettle.

"We haven't had our backs against the wall all year, until now, because even during all that panic stuff about the division at the end of [September], we were never in danger of missing the playoffs," Schilling, a two-time World Series winner at the time, said rather matter-of-factly. "I think this is our first true character test given our lead all year."

Given that the observation this time came from a trusted member of his roster—and not a member of the media—even Francona didn't disagree.

Along with Schilling, Red Sox sluggers Ortiz and Ramirez took a similar stance on the 3-1 series deficit, refusing to acknowledge it as any sign of defeat. While the carefree Ramirez shrugged off the defeat with a "sun will rise either way" mentality, Ortiz was far more defiant. According to Tom Verducci, Ortiz stood in the center of a team meeting and tugged on his Red Sox jersey, assuring his less accomplished teammates that winning—and not losing—was now embroidered in the Boston uniform. "We're a great team—and don't you fucking forget that," Ortiz bellowed, adding that the Red Sox, collectively, were a "bad motherfucker," which would make them difficult to eliminate.

And so, predictably, the comeback began behind ace Beckett, who would prove to be the baddest *MFer* on any roster that postseason.

Three years after Schilling backboned the Red Sox on a bad, bloody ankle, Beckett dominated the Indians in Game 5, on the road, turning in an epic performance that established his place in the Red Sox line of kings, a series of aces that began with Roger Clemens and continued—with only minor disruptions—with Pedro Martinez and Schilling, who handed the baton to Beckett. The Indians even tried psychological warfare by having Beckett's former girlfriend and country singer Danielle Peck sing both the national anthem before the game and "God Bless America" during the seventh-inning stretch, neither of which derailed Beckett from running over the Indians as if he were the Polar Express.

In a 7–1 Red Sox victory, Beckett threw a whopping 74 of his 109 pitches for strikes and struck out eleven overmatched Indians. To that point, both Boston victories in the series had come behind their ace, a man acquired during Theo Epstein's resignation, further evidence that the Red Sox were in the midst of an age when everything went right—even when they went wrong.

Like Schilling, Ortiz, and Ramirez, Beckett already had a World Series championship on his résumé before the 2007 season—from 2003, when he was the MVP of the World Series with the Florida Marlins. Beckett prided himself on being at his best in the biggest moments, and he responded to the presence of Peck demonstrating the same brashness with which Ortiz had addressed teammates.

"I don't get paid to make those fucking decisions," he snickered. "She's a friend of mine. That doesn't bother me at all. Thanks for flying one of my friends to the game so she could watch it for me."

Translation: *I'd like to personally thank the Indians for bringing her here so she could watch me beat their sorry asses.*

With Games 6 and 7 of the series set for Fenway Park, the Indians never had a chance. Under Theo Epstein—and with Ortiz and Ramirez in the center of the Boston lineup as if they were a modern-day version of Ruth and Gehrig—the Red Sox had built a prolific offense, particularly in their home ballpark, where they were extremely difficult to beat. From the time Epstein began as general manager prior to the 2003 season, the Red Sox had scored more runs at home than any team in baseball—including the Yankees—and they possessed a .644 winning percentage that was second only to New York (.645). Even then, the Yankees' microscopic advantage in the latter was the result of New York having played one more game over the five-year span.

In Game 6, the Red Sox struck early and often, the first haymaker of the game delivered by right fielder J. D. Drew, who blasted a 3-1 offering from right-hander Roberto Hernandez into the center field seats for a first-inning grand slam that immediately made the score 4–0. The Sox added six more runs in a third inning during which they sent eleven batters to the plate, opening up a whopping 10–1 lead en route to a 12–2 victory that sent the series to a decisive seventh game.

Once there, the results were frighteningly similar.

Though the Indians managed to get to the later innings this time—the Red Sox scored only single runs in the first, second, and third innings—the score was still 3–2 in favor of the Red Sox when the team entered the seventh. The Red Sox then erupted for eight runs over the next two innings to completely blow the game open, cruising to an 11–2 victory that left the Indians looking like they'd been hit by a truck. In the final three games of the series, Boston outscored Cleveland 30–5, leaving little doubt as to which team deserved to represent the American League in the World Series.

Officially, the 2007 ALCS was a seven-game series, but the margin between the teams hardly felt so slim.

"I think the veteran guys have kind of instilled belief in us," rookie second baseman Dustin Pedroia told reporters after the game. "They kind of set the tone early in the season—'We want to win the American League East, we want to win the World Series.' You know, when your season is almost over . . . you get that sense of urgency that we're going to play every inning, every pitch, everything as hard as we can, and we did that the last three games."

Indeed, for as much as losing was an accepted part of baseball, the game's measures could be deceiving. Once the urgency of postseason play—and potential elimination—was introduced, gaps in talent could become far more apparent.

As such, when the World Series began, the Red Sox encountered a Colorado Rockies team that had seemingly appeared from nowhere, a relatively average club that had caught fire at the end of the year. With just two weeks remaining in the regular season, the Rockies were the possessors of a 76-72 record that was good for just fourth place in their own division, the National League West. But then, defying all logic, Colorado won twelve of its final thirteen games to finish 89-73 and force a one-game play-in with the San Diego Padres for the final National League playoff spot, a place Colorado secured with a 9–8, thirteen-inning victory.

Incredibly, the Rockies subsequently swept the Philadelphia Phillies in the NL Division Series before sweeping the Arizona Diamondbacks in the NLCS, giving Colorado an incredible 21-1 record over a twenty-two-game stretch entering the World Series against the Red Sox. The Rockies were so hot that they had to be taken seriously.

"I know enough about them now to know that they've won a lot of games out of a lot of games," cracked Red Sox manager Francona during a pre-series press conference that drew an abundance of laughter.

Nonetheless, because the Rockies had been winning with such regularity, they were faced with an odd reality entering the World Series: they had almost been *too* good. Amid a season during which they had effectively played every day for roughly seven months since the start of March, Colorado's first- and second-round sweeps meant that the Rockies had a wild, unusual eight days off between games. Any momentum the Rockies possessed at the end of the year—and they had plenty—was subsequently claimed by the Red Sox during the final games of the Cleveland series, an odd paradox that further proved that the Red Sox had entered a different (and luckier) era in their history.

Prior to 2004, the Red Sox might have been the Rockies—victimized by their own success. But in 2007 the Red Sox were now *far better off* for having been pushed to seven games by the Indians, though the simple truth is that the Red Sox were the better team, too.

In Game 1 at Fenway Park, picking up precisely where they left off against the Indians, the Red Sox absolutely bludgeoned the Rockies by a 13–1 score, backing the superhuman Beckett with a seventeen-hit attack. The Red Sox won Game 2 by a far more competitive 2–1 margin before blasting the Rockies again in Game 3, this time by a 10–5 final at Coors Field in Denver. Game 4, like Game 2, proved far more competitive, but the Red Sox nonetheless claimed a 4–3 victory behind young left-hander Jon Lester, completing a second consecutive World Series sweep after having gone eighty-six years without a world championship.

When the final out was recorded, the Red Sox had followed a 96-66 regular season with an 11-3 mark in the AL playoffs and World Series, cementing the team's place atop the baseball world during the first five years of Epstein's tenure. Overall, in eight postseason home games during the 2007 postseason, the Red Sox had gone 7-1 while batting an incredible .326 with a .941 OPS while averaging exactly eight runs per game, the kind of performance that made them downright unbeatable, particularly with Beckett (4-0, 1.20 ERA, thirty-five strikeouts, and two walks in thirty innings) turning in one of the great postseason performances in team and baseball history. Meanwhile, third baseman Mike Lowell—the other player acquired from Florida in the trade made during Epstein's absence—was named MVP of the World Series.

Everything—absolutely *everything*—was turning up Red Sox.

"We were talking about this in the office the other day," said Epstein at the time. "If you look at it, I think our last five years have been better than anybody else's in baseball. At the same time, I'm not sure we'd trade our next five for anyone else's, either."

As incredible as it seemed, it was true.

Once weighed down by their past, the Red Sox were now skipping along toward their future.

* * *

In Boston, in the twenty-first century, one question is almost always asked: When did things change? When did Boston morph from a baseball town to a football town, joining much of America in transitioning from America's *pastime*, as NFL analyst Howie Long once articulated, to America's *passion*? When did the Patriots overtake the Red Sox and become the dominant force on the Boston sports landscape, *the* franchise that New Englanders obsessed over twenty-four hours a day, seven days a week, fifty-two weeks a year, including leap days?

The right answer, of course, was that Boston's evolution was gradual, less the result of a cataclysm and more akin to something like climate change—or the end of the Ice Age. But if you're looking for a specific date, the answer might be October 28, 2007, the night the Red Sox claimed their second world title under the ownership spearheaded by John Henry. Earlier that day, after all, the Patriots had defeated the Washington Redskins in a 52–7 landslide that moved the Patriots to a perfect 8-0, driving a stake into the exact midpoint of a sixteen-game season that would prove to be, simultaneously, one of the best and worst seasons by any team in modern sports history.

On October 28, 2007, any remaining eyes on the Red Sox quickly moved to the Patriots, who were both fueled by controversy and motivated by their previous season's failure, resulting in the kind of all-or-nothing campaign that threatened the power structure of the NFL and some of its most sacred history. The 2007 Patriots, for lack of a better term, played and acted like a team on a mission.

And while overtaking the Red Sox to assume control of Boston and New England, they set their sights on something far grander and, perhaps, impossible.

Perfection.

CHAPTER 5

THE PERFECT NIGHTMARE

"Any season that doesn't end in a Super Bowl championship is ultimately a failure."

—Patriots linebacker Ted Johnson, spring of 2021

IN BOSTON SPORTS HISTORY, THE story of the 2007 New England Patriots stands, perhaps, as the most complex of tales, a lesson in the tantalizing, treacherous lure of perfection. The 2007 football season in New England was, in many ways, the sports world equivalent of the search for the fountain of youth, the quest for the Holy Grail, the pursuit of everlasting life. In the end, those stories all share a moral.

Be careful what you wish for.

In the aftermath of a 2006 season that ended with a loss to the Indianapolis Colts in the AFC Championship Game, Patriots coach Bill Belichick found himself in unfamiliar territory. Having taken over the Patriots in 2000 and stumbled upon the brilliance of Tom Brady in 2001, Belichick and his team had won three Super Bowls in four years from 2001 to 2004. New England was then ousted from the playoffs in 2005 and 2006, the first time Belichick's Patriots had gone consecutive years without winning a championship, which was hardly cause for alarm given the low odds of *any* team winning *any* championship at *any* time. Yet, Belichick nonetheless seemed to respond as if something had been taken from him, embarking on an off-season that turned the Patriots from perennial championship contenders into a downright frightening force.

In the span of weeks, the Patriots addressed a wide range of deficiencies on their roster, fortifying most every weakness they possessed to both avenge their loss to the Colts—again, New England had held a 21–3 lead—and surround Brady with a far more talented cast of pass catchers. As if fueled by rage, Belichick signed multitalented free-agent linebacker Adalius Thomas from the Baltimore Ravens and traded for two skilled, complementary receivers—slot man Wes Welker and deep threat Randy Moss. He signed another explosive receiver, Donté Stallworth, from the Philadelphia Eagles, and a massive tight end, Kyle Brady, from the New York Jets. The Patriots retained cornerback Asante Samuel on a one-year contract by using a roster mechanism known as the franchise tag—the move paid Samuel handsomely—and the team swapped out fading running back Corey Dillon for Sammy Morris, whom, like Welker, was lured from the divisional rival Miami Dolphins.

When the dust settled, the Patriots had arguably the deepest and most talented roster in their history to go along with their best coach and quarterback, not to mention the kind of motivation that fueled most any gifted team to its greatest heights. In a word, they were stacked.

Or as Patriots fans might have said . . . *we're fuckin' loaded.*

For all the mind games Belichick played with his team during the course of a season—one week at a time, game by game, quarter by quarter, play by play—the potential from the pairing of the brilliant, detail-oriented coach with a supremely talented roster was difficult to harness. Prior to 2007, Belichick's best team had come in 2004, where the Patriots effectively lost one meaningful game, at Pittsburgh, to a Steelers club they later dismantled (on the road) in the AFC Championship Game. The 2004 Patriots had finished 17-2—their other defeat came at Miami in a relatively meaningless and fluky 29–28 loss in Week 15—and, with a little luck, might have challenged the 1972 Miami Dolphins as the only team in NFL history to complete a perfect season. (Miami went 14-0 in the regular season and 3-0 in the playoffs en route to a perfect 17-0 record and Super Bowl championship.) And while a handful of teams in the mid-1980s were worthy—the 1984 San Francisco 49ers (18-1), the 1985 Chicago Bears (18-1), and the 1986 New York Giants (17-2)—both the Niners (Week 7) and Giants (Week 1) suffered early- or mid-season defeats that prevented any real buildup or hype; only the '85 Bears, who were 12-0 before losing at Miami in Week 13, took a perfect record into the final weeks.

Since then, prior to 2007, only the 1998 Minnesota Vikings (15-1, the only loss in Week 7) and the 2004 Steelers (15-1, the loss in Week 2) had recorded fifteen wins during the regular season—and both teams suffered a second loss in the playoffs before even reaching the Super Bowl.

As such, in the age of a sixteen-game schedule, many regarded the idea of an undefeated season to be pure fantasy—and not solely because of the math. The human condition, too, was a significant factor. For one, even great teams often *needed* a loss to hone their motivation, sharpen their focus, stay hungry. Second, the mounting pressure that came with each successive victory could create a psychological burden that was crippling. As most any person could testify to, walking heel to toe on a curbstone for the length of a city block is hardly a challenging task. But try the same thing on the rooftop of an apartment building and, well, the task grows infinitely harder.

But Belichick being Bill Belichick—particularly with three championships already to his credit—he was inclined to challenge both conventional wisdom and faulty preconceptions, even to his own detriment. Before the 2007 season, in fact, Belichick knew that his team had extraordinary potential—*Wait until we go undefeated,* he is purported to have told some listeners in private conversations during the preseason—though that is something he would never, ever admit to his team or to the public. To do so do would create a perception of insulting arrogance and boundless ambition, the kind of sin that philosophers and historians warned of through fables, parables, and mythology.

In a way, Bill Belichick was, perhaps, like Sisyphus, whose cheating of the Greek gods earned him the eternal task of pushing a boulder up a hill only to have it repeatedly roll all the way back down just before he reached the peak. Or Tantalus, who was eternally kept at arm's length of water and food after similarly insulting the gods. Or perhaps Icarus, who defied his father's warnings of flying too high with wings made of wax, only to plummet to his demise when the wings melted after he flew too close to the sun.

In the world of professional football, Bill Belichick, too, wanted his special place. He wanted to fly where no coach or team had flown, the sun be damned.

* * *

At the start, the 2007 New England Patriots played as if shot from a cannon, taking the league by such force that opponents were left devastated. For all of the talent that Bill Belichick had accumulated during the off-season, there were still questions—some concerning the health and age of Patriots players, some concerning the time it would likely take for new pieces to coalesce. Quarterback Tom Brady would likely need time to build chemistry with newcomers like the supremely talented Randy Moss, and that was assuming that Moss still had jump in his thirty-year-old legs.

This kind of thinking was quite standard in sports—and it took the Patriots no less than one game to dismiss it all as hot garbage.

Despite having missed the entire preseason—something Belichick did largely by design—Moss made his debut for the Patriots in spectacular fashion, catching nine passes for 183 yards and a touchdown in his very first game, a 38–14 Patriots win over the New York Jets that proved he still possessed the speed that made him one of the most explosive weapons in NFL history. His lone touchdown came at the back end of a 51-yard pass from Brady on which Moss easily outran multiple members of the Jets secondary, a laughably easy play that gave the Patriots a 28–7 advantage and served notice to the other thirty-one teams in the league.

The Patriots weren't just loaded. They were already clicking on all cylinders.

By that point, no matter what Belichick was saying publicly about his team's need to stay focused and to concentrate on each individual week, the coach understood the talent at his disposal. Already, privately, he was telling people that Moss was among the best athletes he had ever coached. And Brady, with better weapons surrounding him than at any other stage of his career, finished Week 1 by completing twenty-two of twenty-eight passes for 298 yards and 3 touchdowns, a quarterback rating of 146.6 that came close to a perfect 158.3 rating. And if the final numbers in and of themselves weren't eye-popping, the potency was. When Brady threw it, he completed it, often for significant chunks of yardage. He did not turn the ball over. And he scored when he had the chance.

Frankly, it all looked so easy that one couldn't help but wonder if the Patriots had somehow stolen the Jets' game plan.

Of course, as much as the season-opening win over the Jets signaled the start of the only perfect 16-0 regular season in NFL history, it will forever be remembered for the day that spawned Spygate, the infamous scandal that forever tainted the franchise. And like the rift between Red Sox president Larry Lucchino and young general manager Theo Epstein that exploited the cracks between mentor and protégé, the Spygate scandal was born out of a fractured relationship between Belichick and Eric Mangini, a former Cleveland Browns ball boy whose work ethic had inspired Belichick to add him to his coaching staff.

Once the Patriots began winning championships, of course, Belichick was not the only one garnering attention in the football world; his assistant coaches almost immediately became head coaching candidates. Owners and high-ranking executives from organizations throughout college football and the NFL wanted to tap into New England's secret to success, the belief being that Belichick's wisdom and magic had at least partly rubbed off on his aides. In late 2004 and early 2005, offensive coordinator Charlie Weis and defensive coordinator Romeo Crennel were hired as head coaches by the University of Notre Dame and the Cleveland Browns, respectively. Eventually, the focus turned to younger members of the New England operation like Mangini (then the Patriots defensive coordinator) and Scott Pioli, the team's vice president of player personnel, who had similarly caught Belichick's eye as a youngster, albeit during Belichick's tenure as the defensive coordinator of the New York Giants.

In the case of Mangini, one of his suitors was the New York Jets, the same organization with whom Belichick had a bad breakup following the 1999 season, when Bill Parcells tried to block Belichick's departure for New England. Mangini's subsequent decision to take the Jets job was seen as an act of treason by Belichick, whose response was vindictive. Among other things, Belichick had Mangini's access card to the Patriots' home at Gillette Stadium deactivated, delivering a simple, strong message that many would come to learn over Belichick's tenure in New England.

You're either with me or against me.

Mangini immediately became persona non grata, Belichick going so far as to snub him during the traditional postgame handshake between coaches following the first meeting between Belichick's Patriots and Mangini's Jets. A year later, at Randy Moss's debut, Mangini had advised Jets team security that the Pats had a practice of videotaping the opposing sideline, something that NFL officials had deemed a violation of the rules. Additionally, the league sent a memo to all teams explicitly stating that videotaping was to stop, largely because—as the Patriots were building a dynasty—teams were getting wary of their practices and tired of Belichick's sheer brashness. True to form, Belichick ignored the memo.

As such, while the Patriots were thoroughly beating the Jets, New England underling Matt Estrella was apprehended by Jets security toting a video camera and recording the Jets' defensive signals during the first half of the game. According to a story on ESPN.com, Estrella told Jets security that he was working for "Kraft Productions," an arm of the Kraft ownership that produced internet and media content for the club's fan base. Further, Estrella was wearing a polo shirt on which the Patriots team logo had been taped over to conceal his affiliation, and he also had a phony credential identifying him as "NFL photographer 138." No matter what the Patriots claimed to be doing, they went to significant lengths to hide it.

And despite that, the Patriots had been caught red-handed.

Mangini, for his part, wanted the incident to effectively end there, but it did not. Jets general manager Mike Tannenbaum, who had also been apprised of the Patriots videotaping tactics, reported the matter to officials and allies in the league office. The subsequent fallout mushroomed into one of the great scandals and controversies in the history of sports.

Said Mangini to the *New York Post* almost ten years after the incident, while revealing that he had not had a substantive conversation with Belichick in ten years: "Spygate is a big regret. It wasn't supposed to go down the way it went down."

Given the Patriots' success during the millennium and the generally boorish behavior of Belichick, the incident triggered a predictable avalanche. The league launched an immediate investigation and the Patriots' accomplishments were called into question, much to the chagrin of nouveau Patriots fans, who felt they were being singled out for sign-stealing practices that were regarded by many as an accepted part of professional sports. Stories abounded of coaches doing things like sifting through trash bins in the opposing coaches' box on game days, looking for any hint of a team's playbook.

Regardless of whether such defenses were true, that excuse-making conveniently overlooked a simple truth regarding Belichick's behavior: Because opposing teams had been complaining about the Patriots' filming practices—and about the Patriots' practices in general—the NFL had ordered all clubs to stop. Belichick ignored the missive. He then brazenly sent his spies to resume their practices in the stadium of a longtime protégé, who was well aware of the Patriots' tactics and who had similarly told them to cease. Belichick effectively gave the middle finger to both Mangini and the league, an incredibly stupid and ultimately selfish act that left a major stain on what could have been an otherwise spotless run of greatness.

Within days of the Jets game, NFL commissioner Roger Goodell announced that the Patriots had violated rules, demanded the team turn over any videotapes and other material relating to sign stealing, then levied significant penalties against both Belichick and the organization. In the case of the coach, Belichick was fined a whopping $500,000. In the case of the franchise, the Patriots were hit with an additional $250,000 fine and—far more significantly—the forfeiture of a first-round draft pick, a fundamental building block in the NFL.

At his first press conference following the fallout, Belichick issued only a short statement, apologizing to people inside the organization specifically but really no one else.

"Although it remains a league matter, I want to apologize to everyone who has been affected, most of all ownership, staff and players," said the coach.

There was, of course, no specific mention of the Patriots' opponents, the league, or the Jets, least of all Mangini. Such was often the case with Belichick, who often gave the bare minimum or nothing at all to anyone who didn't have something to give back, at least when it came to his football operation. There was really no such thing as common courtesy, even human decency. To outsiders, everything felt like a leverage play. When it came to his job, Belichick acted like everyone needed him more than he needed them, which was often true. But it earned him little or no compassion or latitude when things went sideways.

Of course, in the eyes of the Patriots fan base, Belichick was beyond reproach no matter what he did. By the time 2007 rolled around, "In Bill We Trust" had become something of a mantra to hard-core Patriots fans, a punch line to those who mocked blind loyalty. The coach had made a succession of controversial personnel moves that shocked people at times, but he had been proven right. And Patriots fans had been so beaten down by the first forty years of the team's existence that they looked at Belichick like a winning lottery ticket that lifted them out of homelessness and into a Back Bay brownstone on Marlborough Street.

Patriots fans seemingly had little understanding of how to handle their newfound wealth or success, or even how to act in a dignified manner. Winning had become their birthright. And Belichick seemingly reveled in it, never more so than at the start of the Week 2 game against the San Diego Chargers in the immediate aftermath of the Goodell decision to discipline both him and the team.

When Belichick was shown on the stadium's massive video screen and scoreboard just before kickoff, the home crowd in Foxboro roared with approval for their embattled coach. Belichick acknowledged the crowd and then watched his team dismantle the Chargers by the same 38–14 score by which the Patriots shredded the Jets, the win highlighted by a 65-yard interception return for a touchdown by newcomer Adalius Thomas. The defense held the Chargers to just 201 yards and forced three turnovers. Moss scored twice and the Patriots had a 31–7 lead entering the fourth quarter against a team that had finished 2006 with the best record in football during the regular season.

Given the victory, many debated the impact of the Patriots' cheating. Owner Kraft told longtime *New York Daily News* football columnist Gary Myers that he asked Belichick how much of a competitive edge the Patriots gained by videotaping the opposing coaches, and, according to Kraft, the gain was trivial.

"How much did this help us on a scale of 1 to 100?" Kraft reportedly asked Belichick.

"One," a typically terse Belichick replied.

"Then you're a real schmuck," Kraft claimed to have answered.

Which begged the obvious question: Why even risk it all?

As for Mangini, his career in football, like his relationship with Belichick, deteriorated rapidly after Spygate. After going 10-6 in his first season, he went 4-12 and 9-7 in his next two seasons—the latter with Brett Favre at quarterback—and was subsequently fired. He then spent two years with the Cleveland Browns and went a combined 10-22, leaving his career record through five seasons at a woeful 33-47, losing more than just football games.

Meanwhile, without so much as looking in his rearview mirror, Bill Belichick and the 2007 New England Patriots continued to rise.

* * *

In the immediate aftermath of New England's Week 2 win over San Diego, the resentment in the New England locker room was palpable, particularly among the coach's most loyal players. Belichick, after all, understood the pressure points of his locker room better than anyone, which is to say that he understood which players wielded influence and which did not. The coach knew that he just needed to win the trust of those influencers—get their full *buy-in*. In the end, you were either with the program or you were not, and those who were not were usually jettisoned—sooner or later.

As quarterback, Tom Brady was an obvious pressure point. Linebacker Tedy Bruschi was another.

Following the Chargers' win that concluded a tense week, Bruschi stood in front of his locker at Gillette Stadium and customarily answered questions from a media corps that had one real storyline on its mind: Spygate. *Did the Patriots feel their championships had been tainted? Did the scandal call into question their accomplishments? Was the performance against the Chargers some sort of statement back to the naysayers, critics, and doubters?*

Bruschi spoke angrily, his head seemingly swelling as if it were about to explode.

"I don't want to punch all of you in the face for what you were saying. *I don't*," Bruschi said forcefully and sarcastically, implying quite the opposite. "I just wanted to win a game."

Said Brady when asked about the overall clandestine manner in which Belichick ran his operation, a canopy of secrecy that contributed to many wondering what the Patriots were up to—even before the Spygate explosion: "He doesn't sit here and give everyone a lot of information, talk about injuries and tell people what they want to know—and that's for us. That's to protect us. If you want to know, go figure it out."

In retrospect, on this occasion, Brady's words were especially noteworthy. For one, they revealed the reverence with which Belichick's leaders—his pressure points—regarded their coach. *Bill was doing it all for us.* Anyone questioning the coach was out of bounds. And while that sort of cultlike commitment was useful in football, it also demonstrated the kind of sometimes worrisome control Belichick had over his organization, especially over many young men who didn't know any better than to do what their coach told them. Over his years in New England, in fact, Belichick's coaching staff largely comprised ambitious young men similarly eager to please a coach who had been widely acclaimed as a genius. Belichick knew this and exploited it, and much of a long-deprived New England fan base was similarly willing to look the other way if and when there were transgressions.

"I did notice, sure," an atypically candid Belichick said when asked about the support of the crowd when he was shown on the scoreboard before the game. "We've got great fans. They showed and supported the team and I felt something personally, too."

In the end, there was indisputable fact. Aside from owner Kraft, who was thrilled with the results on the field and in the proverbial box office, there was no one but the media to question Belichick's methods. As such, reporters—like opposing teams—became (even more so) a threat to the Patriots' greatness. Players and fans rallied around their coach like never before, the wagons circling so tightly that anyone outside of a very small radius was considered a threat.

On the field, too, the Patriots played as if angry and threatened, opponents routinely feeling the full wrath of New England's mission.

Over the of the next six weeks, culminating with a 52–7 beatdown of the Washington Redskins on their home field in Foxboro, the Patriots dismantled opponents with astonish potency. Coupled with their two wins to start the season, the Patriots went a perfect 8-0 and averaged 41.4 points per game with average margin of victory of nearly 26 points. Brady was averaging more than 300 yards per game while completing more than 74 percent of his passes with thirty touchdowns and two interceptions, numbers that were, at the time, unheard-of. His quarterback rating for the season was an inhuman 136.2, a number that would still obliterate the current single-season passer rating of 122.5, set by Aaron Rodgers in 2011.

Simply put, Belichick, Brady, and the Patriots were unstoppable, blessed with a deep and talented roster, not to mention a coach who was intent on exacting revenge on the league before anyone accused him of cheating.

By then, everyone knew the Patriots had a realistic chance to go undefeated. But there were still critical games to be played. And one of them was against another undefeated team, the reigning Super Bowl champion Indianapolis Colts, the opponent whose victory over the Patriots in the 2006 AFC Championship Game had triggered Bill Belichick's rampage in the first place.

* * *

During the first fifteen years of the new millennium, Tom Brady and Peyton Manning were the NFL equivalent of Muhammad Ali and Joe Frazier, the heaviest of heavyweights who routinely produced epic confrontations. Beginning in February 2002 and ending with Manning's retirement in early 2016, Brady or Manning represented the AFC in a stunning ten of fifteen Super Bowls. (Brady was in six, Manning four.) That fact also heightened the regular-season meetings between the two, where the winner was almost certain to hold home field advantage if the two teams met in the playoffs.

The 2007 meeting between them was perhaps the most significant and remains one of the most watched regular-season games in NFL history. And yet, because football is at its core a physical game that demands power and strength as much as skill and athleticism, the game was less about fireworks and confetti than it was about will and determination.

Despite playing without brilliant wide receiver Marvin Harrison, the Colts foiled the Patriots in the early going and held a 13–7 lead at halftime, thanks largely to an improbable 73-yard touchdown pass from Manning to running back Joseph Addai at the end of the first half. The play came just seconds after Manning completed a key third-down pass to wide receiver Reggie Wayne, giving Indianapolis a first down and preventing the Colts from having to punt the ball away to Brady and New England with less than a minute remaining in the second quarter.

On the ensuing snap, Manning dumped the ball off to Addai, who then darted and weaved his way through an uncharacteristically porous but aging New England defense coached and drilled to prevent such breakdowns. The third quarter featured only a field goal by Patriots kicker Stephen Gostkowski to make the score 13–10 when, on the second snap of the fourth quarter, Brady threw an interception—his second of the game, matching his season total to that point—that linebacker Gary Brackett returned to the Patriots' 32-yard line. Eight plays later, concluding a drive on which Manning threw just two passes and handed the ball off to Addai four times, the Indy quarterback plowed behind his offensive line for a touchdown on a 1-yard quarterback sneak, giving the Colts a 20–10 advantage with less than ten minutes remaining in the game. The Patriots' undefeated season, it seemed, was about to turn to dust.

And then, in the final ten minutes, Brady and the Patriots completely took the game over, clearing what would be the biggest hurdle—but hardly the only one—during what would prove to be a historic regular season.

Taking the field with 9:42 left, Brady led the Patriots on a seven-play, 73-yard touchdown drive that took a mere 1:43 off the game clock thanks largely to a 55-yard strike to Randy Moss that placed the ball at the Indianapolis 3-yard line. Shortly thereafter, Brady completed a 3-yard touchdown pass to Wes Welker that closed the gap to 20–17, when Manning and the Indy offense partly self-destructed and partly succumbed to the pressure applied by New England.

On second-and-7 from the Indy 37 with 6:09 left, Manning completed a 6-yard pass . . . but the Colts were called for holding. The Colts then ended up with a third-and-10 with roughly five minutes remaining . . . when they had a false start. On third-and-15—after moving backward and stalling the game clock—Manning was sacked for a 7-yard loss all the way back at the Indianapolis 21-yard line, necessitating a punt back that Wes Welker returned 23 yards to the New England 49-yard line, a stunning flip of field position that completely turned the game in New England's favor.

In just a few plays, Manning and the Colts went from a potential third-and-1 at their own 43-yard line to the Patriots possessing the ball for a first-and-10 at the New England 49.

Brady needed just three plays to make the reeling Colts pay, connecting with three different pass catchers—Moss, wide receiver Donté Stallworth, and running back Kevin Faulk—for gains of 5, 33, and 13 yards, the last distance producing a touchdown that gave the Patriots their first lead of the second half. And though Indy regained possession on its own 24-yard line with 3:10 left following the ensuing kickoff—the Patriots, if anything, had scored too quickly and left too much time on the clock—the Colts advanced only as far as their own 49-yard line before Patriots lineman Jarvis Green strip-sacked Manning, the resulting fumble recovered by linebacker Rosevelt Colvin to seal the victory.

The Pats were 9-0 and it seemed like no one could stop them.

Said Bruschi after the victory: "It showed we still know how to win, even when things aren't going our way. Face it, a lot of things have gone our way this year. It's nice to see we can still dig deep." Added veteran linebacker Junior Seau: "We answered the call. There was a lot of questions going into the game about our defense and everything else, but when you look at the whole picture of this game, it was basically resilience and perseverance. It was a gut check for all of us to see what we were going to do. And the character of this team really stood out."

And the more the Patriots neared the end of the regular season—the more they inched toward *history*—the more they would need to rely on that very same attribute.

After the Indy game, the Pats enjoyed their bye week and then obliterated the Buffalo Bills 56-10 to improve to 10-0. With a worrisome game at Baltimore scheduled for Week 12, the team then stumbled through a home victory over the mediocre Philadelphia Eagles in Week 11, needing a touchdown run by Laurence Maroney and subsequent interception by defensive back Asante Samuel late in the game to escape with a 31-28 win. In the aftermath of the victory that sent the Pats to 11-0—"People built them up to be Goliath, and they're a good team, don't get me wrong, [but] at the same time . . . we know they're not that much better than us," said Philly offensive lineman Shawn Andrews—NFL experts and analysts began talking of a "blueprint" to beat a Patriots team that suddenly seemed more vulnerable than it had all season.

Said Bruschi at the time: "I hope that a lot of guys who haven't been around here learned that this is how it is playing in November and December. This is the NFL and there are a lot of good teams out there. More importantly, there are a lot of good players. It's going to be close going down the stretch, believe me."

He had no idea how right he would be.

Had the Patriots lost in Week 13 at Baltimore, there is no telling how much differently things might have played out—whether the Patriots might have gone on to win the Super Bowl once stripped of the increasing weight of an undefeated season. As NFL history had proven, the cloak of invincibility could be quite heavy. Victories were absorbed like leaden raindrops draped over the shoulders of a coach . . . or a quarterback . . . even a fan base. The 2007 season slowly became a joyless endeavor where victories could feel like losses—the Week 12 victory over the Eagles, for instance—because winning was no longer the objective. The goal was to avoid defeat.

But when the Patriots won at Baltimore, well, the gods certainly seemed to be on their side.

As was the case in Indianapolis, the Patriots trailed for much of the night and were behind 24–17 early in the fourth quarter. New England managed a field goal with just under nine minutes to play that made the score 24–20, setting the stage for a frantic final sequence during which the Patriots avoided three fourth-down failures—yes, they failed on fourth down *three times*—only to be granted an additional chance thanks to a variety of circumstances that included one time-out and two penalties, one of which they themselves had committed.

After taking over at the New England 27-yard line with 3:30 to play, Brady had led the Patriots to the Baltimore 30 when New England encountered the first such situation, a fourth-and-1. Brady attempted a quarterback sneak on the play and was stuffed short of the first-down marker—only to learn the play had been blown because Ravens defensive coordinator Rex Ryan, a future head coach of the New York Jets, had called time-out just before the snap. When the teams subsequently lined up again, Brady handed the ball off to fullback Heath Evans, who slammed into the middle of the line for a 1-yard loss . . . or so it seemed.

This time, it was *the officials* who had blown the play dead, whistling New England lineman Russ Hochstein for a false start penalty that again negated the play entirely. Unable to decline the transgression by league rule, the Ravens then saw Brady scramble for 12 yards and a new set of downs on fourth-and-6, a play that also included a Baltimore penalty, which the Patriots declined.

All in all, the Patriots—the best team in football to that stage and possessors of a perfect 11-0 record—were given three attempts to convert on the play.

"I've got skin like an armadillo—I can take it," the colorful Ryan told reporters days after the loss when reporters questioned his decision to call time-out just before the first attempt. "We have our speed team on the field at the time, which is only one defensive tackle. We have all linebackers and defensive backs filling out the other 10 spots. Obviously, they are going to run a sneak and you probably don't want that personnel grouping on the field. If I would have had a crystal ball, I obviously would have left that group on the field and won the game."

The only ball that night was made of leather.

And the Patriots ended up winning the game, albeit after another controversial fourth down. With fifty-five seconds to play, Brady lined up in the shotgun and took a fourth-down snap from the Baltimore 13-yard line, then fired over the middle toward tight end Benjamin Watson, who was wedged between two defenders. The pass incomplete, the ball bounced to the ground—along with a penalty flag. In defending Watson from the line of scrimmage, Baltimore defensive back Jermaine Winborne had grabbed the Patriots tight end and held him from behind, a 5-yard penalty that came with an automatic first down.

Now at the Baltimore 8-yard line with four plays and fifty seconds left, Brady took the snap, surveyed the field, then rifled a pass to wide receiver Jabar Gaffney, who tapped his toes inside the back left corner of the end zone to lift the Patriots to a 27–24 lead. As the Ravens erupted, the Ravens drew *two* 15-yard unsportsmanlike conduct penalties, the second on irate Baltimore linebacker Bart Scott, who had taken the officials' first flag and thrown it into the stands. Even then, after the Patriots kicked off from the *Baltimore* 35-yard line, the Ravens advanced to their own 45 when—after safety Brandon Meriweather dropped what should have been a game-ending interception—Ravens quarterback Kyle Boller completed a 52-yard heave that receiver Mark Clayton caught at the New England 3-yard line, where he was tackled as time expired.

In the end, the final few minutes of the game included four fourth-down attempts (including three that failed), three critical Baltimore penalties (including two resulting from meltdowns), one fortuitous Patriots mistake (that killed a failed fourth down), an ill-advised time-out (by Ryan), and a 52-yard pass that ended near the goal line.

Other than that, the Pats had it all the way.

Final score: New England 27, Baltimore 24. The Patriots were 12-0.

"It's hard to go out there and play the Patriots and the refs at the same time," Baltimore defensive back Chris McAlister grumbled after the game. "They put the crown on top of them, they want them to win. They won."

Said Brady: "We made enough plays at the end—a lot of questionable calls and we made some plays. There's a lot of room to improve in the final four weeks. There's things we could've certainly done better . . . we kept clawing back."

As a reward for those efforts, the Patriots then got three relatively easy victories over the next three weeks, defeating the Pittsburgh Steelers, Miami Dolphins, and New York Jets by a combined 86–52, finishing their home schedule with an 8-0 record and improving to 15-0. That set the stage for the regular-season finale, a Week 17 meeting in New York against a Giants team that had already clinched a second-place finish in its division and was locked into its position as the No. 5 seed in the NFC.

The Giants had nothing but the role of spoiler to play, but that was plenty for head coach Tom Coughlin, who elected to play his starters—much to the surprise of Giants fans and media, some of whom asked whether he consulted players or other voices in the organization before making his decision.

"The janitor went by once and I grabbed him—I wanted to make it sure I could bounce it off him," said a sarcastic Coughlin, who added, "Our objective is to win. That's what we work for, that's what we prepare for, that's what we practice for. And it will be no different this week."

While that seemed shocking or downright stupid to many, it was hardly surprising to Patriots coach Bill Belichick. Coughlin and Belichick had been assistants together in the championship Giants teams under Bill Parcells—and they were cut from the same cloth. After leaving the Giants, Coughlin had become the head coach at Boston College and elevated the program to national status, which means Bostonians similarly understood the mentality and philosophies of the old-school, hard-nosed coach. In 1992, Coughlin had an unbeaten BC ranked No. 9 entering an enormously hyped game at Notre Dame, where the Eagles were then destroyed by the Irish 54–7. Coughlin later said he felt "violated" by the defeat, crass terminology that nonetheless delivered the message.

A year later, with Notre Dame ranked No. 1 in the country, Boston College went in and won 41–39 on a last-second field goal by kicker David Gordon, claiming perhaps the biggest victory in school history.

More than fourteen years later, Coughlin was fully prepared to similarly give the Patriots everything he had.

As had been the case repeatedly throughout the second half of the season, the Patriots trailed in the second half, this time by a 28–16 score late in the third quarter. New England then scored the next three touchdowns of the game, two on runs by Laurence Maroney. The other score came on a 65-yard strike from Brady to Randy Moss—the receiver's second touchdown of the night—and gave Moss twenty-three touchdown receptions for the season while elevating Brady to fifty touchdown passes, NFL single-season records for both a receiver and quarterback at that time.

Though the Giants scored late on a touchdown pass from quarterback Eli Manning to wide receiver Plaxico Burress with slightly more than a minute left—remember that combination—the Patriots recovered the ensuing onside kick and completed the first 16-0 regular season in NFL history.

Said an unusually introspective Belichick after the victory: "I'll get back to something that a coach that I worked for used to say, and I certainly believe every word of it. What Bill [Parcells] said was that there are no meaningless games when you're [the ones] playing 'em. If we're playing in a game, it means something to us and I know it meant something to the Giants, too. It might not mean anything to you or it might not mean anything to the standings, but if you're playing and you're a competitor, it means something to you. And I think that was reflected out on the field." He added: "Giants Stadium has always been a special place for me. I spent 12 years here and they were 12 great years. We had some great seasons, some championship seasons, and some of the units that I was involved in, special teams and defense, I think were very productive and it was a thrill to be a part of some of those units as well. It's always special to come back here and the fact that what happened today was here, I don't have any complaints about it, let's put it that way."

For Coughlin, who also cut his teeth in the depths of the Meadowlands, the postgame questions were altogether different. The Giants suffered injuries to three starting players—center Shaun O'Hara, linebacker Kawika Mitchell, and cornerback Sam Madison—and an additional injury to backup safety Craig Dahl. The cost for integrity was high. Giants followers understandably blamed the coach and questioned his judgment, particularly when Coughlin's job security was tenuous at best in the wake of a prove-it-or-lose-it one-year contract he had signed before the beginning of the year.

In some ways, all of that made Coughlin's insistence on playing his starters extraordinarily noble, though he certainly appeared to put his team's playoff chances at risk in the process.

"As far as whether we would play it any differently? No," Coughlin said two days after the game, on the day of New Year's Eve. "I don't know that you can move toward the playoffs in a better way than to play against the No. 1 team in the league, a team that's 16-0, and hold your own, at least for the majority of the evening. I think those are all positives."

As the Giants entered the playoffs, many onlookers disagreed, their chances in the postseason now in significant doubt. And nobody, least of all anyone in New England, believed that the Patriots would see Coughlin and his team again.

* * *

For most of the country, the final game of the 2007 NFL season was perhaps the most memorable Super Bowl in history, a most American story in which revolutionaries toppled an oppressive monarchy. If that sounds overly dramatic, it is. But in the wake of Spygate and an undefeated season, Bill Belichick, Tom Brady, and the rest of the Patriots might as well have been been dressed as redcoats.

In New England in general—and Boston, in particular—Super Bowl XLII was a tragedy that might have been written by Bernard Malamud, author of *The Natural*, a story about indisputable greatness and its accompanying side effect: hubris.

After defeating the Giants to go 16-0, the Patriots defeated both the Jacksonville Jaguars and San Diego Chargers in the AFC playoffs—the first behind a near-perfect, 26-of-28, three-touchdown performance by Brady, the latter by 21–12 score on a wintry New England day in which the opposing quarterback, Philip Rivers, played on a torn knee ligament. Both victories felt like formalities, expected wins that delivered the Patriots to the game where everyone expected—or demanded—them to be: the Super Bowl. New England was now 18-0 and had not played its best football in some time, but the combination of coach and quarterback with a talented, experienced roster was still proving unbeatable.

"There was history on the line—we recognize it, we acknowledge it," said Bruschi.

Added Brady: "We'll try to elevate our game for one last performance."

For perhaps the only time during the Brady-Belichick combination, the AFC Championship felt like a necessary task more than an achievement to be celebrated. With each passing week of the season, particularly toward the end, the Patriots felt like a gambler at the blackjack table, riding a hot streak while parlaying their winnings. Winnings of $1 million became $2 million, then $4 million, then $8 million. Now there was one final wager to be placed—all or nothing, and the weeks leading up to the final judgment were like waiting for the jury to come in.

Waiting in Glendale, Arizona, were the Giants, unlikely Super Bowl participants who had beaten Tampa Bay, Dallas, and Green Bay—all on the road—to meet the Patriots again for the second time in five games. Curiously, the Giants arrived in Arizona wearing all black. When wide receiver Plaxico Burress was asked if the Giants were preparing to dispatch the Patriots to their eternal rest, he replied that the team had arrived for "a business trip," adding, "It could be both." Burress then predicted a 23–17 Giants win, a remark that the media gleefully presented to Brady for a response.

"Only going to score 17 points? Is Plax playing defense?" Brady smirked. "I wish he'd said like 45–42 or something like that. At least he'd give us a little more credit for scoring a few points."

But why diss the Giants defense when he could just as easily diss the Patriots offense?

One day before the game, the *Boston Herald* published a story indicating that Spygate was hardly dead—that the Patriots had videotaped the St. Louis Rams during the final walkthrough before Super Bowl XXXVI, the New England victory that had launched the greatest dynasty in Super Bowl history. The Patriots adamantly denied the claim and no tape was ever produced. At the same time, what was indisputable was that Patriots staffer Matt Walsh had watched the walkthrough while packing up his equipment following the Patriots' walkthrough, then relayed what he had seen to Belichick confidant Ernie Adams.

Though the Patriots later threatened legal action against the paper and demanded a retraction—many believed that the distraction contributed to the team's performance the following day—the truth, as Belichick often liked to say, was that *the hay was in the barn*. They hadn't played their best football in weeks. Other teams, like the Giants, had improved, while New England had not. And Brady had an injury that required him to a wear a protective boot on his right ankle just days before the game.

Though the Giants scored only a field goal on their opening possession, they set the game's tempo with a sixteen-play, 63-yard drive that consumed an incredible 9:59 off the play clock. And while the Patriots promptly scored a touchdown on their first possession, the play came on the first snap of the second quarter, when Maroney ran over right guard for a one-yard touchdown run that gave New England a 7-3 advantage. The score remained the same into the third quarter, when the Patriots held the ball for more than eight minutes before a third-and-7 at the Giants 25-yard line. When Brady was sacked—one of five on the day by a New York defense front that dominated the game—the Patriots curiously chose to go for it on fourth-and-13 rather than to attempt a 49-yard field goal, Brady throwing incomplete to turn the ball over on downs.

A defensive grind for the majority of the night to that point, the game suddenly opened up.

On New York's first play of the fourth quarter, quarterback Eli Manning hit tight end Kevin Boss for a 45-yard gain that moved the Giants to the New England 35. Five plays later, Manning hit David Tyree for a 5-yard touchdown and a 10-7 New York lead. The teams then exchanged possessions when, with 7:54 left, Brady and the Patriots took over on their own 20-yard line, where New England began its best drive since its first possession of the game. Brady threw eleven times in twelve plays, completing eight of them for 71 yards. He was not sacked. The Patriots ran once. The final throw was a 6-yard touchdown pass to—who else?—Moss on third-and-goal from the Giants' 6-yard line, giving New England a 14-10 lead with less than three minutes to play.

On the final New York Giants drive of the 2007 season, New York ran twelve plays, three of them on third down, one of them on fourth. As New England so often had done—and would continue to do under Brady and Belichick—the Giants converted them all. On third-and-10 with 1:59 to play, Manning completed a 9-yard pass to wide receiver Amani Toomer; on fourth-and-1, bell cow running back Brandon Jacobs thundered for 2 yards. And then, on third-and-5 from the Giants 44-yard line with 1:15 left—one play after Patriots cornerback Asante Samuel let a potential history-sealing interception glance off his hands—Manning took the snap, somehow avoided being sacked by both Adalius Thomas and Jarvis Green, and heaved a pass downfield that was effectively a jump ball between David Tyree and Patriots safety Rodney Harrison.

With both hands above his head and Harrison stuck to him like Velcro, Tyree somehow pinned the ball against his helmet with his right hand, resisted

Harrison's attempts to knock the ball free, and prevented the ball from touching the ground as he fell backward onto the turf.

Complete.

First down.

Said Giants defensive lineman Michael Strahan much later: "This guy clamps it to his helmet with one hand and then brings his other hand back and pins it—and then lands on his back and keeps the ball off the ground. That right there let me know, 'We're going to win this game.' Because, for something that magical to happen in a season that's been so magical, you could not lose."

Three plays later, after a sack of Manning by Thomas forced the Giants to use their final time-out, Manning completed another third-down pass—this one a 12-yard completion to Steve Smith on third-and-11. There were thirty-nine seconds to play. The Giants lined up on first-and-10 when Belichick called for something he often liked to do—a blitz inside his own red zone—that Coughlin and the Giants were prepared for. With the six-foot-five Plaxico Burress lined up against five-foot-nine Patriots cornerback Ellis Hobbs in one-on-one coverage to his left, Manning lofted a simple, easy touchdown pass to give the Giants a 17–14 lead that proved the final points in the game.

Still, *with twenty-nine seconds on the clock, possessing all three time-outs and needing only a field goal to tie*, the Patriots panicked. Brady threw deep on first down, was sacked on second down, then threw deep again twice—both intended for Moss—on the final plays. All fell incomplete.

And incomplete, too, was New England's run at history, the Patriots finishing as the only one-loss team in NFL history that failed to win the Super Bowl.

Understandably, New England was disconsolate after the defeat. A devastated Belichick was rude and abrupt. Moss questioned the New England game plan. The Patriots were sick to their stomachs.

Today, at the team's home of Gillette Stadium, a "16-0" banner hangs to commemorate the team's undefeated regular season, though it has its own location, away from the banners that celebrate the franchise's six Super Bowl victories. Years after the defeat, linebacker Bruschi was asked if he regarded the season as a success or a failure, causing the longtime Patriot to pause.

"That's a good question," Bruschi replied in 2020. "I think the perspective of [each of] the players, [depending on] how many championships they won, is going to be different—because I'd won three championships going in. I can look at that year [and] I can say it was a good year because we attempted to do something that had never been done before, and I just—I respect that type of effort and that type of mentality of 'Screw everybody else. We're going to beat everyone and we're going to go for it and we don't want to be taken out.' I remember captains' meetings and we'd tell him, 'Bill, we want to win, we know they're talking about resting, we want to do it this way, we want to win every one. We've won championships. Now we want to win *the* championship.' So to try to complete that task, it's monumental in itself to go 19-0 and, looking back, I wouldn't change anything. So, I would say that's a good year. I mean, in terms of what we tried to accomplish, failure in the end . . . yes. Did we lose? Absolutely. But, man, I wouldn't trade it for the world because we try to do something that people can't even think about."

He added: "On the last drive, there was a fourth down-and-short where, I mean, I just couldn't get it done against [Giants fullback and blocker Madison] Hedgecock and [Brandon] Jacobs was able to fall forward [for the first down on fourth-and-1]. I mean, various plays like that, that we couldn't get done. I don't think it was fatigue. I don't think it was lack of focus or anything like that. I've lived the other side. So the only thing I point to is that the plays that we made to win championships were made by the Giants that day."

In the end, Plaxico Burress was wrong. The Patriots didn't score 17 points. They scored only 14.

Little did anyone know that the air of invincibility that the Patriots had built beginning in 2001 had been punctured.

And it would take some time to repair.

CHAPTER 6

GREEN DAYS

"Doc was all about creative motivation. Also creative language. What words you use. What words you don't use. Take the phrase 'Boston culture.' There's always been talk about Boston being a basically racist city. Of course Doc knew that, but Doc had his own way of dealing with it. He didn't bring up Boston culture or racism. He used one word, a word that captured our imagination: Ubuntu."

—former Celtics center and NBA Hall of Famer Kevin Garnett
in his memoir, *KG A to Z: An Uncensored Encyclopedia
of Life, Basketball, and Everything in Between*

IN BOSTON, IN THE NEW millennium, the heartache from a painful loss rarely lasted long. And while the toppling of the 2007 Patriots forever left an indelible mark on New England, Boston did what it always did at the end of every long winter. It embraced another spring.

And this time, that meant basketball.

Long before the grass turned green again, the Celtics had joined the Red Sox and Patriots as legitimate championship threats during the summer of 2007, most notably on July 31, the date of the annual MLB trading deadline. On that day, while the Red Sox acquired closer Eric Gagne from the Dodgers in hopes of fortifying their relief corps en route to another (successful) World Series run, the Celtics' head of basketball operations, Danny Ainge, executed one of the great blockbuster trades in team history, acquiring center Kevin Garnett from the Minnesota Timberwolves (former Celtics teammate Kevin McHale was then the GM in Minnesota) for a collection of would-be spare parts that included promising power forward Al Jefferson.

Ainge, to borrow a phrase, traded ponies for a horse, in this case Garnett, a premium Thoroughbred and one of the few basketball players in the world who could greatly impact a game on both the offensive and defensive ends of the floor. Garnett was a competitor and leader, the kind of true centerpiece that championship rosters were built around.

"We're not talking about potential today," Celtics coach Doc Rivers said upon completion of the deal, in which the Celtics sent a combination of seven players and draft picks to the Minnesota Timberwolves for Garnett. "We're talking about what we have and the jobs we have to do to be a team that contends right now. I'd rather have that."

With Garnett in town, it truly seemed like Boston had it all.

Three months after the Patriots had reshaped their roster around a collection of players that included, most notably, wide receiver Randy Moss, the acquisitions of Garnett and Gagne—on the same day—signified Boston's place not only as a sports mecca but as true power. It suddenly felt as if everyone wanted to play there. Moss salivated at the idea of resurrecting his career with quarterback Tom Brady. Gagne, the 2003 National League Cy Young Award winner and possessor of a major-league-leading 152 saves from 2002 to 2004, waived a no-trade clause to serve as a setup man to closer Jonathan Papelbon. Team executives were wheeling and dealing all over the country with a seeming avalanche of maneuvers that always seemed to end in Boston.

In the case of the Celtics, the Garnett deal was the biggest in a series of maneuvers made by Ainge, who had reached a critical stage with forward Paul Pierce, who had grown frustrated by the team's inability to surround him with comparable talent. The No. 10 overall selection by the Celtics in the 1998 NBA draft, Pierce had an immediate impact in the NBA, averaging 16.5 points a game in his rookie season. By the end of the 2006–2007 campaign, Pierce had scored more points during his nine years than all but three players in the NBA—Kobe Bryant, Allen Iverson, and Garnett. Meanwhile, the Celtics had lost more games than they had won, and in '06–'07 they went an abysmal 24-58, at one point losing an incredible eighteen straight and 22-of-23, mostly while Pierce was (allegedly) injured. The message was clear: Without Pierce, the Celtics were a laughingstock.

Thanks to the losing streak—many believed the Celtics extended Pierce's absence to improve their standing for the NBA draft—the Celtics easily qualified for the NBA draft lottery and ended up with the No. 5 overall selection. They drafted Georgetown's Jeff Green, who they traded to the Seattle SuperSonics as part of the deal for accomplished guard Ray Allen, widely regarded as one of the best pure shooters in the NBA. The move was a necessary step to lure Garnett, who shared a frustration with Pierce and Allen both—the inability of their respective franchises to surround each player with the necessary pieces to win a championship.

Individually, Pierce, Allen, and Garnett were looked upon at least partly as failures, if only because none of them had won a championship. (Such is the pass-fail grading system for NBA greats.) Allen, like Garnett, was a No. 5 overall selection in the draft. All of them had played in numerous All-Star Games. But none of them had really played with talents like the other two, an enticing lure that Ainge ultimately used to leverage Garnett out of Minnesota.

To that point of the NBA off-season, after all, Garnett had resisted accepting a trade to Boston. His preference was to join Kobe Bryant in Los Angeles, but the Lakers did not have the necessary assets or payroll flexibility to orchestrate the maneuver. Ainge and the Celtics also had to combat Boston's tarnished image as an unwelcoming place for African Americans, a reputation the city had earned over a period of decades for an assortment of reasons. One of the most damaging and more recent examples had come in mid-1970s, when court-ordered desegregation of the Boston schools triggered a succession of riots, one of the enduring images of which was a white Boston man attempting to use a flagpole, with the American flag waving from it, to spear a young black man named Ted Landsmark.

The unforgettable photo, taken by former *Boston Herald American* photographer Stanley Forman, was appropriately dubbed *The Soiling of Old Glory*.

Coupled with Boston's history in other areas—the Red Sox were the last major-league team to integrate under longtime owner Thomas A. Yawkey, widely regarded as a racist—the stain on Boston proved far more enduring.

Faced with few options, Garnett consulted most everyone he could, from Allen and Pierce to former Celtic forward Antoine Walker. For all of the shame that Boston had brought upon itself, the Celtics were forerunners when it came to integration, establishing themselves as everything the Red Sox were not. In 1950, the Celtics had been the first NBA team to draft a Black player, Chuck Cooper. In 1964, the Celtics became the first team to start five Black players in an NBA game. And in 1966, the Celtics became the first team with a Black coach, the great Bill Russell, whom Celtics patriarch Red Auerbach named player-coach in 1966 and who led the Celtics to two championships in that role, in 1968 and 1969. Even so, the city's reputation was impossible to ignore.

As noted in a story by African American reporter Marc Spears of the website the Undefeated in 2020: "Russell, who declined to be interviewed for this story, once called Boston 'a flea market of racism' in his 1979 memoir, *Second Wind: The Memoirs of an Opinionated Man.* 'It had all varieties, old and new, and in their most virulent form,' Russell wrote. 'The city had corrupt, city hall-crony racists, send-'em-back-to-Africa racists, and in the university areas phony radical-chic racists. . . . Other than that, I liked the city.'"

In the end, Kevin Garnett agreed to the trade, though the entire process took more than a month after the acquisition of Ray Allen. Garnett required some arm-twisting, an ironic truth given that, in some ways, he was the perfect Boston athlete: committed, intense, hardworking.

And, of course, championship-driven.

"Garnett, through many, many discussions, was [eventually] convinced that this was a good place to play . . . and so he decided to take a leap of faith and come," Celtics co-owner Steve Pagliuca said in May 2020. "Garnett would tell you today that he developed a whole new appreciation for being an NBA player when he came to Boston. There are players that wilt when they come to a market like New York or Boston with the high fan intensity and media scrutiny—and sports are the topic of the day every day in Boston. Garnett was a quintessential guy that actually loved and fed into that. His intensity, which was already high, increased even higher when he came here. He really embraced the scrutiny and embraced the will to win and the grit that it takes in Boston. He is almost your perfect example of someone who thrived in Boston."

For the Celtics—nay, for the *city*—the trade was a reason to be proud, a reason to believe that things were changing. Moss had come to New England, and now Garnett and Gagne were doing the same for one thing: opportunity.

Or, more specifically, a real chance to win.

* * *

A mere five days after the Red Sox won the 2007 World Series and on the same day the Patriots obliterated the Washington Redskins by a 52–7 score to improve to a perfect 8-0, Boston unveiled a new-and-improved Celtics team with potential that was, at the time, unclear. After the Celtics took a one-week preseason trip to Europe as part of the NBA Europe Live Tour, many still wondered about the team's true potential. Celtics officials believed the trip would provide the newly constructed roster an opportunity to bond, something coach Doc Rivers saw as critical to the team's success. Rivers promoted the concept

of *ubuntu*, a Nguni Bantu term that was at the core of his message to his three
newly joined All-Stars. Roughly translated it means:

I am because we are.

While Rivers focused on the need for his players to set aside their egos,
others wondered whether the new "Big Three" of the Celtics had the necessary support, largely because the head of basketball operations, Danny Ainge,
had traded most everything else on his roster to assemble the team's nucleus.
(Longtime *Boston Globe* columnist Bob Ryan, one of the most widely respected
basketball writers and sports columnists of his time, went so far as to suggest
the Celtics had the worst bench in the league.) Yet, with a handful of shrewd
signings—most notably swingman James Posey and guard Eddie House—Ainge
bet that the trio of Garnett, Pierce, and Allen (in that order) would both elevate
the play of existing players of the roster and, simultaneously, lure others to
Boston for the chance to play with the best threesome in the league.

A longtime player, broadcaster, coach, and executive, Ainge knew how
the NBA worked as well as anyone. And he was right.

Though an amped-up Garnett's first shot as a Celtic was a cinder block
that nearly felled the backboard at the TD Garden, Boston opened with an easy
103–83 victory over a Washington Wizards team regarded as, at best, below
average. A relatively lackluster Celtics performance followed in a 98–95 victory
at Toronto over the inferior Raptors, a game that further validated the belief
that the Celtics, as potent as they might be, would likely encounter a learning
curve through the early part of the season. From the time of the deal, many
regarded the Celtics as having a championship window of roughly three years,
which left some question as to whether the 2007–2008 Celtics would be ready
to make a real run at Boston's next title.

Rivers, for his part, was having none of such talk. "I don't look at it that
way," the coach said, dismissing out of hand any and all suggestion that the
Celtics had time on their side.

And then it happened.

On Wednesday, November 7, three days after the Patriots defeated the
Indianapolis Colts to improve to 9-0, the Celtics had Boston's full attention
for a meeting with the Denver Nuggets, a talented Western Conference opponent that was to provide the Celtics with their first real test of the season. In a
positively scintillating first-half performance, Boston outscored Denver 77–38,
dominating both ends of the floor with such efficiency that the entire league
took notice. Despite little reason to play the second half, the Celtics finished

the night making 64.5 percent of their shot attempts (an absurd 64.5 percent) while out-rebounding the Nuggets 38–27 and amassing thirty-two assists to go along with twenty steals. The victory was so impressive that it led to an immediate recalibration of expectations, even Bostonians awakening to the reality of how good the Celtics really were.

Said a succinct Carmelo Anthony, the multitalented Nuggets forward who accurately summarized the events of the alleged contest: "They beat the shit out of us tonight."

Did they ever.

Said Rivers of his players: "They're playing together, there's no doubt about that. They like each other. If I had to simplify it, I really think it comes down to that. They like each other and they've decided that they don't need anything for them individually. They want to win for a team."

Veteran Pierce, with whom Rivers had clashed out the outset of their time in Boston, agreed: "Nobody really cares who gets the credit on this team. We just want to go out there and have some fun. We're just scratching the surface of where we can be. "

Indeed, for all that Garnett, Pierce, and Allen had accomplished individually during their careers, not one of them had ever played a single game in the NBA Finals. Rivers, a veteran of fourteen NBA seasons who made one All-Star team and played in eighty-one career postseason games over nine playoff series, similarly had never played in the Finals. Rivers knew he needed to stoke the confidence of his three star players and stress the importance of winning in the regular season to secure home-court advantage through the playoffs. Before the season began, in fact, Rivers had gone so far as to take Garnett, Pierce, and Allen on a tour of the parade route that Boston teams had taken to celebrate their championships in recent years—the three Super Bowl titles by the Patriots and the two by the Red Sox.

Together with his star players, Rivers also had set the lofty goal of going undefeated in the 41-game home schedule, something never achieved in the history of the NBA. (The 1986 Celtics, who were the last team in franchise history to win a title, went an incredible 40-1 during the 1985–86 regular season and 10-0 in the playoffs.) While most everyone was waiting for the Celtics to jell, the team essentially came out with its foot on the accelerator, winning its first eight games to start the season on the way to a blistering 29-3 start. The last of those victories was a 92–85 win at Detroit, a team that had established itself as the class in the Eastern Conference over the previous six seasons. During that time, the Pistons had won an NBA championship while also losing a finals series to the dynastic San Antonio Spurs. They had been to the conference finals (or better) for five straight years.

For the Celtics, the victory over Detroit proved invaluable, and not solely for the fact that the Pistons were a measuring stick. Despite the lofty goal of going undefeated at home, the Celtics had lost to the Pistons 87–85 in the first meeting of the season between the teams, in Boston. In the rematch in Detroit, the Celtics outscored the Pistons 29–19 in the fourth quarter to claim a 92–85 victory.

"This was a test game," noted Pierce. "We needed to find out a lot about ourselves in this game. It was on the road. Detroit's the hottest team in the league. There were all kinds of excuses you could have about losing this game. We're still growing up as a team. We're still learning about ourselves. But this is a character win. This is a look-deep-inside-you-and-see-what-you're-about type of win."

Said a more direct Rivers: "Our team needed it."

Truth be told, over the balance of the regular season, the Celtics did not need much else. While the team went through one minor midseason malaise that dropped its record to 41-12, the Celtics closed the regular season by going 25-6 in their final thirty-one contests, finishing the regular season with a sterling 66-16 mark that was easily the best in the NBA.

Just as Boston was overcoming the Patriots' backbreaking loss in the Super Bowl, as the Red Sox were to embark on a defense of their second world title in four seasons, the Celtics were about to begin the postseason. Nobody was talking about three-year windows anymore. The goal was simple.

Championship or bust.

* * *

In the National Basketball Association, the first round of the playoffs is largely a formality. The NBA was, is, and always will be an oligarchy, a league dominated each season—and, perhaps, throughout history—by a few clubs. No other sport allows a singularly great player to dominate the play, largely because of the simple math. Each team has only five players on the floor at a time, and a dominant player can remain on the floor for as much as 85 to 100 percent of the time. And so a team like the Cleveland Cavaliers, perennially one of the true doormats in all of professional sports, can go from laughingstock to championship contender almost overnight purely by the acquisition of a dominant player like, say, LeBron James.

In the case of James, specifically, he was in his fifth NBA season in 2007–2008, having just made his first career appearance in the NBA Finals in 2007. And while the Cavaliers were swept by the peerless San Antonio Spurs, Cleveland's ascension was proof that one player could alter the landscape of professional basketball like no other athlete in any other sport.

For Boston, that athlete was the Big Ticket, the brilliant Garnett, who had stellar wingmen in Pierce and Allen. And yet, for as dominant as Boston had been during the regular season and as heavily favored as the Celtics were to breeze through the early round of the playoffs, a funny thing happened on the way to Boston's seeming coronation, what would be the seventeenth championship in franchise history. The Celtics nearly choked in the first round.

Matched with easily the worst team to qualify for the playoffs, the forever mediocre and anonymous Atlanta Hawks, the Celtics won both Games 1 and 2 at home by sizable margins before dropping both Games 3 and 4 in Atlanta. Game 5 was a Boston blowout, but they lost Game 6 by three points—delivering the Celtics to a seemingly unfathomable Game 7 against the worst of the sixteen teams in the NBA playoff field. The series pattern suggested Game 7 would be a blowout—and it was—but the 99–65 victory did little to quell the doubt that crept into the equation for the simple fact that 2007–2008 Hawks did not belong on the same planet as the Celtics, let alone in a Game 7.

The cause of the Celtics' troubles? "It's hard to put a finger on," Allen said after Game 6.

Actually, it wasn't. They were tight, at least on the road, where NBA weaknesses were typically exposed. And for a Celtics team built around three veteran All-Stars saddled with the sandbags that belong to the Best Players Without a Championship, the doubt was palpable. The Celtics suddenly seemed unsure of themselves. They seemed timid at times. They seemed like the epitome of paper tigers, a team that could rampage through the regular season only to wilt when the stakes reached their highest.

In Round 2, with the estimable James now leading the opposition, the series again followed a disturbing pattern. The Celtics won at home and lost on the road in Cleveland, leading to another Game 7, also on the fabled parquet floor of the TD Garden. But where the badly overmatched Hawks had folded, the Cavaliers would do not such thing, thanks largely to James, who single-handedly had the Cavaliers within a point, 89–88, with roughly two minutes remaining in the game.

And then, as often was the case in Celtics history, it was if the Celtics team logo came to life, the leprechaun peeling itself up off the floor to at least temporarily delay what would eventually become LeBron James's stranglehold on the NBA Eastern Conference.

After James missed a long 3-pointer that would have put the Cavs ahead for the first time in the game, the Celtics used most of the twenty-four-second shot clock on their next possession. The ball ended up in the hands of Pierce beyond the top of the key, where he began dribbling to his left as the Cleveland defense surrounded him. Pierce carefully bounced a pass to an open Eddie House near the left corner, where House might have fired a jumper over Cleveland center Zydrunas Ilgauskas with less than ten seconds on the shot clock. Instead, House funneled the ball to P. J. Brown, a six-foot-eleven power forward who had spent a nomadic fifteen-year professional career playing in both Greece and the NBA, the latter with five different franchises. Never regarded as a scorer, Brown had been out of basketball, weighing his options, when Pierce and Allen convinced him to join the Celtics near the end of the regular season, when he appeared in eighteen games without much of a real impact.

And yet, amid a winner-take-all affair with the budding LeBron James, the Celtics' season was in his hands. Without hesitation, from the left elbow and about three feet inside the 3-point line, Brown buried a jump shot officially listed at twenty feet, though it was probably closer to eighteen. Regardless, the field goal was part of a four-for-four shooting performance—including three-for-three in the third quarter—that propelled the Celtics to an eventual 97–92 win and a meeting with Detroit in the NBA Eastern Conference Finals. Garnett, Pierce, and Allen were all on the floor when the ball ended up in Brown's hands, hardly the scenario anyone in Boston had envisioned when Ainge had assembled the roster in the first place.

"That shot, hey, probably I would say the biggest shot of my career," Brown admitted.

"I wasn't brought here to hit shots like that."

Nonetheless, he made it—without the slightest rattle—only adding to an epic duel between James (45 points) and Pierce (41) that otherwise highlighted the afternoon. And in the process, Brown validated Rivers's mantra for the team from the beginning: to believe in one another, to share the burden, to trust.

I am because we are.

Now the Celtics squared off against the Pistons in what promised to be a grueling affair. The Pistons promptly served notice that they were superior to both the Hawks and Cavs when they won Game 2 in Boston, handing the Celtics their first home loss of the playoffs, and sending the Celtics back on the road, where they had failed to win once during the entire postseason.

Boston had yet to trail in any series, but now they were facing a seasoned, hardened, and accomplished Pistons team that had one of the best records in the NBA at both home and on the road.

"Well, this is a test for us," acknowledged Allen. "We talked about all the things that happened in the first two rounds, and now we're in a situation where we can't move on without winning on the road."

Rivers, for his part, preached defense. The games in Detroit were likely to be intense and physical, the crowd intimidating. Under such conditions, scoring was usually at a premium. That made Garnett perhaps the perfect centerpiece, amid a Hall of Fame career that would include twelve NBA All-Defensive selections and nine on the All-Defensive First Team. In his first year with the Celtics, he was the NBA Defensive Player of the Year. And with a trip to the finals at stake, the Celtics now needed him to dominate the interior more than he had at any point during the season.

Given the spotlight, the Big Ticket delivered.

In Game 3, facing their first potential series deficit of the postseason, the Celtics limited the Pistons to 17 points in the first quarter and just 15 in the second. They held a 50–32 lead at half and controlled play throughout the whole game, posting a 94–80 victory that was easily their most impressive and important of the season. There was nothing particularly fancy about it. Garnett finished with 22 points, 13 rebounds, and 6 assists, and the Celtics had control of the series again, something that felt true even when Detroit won Game 4 by a 94–75 count to send the series back to Boston tied at two games apiece.

Said Rivers after the team's first road win of the playoffs: "Maybe somebody taking away our security blanket is what we needed."

Indeed, the win at Detroit seemed like a breakthrough, the kind of win that infused the team with confidence and led virtually the entire basketball world to the same conclusion. During the 2007–2008 season, Boston had won absolutely every game they needed to, controlling their own destiny from the very start.

With Garnett (33 points) again leading the way, the Celtics won Game 5 at home by a 106–102 score, then returned to Detroit and closed out the Pistons on their own floor. This time, the Celtics completely dominated the fourth quarter, turning a 70–60 deficit into an 89–81 victory, clinching the series (and a trip to the finals) and effectively ending Detroit's grasp on the East. The following season, the Pistons finished with a 39-43 record and missed the playoffs. Entering the fall of 2021, they had yet to win a single playoff series since the Celtics toppled them on May 31, 2008.

For the Celtics, on the other hand, the victory marked a new beginning, the team's first trip to the Finals since 1987, when Boston suffered a six-game defeat to the same franchise that awaited them now: the Los Angeles Lakers. And the Lakers, of course, were the same team that had been Garnett's first choice during the off-season, when Ainge ultimately rescued him from the Minnesota Timberwolves. Throughout the Pistons series, Garnett had been the Celtics' best player, finishing with averages of 22.8 points and 9.7 rebounds that led all players in the six games. He had shot 52.5 from the field and 81.1 percent from the free-throw line, playing like a man intent on capturing his best career opportunity at a championship.

"I give credit where credit is due," Pistons point guard Chauncey Billups said of the Celtics as a whole. "That team is good. They're locked in, they're focused. From the coaches to the players to the bench, they're together, man. That's why you see them playing the way they played all season, and beating us in this series. Yeah, we've got a lot of respect for them."

Added Billups of Garnett: "I told him, 'Man, [you've] been waiting a long time—waiting a long time for this.' He deserved it—and I'm pulling for him."

The Pistons, for certain, sounded like a team that realized its multiyear journey was complete.

Fifteen years into *his* illustrious NBA career, meanwhile, Kevin Garnett still had another stop to make.

* * *

The Boston Celtics and Los Angeles Lakers are, without dispute, the NBA blue bloods, franchises with histories so rich that it borders on embarrassing. Between them, entering the 2022-23 NBA season, the Celtics and Lakers had combined for thirty-four of the league's seventy-five championships, an absurd 45 percent. And the teams had amassed roughly 36 percent of all Finals *appearances.* And when both were in the Finals at the same time, the basketball world braced for what amounted to a clash of the titans.

As such, the NBA summoned the gods of a bygone era to hype the series, most notably Larry Bird and Magic Johnson, who had led the Celtics and Lakers, respectively, who combined to win eight of the nine NBA championships from 1980 to 1988. Now, with both teams back, the focus shifted from Garnett to Pierce, the longtime Celtic, and Kobe Bryant, the Lakers star against whom he would be matched up. The franchise players perfectly reflected the values of their cities: Bryant was more glitz and glamour, Pierce more solid and workmanlike, deceptively strong, sneakily effective. Most everyone in the basketball world regarded Bryant as a superior player—and he was. But the 2007–2008 Finals proved to be Pierce's show.

Seen almost exclusively as a scorer to that point in his career, Pierce's final numbers in the series seemed modest on paper—21.8 points, 4.5 rebounds, 6.3 assists, and 1.2 steals—but they reflected comprehensive contributions that many never knew to be part of his game. He scored 38 points one game, had 10 assists the next. He defended Bryant. And he helped spearhead the indisputable turning point of the series in Game 4, when the Lakers went from having a real chance at winning the championship to losing it within a matter of minutes.

After the Celtics won the first two games of the series in Boston by scores of 98–88 and 108–102, Los Angeles claimed Game 3 87–81. The Lakers then blistered the Celtics by a 35–14 margin in the first quarter of Game 4, increasing their advantage to as many as 24 points in the second quarter. Trailing 58–40 at halftime, the Celtics had just four assists as a team. Boston couldn't make shots, couldn't rebound, couldn't defend. While law enforcement officials had cordoned off the area outside the Staples Center to investigate a bomb threat—it proved phony—the Lakers absolutely had their way with the Celtics in such dominating fashion that most everyone was assuming the series would soon be tied at two wins apiece.

Instead, the Celtics executed one of the great, improbable comebacks in team history, rallying for a 97–91 victory that stunned LA and all but made Boston's seventeenth world title a formality. Decades earlier, when Bird and Johnson (more commonly referred to in NBA lore as "Larry" and "Magic") first met in the Finals, the series had been structured differently. The team with home-court advantage would host Games 1, 2, 5, and 7, what was customarily referred to as the 2-2-1-1-1 format. But, to help minimize travel, the NBA switched to a 2-3-2 format in 1985.

That only amplified home-court advantage. In 2008, the Lakers knew upon returning to LA that they needed to win three straight home games to have any chance at all of winning the series. The Celtics, by contrast, needed only one win in LA to return home with a 3-2 series edge and the knowledge that one victory in the final two home games would secure the club a championship. If the Lakers failed to sweep at home, they were pretty much cooked.

Though the Celtics had trimmed the Lakers lead some in the third quarter of Game 4, Los Angeles still had a 73-61 advantage with roughly two minutes remaining in the third when the Celtics ripped off a 10-0 run. The LA lead was still 73-71 two minutes into the fourth when Leon Powe—pronounced *Poe*, though arrogant Lakers coach Phil Jackson referred to him as *Pow*—flipped in a six-footer to tie the game at 73. The teams then exchanged buckets: 75-75, then 77-77. Thanks to some key contributions by the unheralded James Posey, the Celtics pulled ahead 94-91 with forty seconds left before the Celtics isolated Allen on the far less athletic Sasha Vujacic with roughly twenty seconds to play. A historically good sniper whose range was to be respected, Allen executed a crossover dribble that left Vujacic staggering—an "ankle breaker," as the saying goes—that produced an easy layup and a 97-91 Boston victory.

Los Angeles was stunned—and the Lakers were effectively done.

"We just wet the bed—a nice big one, too," Bryant told the assembled media in response to a question from a radio personality with whom he jousted. "One of those you have to put a towel over."

In retrospect, the basketball world might just as well have thrown a sheet over the Lakers, who were toast.

While Los Angeles won Game 5 by a 103-98 score, there was nonetheless an air of inevitability as the teams boarded their respective flights and returned to Boston. Game 6, to almost no one's surprise, was the sports equivalent of a bloodbath, the Celtics exploding in a 34-15 second quarter that gave them a 58-35 lead at intermission. The Boston lead peaked at a preposterous 42 points on a free throw by Eddie House late in the fourth quarter before the Lakers scored the final three points of the game, making the final score 131-92, a 39-point margin, and the second biggest blowout in NBA Finals history.

Pierce, unsurprisingly, was named MVP of the Finals, a fitting development for an assortment of reasons. Only a year or two earlier, while fans at the TD Garden chanted for the dismissal of coach Rivers during an ugly loss amid an ugly season—"Fi-re Doc! Fi-re Doc!" they thundered—an immature Pierce openly laughed on the Boston bench. His frustration with the organization later grew palpable. But after the arrival of both Garnett and Allen, Pierce subjugated his game more than anyone. In the seven seasons before Garnett and Allen arrived in Boston, Pierce averaged 24.8 points and 18.3 shots per game, largely out of necessity. But in the championship season, those numbers dipped to a respective 19.6 and 13.7, further evidence that statistics in sports can be terribly, terribly deceiving.

As one NBA official remarked of Pierce during the Celtics' three-game stint in Los Angeles, "I had no idea he was this good."

Many nodded in agreement.

"No doubt," agreed Rivers, whose relationship with Pierce improved greatly over their time together in Boston. "I think Paul was viewed only as a scorer and now I think people see him as a complete basketball player. He had eight assists the other night [in Game 5]. The game before that, he guarded Kobe and did a terrific job. I think he's one of the best rebounders at small forward in our league and he's a lethal scorer. He did it all."

Offered team architect Danny Ainge: "He's had his ups and downs, and he really hasn't had any of the opportunities to build on his legacy. I've always thought that Paul was one of the top handful of players in Celtics history, and these are the kinds of games he can build on that legacy. And they're the kinds of games he lives for."

They were the kind of games, too, that redefined careers—for Pierce, for Garnett, and for Allen, all of whom united for a singular purpose: to shed the burden of being labeled a great player who couldn't win it all.

Now, each was a champion.

I am because we are.

In Boston, from the gridiron to the diamond to the court, *ubuntu* was everywhere.

CHAPTER 7

THE PUCK STOPS HERE

This one's for our favorite game
Black and gold, we wave the flag

—"Rose Tattoo" by the Dropkick Murphys

HOCKEY DEMANDS COMMITMENT. THERE ARE no shortcuts. The game requires, first and foremost, ice, which must be man-made or naturally formed. Relative to a patch of grass, an open field, or a neighborhood basketball hoop, ice can be hard to find, even harder to reserve. Securing it requires time, effort, and often money, a process that immediately thins the herd and filters out those whose interest in the sport is something less than an obsession.

And let there be no doubt: at its core, beneath all the layers and hurdles, Boston is a legitimate, bona fide *hockey town*.

Aside from Boston being home to one of the famed Original Six franchises of the National Hockey League, New England has claimed sixteen national college hockey champions. In New England college lore, hockey is the one sport that has truly and almost always mattered. The sport has always played to smaller crowds and viewing audiences, garnered less media attention, and generated less revenue, but those who care about it care deeply. Hockey is a way of life far more than a hobby or casual interest.

"Since the thirties and forties, it's been a huge sport in our area," said Jack Parker, a Somerville, Massachusetts, native who grew up in Boston as a hockey player, went to school in Boston as hockey player, and became one of the most accomplished men in the sport's history as a hockey coach at Boston University.

For a long time, it was very colloquial. It was New England—mostly Eastern Massachusetts—and Minnesota with a little bit of Michigan stuck in there. For years, that's the way it was. And the only reason we had the sport was because of the Bruins.

We've had professional hockey here for a long, long time and people went to the games and were enamored with the games. And then they thought, *It might be fun to play.* We had some lakes that were frozen and people were playing. All of a sudden, they were putting together high school hockey teams. From then on, it's been in the fabric of our social, economic and educational philosophy, I think, because kids were going to play high school hockey. They didn't have high school hockey teams in New Jersey. They didn't have high school hockey teams in Ohio, but we had high school hockey teams here. And then, because they're playing high school hockey, they thought maybe we could play college hockey. . . . All those schools always had hockey for a long time because, I believe, we were exposed to the Boston Bruins in the old six-team NHL that was so exciting and so different than any other sport we were watching.

Even in Boston, there is a line of demarcation when it comes to the Bruins. Born in 1924, they are the oldest of the four American teams included in the Original Six. To borrow a collegiate term, hockey in the United States was still generally a club sport through 1966, when the league comprised just the Original Six. In 1967, that total doubled. And the growth of the league coincided with the arrival of a young man who remains arguably the greatest player in the history of the sport, an exquisitely talented skater from Parry Sound, Ontario, who would revolutionize the sport. His name, of course, was Robert Gordon Orr, the kind of historic talent who warranted one-name status.

Bobby.

Wearing his seemingly emblazoned No. 4, Orr took both Boston and the hockey world by storm and, according to longtime Bruins executive Harry Sinden, was "a star from the moment they played the national anthem in the first game of the season." Signed by the Bruins when he was just thirteen—he was, at a much earlier time, the LeBron James of hockey—Orr had speed, skill, size (six feet, two hundred pounds), and toughness. There had never really been anyone like him. Beginning in Orr's second season, over a span of eight years, the Bruins won two Stanley Cup championships and appeared in the finals three times. They began a stretch of twenty-nine consecutive postseason appearances, one of the most astonishing runs of consistency in the history of all professional sports. Orr was the indisputable axis of a team that became known as the "Big Bad Bruins," the proverbial straw that stirred the drink, a breathtaking performer on the ice who was endearing and humble off it, the embodiment of everything hockey was about. Commitment, teamwork, talent, and, as important as anything else, humility.

On May 10, 1970—Mother's Day, as it was—Orr scored arguably the most famous goal in NHL history, an overtime winner against the St. Louis Blues that completed a four-game-series sweep and handed the Bruins their first championship in twenty-nine years. Just forty seconds into overtime, Orr perfectly executed a give-and-go with teammate Derek Sanderson, who fed Orr for the overtime goal that triggered a Bruins celebration. As the puck zipped into the net and Orr raised his hands, Blues defenseman Noel Picard helped launch Orr into the air by using his stick to lift Orr's skate, sending Orr flying—arms extended above his and body parallel to the ground—as if he were Superman. And in the eyes of New Englanders, of course, that is exactly who Bobby Orr was. Superman on the ice, as unassuming as Clark Kent off it.

The photo, forever etched in history and the inspiration for a statue at the Bruins' home arena at TD Garden, is, of course, nothing more than a snapshot taken by Ray Lussier, the Boston-area photographer who captured the moment. But it remains an enduring symbol of the Bruins' ascension to greatness during the Orr years—and it serves, too, as documentation of the moment when hockey in New England catapulted into another stratosphere.

During the late 1960s and throughout the 1970s, the Metropolitan District Commission in Boston (among others) benefited from the inevitable: a demand for ice. Suddenly, everybody wanted to play hockey. Plastics companies in the Boston area got waves of orders for plexiglass—white for the boards, red for the dashers, yellow for the kickplates—and new facilities went up all over New England as if they were clam shacks and lobster huts along the North and South Shores. Long before Gatorade marketed a campaign around Michael Jordan, New England boys and girls wanted to be like Bobby, the affable and endearing Bruins demigod who could skate and smile like Dorothy Hamill—and score like Rocket Richard.

Said Parker: "When I was a kid, there really were only three rinks in Boston that you could use. You couldn't use the Boston Garden, but there was the Boston Arena, there was the Boston Skating Club and there was the sports center in Lynn, otherwise known as Lynn Arena. Those three places were the only places there was ice. You had to get ice time at two o'clock in the morning sometimes. . . . When Orr came around in the late '60s, I was still in college but immediately I started to get into coaching. All of a sudden, there were rinks everywhere and there was plenty of ice available to everybody, all around, and everybody was so enthusiastic about the sport because the Bruins are unbelievable. . . . We always produced really good players, but the [volume increase] in the quality players we were producing that could compete against anybody in the world at 18 years old was because of all those kids getting in love with the sport of ice hockey—because of the Boston Bruins and Robert Gordon Orr."

Following the 1974–75 season, Orr's career rapidly deteriorated. Plagued by knee injuries throughout his career, his health worsened. The Bruins did the seemingly unthinkable following the 1975–76 season—Orr played just ten games that year—allowing him to leave via free agency to sign with the Chicago Blackhawks, for whom Orr played just twenty-six games over three seasons. Orr retired at the age of just thirty, a premature end that might have been deemed tragic were it not for simple fact that his mark on the sport was indelible—though even calling it a *mark* seems grossly unfair and does nothing but trivialize it.

During his ten years with the Bruins, Bobby Orr was a force, off the ice even more than on, who changed the game of hockey forever, changed Boston forever, changed the lives of countless children and parents who awoke before dawn, loaded the car, and drove miles in search of not a dream—though many certainly were—but rather a simple, common substance: ice.

And they didn't just want to play hockey. They *needed* to.

* * *

Post–Bobby Orr, the Bruins seemed to get *this close* to a championship, only to suffer defeat in the kind of tragic fashion that felt like it defined the city's sports teams. The Bruins, even without Orr, made consecutive trips to the Stanley Cup finals in both 1977 and 1978, only to lose to the hated Montreal Canadiens, the second such defeat coming when Boston opened the door for a Canadiens comeback by being called for a penalty after the embarrassing mistake of having too many men on the ice.

But from the fall of 1967 through the spring of 1996, the Bruins were Boston's mainstay, its bread and butter, the one franchise that routinely operated at an above-average level, albeit without a championship. As if passing the baton in a relay race, the Bruins essentially went from Orr to Raymond Bourque, among the greatest all-around defenseman of all time. During a twenty-one-year career with the Bruins that led him to the Hall of Fame, Bourque played in seventeen All-Star Games and became the franchise's all-time leader in games, points, and assists. He won five Norris Trophies as the best defenseman in the NHL and played in nineteen postseasons. His only failing was that he never led the Bruins to a Stanley Cup championship, twice reaching the finals only to lose to the dynastic Edmonton Oilers.

Had the story been merely a case of bad timing, that would have been one thing. But there was so much more to the story.

As brilliant as the Bruins were during the Bourque years, their inability to win a championship was the prevailing theme, a failure that landed squarely at the feet of team owner Jeremy Jacobs, at least in the eyes of Boston hockey fans and, for that matter, many Bruins players, coaches, and employees. The owner of the franchise beginning in 1975, Jacobs was a Buffalo-based entrepreneur who built an empire as a concessionaire through his company, Delaware North. And to Bruins fans he was, in many ways, a precursor to Red Sox principal owner John Henry, perceived as a carpetbagger who had no emotional stake in the team and who treated hockey as a business more than a passion. Routinely during the Bruins' twenty-nine-year playoff run, fans criticized the team for failing to go all in, adhering to strict budgets and economic principles, all with the goal of enhancing the bottom line. The Stanley Cup certainly seemed secondary, especially when the Bruins repeatedly reached a stage where they were often one player short.

Yet, the Bruins always competed, thanks largely to some shrewd maneuvering by general manager Harry Sinden and a star-studded nucleus that also included, along with Bourque, right-winger Cam Neely, a six-foot-one, 220-behemoth who played even bigger (and angrier). Neely, the selection of his hometown Vancouver Canucks with the ninth overall selection in the 1983 draft, played for four coaches during his three years with the Canucks, during which his stock dropped and his anger intensified.

Ever the opportunist, Sinden acquired Neely and a first-round pick (which became defenseman Glen Wesley) for skilled center Barry Pederson, one of the great trades in Boston sports history. Given Neely's playing style and frustration in Vancouver, the Bruins and Boston provided him a new home that was, in a word, perfect.

"It really ended up being just that," Neely said in early 2021. "At the time, the size of the building and the [smaller] ice surface were perfect for me because I liked contact. I enjoyed hitting people. It was a little easier to do that in the Garden than other buildings. . . . At the time, the coach [in Vancouver] was not enamored with me. I think I played more my rookie year than my third year. I remember one game I was centering the fourth line and I'm like, 'OK, things are going backwards here.' It's still the best birthday gift I've received."

Indeed, the trade was officially completed on June 6, 1986, Neely's twenty-first birthday.

Nonetheless, the Bruins being the Bruins, things hardly went perfectly. In 1996–97, for the first time in nearly two generations, the Bruins missed the playoffs. Two years later they missed again, prompting the the aging Bourque to seek—and receive—a trade to the Colorado Avalanche in hopes of finally winning a Stanley Cup. It was one of the true low points in modern Boston sports history, a Boston franchise being forced to trade away an iconic player because the team couldn't give him a championship.

For Neely, the end was, in many ways, much sadder, his career cut short by an injury that originated when Pittsburgh Penguins defenseman Ulf Samuelsson, a Swedish brute regarded as dirty and predatory, extended his right leg into Neely's right knee and quadriceps during Game 3 of the 1991 Wales Conference Championship series. Neely had just completed a second consecutive regular season during which he had eclipsed the magical 50-goal plateau, establishing him as a force so physically and statistically lethal that the game essentially created a new term for players like him: "power forward."

Following the hit by Samuelsson, Neely hobbled to the bench. The next season, he played in just nine games. And while he remained remarkably proficient over the final four years of his career—he scored 123 goals in 162 games, including 50 in 49 games during the 1993–94 season—he played his last game in 1996, ten years after the Bruins acquired him and, not coincidentally, the final season of the Bruins' twenty-nine-year playoff run. Like Bobby Orr, Cam Neely was thirty when he retired.

* * *

Following the departures of Cam Neely and Raymond Bourque, Boston hockey entered what can only be described as its Dark Ages. Beginning with the 1999–2000 season, in which Bourque was traded, the Bruins went an astonishing seven consecutive seasons without winning a playoff series—eight if one were to include the work stoppage that eliminated the 2004–2005 season. Overall, the stretch concluded an eleven-year period during which the Bruins won only one playoff series—and missed the playoffs entirely a disturbing five times—an on-ice ineptitude that was matched only in off-ice futility.

During those same years, the Bruins earned and used the No. 1 overall selection in the 1997 NHL draft on center Joe Thornton, a six-foot-four, 220-pound Range Rover who was to be the foundation of their renaissance. Eight years later, after the work stoppage and though Thornton had qualified for two All-Star Games while posting his first 100-point season, the Bruins traded him to the San Jose Sharks for a collection of parts: center Wayne Primeau, defenseman Brad Stuart, and winger Marco Sturm. It was a horrendous trade that only got worse when Thornton won the Hart Trophy as the league's MVP during his first *partial* season with the Sharks. And though Thornton never won a title during a long career in San Jose, the deal, like the Bourque move, defined a sorry time in Bruins history, the team trading away its best player—and to *San Jose* of all places—because the Boston organization was otherwise in a desperate, decrepit state. As the world was entering its next millennium, it was as if the Bruins had gone back a thousand years.

"I would have to say, whenever you're struggling like we've been, you throw different scenarios out. It wasn't really like our focus was to trade Joe Thornton," Bruins general manager Mike O'Connell admitted at the time. "Our focus was to try to see if we could better the hockey club. Then this scenario came up." Added the Bruins chief hockey executive, explaining the deterioration of the organization under his watch: "Maybe our strategy was flawed. . . . I bear all the responsibility."

Indeed, while the Bruins' problems were largely attributable to poor management and a gross misjudgment centered around the work stoppage—Bruins owner Jacobs was among the chief hard-liners who guided the league into a salary-cap era—the Thornton deal essentially triggered an organizational rebuild from the ground up. The Bruins signed marquee free agents Zdeno Chara and Marc Savard prior to the 2006–2007 season and, after a horrendous year under newly hired coach Dave Lewis, brought in the respected, more disciplined Claude Julien to oversee a roster and player development operation that had produced Patrice Bergeron, David Krejci, Milan Lucic, Phil Kessel, and Brad Marchand, among others. By the end of the 2007–2008 season, the Bruins had returned to the playoffs, even though they were deemed cannon fodder against a rival, hated Montreal Canadiens team that had designs on the Stanley Cup.

But then a funny thing happened. The Bruins gave the Canadiens all they could handle, nearly overcoming a 3-1 series deficit before succumbing to the Canadiens in a decisive seventh game.

As it was, Game 6 of the series between Boston and Montreal became a pivotal moment in modern Bruins history, an axis on which the fortunes of the franchise changed. After a surprising 5–1 win in Montreal in Game 5, the Bruins returned home. Relentlessly chasing the heavily favored Canadiens throughout the night, the Bruins trailed by scores of 1–0, 2–1, and 3–2 before rallying for a blood-pumping 5–4 victory that sent Boston fans into a state of delirium. The Bruins scored four times in the third period, three times in the final eight minutes. Two of their five goals were scored by Kessel, a young, supremely talented but enigmatic right-winger whom the Bruins had selected with the No. 5 overall pick in the 2006 draft—and whom head coach Julien had benched for Games 2, 3, and 4 of the series for being lazy and careless. Kessel returned to score a combined three goals in Games 5 and 6, fueling the two-game onslaught during which the Bruins scored a stunning ten times.

And while Game 7 was a one-sided affair that the Canadiens won by a 5–0 score in Montreal, the series—or specifically Game 6—is remembered as the genesis of the next must-see era in Bruins history, one built around defenseman Chara and centers Bergeron and Krejci, eventually winger Marchand, and a cast of others. The Bruins were back. And, in Boston, so was hockey.

"It was awesome," rugged winger Lucic said in the aftermath of Game 6. "This is what I've heard about, this is what everybody talks about—about the Garden being a loud place, about being a hard place to play. I give our fans total credit. They were like a seventh man out there the way they were cheering."

Just the same, passion manifests itself in various forms, which is to say that all Bruins experiences—even during a renaissance—were not necessarily welcomed with an embrace. A year after pushing the Canadiens to the brink, the Bruins finished first in their division and amassed a whopping 116 points, a total that earned them the Presidents' Trophy as the NHL team with the best regular-season record. The Bruins then wiped out the Canadiens in four games before losing to the Carolina Hurricanes in the second round of the playoffs, a defeat that was simultaneously disappointing (in the short term) and promising (in the long), the season's entire performance indicative of what was to come.

The Bruins were back. They were young, talented, and developing. Their future was filled with promise. And while there was the requisite drama that centered around aloof winger Kessel—general manager Peter Chiarelli traded him to the Toronto Maple Leafs after the Bruins were unable to sign the player to a new contract—the return (unlike the Thornton deal) seemed considerable. In exchange for Kessel, the Bruins received two first-round picks and a second-rounder from Toronto, assets that would soar in value when the Leafs proved to be one of the worst teams in the league over the next two seasons.

And then there was this: While the 2009–2010 season produced a relatively disappointing 91-point total during which the Bruins, in the absence of Kessel, lacked offensive firepower, they were seemingly more prepared for the playoffs. In the NHL, the regular season is nothing more than a qualifying heat; the real hockey happens in the playoffs. The NHL postseason, more than any other sport, was a brutally demanding war of attrition that required physical and mental toughness, immeasurable sacrifice, and, as much as anything else, luck. Wasting ammunition during the regular season, as such, could be downright foolish.

As if on cue, the 2009–2010 Bruins dispatched the Buffalo Sabres in six games in the first round of the playoffs. They subsequently bolted to a 3-0 series lead against the Philadelphia Flyers in the second round and seemed destined for a trip to the conference finals against either the Canadiens or the Pittsburgh Penguins. The Stanley Cup, incredibly, was in sight.

"We realize they're going to be pretty desperate," Bergeron said of the Flyers following the victory. "We have to make sure we're ready. You don't win a series with three games."

As it turned out, nobody knew how right he would be. During Game 3, the Bruins had lost center Krejci and defenseman Adam McQuaid to first-period injuries, the former when Flyers center Mike Richards dealt him a devastating mid-ice check that dislocated Krejci's wrist and ended his season. The loss of McQuaid further compounded the loss of Dennis Seidenberg, a trade-deadline acquisition who had been injured late in the regular season when the skate of an opposing player (Toronto's Nikolai Kulemin) cut into Seidenberg's forearm and sliced a tendon. The mounting injuries on defense were an obvious concern, particularly against a Flyers team that had, if nothing else, excellent frontline firepower.

Facing elimination on their home ice, the Flyers narrowly escaped in Game 4, claiming a 5–4 victory in overtime when Simon Gagne redirected a pass from Jeff Carter past the left skate of goaltender Tuukka Rask, who had taken over from Tim Thomas. Two nights later the Flyers went to Boston and claimed a 4–0 shutout victory. Minus Krejci, the Bruins were held scoreless again for the large majority of Game 6, in Philadelphia, where only a goal by Bruins winger Milan Lucic with a minute remaining in the game prevented another shutout loss. The final score was 2–1 this time, leveling the series at three games apiece and bringing the Bruins to the cusp of one of the more ignominious feats in all of professional sports.

With another loss, they would join a handful of teams in professional sports history to blow a 3-0 series lead in a best-of-seven affair, the kind of collapse that left an indelible mark on any franchise.

And in the case of the 2009–2010 Bruins, the worst-case scenario was somehow even worse. Playing before a home crowd of nearly 18,000, the Bruins surged from the very start of Game 7, capitalizing on a pair of Philadelphia penalties to strike quickly. Their first goal, from Michael Ryder, came slightly more than five minutes into play. A second, from Lucic, came less than four minutes later. When Lucic scored again just 14:10 into the game, the Bruins had a 3-0 lead, an eerie parallel to their earlier 3-0 series advantage that at another time in the long history of Boston sports might have sent the locals scrambling for elixirs and antidotes.

The crowd roared. But if the building shook, the Flyers did not. Undeterred, they scored late in the first period to make the score 3–1. They then potted a pair of goals in the second to tie it up. And then, with slightly more than seven minutes to play, and after the Bruins committed the egregious sin of having too many men on the ice—words that would once again echo forever in Boston's history—Boston allowed a power-play goal to the man who beat them in Game 4, the omnipresent Gagne, whose return to the series from injury gave the Flyers everything the Bruins lost with the injury to Krejci. After collecting a loose puck just to the right of goaltender Rask, Gagne snapped a puck into the net for his fourth goal—and fifth point—in four games since returning to the lineup, propelling the Flyers to a 4–3 lead and, ultimately, a 4–3 series victory that left Boston stunned and ashamed.

"The bottom line is that we had a 3-0 lead in the series and we had a 3-0 lead tonight—and we blew both," said a blunt Julien, the coach. "There's no excuses. We have to take the responsibility that goes with it. Everyone."

Said veteran Mark Recchi: "You have to have that killer instinct, and it didn't happen."

Amid the ensuing rubble, the Bruins joined, at the time, three other teams in sports history to have collapsed following a 3-0 series lead, two of them hockey clubs: the 1942 Toronto Maple Leafs and the 1975 New York Islanders.

In all of sports history, the only other team to blow such an advantage was, of course, the 2004 New York Yankees. Bostonians were in no mood to rationalize at the time—live by the sword, die by the sword—though there were other comparisons to be drawn to the Red Sox had anyone been interested.

A year prior to the comeback against the Yankees, the Red Sox had suffered a devastating defeat in a similar Game 7 at New York, furthering a near century of heartache, but in the aftermath of yet another organizational trauma, they returned in 2004 with even greater resolve. They fortified the roster. And then, after falling behind the Yankees by a 3–0 series score, as if they were the hardball incarnation of Job, they rose, dusted themselves off, and hit back. Nobody in Boston could have possibly imagined it at the time, but the Bruins were about to do essentially the same thing.

* * *

In retrospect, at least some of what took place in the 2009–2010 season was consistent with the development of a new and young roster. They needed maturity. The Bruins of 2010–2011, by consequence, were a team seemingly prepared to take the next step in its development, winning seven of the season's first nine games. By the time they embarked in February on a six-game road trip that coincided with the annual NHL trading deadline, they were the possessors of a 31-19-7 record, tied for first place in the Northeast Division and on pace for 99 points. Club officials very much deemed them contenders to win the team's first Stanley Cup since 1972, something they validated with a series of moves to bolster the lineup.

In need of help on defense as well as depth in their group of forwards, Bruins general manager Peter Chiarelli made a series of trades to acquire defenseman Tomas Kaberle, defensive-minded center Chris Kelly, and forward Rich Peverley, an aggressive series of maneuvers that prompted the following headline in the *Boston Herald* on February 19, 2011: ALL PARTS NOW IN PLACE—PLAYOFF RUN A MUST.

"It's a strong message to our fans that we want to win," said Chiarelli, an Ontario native who played his collegiate career at Harvard. "[Kaberle] was an important piece for us to get. We just felt the time was right."

Said Cam Neely ten years after having been named team president just before the start of the 2010–2011 championship season: "I think you recognize that your team could have a chance. There are so many factors (in winning a championship), but you want to put yourself in a position where you can compete with the best teams. You hope you can stay healthy and you certainly need some breaks along the way. Your best players need to be your best—all those things need to happen for you to win. And until those things happens in the playoffs, you find yourself saying, 'We have a chance to really do something here if we get all those (other) things. We all thought we had a pretty deep team both in the forward group and on the back end."

Indeed, for all of the building the Bruins had done since the trading of Thornton, the team had amassed a wealth of young assets, including talented forward Blake Wheeler, who was traded with defenseman Mark Stuart to the Atlanta Thrashers for Peverley. For Kelly, the Bruins sacrificed a second-round draft pick. For Kaberle, the price was a first-rounder, second-rounder, and former first-round selection Joe Colborne, a player whose path to Boston was blocked by Krejci, Bergeron, and Tyler Seguin.

That same night, having defeated the New York Islanders in the trip opener on February 17, the Bruins beat Ottawa by a 4–2 score. Four nights later, they defeated Calgary 3–1. The team subsequently won at Vancouver and Edmonton on consecutive nights—February 26 and 27—before returning to Ottawa for a 1–0 victory that made every bit the same statement as Chiarelli's acquisitions at the trade deadline. When all was said and done, the Bruins had dusted the field, winning all six games by a combined score of 20–9, the most impressive a 3–1 victory against a Vancouver team that would finish with the best record in the NHL. And when historians leafed through Bruins records to find the last time the Bruins were perfect on a trip of the like, they stumbled upon a rather heartening fact: It had been in 1972, the last time the Bruins had won the Stanley Cup.

"We know what situation we are in," said team captain Chara. "Even though we are on top of the standings, we still want to climb and get ourselves in the best possible position to finish the season, and every game is important for us. We're really looking at it as a challenge and we just want to focus on our game and how we play."

The Bruins, it seemed, had learned their lesson.

The regular season didn't mean everything, but it still meant *something*.

Now the possessors of the fourth-best record in the league, the Bruins effectively treaded water for the balance of the regular season, finishing with 103 points, neatly placed between their totals of 116 and 91 from the two previous years. *The happy medium.* Chiarelli's acquisitions at the deadline had similarly dealt the Bruins a combination of speed (Peverley), grit (Kelly), and skill (Kaberle), the three veteran players dispersed across the roster in areas of need. In the locker room, too, the Bruins were a nice combination of experience and youth, poise and energy, toughness and skill, the kind of elements that would afford them the opportunity to play a game of virtually any style, against any opponent, at any time.

And then there was this, noted often by team president Neely, who filtered out the variables: during the 2010–11 season, the Bruins had proven to be the best five-on-five team in the NHL. Though that was a simple statistic, the detail also spoke volumes. Hockey, after all, was a game designed to be played by five skaters against five others, each team afforded the sixth man of a goalie. That was the game at its purest form. For the large majority of any game, that was the way the game would be played. If the Bruins could win those minutes, if they could control those long occasions when the manpower on both was equal, they believed they could deliver something to Boston that no Bruins hockey team had done since the Nixon administration. The Bruins believed they could win the Stanley Cup.

Now they actually had to do it.

* * *

The hockey playoffs, by all accounts, are a war of attrition. As much as they are about talent and skill, they are also about toughness, durability, sheer will. The games can be immeasurably intense, physical, even destructive. They can feel like Roller Derby on ice, teams taking any opportunity to quite literally knock an opponent out of play. In a seven-game series, the goal is not to injure so much as it is to beat opponents into submission, wear them down, break their spirit. And, of course, you have to score more goals than the other guys.

For the Bruins, the challenge also included the weight of history, specifically in the form of their first-round opponents, the Montreal Canadiens, who had treated the Bruins like footrests for the large majority of their existence. Montreal that season relied heavily on a power play unit and penalty-killing operation that were among the best in the league, so the goal for the Bruins was to keep as many skaters on the ice as possible—for either team.

But there was the matter of the games to be played north of the border, in Canada, where hockey folks often complained about the officiating in Montreal to the point of amusement. As the saying went, there are three certainties in life: *death, taxes, and the first penalty in Montreal.*

The good news for the Bruins was that Boston had earned the home ice advantage by virtue of their regular season performance, meaning that the series would begin in Boston—where the team promptly lost both Games 1 and 2. The Bruins fired a combined sixty-six shots at Canadiens goaltender Carey Price and scored on just one of them, a strike by Patrice Bergeron in the second period of Game 2 that trimmed the Montreal advantage to 2–1. The Bruins never led in either game and played the second without team captain Chara, who missed the game due to illness and had to be treated at Mass General for dehydration. From the start, the Bruins prospects looked so dire—historically, teams that lost the first two games of a playoff series at home were eliminated more than 85 percent of the time—that the *Boston Herald*, for one, suggested the Bruins needed a "miracle."

"We'll see at the end of the series," said Recchi. "We've got a long way to go."

As it turned out, no one could have imagined how right he was.

Seeking to fortify his backline after the Bruins allowed two goals to the Canadiens within the first two minutes and twenty seconds of Game 2, Bruins coach Claude Julien responded by pairing stalwart defenders Chara and Dennis Seidenberg—the defenseman lost to injury a year earlier—for the start of Game 3 in Montreal. The move proved to be series altering. The Bruins won both games in Montreal, the latter on an overtime goal by Michael Ryder to claim a 5–4 victory that sent the series back to Boston all even. While Bruins president Neely beamed before the game—"I think a lot of people probably wrote us off, figured we were out of the series," he mused—the Bruins benefited from a second, significant development that would similarly alter the series and, for that matter, the entire postseason. Goaltender Tim Thomas had awoken.

Originally a ninth-round selection in an NHL draft that longer has nine rounds, Thomas had built a career defying logic and explanation. In an age when goaltenders were become bigger and more fundamentally sound—rather boring, frankly—Thomas was undersized (five-foot-eleven) and unheralded. Unlike Montreal counterpart and twenty-three-year-old phenom Price, a six-foot-three Canadian taken with the No. 5 overall selection in a first round that will always have a first round, Thomas was born in Michigan and attended the University of Vermont. He did not play in an NHL game until he was twenty-eight. He did not become a starter until he was thirty-three. By the spring of 2011 he was thirty-seven years old, an unorthodox, sprawling goaltender who often kept the puck out of the net through sheer relentlessness.

"Tim just battles," Neely once observed.

But then, who better for the grind of the NHL postseason?

In Game 6 at Montreal, despite not allowing an even-strength goal, Thomas was not enough. The Canadiens had seven power play chances and scored twice, securing a 2–1 victory and sending the series back to Boston for a decisive seventh game. Game 7 was 2–2 entering the third period—Montreal's scores, of course, had both come on special teams, including one shorthanded goal—when the recently acquired Kelly snagged a rebound and slipped a backhander under the left arm of a lunging Price, giving the Bruins a 3–2 lead with precisely 10:16 left. The Bruins held the same advantage until there were fewer than three minutes remaining in the game, when the typically impeccable Bergeron—one of the Bruins' most reliable players—was called for a high-sticking penalty that placed the Canadiens on the power play.

Precisely forty seconds later, with the defenders in front of Thomas over-shifted on the ice to the goalie's left, Canadiens center Tomas Plekanec placed a perfect pass for defenseman P. K. Subban on the opposite side of the zone, from where Subban launched a rocket so vicious that it might have decapitated Thomas. Instead, it tied the game at 3, which then went to overtime.

Had things transpired differently from there, there is no telling what might have happened to the Bruins, to their coach, Julien, or to the legacies of countless players, including Bergeron, whose mistake might have lived in infamy. As it was, following a face-off in the Montreal zone to the right of Price with 14:37 left in the first overtime period, the teams battled for the puck along the boards, behind Price, to the opposite corner. Bruins defenseman Adam McQuaid pinched from his station at the right point and kept the puck in the zone, now to Price's left. Subban made a backhanded flick at the puck but could not clear past McQuaid, the puck popping straight into the air and then into the hand of Bruins winger Milan Lucic, who dropped it onto his stick and eyed teammate Nathan Horton, who was drifting toward the net in an area known as the high slot, between the face-off circles, slightly to the right of where Subban had been positioned when he scored late in the third period.

Horton collected the puck, settled it, and then, drifting to his left, blasted a slapshot that beat Price to the goaltender's left, giving the Bruins a 4–3 victory and ending both the game and the series.

The die was cast. And the Bruins were on their way.

"It was pretty special," Horton later said of his game winner. "It doesn't get any better."

He was wrong, of course. For the Bruins, the good times were just beginning.

* * *

After blowing a 3-0 series lead and losing to the Philadelphia Flyers in the second round of the 2009–2010 season, the Bruins could rationalize the defeat only in so many ways. Minus the injured Krejci and Seidenberg, the Bruins were probably in no shape to win the Stanley Cup anyway. Had the Bruins somehow defeated the Canadiens in the Eastern Conference championship series, as the Flyers did, they would likely have succumbed to the eventual Stanley Cup champion Chicago Blackhawks, who felled the Flyers in six games to win the first of what would become three Cup titles during a six-year span over which they proved to be the most dominant team in the NHL. Just the same, rationalizations do not heal all wounds as much as they help to live with them.

One year later, however, the Bruins had the opportunity for something far more meaningful: a rematch. The Flyers similarly had begun the playoffs with a long, seven-game series that ended with a 5-2 win over the Buffalo Sabres, propelling them into the second round for yet another series with a motivated, fortified, and suddenly emboldened Boston team.

"I'm not going to lie—it's a good opportunity for us to hopefully exorcise some demons," defenseman Andrew Ference said in the immediate aftermath of the Game 7 win over Montreal. "I don't put too much stock in history. There are new guys on this team, new guys on that team. This is a fresh start for us. But we learned lessons from last year, no doubt about it."

Such statements are rare from athletes in modern sports, if no other reason than they run the risk of motivating the opposition. Ference was speaking purely in terms of the *opportunity* that awaited the Bruins a year after their implosion, but the Flyers might have taken the comment anyway and twisted it into something altogether different. *You mean they want to play us again? Even after what we did to them last year? Well, I guess we'll just have to show them who's boss once more.* But if there was any chance of that, the notion was dispelled quickly and decisively, this time against a Flyers team that, though explosive offensively, had suspect defense and goaltending while being mediocre, at best, in special teams.

From the start, the series proved no match at all. Less than two minutes after the puck dropped in Game 1, the Bruins claimed a 1-0 lead on a goal by Krejci, who had posted an astonishingly quiet series against the Canadiens. (He had totaled just one assist in the seven games.) And yet, marking his presence against the Flyers from the very start as if carrying a grudge from his injury the previous year, he amassed a pair of goals and a pair of assists in a 7–3 blowout during the which the Bruins never trailed, setting the tone for what would be a thorough dismantling. Philadelphia's only real chance in the series came in Game 2, when the Flyers jumped to a 1–0 lead just twenty-nine seconds into play and doubled the lead less than halfway through the first period—but that blip lasted a relative instant. The Bruins immediately answered with a pair of goals in the next five minutes to lock the game at 2–2, where the score remained for the balance of regulation and into sudden-death overtime.

Fourteen minutes into what amounted to the fourth period, the Flyers' greatest weakness—their play in their defensive zone—proved fatal. After the Flyers failed to clear the puck, Bruins winger Nathan Horton quickly shuttled a pass to Krejci, who drifted down the center of the ice directly in front of Flyers goaltender Brian Boucher, preparing to shoot. As soon as the puck slid into his reach, Krejci blasted a one-timer over Boucher's right shoulder and into the upper back of the net, upon which Bruins winger Milan Lucic, stationed just to Boucher's left, raised his arms to celebrate what was the game-winning goal.

Or was it?

Seemingly stunned by the swiftness of the Flyers blunder and the Bruins ability to capitalize on it, officials on the ice initially ruled that the puck hit the crossbar behind Boucher before popping back onto the ice. Consequently, the teams played on for the next eighteen seconds. The whistle finally blew with 5:42 showing on the game clock, at which point an official review officially validated what television replays confirmed: that Krejci had struck again, making a winner of both the Bruins and goaltender Tim Thomas, who had similarly missed the series against Philadelphia only a year earlier.

The omens were everywhere. The Bruins were a different team from the club that collapsed in 2010—and they were intent on proving it.

"He's really been motivated to play this series, obviously, with what happened to him last year," Julien said of the highly skilled Krejci. "He's a determined player, he's playing hard and he's playing well, and obviously we need that contribution from him and his line."

Suddenly, the Bruins were in the exact opposite position they had been roughly two weeks earlier, possessors of a 2–0 series lead after *winning* the first two games on the opponent's ice.

With the series now shifting to Boston and Thomas continuing to play at a high level, the Bruins won both Games 3 and 4 by identical 5–1 scores, the final affair featuring a pair of empty-net goals that ended Philadelphia's season. All in all, the Bruins trailed for just 13 minutes and 46 seconds of the nearly 254 minutes played in the series. Overall, they outscored the Flyers 20–7. Krejci was the leading score in the series with 9 points and defensive stalwart Seidenberg—after missing the entire postseason a year prior—led the Bruins with a whopping 119 minutes and 27 seconds of ice time—an average of just under 30 minutes per game—while Thomas posted a brilliant save percentage of .953.

The three biggest absences from the 2010 breakdown had arguably been the three most important Bruins of the series, the Bruins delivering a message that was impossible to overlook.

We had some bad luck last year, too. Let's see if you can beat us now.

"There's a learning process along the way," said team president Neely. "We've gained some experience in some of those series in past years and carried them into this year, and it showed. You get down 2–0 in the first series and you win that. We had some similar situations this year that we did last year, but guys learned from it. History's great—great if you can learn from it."

Said the typically understated Julien: "You come from all over the place, but you are representing the city of Boston and the one thing you want to do is do them proud. We know baseball, football and obviously basketball have done very well lately. And now it's time for hockey to step up and do the same thing."

Following the defeats to Montreal in Games 1 and 2 of their playoff-opening series, they had gone 8-1. In even-strength, five-on-five play for the entire postseason, the Bruins had outscored opponents by a whopping 35–15 in their first eleven games. Even in their seven-game grind against Montreal, the Bruins had outscored the Canadiens by a 17–10 gap in five-on-five play, allowing six power plays and a shorthanded score in the seven games. Headed to the Eastern Conference championship, when everyone had been on the ice, the Bruins had been virtually unbeatable.

* * *

In the world of sports radio, particularly in a place like Boston, there is always a negative. And the downside of sweeping the Philadelphia Flyers, if there was one, invariably involved the notion that the Bruins disposed of the Flyers *too* quickly. By defeating the Flyers in four games, the Bruins earned an eight-day layoff before resuming their quest against the Tampa Bay Lightning. Never mind the fact that Tampa had similarly disposed of the Washington Capitals in four games and actually had a *longer* layoff than the Bruins—because Bruins fans, especially, could always find something to worry about as they closed in on a half century without a championship.

The truth, of course, was that the rest would benefit both teams in the long run, particularly the one that emerged from the series to reach the Stanley Cup finals. In the NHL playoffs, any additional recovery time was critical. Bumps and bruises had more time to heal. Heavy legs lightened. Emotional and psychological balance was restored during a potential two-month slog that could sometimes feel like an interminable Arctic expedition.

And so, effectively, the Bruins and the Lightning each set up what amounted to base camp, waiting for the signal to resume the most challenging quest in sports.

For the Bruins, the break was especially important given the absence of center Bergeron, who suffered a concussion in Game 4 against Philadelphia that prompted immediate concerns. As a twenty-two-year-old only three years prior, Bergeron had suffered a severe concussion that wiped out all but ten games of his 2007–2008 season and jeopardized his career. He was not quite the same player the following season but had made strides in each year since. During the 2010–2011 campaign, he had fully returned to form, finishing with 22 goals, 57 points, and a +20 rating while establishing himself as Boston's best two-way center and one of the best defensive forwards in all of hockey.

And then he took another hit to the head.

In retrospect, it was unsurprising when the Bruins looked rather detached in Game 1, foiled by their own blunders and the trapping style of the Lightning, who baited opponents into sloppy errors and then converted them into goals. Tampa scored three times in the span of one minute and twenty-five seconds during the first period and was never threatened. The only good news for the Bruins came in the form of budding nineteen-year-old prospect Tyler Seguin, a speedy and talented youngster whom the Bruins had selected with the No. 2 overall selection in the 2010 draft. Seguin's presence in the lineup was a ripple effect from Bergeron's absence, but his play alone was hardly enough against a Tampa team that effectively gummed up the ice.

After emotional series with the Canadiens and Flyers, the Lightning presented an entirely different challenge, one in which the Bruins had to tussle with themselves as much as the opposition.

"I guess we don't have the history that we do with the others," noted Bruins defenseman Adam McQuaid. "But each team is trying to keep each other from getting to where we want to go. If that's not enough reason to go out and play hard, I don't know what is."

To their credit, the Bruins responded. Seguin provided a jolt of energy and the Bruins opened up a 6–3 lead in Game 2 and eventually closed out a 6–5 win, Seguin totaling two goals and two assists in the outburst. By the time the series shifted to Tampa for Game 3, Bergeron had returned to the lineup and the Bruins played their most disciplined game of the series to that point, claiming a 2–0 victory on goals by Krejci (his seventh of the postseason) and Ference in front of thirty-one saves by Thomas. The Bruins then raced to a 3–0 advantage in the first period of Game 4, culminating in a shorthanded score by Bergeron, to seemingly grab a stranglehold on the series as they moved toward a 3-1 series advantage.

And then, stunningly, the tables turned. With the Tampa season in jeopardy, the Lightning struck three times in the second period—all during five-on-five play. It was an uncharacteristic breakdown for the Bruins. The Lightning took a 4–3 lead early in the third period and then completed the game's scoring with an empty-netter that produced a 5–3 victory, turning a potential 3-1 series deficit into a 2-2 deadlock, sending the series back to Boston.

Bruins winger Brad Marchand said precisely what many Bruins fans felt: "I think we might have taken it for granted and it bit us in the butt."

Goaltender Thomas, however, displayed the utmost confidence when asked if he could possibly guess how the topsy-turvy series might end. "Yeah," he said. "We're going to win." And then he went out and made sure of it.

After Tampa scored just 1:09 into the pivotal fifth game to take a 1–0 lead, Thomas was, in a word, sensational. The Michigan native ultimately stopped thirty-three of thirty-four Tampa shots, none more threatening than a rebound off the stick of Tampa's Steve Downie roughly halfway through the third period. With the Bruins clinging to a 2–1 lead thanks to second-period goals by Horton and Marchand, Tampa was pressing in the Boston zone when defenseman Eric Brewer fired a shot to Thomas's right, away from a crowd in front of the net, that deflected off the backboards and directly toward the left-wing side of the goal mouth. The puck landed squarely on the stick of the right-handed Downie, who flicked the puck toward an open side of the net for what seemed like a certain game-tying goal.

And yet, as Downie's puck drifted toward the goal and just inside the post to Thomas's right, a scrambling Thomas lunged and extended his stick, paddling the puck out of midair and back into play as if he were executing a volley at the net at Wimbledon. In real time, the events happened so quickly that the save was nearly impossible to see, something that held true until a subsequent whistle allowed spectators to witness the play on the TD Garden video board, at which point the crowd erupted as Thomas hunched forward, humbly lowered his head. and stared forward.

"The way I remember it, [the puck] got out to the point and there were a couple of different sets of screens," Thomas recounted. "There was one set of our forward and their guy up top, and there was one set of their guy and our guy closer to me. I saw [Brewer] getting ready to take the shot, but I couldn't see the puck. . . . I picked it up when it was about halfway to me. I saw it was going wide. I was out toward the top of the crease. I didn't have time to get my whole body back. With the way the new boards are nowadays in all the arenas, you've got to be on your toes for those big bounces. The big bounce came out. It was just, you know, a reaction, a desperation. I'll admit, I got a little bit lucky there."

Chris Kelly, one of the players acquired at the trade deadline, offered a far more succinct observation: "That was a game-saver. It was unbelievable."

Indeed, for all the time athletes and teams spend on preparation, there was simply no way for any coach or player to account for a moment like the one that remains perhaps the single, most memorable highlight of the Bruins 2010–11 season. Oft criticized for his goaltending technique—or lack thereof—Thomas's greatest asset at that moment was his sheer resolve, plain and simple. The save against Downie was not the kind of play that any goaltender could necessarily teach or that any coach would ever want to, though Thomas certainly did some things right, most notably by extending his stick. His general approach was to do anything and everything to simply keep the puck out of the net, however possible, fundamentals and techniques be damned. The idea was to keep competing until something or someone prevented it, which is how Thomas had built a career in the first place. If Tim Thomas, in particular, was going to lose, well, you had to beat him.

After finishing off Game 5 with an empty-net goal by Peverley to secure the 3–1 victory and 3–2 series advantage, the Bruins tumbled to a 5–4 defeat in Game 6 at Tampa, the Lightning scoring three times on the power play to force yet another decisive seventh game on the TD Garden ice. In a game that featured not a single penalty—the entire game was played five on five—the Bruins outshot the Lightning 38–24, including 29–17 through the first two periods. And yet, the game remained scoreless thanks in large part to the play of Tampa goaltender Dwayne Roloson.

And then, with less than eight minutes remaining in a 0–0, penalty-free affair in Game 7 of an Eastern Conference semifinal series that had rhythmically rocked back and forth, the Bruins executed the kind of play that made goal scoring under the most pressurized circumstances look astonishingly easy. Skating out of his zone against the Tampa trap, defenseman Ference slid a tidy pass onto the stick of Krejci, Horton flanked just to Krejci's left as the teammates crossed the Tampa blue line. As Krejci skated out wide toward the left-wing boards, the players crossed, the right-handed Horton darting toward the front of the net. Krejci shifted the puck to his forehand and squared his body to the middle of the ice, placing a pass that landed squarely on the stick of his driving teammate, who simply redirected the puck past Roloson for a 1–0 Bruins advantage that triggered a roar from the Garden crowd bordering on a sonic boom.

There was no other scoring. The Lightning pulled Roloson in hopes of pressing late, but Chara and Seidenberg led a cast of Bruins who policed the Garden ice and snuffed out any real threat. As was the case in the Montreal series, Horton had scored the decisive goal. He and Krejci (again) each had amassed seven points to lead the Bruins in scoring during the series. The Bruins once again had held an edge in five-on-five scoring—this time by a narrow, 18–16 margin—and persevered despite playing an inconsistent series against an opponent that generated no real ill will.

Regardless, the Bruins now had a chance. Winners of the Prince of Wales Trophy as Eastern Conference champions, they had advanced to the Stanley Cup finals for the first time since 1990, when they had been dispatched by the juggernaut Edmonton Oilers in five games. Their opponent would be the NHL's indisputable best team in 2010-11—the Vancouver Canucks—and they would attempt to become the fourth Boston team to win a championship in the new millennium, an astonishing and comprehensive run of success for the city that was already unlike perhaps any other in Boston's history.

"It's something that this team, this organization, this city has been waiting for—for a long time," said Chara. "So obviously, we are very excited. We can enjoy the moment but we are going to go back to work."

In Boston, for a long time, the idea of the Bruins working into summer was preposterous. The final victory over the Lightning had come on May 28, a Saturday night. The region was celebrating Memorial Day weekend, the unofficial start of summer, with weekends on Cape Cod or trips to Maine, Vermont, even Lake Winnipesaukee. By the end of winter, New Englanders typically flocked to the water, to the south and the north, eager to embrace the benefits of coastal proximity. There would be plenty of time to return to the rinks in the fall, to lace up the skates again, to turn to hockey to help endure the typically cold, dark winters.

But this? This was different. A Stanley Cup was at stake.

And so, dressed in shorts and flip-flops, fans were willing to forgo beach traffic on the Sagamore and Bourne Bridges for the foot traffic funneling into TD Garden—all because, this year, hockey season was running a little longer than usual.

* * *

The 2010–11 Vancouver Canucks were hardly the Edmonton Oilers team that dominated the NHL in the mid- to late 1980s while winning five Stanley Cups over the span of seven seasons, twice defeating the Bruins, in both 1988 and 1990. The Canucks had no history of winning whatsoever, remaining to this day one of the handful of franchises never to hoist the cherished Stanley Cup. But during the 2010–11 season they were nothing short of a juggernaut, a team that excelled in every area of play. The Canucks finished first in the league in an array of key indicators: overall wins (54), home wins (27), road wins (27), most goals for (262), fewest goals against (185), goal differential (+77), and power play percentage. The Canucks also ranked third in penalty killing percentage. And after nearly blowing a 3–0 first-round series lead to unseat the reigning world champion Blackhawks, the Canucks had dispatched the Nashville Predators and San Jose Sharks in just eleven games total, by series counts of 4–2 and 4–1. The Canucks never found themselves behind in any of their three series.

The Bruins had two areas in which they could match the Canucks: five-on-five play, where Vancouver had ranked second to Boston during the regular season; and goaltending, where Thomas had the league in both goals against average (2.00) and save percentage (a sterling .938), placing him just ahead of Vancouver goaltender Roberto Luongo, who ranked second and third, respectively, in those two categories.

The point? The Bruins' margin for error was as thin as the skate blades on which their season rested.

"It's fair to say we have a team that's more station-to-station in Boston vs. a team in Vancouver that likes to go from one zone to the next very quickly.

That's the strength of each team," respected NBC analyst Eddie Olczyk told the *Boston Herald*. "When you get to this stage you've got to play to your strengths. I mean, at the end of the day, the Bruins beat Tampa because they out-defended them. Can they outscore Vancouver? Sure, because they've proven they can score. But that's not their strength. Over a long series, it would not be beneficial if they tried to play that way."

A sixteen-year NHL veteran who had scored 342 career goals and won a Stanley Cup as a member of the historic 1993–94 New York Rangers, Olczyk had long since polished his skills as a broadcaster, leaving the coarser message between the lines. The Canucks were seen as fast and skilled, as flashy and dynamic as a European sports car. The Bruins were a pickup truck.

The stereotypes of the clubs existed for a reason, but they were hardly absolute. And the early games proved it.

Trading hit for hit with the Bruins throughout Game 1, the Canucks pulled out a dramatic 1–0 victory when winger Raffi Torres scored with just nineteen seconds remaining in regulation. Multitalented Canucks center Ryan Kesler began the play by poking the puck away from Bruins defenseman Johnny Boychuk just as Boychuk was hoping to leave the Bruins zone, then collecting the puck along the boards just to the right of goalie Thomas. Kesler then fed teammate Jannik Hansen as he drifted through the high slot, after which Hansen placed a pass perfectly on the stick of a surging Torres, who merely needed to deflect the puck past Thomas. The goal, at the finish, was roughly the mirror image of the goal Horton had scored in the Bruins' Game 7 win against Tampa Bay only a few days earlier.

Three days later, on June 4, the Bruins suffered a similarly crushing defeat. The Canucks even outhit the Bruins this time, 40–31, and again scored the first goal of the game, a strike by chippy winger Alexandre Burrows. The Bruins took their first lead of the series on strikes by wingers Milan Lucic and Recchi in the middle of the second before Vancouver's Daniel Sedin evened the score in the middle of third, leaving the teams knotted at 2 headed into overtime.

Once there, just eleven seconds in, the Canucks snapped at the Bruins with the speed of a viper. Following the face-off, the puck rested with defenseman Ference, who tried to bank it off the boards at center ice and into the Vancouver zone. In an instant, Canucks defenseman Alex Edler corralled the pass and pushed it to Sedin, who then funneled past Ference and onto the stick of Burrows. The winger then skated wide to his left, protecting the puck against the reach of the six-foot-nine Chara, drawing goaltender Thomas to the right side of his crease. As the goaltender anticipated a shot and overcommitted, the puck slid behind the Bruins goal, where Burrows collected it and quickly tucked it into the opposite corner in wraparound fashion to give the Canucks a 2-0 series advantage.

The sight of a celebration by Burrows was especially frustrating, if only for the fact that he had been a central participant during one of the more controversial moments of Game 1, when he was involved in a small scrum with Bergeron following a whistle. With an official stationed between them, Burrows and Bergeron took turns jamming a glove in each other's face before Burrows then chomped down on one of Bergeron's fingers, an act both dirty and disrespectful. For all the stereotypical portrayals of the teams entering the series—the flashy Canucks and the fearsome Bruins—Vancouver was the team that played the first two games with, well, bite.

"I think people look at our team and see the skill we have . . . and automatically think this is a high-end, run-and-gun kind of team," Canucks defenseman Keith Ballard had said before Game 1. "In reality, we were the best defensive team in the league this year. Inside the room, we know what we pride our game on: our defense."

And the Canucks also, it seemed, were intent on proving that they would not be intimidated by a Bruins team perceived to be tougher and more physical. Unsurprisingly, the Canucks went too far.

Hoping to give his team a jolt prior to Game 3, Bruins coach Claude Julien called upon tough guy and inspirational leader Shawn Thornton, whom he inserted back into the Boston lineup into the place of Seguin, whose speed had not been as effective against the quicker Canucks. The move was simple but spoke volumes: *Instead of playing your game, we're going to play ours.* Agitated by the antics of Burrows—to whom the NHL had dealt no disciplinary action or suspension after the biting incident—the Bruins took matters into their own hands. In the span of roughly a minute early in the first period, the Bruins dealt Burrows two hard body checks—the first from Recchi knocked Burrows's stick loose, the second from Thornton knocked Burrows to the ice—to inspire the home crowd. Thornton followed his check by talking trash to the Canucks bench, intimidation tactics that he had started during the pregame, making it clear to the Canucks that they were no longer on their own turf.

The Canucks took the bait—to a fault. With just over five minutes gone in the first period, Bruins forward Nathan Horton had skated across center ice, head down and puck on his stick, sliding a pass to teammate Milan Lucic, on

Horton's left, just before the Vancouver blue line. Vancouver defenseman Aaron Rome then dealt Horton a vicious blindside blow to the head that knocked Horton on his back. Horton oddly crumpled to the ice with his right arm and hand extended out in front of his chest as if he were trying to ward off a defender who had long since delivered a blow. Television cameras captured a worrisome look on Horton's face—eyes fixed, looking straight ahead, entirely oblivious as to what had just happened. At a time when the NHL was beginning to legislate against predatory hits, Rome had dealt Horton the kind of blow that, as the saying goes, knocked Horton *into next week.*

Horton was done for the series, as it turned out—and so was Rome, who garnered a game misconduct to bounce him from Game 3 and a suspension that would wipe him out for the balance of the postseason.

An eye for an eye, as the ancient law code of Hammurabi might have demanded, but a loss for the Bruins nonetheless.

"My initial reaction was anger, and then we were worried if he was OK," Thornton said after the game. "We talk about it all the time as players. That's the shit we've got to get out of the game—head shots, blindsides. That's what the rule's there for."

In the wake of the Horton injury, momentum shifted—and so did the series. After a scoreless first period, the Bruins scored four times in the second period of Game 3, including goals on both the power play (by Recchi) and the penalty kill (by Marchand). They repeated the pattern in the third with four more goals—two even-strength, one power play, one shorty—and blistered the Canucks in an 8–1 victory. A night later, despite being outshot by the Canucks 38–29, the Bruins claimed a 4–0 victory in which Vancouver goalie Luongo was pulled from the game in the third period, the ultimate indignity. Thomas, meanwhile, was putting together a brilliant series despite some missteps in Vancouver, having stopped a remarkable 96.6 percent of all Vancouver shots. The Canucks had rifled seventy-nine shots on goal during Games 3 and 4 in Boston and Thomas had stopped seventy-eight of them, Vancouver's only score coming with a little more than six minutes remaining in Game 3, when the Bruins already held a 5–0 lead.

When they had left Vancouver after losses in Games 1 and 2, the Bruins had said all the right things, seized upon all the obvious points. But they were nothing more than rationalizations. What the Bruins subsequently did in Boston was to show *resolve*, hit back with impressive force, obliterating the Canucks in Games 3 and 4 by a combined 12–1 count while Vancouver's highly drafted, world-class goalie was outplayed and downright humiliated by the scrappy, overlooked Thomas.

Late in the third period of Game 4, even the feisty Thomas hacked at the leg of the ratty Burrows as retaliation for what he perceived as gamesmanship.

"They'd been getting [at] the butt end of my stick," Thomas said. "Actually, they did it a couple of times on a power play in the first period. That was like the third time he hit my butt end on that power play. . . . The game was getting down toward the end, so I thought I'd give him a little love tap to let him know, 'I know what you're doing. I'm not going to let you keep doing it forever.'"

So, too, was the larger message as pertained to the series: *Okay, we're even.*

By the time teams traveled back across the continent to Vancouver, an obvious pattern had formed: The games in Vancouver were tighter, lower scoring; the games in Boston were one-sided routs. The home team had been victorious in all four. Game 5, subsequently, fell neatly into line, the teams tied at 0–0 entering the third period, when the Canucks scored the only goal they would need. With Vancouver pressing in the Boston zone, Canucks defenseman Kevin Bieksa snapped a shot from the right point that zipped past the left side of the net and came out the other side. Former Canadiens forward Maxim Lapierre corralled the puck at the post to Thomas's right—almost exactly where Tampa's Steve Downie had been stationed when Thomas made the save of the postseason—and slipped it into the net to give Vancouver a 1–0 edge. Vancouver kept the Bruins off the scoresheet for the balance of the 15:25 remaining to claim a 1–0 victory and 3–2 series edge, moving to within one win of its first-ever championship.

On the play, for Thomas, there would be no circus save this time. And the play marked the second late game-winner for Vancouver in which the aggressive Thomas had drifted from the net—perhaps too far—though the Boston goalie's play overall had remained stellar.

Nonetheless, after taking a beating in Games 3 and 4 while Thomas tanned in the spotlight, Vancouver goalie Luongo seemed all too eager to take a jab at his counterpart, a decision he would regret on multiple levels.

"It's not hard if you're playing in the paint [or crease]. It's an easy save for me, but if you're wandering out and aggressive like he does, that's going to happen," Luongo said. "He might make some saves that I won't, but in a case like that, we want to take advantage of a bounce like that and make sure we're in a good position to bury those."

The words hung in the air. *Sure, he might make some saves that I don't . . . but I'm as good or better.*

A day later, undoubtedly still burdened by a reputation that he could not excel under pressure, Luongo made the matter worse. After initially attempting to walk back the comments—"I also said that he might make some saves that I don't," said the goalie—he further revealed his insecurities, rambling on about seemingly childish matters with Vancouver just win one from a Stanley Cup. "I've been pumping his tires ever since the series started," he said, "and I haven't heard one nice thing he had to say about me, so that's the way it is."

The conclusion was clear. Tim Thomas was squarely stationed between the ears of the conflicted Roberto Luongo. And, for that matter, the Bruins were similarly in the heads of the Canucks. At least in Boston.

* * *

Game 6, too, was a blowout, and one in which Luongo was once again pulled from the ice—this time in the *first* period. He lasted just eight minutes and thirty-five seconds—allowing three goals on eight shots, the last a power play that gave the Bruins a 3–0 lead and completed a surge during which Boston scored three times in a whisker more than three minutes. Backup Corey Schneider once again replaced Luongo and promptly surrendered another goal just 1:10 after entering the game, giving the Bruins a 4–0 lead they eventually turned into a 5–2 defeat, the Canucks never getting closer than three goals after the initial breakdown by Luongo.

Thomas once again was stellar—both on and off the ice. The goalie remained both humble and focused the day prior to the game, then went out and backboned his team to another victory, bringing the Bruins within one game of the Stanley Cup.

"I guess I didn't realize it was my job to pump his tires. I guess I have to apologize for that," Thomas mused in a very matter-of-fact manner. "I still think I'm a goaltender and I stick with all the other goalies. In being one and knowing what it takes to perform at this level and with this amount of pressure, I understand to a certain extent what every other goaltender is going through." He paused. "I guess that's that," he said.

Indeed, as Luongo's feet seemingly tapped and his wheels seemingly spun, the Vancouver goalie had broken a critical rule: *Never forget how hard this job is.* Hockey—and life—had a way of biting you in the ass if you weren't careful.

Meanwhile, as the teams flew across the continent yet again and prepared for Game 7—the Bruins' third winner-take-all game of the postseason—one thing had grown clear and apparent to everyone: Tim Thomas was the more confident goalie.

Nonetheless, there was the matter of home ice: Every game had been won at home. The most obvious difference was that the three Vancouver games all had been tight and fought to the finish; the Boston games had been full-fledged blowouts. The Bruins faced the unusual reality of potentially losing a series in which they outscored the opposition by a better than two-to-one margin—the totals were Boston 19, Vancouver 8, after three games—unless they figured out how to win on the road.

Relegated to the role of spectator following the knockout hit by Vancouver defenseman Aaron Rome, Bruins forward Nathan Horton took it upon himself to solve the problem. Before the Bruins left Boston for the return flight to Vancouver, Horton grabbed some of the ice shavings from the surface at TD Garden and placed them in a water bottle he brought with him on the long flight. Just before Game 7 on June 15, 2011, Horton strode out to the Bruins bench at Rogers Arena, unscrewed the lid, and poured the water onto the surface, thereby bringing at least a little bit of Boston onto the ice where the 2011 Stanley Cup would be decided.

"It's our ice now," Horton said.

And then the Bruins went out and played like it.

Fueled by the duo or Bergeron and Marchand, who scored two goals each—and more brilliant play by Thomas—the Bruins rolled to a 4–0 victory that crystallized a series of indisputable truths. First, after trailing 2–0 and 3–2 in the series, the Bruins had played under far greater pressure than the Canucks—and handled it far, far better. Boston had outscored the Canucks overall, 23–8. They had outscored them in 5-on-5 play, 15–6. They outscored them on the power play, 5–2. And they also had tallied three shorthanded goals in the series, including one in Game 7, when a Bergeron tally had made the score 3–0.

Thomas was named the winner of the Conn Smythe Trophy as the MVP of the entire playoffs, during which he posted a .940 save percentage and 1.98 goals against average. His numbers in the finals were simply otherworldly—a .967 save percentage and a 1.15 goals against average—and immortalized him in Boston forever, completing a rags-to-riches story that anyone could embrace. When Thomas was a child, his parents sold their wedding rings so that he could attend goalie camp. Now he could replace them with a championship ring that he could place inside the Vezina Trophy (as the league's best goaltender during the regular season), which he could place inside the Conn Smythe, which he could place inside the Stanley Cup as if they were Matryoshka dolls.

Said Julien of his goalie: "He's so deserving of everything he's gotten."

As for the rest of the Bruins, their names would similarly be etched on the side of the Stanley Cup, which captain Zdeno Chara accepted on behalf of the team while towering on the Vancouver ice—*It's our ice now*—and emitting a guttural roar. One by one, the Bruins passed the trophy on to one another, perhaps the greatest trophy in sports, a fitting reward for the most challenging tournament. All in all, the Bruins had played twenty-five postseason games, including three seven-game series. The Bruins had received contributions from top to bottom, the kind of total team effort required to end a drought—like the 2001 Patriots or the 2004 Red Sox, everlasting teams that had become part of Boston lore. Krejci, who had been knocked out of the Flyers series a year earlier, had led all postseason players in both goals (12) and scoring (23 points) and easily could have won the Conn Smythe; defenseman Seidenberg, who had been injured before the previous postseason, played more total minutes (691) than any other Bruin and, along with Chara, anchored the back line; Bergeron rebounded from a concussion and finished with 20 points in twenty-three postseason games, dominating Game 7 of the finals with linemate Marchand (19 points).

"Best feeling in the world," said a succinct Thornton when asked about the achievement in the postgame euphoria.

By that point, it was a feeling Boston had grown to know quite well.

* * *

After a thirteen-year career during which he established himself as one of the best players ever to play his position, Cam Neely began his first postseason as team president in much the same the way a fan would: nervously watching from his seat. He had begun his executive career as a vice president three years earlier, but his promotion to president in 2010 changed things. This was his organization now. And throughout the playoffs, television cameras routinely captured Neely watching from above, flanked by Bruins executives that included general manager Peter Chiarelli, pumping his fist and gritting his teeth as the Bruins pushed their way toward their first championship since 1972.

Three days after the Bruins won Game 7, Boston celebrated another championship—its seventh in ten years—with a rally and parade, the latter becoming to Boston what the Macy's Thanksgiving Day Parade was to New York: an annual tradition. Boston had now won titles in all four major sports to start the millennium—the Bruins' title completed the set, in a manner of speaking—and the city could now at least chuckle about many of its previous failures, like championship droughts and blown series leads.

"I think I have communicated more than once that, all along, he is such a great role model for the players and for the organization. He is the heart and soul of what a Bruins means. You couldn't have a better leader," team owner Jeremy Jacobs said of Neely to an assembled crowd. "On top of it, he brought us a Stanley Cup—something he couldn't do while he was playing."

The crowd groaned at that line, but Neely, to his credit, accepted the barb tactfully—and was all too willing to return serve. Less than four months later, as the Bruins opened the defense of their title at home against Philadelphia, the team raised its championship banner to the TD Garden rafters. Neely spoke to a capacity crowd and thanked ownership for committing the "resources" to build a winner, holding his hand in the air and rubbing his thumb against his forefingers. The gesture drew laughter and was an obvious reference to Neely's playing days, when the Bruins were too often one player short and ownership was criticized for its unwillingness to commit financially.

"He kind of busted my balls just before the parade. And knowing him, that's his sense of humor—even though I was like, 'Whoa, okay,'" Neely chuckled a decade later. "It was more to just return fire. But he has allowed us to do what we think is best to put the best team on the ice."

Over the years that preceded the Stanley Cup run, as the drought neared four decades without a championship, Neely admitted that the public dissatisfaction did "get a little louder," at least in the ears and minds of players, for whom the Bruins uniform grew a little heavier. The 2011 Cup eased that burden. The Bruins could start anew. Instead of serving as yet another epilogue on a Bruins season, blowing the 3–0 lead against the Flyers became a *prologue* that fueled the Bruins to a title. And rather than being the outsider, the one local franchise that hadn't won, the Bruins, too, now belonged.

"Feeding off the success of the other teams—that helped us," Neely said in 2021. "We were saying, 'We can't be the ugly stepchild.'"

During the summer of 2011, Boston's children were anything but ugly. The Patriots had won three titles, the Red Sox two, the Celtics and Bruins one each. There had been no other decade like it in the history of Boston sports. Had the teams lined up shoulder to shoulder, like siblings, they might have been the subjects of a most splendid family photo, the kind that rests above the mantel, an instant that suggests perfect harmony in a world and a city that often lack any.

At that moment, winning in Boston seemed absurdly simple and easy. As most everyone in Boston would soon remember, it is anything but.

CHAPTER 8

BROKEN WINDOWS

"Yeah, but it's a bad place to lose."
—former Red Sox shortstop John Valentin during the 1995 baseball
season, after a member of the media said "This is a great place to win"
before a home game at Fenway Park

IN THE WORLD OF PROFESSIONAL sports, teams, executives, players, and fans often speak of competitive "windows," a term used to identify those relatively limited periods of time when an organization can compete at its highest levels and, ultimately, challenge for championships. As salary caps and payroll restrictions became more and more prevalent in sports, decision-makers more often found themselves handcuffed, unable to make the roster changes and alterations that were often critical to winning. As such, teams and executives had less margin for error and sought to optimize the peak years of their very best players, hoping to extend one *window* while, simultaneously, opening another.

In Boston as the new millennium went from a first decade to a second, Boston's four major teams were in various stages of managing their differently sized windows. The Bruins were just opening one that seemed gigantic. The Celtics, by contrast, knew from the start that theirs would be very small. And the Patriots, thanks to the presence of a fiscally cooperative, once-in-a-lifetime player who played the most important position in sports—"He gets it," team executives were fond of saying when asked why quarterback Tom Brady took less money to stay in New England—were hoping to make theirs big picture–sized.

But for the Red Sox, in retrospect, the reality was simple. The window was closing.

After winning two World Series and reaching four American League Championship Series during Theo Epstein's first six years as the team's chief baseball executive—more championships and more games (regular- and post-season combined) than any team in baseball over that six-year span—the Red Sox had started to slide. Boston made the playoffs in 2009 but was swept by the Los Angeles Angels in the first round of the playoffs. In 2010 they missed the playoffs entirely. And, after having set a franchise record with positively astronomical television ratings during the championship 2007 season, Boston had seen a decline in local television viewership during subsequent years. The team was getting worse—and interest was waning.

In retrospect, the popularity drop-off was inevitable, merely the result of what team executives often liked to refer to as a *market correction*. From a baseball standpoint, Epstein seemed to fully understand the ebbs and flows that came with roster management, calling the 2010 season a "bridge year" even before it began. But the business side of the Boston baseball operation bristled at the mere existence of that term, believing it would undermine their ability to attract fans and viewers. It wasn't a wholesale rebuilding like the Houston Astros would later pursue, but every few years or so, Epstein believed, the Red Sox would benefit from taking a small step backward so that they could again push forward. The concept hardly meshed with that of team president Larry Lucchino, who oversaw the *business* of the Red Sox and whose general approach in most things was, at once, both admirable and unrealistic.

Push, push, push. Go, go, go.

"I think that when you have a city going through the time period that Boston was going through, the good news for fans is that there was competition amongst the teams," said Mike Dee, a longtime sports executive who worked for Lucchino as chief operating officer and, later, president of the Fenway Sports Group. "Here you have four teams operating at or near championship levels or at least at serious contention for championship level, so being able to maintain your fifty-two-week high—to use a stock term—I'm sure every ownership group felt pressured to do that. In the case of every sport other than football, you have other considerations like local media rights and local TV ratings. The Red Sox, of course, didn't have to worry about ticket sales during that period. We took care of that. But simply put, the stakes were high to sustain a level of success that fans and, frankly, the front office had become accustomed to. Whether or not that causes you to think differently than you thought five years earlier when you were the upstart . . ." Dee trailed off.

"We used to be Avis and we turned into Hertz along the way," he added. "We were no longer the other guys—we were the guys that people wanted to knock off the pedestal in baseball."

And the people who wanted to knock them off? They, too, were Bostonians.

But whatever the pressures and from wherever they came, the Red Sox decision-making suffered. During an off-season in which Epstein had spoken of a "bridge" year, the Red Sox signed free-agent pitcher John Lackey to a five-year, $82.5 million contract that seemingly came out of nowhere. In Josh Beckett and Jon Lester, the Red Sox already had a one-two punch at the front of their rotation that was among the best in baseball. But amid the rise of Boston's other teams, the Red Sox suffered. Meanwhile, they also slid behind the rival New York Yankees, who won the 2009 World Series following an off-season spending spree that included the signings of both pitcher CC Sabathia and first baseman Mark Teixeira, who had been an Epstein target.

In the case of Teixeira, the inner workings of the Red Sox—and the seemingly never-ending power struggle between Lucchino and Epstein—had hurt them badly. Epstein believed he was on the verge of a deal when Red Sox ownership—despite having already met with the player—wanted a second sit-down. When the meeting became contentious, Teixeira turned his attention elsewhere and signed with the Yankees, for whom he subsequently batted .292 with a league-leading 39 home runs, 122 RBIs, and 344 total bases. He won both the Silver Slugger (as the league's best hitter at his position) and Gold Glove (as the league's best defensive player at first base), and finished second in the balloting for the American League MVP. And though Teixeira was a bust in the postseason—the balance of his Yankees career, too, never again reached the heights of his first season—the immediate shift in power in the American League East mirrored that of the Red Sox slide in the Boston sports hierarchy.

They were now a second-place team.

Having clashed with Lucchino earlier in the millennium, Epstein was especially careful to call the Teixeira breakdown an organizational failure, but the Lackey signing a year later was also wildly out of character. ("It's not the kind of move Theo would typically make," one voice in the Boston organization hinted at the time.) But at the urging of ownership and Lucchino, the Red Sox made it anyway—and despite the fact that there were concerns about the long-term health of Lackey's right elbow. As such, the Red Sox negotiated a sixth-year option year on the contract for the major-league minimum salary in the event that Lackey needed elbow surgery—the kind of protective clause for which Lucchino was renowned.

In the end, the Red Sox were making baseball decisions for business reasons, a combination that often proved fatal in any organization in any market. Lackey was a disappointment in 2010, going 14-11 with a 4.40 ERA, his worst season in six years. Once again, the Red Sox missed the playoffs, finishing 89-73 and now slipping to *third place* in the division behind Tampa Bay and the Yankees. During the ensuing off-season, the Red Sox further abandoned Epstein's longer-term thinking for the quick fix, this time signing multitalented outfielder Carl Crawford for a preposterous $142 million over seven seasons while executing a blockbuster trade with the San Diego Padres, sending four prospects including Anthony Rizzo for first baseman Adrian Gonzalez, whom they then signed to a seven-year, $154 million extension (on top of the $6.3 million Gonzalez already was set to earn in 2011). Boston's investment in the two players topped $300 million. The Red Sox had gone all in, but it was reckless and self-destructive, the kind of spendthrift behavior for which, privately, Patriots officials had mocked the Red Sox for years.

Still, entering the 2011 season—at least on paper—the Red Sox looked absolutely loaded. The *Boston Herald* season preview labeled the star-laden squad the BEST TEAM EVER! In spring training, pitcher Josh Beckett openly wondered about the team's prowess: "I've never been on a team that won 100 games," he said. That was the kind of faux pas that organizations, executives, and managers frowned upon, because they believed it warranted the simplest and most obvious warning.

Don't take anything for granted.

On paper, the 2011 Red Sox appeared to be like, in some ways, the 2007 Patriots. As such, they would suffer an even worse fate.

* * *

One of the great dangers of success, of course, is arrogance—and on multiple levels. Fans become insufferable. Decision-makers who pride themselves on being bold go too far and become self-destructive. Players become downright selfish and gluttonous, focusing on things like their personal *brand* rather than controlling the things required to win consistently on any level, independent of talent. Commitment, work ethic, and, most important, attitude. And from the very start, the 2011 Red Sox pretty much lacked them all.

Insultingly cocky from the start, the 2011 Red Sox began the season by losing six straight games and stumbled through the first two weeks like a bunch of fat, inept, and oblivious drunks. They were 2-10 after a dozen games. When the team actually got its act together, the potential of its talent was indisputable. From April 16 through August 9, the Red Sox went a sizzling 70-33, a whopping .680 winning percentage in a sport where merely winning more than half of one's games was often considered an achievement. And yet, the team and season often seemed utterly joyless.

During the season, comments from the insufferable Gonzalez—"He's a know-it-all," one voice in the organization would later say of the opinionated first baseman—reflected an out-of-touch arrogance that was further indication of the team's hubris, particularly among the players. A talented hitter who had generally played on bad or mediocre teams, Gonzalez complained about things that came along with playing for a highly competitive, championship-driven organization, particularly on the East Coast.

"We play too many night games on getaway days and get into places at four in the morning," Gonzalez whined to reporters. "This has been my toughest season physically because of that. We play a lot of night games on Sunday for television and those things take a lot out of you." When essentially told that the Sunday night games were part of playing in places like Boston and New York, Gonzalez replied: "Why does it have to be? They can put the Padres on ESPN, too. Nobody is really reporting that."

Traded from San Diego to Boston largely because the Padres could not afford to pay him—again, the Red Sox subsequently gave Gonzalez an additional $154 million—Gonzalez's sense of entitlement (or sheer stupidity) was mind-numbing. The reason why the Padres didn't play on Sunday night baseball was because nobody wanted to watch them. But, in retrospect, that was merely the beginning of the team's problems—and the public would soon get a much clearer look at some of the 90 percent hiding beneath the surface.

Miserable as they were, the Red Sox still possessed arguably the most important asset on any sports team: talent. With roughly a month to go in the 2011 season, the Red Sox were 82-51, on pace for the one hundred wins that would have satisfied Josh Beckett's preseason goal. Entering play on August 27—after having trailed in the division by as many as five games early in the season—the Red Sox led the American League East by two. And while Boston certainly would have to play well to hold off the second-place Yankees, the playoffs seemed a foregone conclusion: The Rays, in third place, were a whopping nine games behind.

And then, incredibly, it all fell apart.

Beginning with a loss to the Yankees on August 29, the Red Sox went a dreadful 8-21 over their final twenty-nine games. They did not win a single series they played. Tampa Bay won six of seven head-to-head meetings between the clubs over the final weeks, putting the Red Sox in the position of needing a victory on the final day of the season, against the wretched Baltimore Orioles, to make the postseason at all. Either a Boston victory or a Tampa Bay loss—they were playing the Yankees—would have qualified the Red Sox for the playoffs. As the games unrolled, it seemed a lock: the Sox led the Orioles 3-2, and the Rays trailed the Yankees by a whopping 7-0 score through seven innings.

But in Baltimore, pitching for the third time in four nights, Red Sox closer Jonathan Papelbon melted down in the ninth inning. After a pair of strikeouts, Papelbon allowed a first-pitch double to first baseman Chris Davis; then, down to Baltimore's last strike, Nolan Reimold hit a ground-rule double to tie the game at 3. Three pitches later, the previously anonymous Robert Andino hit a sinking liner to left field that a sliding Crawford allowed to squirt out of his glove, delivering the final run of a 4-3 Baltimore victory that was, in a word, embarrassing. Meanwhile, the Rays rallied for an 8-7 win that featured two home runs by third baseman Evan Longoria, the latter a line drive that barely cleared a short wall in the left field corner at Tropicana Field. It was the coup de grâce that ended the Red Sox season and, as it turned out, so much more.

In the days and weeks following the darkest night during the ownership of John Henry, a disturbing light was shed on the depth of the Red Sox dysfunction by investigative reporter Bob Hohler of the *Boston Globe*. According to Hohler, pitchers Beckett, Lackey, and Jon Lester—the nucleus of the Red Sox pitching staff—reportedly grew so detached during the season that they resorted to consuming beer and fried chicken in the clubhouse during games, ordering takeout from a nearby Popeyes, and even playing video games. Francona, in the midst of marital difficulties, was seemingly helpless when it came to reining in his players. The Red Sox were painted as a fraternity house run amok, a collection of spoiled rich kids with bad grade point averages and no pride. All that was missing was the admonishment of Dean Wormer. Fat, drunk, and stupid might be no way to go through life. It was certainly no way win a baseball championship.

In the aftermath of the on-field collapse, the Red Sox disintegrated into a dumpster fire of resentment. The team and manager mutually parted ways, which is to say that all parties had grown quite sick of each other. Francona had become increasingly frustrated by his inability to get through to his seemingly brain-dead players, some of whom he had shared excellent relationships with and relied on for championships. Beckett, for instance, had been a cornerstone of the 2007 championship team, but he became so disengaged during the 2011 season that one club official (not Francona) sarcastically wondered whether the former ace had undergone "a lobotomy." Lackey, a bad fit in Boston from the start, hated both the city and the organization, not necessarily in that order. He wasn't alone in a simmering distaste; it seemed everybody hated everybody.

As the first Red Sox manager to have won a World Series in nearly a century—and he had, in fact, won two—Francona had become a Boston immortal, someone whom fans had come to hold in the highest regard. Not long after the 2004 championship, for instance, Francona had dined with bench coach Brad Mills at an Italian restaurant near Boston Common. Along with their wives, the two dined without the slightest interruption, but when they rose to depart, customers in the restaurant stood and applauded, something that has been forever etched in the manager's mind.

"That was pretty cool," Francona acknowledged.

When Francona won a second title, his place in Boston lore was forever cemented. For decades, no manager of the Red Sox had ever made it through five full seasons without being fired; Francona made it through eight. Consequently, Red Sox ownership feared a public backlash from firing him, leading to an awkward press conference in which Francona technically announced that it was his decision to move on, though the club essentially had backed him into a corner by failing to address his expiring contract. The tension between Francona and the organization was palpable—Francona and Lucchino, especially, seemed to hold one another in contempt—and the sniping, however veiled, continued as the manager walked out the door.

"To be honest with you, I didn't know, or I'm not sure, how much support there was from ownership," Francona told reporters. "I don't know if I felt real comfortable. You have to be all-in with this job and I voiced that today. There were some things that maybe—going through things here and to make it work—it has to be everybody together and I was questioning some of that a little bit."

Lucchino's counter?

"I was actually puzzled by that comment," responded the club president. "We have done nothing differently this year as we have done in previous years. I think it's a question that you probably have to ask him. I thought he did an exceptional job conveying the strength of his feelings and his frustration and his fatigue with the situation here in Boston. But I must confess to be a little puzzled what was different this year from previous years."

The answer, of course: *Nothing.* That was the point. After all the winning, Francona felt he deserved more. And he felt like he never got it.

As fearful as the Red Sox were of firing Francona, the public backlash from the *Globe* story was worse because it portrayed ownership and management—from John Henry to Lucchino—as cowards who smeared the most accomplished manager in team history behind the shield of anonymity. Francona was portrayed as a desperate soul crumbling beneath the pressure of the job and a failed marriage, and there was even talk about his use of painkillers. On the day the *Globe* story appeared, a Boston television reporter asked Lucchino about the story and the team president called the report "an interesting set of theories." Lucchino went on to say that club officials "have our own [theories]" for the downfall of the Red Sox, but he never dismissed or denounced the report. When the public lashed out at the team and talk radio hosts blasted everyone from Henry on down, the owner made the unprecedented move of driving to the studio, where he confronted the hosts for ninety minutes on air.

Francona was among those listening, even texting questions he wanted asked of Henry to station employees. Such was the life of a manager, coach, executive, or athlete in Boston.

"I mean, if you care—if you're passionate about sports—it's hard to find a better place to be associated with it," Francona said years later, in March 2021. "Because of the passion and because of the energy and the attention, the manager or the head coach is going to have a headache sometimes. That's the way it is. But, man, I remember walking down that tunnel every night before the game thinking, *Goddamn.* I mean, I was there eight years and there wasn't one game that wasn't sold out. There's no day game after a night game where, 'Well, we'll just go through the motions.' I mean, it was an incredible experience. And I mean, the Celtics can say the same thing, the Patriots can say the same thing. Shit, even the Bruins. I mean, that's an incredible amount of winning. . . . I mean, it's kind of a reactionary place. And that's okay. I mean, I get it. Like I said, sometimes, you get a headache, but that's not condemning the place by any means. It is such a special sports town that, I mean, my goodness."

So it was in Boston. The good, the bad and, sometimes, the ugly. As it turned out for the Red Sox as a whole, the bad and the ugly were just beginning.

Within a month of Francona's dismissal and departure—and make no mistake, it was both—general manager Theo Epstein orchestrated his own departure from the club for what amounted to the same job with the Chicago Cubs, albeit with an elevated title. Like Francona, he had experienced enough of the drama in Boston. Epstein's defection to the Cubs had been rumored for months, yet another indication of the discord that started as small chips in the team's windshield. But before long, thanks to the bumps, the wind, the elements that came along with playing professional sports in Boston, the cracks spread into a complex web that ultimately required a full replacement.

Ever eloquent, Epstein outlined the reasons for his departure in an op-ed column he wrote for the *Globe* in which he referenced the philosophies of accomplished and revered football coach Bill Walsh, who recommended that, to prevent burnout and ego-driven conflict, it was beneficial to change jobs every ten years. Nonetheless, the timing of Epstein's departure was impossible to ignore, coming at the end of a season in which the Red Sox had experienced both a historic on-field collapse and imploded internally, the walls collapsing around what once felt like an empire.

"The reason I am leaving has nothing to do with power, pressure, money, or relationships," Epstein wrote. "It has nothing to do with September, either."

In Theo Epstein's mind, after all, those things were symptoms more than they were actual problems. Over time, the fraying of relationships was inevitable. He was in his twenties when he started his career as general manager of the Red Sox, approaching his forties when things began to unravel. His relationships with both Lucchino and Francona had changed. Further, the Red Sox had won—*Boston* had won—and the challenges in the city were changing. At the beginning, the goal for the organization and the entire city was singular—for the Red Sox to win their first championship in nearly one hundred years—and everyone was generally pulling in the same direction. But once the Red Sox accomplished that feat, they had an array of new challenges that took them in multiple directions, the struggles on the inside becoming more consuming and, ultimately, downright detrimental to the kind of synergy that was required to win championships.

Winning, it turned out, often had a shelf life.

For Boston as a whole, that would be a lesson worth remembering.

* * *

Comparatively speaking, the deconstruction of the Boston Celtics was far more tactful, even downright peaceful. Unlike the Red Sox, who constantly tussled weighing the short term versus the long, the Celtics' lines had been much more clearly drawn. Championship windows in the NBA were dictated almost entirely by the age of a great player or players, and the Celtics had been faced with a simple decision regarding Paul Pierce. They could either build around him and win for a short period of time, or trade Pierce for a collection of young players and/or draft picks with the hopes of finding the *next* incarnation of their star player. In a league driven by elite talent, they chose the bird in hand, and they won a championship.

But after the triumphant 2007–2008 season, the Celtics encountered the kinds of problems that NBA teams almost always encounter: age and injury, which often go hand in hand. The NBA was, at its essence, a league dominated by star players in the primes of their careers. Lacking both maturity and breadth of skill, even the best young players usually needed six or seven years to win their first championships. By the time they did, their championship windows were usually short. That was especially true in the case of the Celtics, who had acquired a thirty-something Kevin Garnett and a thirty-something Ray Allen to put alongside a thirty-something Pierce, which made the reality self-evident. Win now. Worry later.

Just the same, there were always challenges—and ones that could allow managers and coaches to form their own support group, to commiserate with one another. In a place like Boston, that was important. Francona, for one, was also a sports *fan* who befriended both Celtics coach Doc Rivers and Patriots executive Scott Pioli, each of whom he regarded as a sounding board. Though Francona remembers being closer to Pioli, he frequently attended basketball games and grew friendly with Rivers, whose challenges were, in some ways, more intense.

Basketball rosters were smaller, star players had enormous influence and power, and it was a game in which players often competed with each other for the ball more than they competed with the opposition, especially when individual accomplishments were at stake.

"I do remember him telling me one time—it was about two weeks before the All-Star Game and they were struggling—and he was like, 'Goddammit, there's not enough basketballs going around,'" Francona recalled. "And I said,

'Well, how come?' And he said, 'Because the All-Star Game is in two weeks.' I started laughing."

For Rivers, at least in 2007–2008, the advantage was that Pierce, Allen, and Garnett had matured to the point where All-Star Games were no longer the priority. But one of the trade-offs was the wear and tear on his stars, most notably Garnett, who was well into a career during which he would ultimately play more than 50,000 minutes, a plateau eclipsed by only seven players in the history of the league. With one championship already in their pockets, the Celtics were 41-9 when they hit the All-Star break during the 2008–2009 season, a 67-win pace that would have eclipsed the 66-win total from the 2007–2008 championship season. Then things literally began to break down.

With Garnett mostly sidelined by a knee injury, the Celtics finished the season by going 21-11 in their final thirty-two games. Good, but more middle-class in a league ruled by the rich and famous. In the playoffs, the Celtics were pushed to seven games in a first-round series victory over the Chicago Bulls before succumbing to the upstart Orlando Magic and center Dwight Howard in the second round, losing a Game 7 on their own floor at the TD Garden by the lopsided score of 101–82.

By the time the Celtics arrived for the 2009–2010 season, their future had been altered. Committed to an aging roster and fearful of Garnett's durability, the Celtics acquired another aging big man, the troubled Rasheed Wallace, as insurance. Rivers subsequently managed Garnett carefully, limiting him just below thirty minutes per game, the first time since Garnett's rookie season (when he was a nineteen-year-old) that he fell below that mark. Once regarded as the best defensive player in the league, Garnett suffered noticeable drops in rebounding and blocked shots, in part because of the diminishing minutes, in part because of a slowly deteriorating body. Consumed with gaining home-court advantage for the playoffs when Garnett first arrived, the Celtics managed their way to a 52-30 record with hopes of elevating their play during the postseason and securing another title. To their credit, they came within a whisker of pulling it off.

After defeating the Miami Heat in five games in the first round, the Celtics played the second round—against the Cleveland Cavaliers—without home-court advantage for the first time during the Garnett era. They defeated an increasingly frustrated Lebron James in six games, and the Magic (and an equally frustrated Howard) again in six games, both times clinching the series on the TD Garden floor to avoid a seventh game on the road. The victories sent the Celtics back to the NBA Finals for the second time in three years.

In the short term, at least, experience had won out, and the Celtics had another chance at a championship.

"The first thing we said when we got into the locker room was this is where we thought we would be," Rivers told reporters after the game. "This is what we talked about before the season started. And you know, we did go through some tough times. We started out so well. I thought after 28 games you could say we were the best team in the NBA, but after that we had injuries and fell apart—we had trouble finding ourselves. But we kept saying as a staff, 'It's in us. We've got to try and get it back out of us.'"

Observed Howard, whose team had lost in the Finals after defeating the Celtics a year earlier: "In games like this or a series like this, it's not about skill or talent, because it's the Eastern Conference championship. Both teams were talented and skilled. It's about who wants it most and who is willing to do it for a series. Those guys played like they wanted to win the championship the whole series. That's why they're in the position they're in now."

In the Finals, the Celtics encountered a familiar foe, the Los Angeles Lakers, who now had some things in their favor. The first was center Pau Gasol, who was now far more acclimated to the team, and star Kobe Bryant—who had entered the prime years of his playing career. The second—and perhaps more significant—was home court advantage, something the Lakers had lacked in 2008, which cost them dearly.

Los Angeles had additional motivation, too, this kind based purely on the opponent: Though the Lakers had won the championship while an injured Garnett and the Celtics were eliminated in 2009, that had come against an inferior Orlando team. The 2010 Finals were against the *Celtics*, the NBA's other blue blood franchise, the team that had last defeated them in a postseason series. That title had been the fourth of Bryant's career, but his first without Shaquille O'Neal as a teammate, an accomplishment that validated Bryant's place as an all-time NBA great. And yet, the media still found a way to tweak him, noting that Bryant had never beaten a team *like Boston* in the Finals.

As it turned out, the greatest advantage the Lakers may have had in their favor was the age of the Celtics' core. After losing Game 1 in LA, the Celtics won Game 2 to promptly claim the upper hand. The next three games were in Boston, but the Lakers reclaimed home court with a victory in Game 3. The

Celtics claimed both Games 4 and 5 to send the series back to Los Angeles, and needed just one victory in the final two games at the Staples Center to claim their NBA-leading eighteenth world championship.

They lost both.

In the end, unsurprisingly, Game 7 was the most frustrating of the lot, the Celtics at one point holding a 13-point lead, albeit in the second quarter. In a series dominated by defensive play, the Celtics had scored only 67 points in a Game 6 loss that also cost the team the tough, defensive-minded center Kendrick Perkins. With Perkins gone to a knee injury, the Celtics started and relied heavily on Wallace, who was hardly in the necessary condition to handle a workload of nearly thirty-six minutes, easily his highest total of the season and nearly double his season average. Unsurprisingly, he tired, then fouled out. The Lakers scored 30 points in the fourth quarter and won by 4 points, 83–79, finishing with a decisive advantage at the free throw line. In the fourth quarter alone, the Lakers attempted twenty-one free throws to the Celtics' six, a frustrating conclusion to a game in which the officials had generally let the players fight it out until the final twelve minutes.

"We had a 13-point lead in the second half and we couldn't hold it, so it's frustrating," said Celtics architect Danny Ainge.

Said Rivers: "I thought the lack of size at the end of the day was the difference in the game. Our guys battled down there, but 23–8 on offensive rebounds and then the 37–17 discrepancy in free throws made it almost impossible to overcome."

Translation: *We missed Perkins—and the officials didn't help.*

It would be Boston's last trip to the Finals with the trio of Garnett, Pierce, and Allen, and the road there would have damaging repercussions. Frustrated by a second playoff loss to Boston in three years—and by the inability of the Cleveland Cavaliers to build a championship cast around him—LeBron James subsequently made a decision that would alter the NBA for years. In retrospect, no team may have been more affected than the Celtics. A native of nearby Akron, native son James turned his back on Ohio's only NBA franchise and left the Cavs for the Miami Heat, a development that left Cleveland in a state of uproar and sent shock waves throughout the league. In an astonishingly tone-deaf, vain, and self-indulgent made-for-TV special known as *The Decision*—James announced his intentions on ESPN to Jim Gray, uttering words that would haunt him forever.

"I'm going to take my talents to South Beach."

Outside of Cleveland, the Celtics were as much to blame as anybody. Over James's final three years in Cleveland, they had twice eliminated James and the Cavs from playoff contention, the last coming in inglorious fashion at the TD Garden.

Though the Celtics enjoyed two more seasons with the Big Three of Garnett, Pierce, and Allen, they were eliminated both times by James, whose move to Miami had united him with superstar Dwyane Wade and talented forward Chris Bosh, forming a new (and younger) Big Three that would redefine the league. In 2011, after Ainge regrettably traded Perkins for Jeff Green in a deal motivated by, among other things, the Celtics' desire to match up better with Miami, the Heat easily dispatched the Celtics in five games. But a year later, thanks to some good fortune that included favorable matchups in the first two rounds of the playoffs, the teams met in the Eastern Conference finals, the Celtics this time jumping to a 3-2 series lead with Game 6 on their home floor at TD Garden.

Facing a season-ending defeat in Boston for the third time in five years, James turned in arguably the greatest performance of his career, scoring 45 points in forty-five minutes of a 98–79 Miami victory that he singularly dominated from start to finish. He made nineteen of twenty-six shots from the floor and collected fifteen rebounds to go along with five assists. Playing at his best, at the peak of his physical ability, he was simply unstoppable. Only one other Miami player (Wade) attempted as many as ten shots and no other player on the floor—for either team—had more than eight rebounds. Miami subsequently outscored the Celtics by 20 points in Game 7 to advance to the Finals for the second straight year, this time winning the championship (James's first) and marking an official changing of the guard.

"Well, it was a matter of too much LeBron," Celtics coach Doc Rivers had reasoned after the Game 6 defeat. "He was absolutely sensational."

And the NBA now belonged to him.

One year later, after slogging through a mediocre 41-40 season, the Celtics had slid to the seventh seed among the eight NBA Eastern Conference playoff teams, neither a contender for the championship nor the No. 1 selection in the annual amateur draft. They were quite literally caught in between. Ainge knew this as well as anyone, so after a first-round series loss to the New York Knicks in six games, he went about deconstructing the roster of one of the proudest franchises in sports, from the coach to his best players, with the hope of building something far more sustainable, something long-lasting, something that would mark the next great era in Celtics history.

But by the time Danny Ainge pushed the metaphorical demolition button in June 2013, Boston was already rebuilding from something far more real and destructive, something far more hurtful and threatening, something that would remind the city, region, and country that sports were ultimately nothing more than entertainment, a freedom, something to celebrate, win or lose, and something to enjoy.

CHAPTER 9

MARATHON MONDAY

Settle down, it'll all be clear
Don't pay no mind to the demons
They fill you with fear

—"Home" by Phillip Phillips

THE BOSTON MARATHON IS THE oldest annual marathon in the world, but to call it a road race is an enormous understatement and disservice to what it truly represents. On a macro level, *the Marathon,* as Bostonians simply and most frequently refer to it, is the city's most prestigious event, an international festival for which Boston opens its doors to the rest of the world. Anyone and everyone is welcome to what has the feel of a massive block party, a one-day event that is, loosely, Boston's version of Mardi Gras.

And on April 15, 2013, it was the backdrop for one of the most tragic events in the city's history.

Years later, the details of the attacks perpetrated by Chechen/Kyrgyzstani brothers Tamerlan and Dzhokhar Tsarnaev are well-known, the memory no less painful. Routinely held on a Monday holiday exclusive to Massachusetts—Patriots Day—the marathon concludes on Boylston Street, at the foot of the Prudential Center, a signature building of the Boston skyline. Onlookers congregate there to celebrate the winners and cheer on family and friends, many of whom run to raise money for charitable endeavors. Every year on Marathon Monday, the finish line is a place to celebrate achievement, to acknowledge the giving to both oneself and others.

According to accounts, the first bomb exploded at 2:49 P.M., the second just fourteen seconds later. The explosions took place slightly more than two hundred yards apart, an attempt to bookend the victims, some of whom darted away from the first explosion and toward the second. Hundreds were injured. Many lost limbs. Three were killed, including eight-year-old Martin Richard, who was at the finish line with his father, mother, older brother, and younger sister. Richard's mother and sister were injured in the first explosion—suffering brain injury and a lost leg, respectively—but survived.

In the ensuing chaos, as first responders tended to victims on the blood-stained pavement, there was confusion, panic, fear. The Tsarnaevs had left behind backpacks containing the bombs, made of pressure cookers, as if they were leaving packages on a stoop. The brothers then walked by storefronts and bystanders and were caught on security cameras—the images soon part of public pleas for any and all information that could explain the events that were, at once, both gruesome and surreal.

The attack struck the city on its most open and inviting day. There were large crowds scattered all across the city and the marathon course. The Red Sox similarly played on that day, more than 30,000 spectators spilling into the city from Fenway Park at the conclusion of the game, which had come within an hour of the explosions. Police were scattered about the marathon route, but there were no metal detectors, and they were there to perform crowd control: The sheer volume of people, over an expanded area, made it virtually impossible to know who was doing what, where, when, and with whom, often college students toting backpacks.

"I was at the ballpark," Red Sox president Larry Lucchino remembered. "I found out [about the explosions] when I was about to walk over to the finish line, which is what I customarily did on Patriots Day. I remember being in L1, the suite that I occupied [during games], trying to get as much information as I could without having to walk over there. But it was my custom and practice to walk over and check out the marathon after our games on that Monday."

That was the routine for many. The Tsarnaev brothers knew it and exploited it.

Local and national newspaper accounts of the attack hit squarely at the heart of the matter. The front page of the *Boston Globe* declared the bombings an act of "Marathon Terror." The *Herald* called it "Terror at the Finish Line." The *New York Post* simply opted for "Terror." But those were just the initial headlines. A local and federal manhunt would soon follow, including an unprecedented ordered lockdown.

At a press conference, FBI special agent Rick DesLauriers released photographs and video of the Tsarnaev brothers as they executed their plan. Realizing their identities had been compromised, Tamerlan and Dzhokhar attempted to escape, and on the night of Thursday, April 18, the brothers attempted to steal the gun of Sean Collier, a university police officer employed by the Massachusetts Institute of Technology. They murdered Collier in the process, then subsequently hijacked an SUV at a gas station from a man who somehow escaped. The brothers were later confronted by police on the streets of East Watertown, an understated Boston suburb. Shortly after midnight, now on the morning of April 19, police shot Tamerlan Tsarnaev, and then his younger, wounded brother, Dzhokhar, drove the stolen SUV over his limp body and through police in an attempt to escape. He soon abandoned the SUV and took refuge in the backyard of a nearby home, where he hid under the cover of Watertown resident David Henneberry's boat.

Noticing that the cover on his boat had been dislodged, Henneberry went out to his backyard to investigate, whereupon he discovered a bloodied Dzhokhar Tsarnaev in his boat. He called 911. A succession of authorities ranging from local police to Boston police to federal investigators then descended on the final freely chosen destination of one of the most notorious figures in Boston's history. They got him, and he's been locked up ever since.

Amid the appreciation for the efforts of law enforcement, public officials in Boston began dealing with the aftermath of the tragedy by preaching, above all else, diligence. Bostonians were encouraged to keep their eyes and ears open, to pay attention, to report anything that might be construed as suspicious behavior. At events like the Big Apple Circus, which was touring through Boston and stationed near City Hall at Boston's Government Center, spectators proceeded far more cautiously, uncertainly, with trepidation. One Tsarnaev was dead and the other was in custody, but the effects of the attack were permanent. New measures would be taken at public events. New awareness would be required. New caution would similarly be mandatory, the residents of one of America's oldest and historic cities forced into a new way of life that included some restriction of freedoms, at least some measure of prolonged fear, and an abundance of unwanted change, particularly to the bombing victims who had been physically harmed.

But emotionally and psychologically, too, Boston had been traumatized. The city needed time to heal, to bond and reconnect, to trust and unite. And Boston being Boston, there was an obvious place to start.

* * *

Between the crime and the capture, before the lockdown, Boston wobbled, the way forward unclear. The Bruins, who had been scheduled to play at home against the Ottawa Senators on the night of April 15, had their game postponed and rescheduled for later in the month. Along with the rest of the NHL, the Bruins already had endured a major disruption, a lockout having wiped out nearly half of the NHL season thanks to the frustration of league owners with the latest collective bargaining agreement. By the time the sides had settled, the NHL had agreed to a forty-eight-game regular season and full playoff schedule, the latter of which was obviously far, far more important. The Bruins had seven games remaining when the bombs exploded at the finish line, forcing another stoppage of play. And though the Bruins would endure another postponement later during Marathon week—the Friday game on April 19 was similarly postponed when the city was in lockdown as the Tsarnaev brothers were hunted down—they resumed play on the night of Wednesday, April 17, against the Buffalo Sabres at TD Garden, home to something infinitely more meaningful than just a hockey game: relative normalcy.

At that moment, the winning or losing really did not matter as much.

"No, it really didn't," said respected Bruins center Patrice Bergeron. "It was about the city coming together. It was very special to be part of it, definitely a night I'll remember."

He was not alone. Honoring those killed, injured, and maimed, the Bruins played a video on the TD Garden scoreboard before the game, highlighting first responders, preaching strength and resolve. "Home" by Phillip Phillips served as the backdrop. A Boston crowd intent on standing up to fear sang the national anthem en masse while players from both the Bruins and the visiting Buffalo Sabres wore helmet decals sporting the phrase "Boston Strong," a refrain that served as a rallying call and that would help Boston back to its feet.

"The one thing that I sense from our team is that we have the ability to maybe help people heal and find some reason to smile again, by giving them that, by representing our city properly," observed dignified Bruins coach Claude Julien.

Said veteran defenseman Andrew Ference, one of the team's emotional leaders: "We all knew this was not just another game. It meant a lot to people as another step [in the healing process]. It was no different for us on the ice with the memory of the last couple of days."

In those remarks, of course, was the essence of professional sports, of
the genesis for how they came to exist in the first place. While Julien spoke of
representing our city, Ference bridged the gap that often existed between players and fans, the former often regarded as celebrities and the latter as nothing
more than civilians. *It was no different for us. . . .* People are people, Ference
acknowledged, and so Bostonians collectively took their places on the ice and
behind the bench as surely as they did in their seats, their neighboring zip codes
serving as the one thing they all had in common.

*Hey, where you from, pal? I'm from Malden. He's from Everett. That guy
is from Stoughton. I'm a plumber and he's a teacher. That one over there does
landscaping. Those guys on the ice play for the Bruins.*

The Bruins ultimately lost the game in an overtime shootout 3–2, though
that was of little consequence. Three days later, on Saturday, April 20, and
after the city breathed a huge sigh of relief following the capture of Dzhokhar
Tsarnaev, they lost again by a 3–2 score, this time to the Pittsburgh Penguins
and this time in regulation. But there was an even greater sense of normalcy.
Boston still had a great deal of rebuilding to do—of confidence, of storefronts,
of trust—but much of the immediate fear had been alleviated. *We got the bad
guys.* Certainly, there was a renewed awareness that others like the Tsarnaev
brothers were out there—for whatever cause, with whatever intentions—but
the most immediate threat had been turned back into something far more
conceptual. Eyes wide-open, people were walking on the city streets again.

On Saturday, April 20, as the Bruins were beginning their 12:30 P.M. game
against the Penguins near North Station, the Red Sox had returned home for
the first time since their Patriots Day victory, a game that concluded just minutes before the bombings. In the immediate aftermath of the attack, the team
had traveled to Cleveland, where they swept a three-game series against the
Indians, extending a surprising early-season winning streak to six games. The
Red Sox were due to open a three-game set against the Kansas City Royals on
Friday night, but that game, too, was postponed while the city was in lockdown
during the frantic pursuit of the bombers. By the time the Red Sox once again
took the field at Fenway Park, the entire incident had played out between their
two home games.

Of course, particularly for the bombing victims, many of the challenges
were just beginning. For them, many of the scars never healed. But in the
short term, for the city, the Red Sox returning to Fenway Park brought at least
a measure of closure to a tragic, chaotic, surreal week that played out like

something from a Hollywood movie. Now nearly ten years removed from the championship that ended eighty-six years of heartbreak and anguish on the field, the Red Sox found themselves eager to promote healing of a different, much realer kind. They had left town almost immediately after the incident and tracked details of the developments en route to Cleveland, where they were due to play a three-game series. Once there, the team arranged a group dinner attended by virtually the entire roster, whose members had something far greater than a just a Red Sox uniform in common. *Boston.*

"Something like 23 or 24 of the guys all went to dinner together in Cleveland that night. They were affected," said Charles Steinberg, a trusted adviser to team president Larry Lucchino. "And it was at that dinner that [Red Sox players] Jonny Gomes and Jarrod Saltalamacchia said to Tommy McLaughlin, the clubhouse [and equipment] manager, 'Let's get a jersey.'"

The following night in Cleveland, when the Red Sox took the field, a traditional, gray Red Sox road jersey was draped on a hanger in the visitors' dugout at Progressive Field. Facing the field, on the back of the uniform top and between the words BOSTON and STRONG, was the number 617—the area code for greater Boston. On short notice, the jersey had letters and numbers that were ironed on, but, at McLaughlin's request, assistant clubhouse manager Edward "Pookie" Jackson (who was still in Boston) had both home and road jerseys made featuring embroidered letters and numbers. Depending on where they played, the Red Sox hung the appropriate jersey in their dugout for every game over the balance of the season.

"There was always a hook or a pipe in the dugout where we could hang it—anything we could find," said McLaughlin, who always packed the jersey for the road games.

The message was clear: *We're thinking of you.* And Boston swept the three-game series.

Four days later, after the lockdown was safely lifted, the Red Sox returned to their home field. Like the Bruins, the Red Sox planned pregame ceremonies to honor first responders and those most affected by the tragedy, though the club took the additional step of having an active player address the home crowd at Fenway Park. Lucchino, for one, remembered a conversation with a friend who had served as team president of the then Washington Bullets, the NBA team now known as the Wizards. The woman frequently attended Opening Day at Fenway Park and, while speaking with Lucchino, expressed one criticism while praising the club for its most recent season-opening production:

She wanted to hear from a player. Lucchino considered the remark as the club planned to reopen Fenway Park for the first time since the bombing, and the player Lucchino wanted was an obvious choice: David Ortiz, nicknamed Big Papi, the man who had backboned two Red Sox championships and resurrected his career in Boston.

"And so we got David as the likely choice," Lucchino recalled. "I remember [Red Sox senior vice president of fan services] Sarah McKenna saying, 'Larry, if you want David to take a live mic and go out on the field or talk, the chances of him dropping an F-bomb are about 100 percent.' I laughed. We all laughed and said, "Sure, he'll be fine, Sarah, and don't worry about it.'"

Of course, Sarah McKenna was right.

In his brief comments to the crowd, Ortiz thanked many of the first responders, the Boston police, the mayor, the governor. Without a script, he spoke to the crowd and from the heart. Ortiz's authenticity was one of his greatest strengths as a person and a player, particularly as he grew into his career as a Red Sox great, a franchise savior. He understood who he was and what he was, and he possessed both compassion and empathy. Ortiz knew what others felt because he felt it himself, and he articulated the hurt and anger shared by an entire city because, ultimately, he felt the same things himself.

"This is our fucking city and nobody is going to dictate our freedom," Ortiz concluded, his words resonating with a Fenway Park crowd that erupted with delight. "Stay strong. Thank you."

In the weeks and years that followed, Ortiz's words became as synonymous with Boston's recovery as *Boston strong*, as the 617 jersey that hung in the Red Sox dugout, as the B STRONG logo the team fashioned from the emblem that decorated the team's classic navy blue cap and helped support the One Fund Boston, a charitable endeavor that provided aid to bombing victims and their families. An accomplished lifelong executive in professional sports, Lucchino called Ortiz's words "one of the most memorable moments in my career," an assessment that has been shared by countless Boston residents, notable or otherwise. "This is our fucking city" became a catchphrase, a source of strength, an approval to get up and fight back. The words forever etched themselves in the city's history, a modern-day version of "The British are coming," inspiring, ultimately, an entire population toward a singular goal:

Recovery.

* * *

The Bruins, by virtue of the calendar, had the first real chance at a championship in the aftermath of the Marathon bombing. And as the city steadied itself and began to rise, the Bruins made one of the great comebacks in hockey and sports history.

The first round of the NHL playoffs, unlike the early rounds in many other sports, can feature extraordinary upsets, something largely attributable to the nature of the game. In 2011, after all, the Stanley Cup champion Bruins had played three Game 7s, winning each of the first two by a single goal—one in overtime—and they could have been eliminated in the first round when a high-sticking penalty against the typically impeccable Patrice Bergeron opened the door for the Montreal Canadiens to score a game-tying goal in the final minutes of regulation. By the late spring of 2013, Bostonians knew quite well—in the arena or outside of it—that things could go awry at any instant.

At the end of the abbreviated 2012–13 regular season, the Bruins possessed the fifth-best record in the NHL. Their finish drew them a first-round meeting with the Toronto Maple Leafs, a franchise that was making its first playoff appearance in eight seasons and had failed to win a championship since 1967. The teams split the first two games in Boston before the Bruins won both Games 3 and 4 in Toronto, sending the series back to Boston with the Bruins holding a seemingly decisive 3-1 series edge with two of the final three games scheduled on home ice.

And then the series flipped. With a chance to close out the Leafs in Game 5, the Bruins were stymied by Leafs goaltender James Reimer, who anchored a 2-1 victory. In Game 6 back in Toronto, it was scoreless entering the third period before the Leafs again jumped in front, the game's first goal coming with 18:12 remaining when a wrist shot by Toronto's Nazem Kadri deflected into the net off teammate Dion Phaneuf, who had been stationed just to the left of Bruins goaltender Tuukka Rask. Slightly more than seven minutes later, former Bruins Phil Kessel collected a loose puck in front of the goal and flipped a backhander by Rask for a 2–0 Toronto lead.

The Bruins finally solved Reimer with twenty-six seconds left in the third period to make it 2–1, then frantically pressed in hopes of tying the score. In the final seconds, Bruins captain Zdeno Chara placed a pass squarely on the stick of teammate Bergeron, who fired a shot from just inside the blue line. But the shot was blocked, never reaching Reimer for what might have a been a dramatic game-tying goal. It would not be the final time that the Bruins cornerstone would find the puck on his stick at a most critical time.

With the series now locked at three games apiece, the teams returned to Boston for a decisive seventh game, the season on the line. The Bruins jumped to a 1–0 lead in the first period on a goal by Matt Bartkowski just 5:39 into play, the Leafs tying the score just under four minutes later on a power play strike by Cody Franson. It was Franson who struck again in the second period to give the Leafs a 2–1 advantage entering the third, when goals by Kessel and the detestable Kadri gave Toronto a whopping 4–1 advantage. The score remained unchanged as the teams approached the midway point of what seemed destined to be a disappointing end to the 2012–13 Bruins hockey season and, perhaps, the team's nucleus.

"At 4–1 with the clock winding down and half a period left, you start thinking to yourself, 'Is this the end of this group here?' Because it probably would have been if we didn't win this game," Bruins left wing Milan Lucic admitted after the game. "But you have to have bounces, you have to have luck, you have to have everything go your way—and that's basically what happened in the third period."

At least, from the perspective of the Bruins.

Entering the final eleven minutes of the third period, the Toronto Maple Leafs had effectively carried the play for the final three games of the series. From the start of Game 5, the Bruins had led for only three minutes and fifty-six seconds. Reimer had been impenetrable, stopping ninety of ninety-three Bruins shots, a sterling save percentage of .968. And in Game 7, through almost fifty minutes, the Bruins had seemed remarkably lifeless, managing just seventeen shots against Reimer.

With 10:42 to play, Nathan Horton scored from just inside the left face-off circle, but the Bruins still trailed by two goals, and time was dwindling. Reimer, in fact, stopped the next seven Bruins shots, leaving the Bruins with a two-goal deficit as the game entered the final two minutes. With little choice, Julien pulled Rask from the net in favor of an additional skater, leaving the Boston goal unguarded. The Bruins entered the Toronto zone before Chara fired a shot that Reimer deflected into the corner to his right, where David Krejci collected it and sent it back to left point, where Bergeron was stationed. Bergeron subsequently slid a pass to Chara, who promptly fired again—a one-timer, as hockey fans call it, that Reimer again saved. But the rebound trickled directly in front of the net, where a well-positioned Lucic quickly hammered it into the top of the net, making the score 4–3.

Almost instantly, as teammates congregated around him to briefly celebrate the strike, Lucic glanced quickly at the TD Garden scoreboard to look at the game clock, which showed 1:22 remaining.

We still have a chance. There's still time.

They didn't need much. Slightly less than 32 seconds later, with 50.2 seconds remaining, the Bruins had won the ensuing face-off, reentered the Toronto zone, and scored again. This time the Bruins moved the puck along the top of the perimeter in front of Reimer, from the right-wing side to the left. Jaromir Jagr, an acquisition at the trading deadline, sent the pass near the center of the blue line, manned by Bergeron, who fed it Krejci, positioned near the face-off circle on the left-wing side. Krejci deftly reversed the flow, sending the pass back to Bergeron, who drifted toward his right, back toward the middle of the ice, before flicking a wrist shot back toward his left, against the grain, to Reimer's right.

This time, unlike in Game 6, Bergeron's shot made it through the cluster of bodies without being blocked. As the puck pierced the goal to the right of a screened Reimer, the Leafs sagged and the TD Garden erupted. The game was tied at 4.

In overtime and to no one's surprise, the Leafs completed their historic collapse—and the Bruins their historic awakening. Just under six minutes into the extra session, after Leafs goalie Reimer steered away a Tyler Seguin shot, Bruins winger Brad Marchand collected the puck in the corner to the goalie's left and fed Bergeron, who immediately fired the puck on net. Reimer made the initial stop, but once again he failed to smother any potential rebound, allowing the puck to drop in front of him. In the ensuing scramble among skates and sticks, the puck dribbled back toward Bergeron, who lifted it over the sprawled-out goalie and into the empty net, ending yet another Toronto season in fruitless fashion and delivering the Bruins into the second round of the playoffs. As a stunned Reimer lay on his belly, Bruins radio voice Dave Goucher led an ecstatic audience in memorializing the most memorable moment of Bergeron's career.

"Bergeron! Bergeron! In Game 7! And the Bruins win the series!"

Just like that, on May 13, 2013, the Bruins were alive and well. Less than a month after the Marathon bombings, Boston was celebrating its black and gold.

* * *

Back in the regular season, Bruins General manager Peter Chiarelli was think-ing about the post season and how to improve the roster. Chiarelli had his eyes set on a big fish: forward Jarome Iginla.

A native of Edmonton and a career member of the Calgary Flames, Iginla was team captain and a surefire Hall of Famer, the franchise's ver-sion of longtime Bruins defenseman and standout Raymond Bourque. Iginla had delivered Calgary most everything he could during a stellar sixteen-year career—production, toughness, leadership, dignity—save for one thing: a Stanley Cup. But as Iginla approached his thirty-sixth birthday and the end of a contract with a Flames organization about to miss the postseason for a fourth consecutive year, he and the Flames had agreed to trade him away from the only professional organization he had ever played for, a decision that could serve both them and him mutually.

The Bruins were perfectly positioned to pounce. Seeking to reinforce a forward group that had underperformed due to the inconsistency of phe-nom Tyler Seguin, the Bruins negotiated a deal with the Flames just before the March 28 deadline that the club believed would deliver Iginla to Boston in exchange for defenseman Matt Bartkowski, minor-league forward Alex Khokhlachev, and a first-round draft pick. According to Chiarelli, the teams agreed to the deal at roughly midday on March 27, the talks so advanced that the clubs removed involved players from their scheduled games that night for fear of injuries or developments that could undermine the trade, as was customary in such situations.

Hours later, after Chiarelli's calls to Calgary general manager Jay Feaster had gone unanswered, the Flames surprisingly dealt Iginla to the Pittsburgh Penguins, the top seed in the Eastern Conference playoffs and one of the Bruins' chief rivals. On the following day, March 28, Chiarelli held a rather embar-rassing press conference in which he had to explain how and why Iginla had slipped through his fingers.

"We were informed around noon [on the twenty-seventh] that we had the player," Chiarelli said. "[Feaster] just had to speak to Jarome and his agent regarding the logistics of everything." Roughly twelve hours later, Feaster called Chiarelli and informed the Bruins GM that Iginla had implemented his right to name his destination, "that it was the player's choice, [that] he opted to go to Pittsburgh and we were out."

Just like that, as the saying goes, Chiarelli and the Bruins were left with their dicks in their hands. They regrouped and traded a lesser collection of players and a first-round pick to the Dallas Stars for Jaromir Jagr, a former league star who was now forty-one years old and something far less attractive: a consolation prize.

Whoever the true culprit was, ultimately Chiarelli, Feaster, and Iginla all deserved at least some blame in a he-said-she-said soap opera that left feelings and reputations damaged, on the ice and off. Iginla could hardly be criticized for choosing the Bruins *or* the Penguins, both of whom were legitimate contenders for the championship. Pittsburgh was built around the supremely talented Sidney Crosby and Evgeni Malkin, the former arguably the league's most recognizable talent. And in 2010, as a member of Team Canada, Crosby had scored what became known as the "golden goal," an overtime strike against the United States that delivered his country the gold medal in a fabulous Olympic tournament hosted in Vancouver.

The player who made the pass to Crosby for the historic tally? Jarome Iginla.

"I knew Pittsburgh was in the mix with Boston and they're both amazing cities, very successful organizations and great teams," Iginla said at the press conference that announced both the trade and his departure from Calgary. "When it comes down to the choice that I had, one or the other, it's really hard as a player to pass up the opportunity to play on a team with Sid and Malkin."

As fate would have it, the teams consequently embarked on a collision course that delivered each to the Eastern Conference finals. The high-powered Penguins advanced there with series wins over the New York Islanders (in six games) and Ottawa Senators (in five), scoring a whopping forty-seven goals in eleven games. The Bruins, after their comeback against the Maple Leafs, subsequently wiped out the New York Rangers in five games, limiting the opposition to just ten goals in the series.

The Eastern Conference Finals, as such, felt like the irresistible force of Pittsburgh's offense against the immovable object of Boston's defense, all circling around Jarome Iginla's decision to back out of his wedding with the Bruins to run off with Crosby. Feeling very much as though they were jilted at the altar, the Bruins responded with an unsurprising vengeance. *Hell hath no fury like a Bruin scorned.*

In a series that many foresaw lasting the maximum seven games, the Bruins completely smothered and suffocated the favored and high-powered

Penguins, never giving so much as an inch. Pittsburgh lost by scores of 3–0, 6–1, 2–1 (in double overtime), and 1–0, managing just two goals in the series. Goaltender Tuukka Rask stopped an incredible 134 of 136 shots for an unfathomable .985 save percentage in his best performance as a member of the Bruins—the Bruins clamping down on Pittsburgh with such consistency and commitment that it seemed, well, *personal.*

No play more perfectly demonstrated the Bruins' relentlessness than a blocked shot by defensive-minded forward Gregory Campbell, who, during a penalty kill, slid to the ice and extended his legs to block a slapshot by the six-foot-three Malkin with just under eight minutes to play in the second period of a 1–1 tie in Game 3. Over the next minute, Campbell struggled to get to his feet, picked up one of his gloves, and hobbled around on one leg to help the Bruins hold off a lethal Pittsburgh power play unit, then labored off the ice, never to return to the series. Malkin's blast had broken the Bruin's leg.

For the series, incredibly, the trio of Crosby (minus 2), Malkin (minus 5), and Iginla (minus 4) were all held scoreless. And while the Bruins generally chose their words tactfully and carefully, the message was clear.

"First off, he's a great player. He's a legend, he's a future Hall of Famer, and I think looking back at that day, he earned the right to make the decision that he made. You can never blame a guy for going with his heart and making that type of decision. I'm not going to insult him in any way," said Bruins forward Milan Lucic, a power forward whose game was modeled after players like Bruins president Cam Neely and, for that matter, Iginla. "He's a guy that I always looked up to as a teenager and seeing the way that he played. As a Canadian, seeing what he did in the Olympics and all that type of stuff, he's definitely an idol of mine. But like I said, he earned that right to make the decision that he made. I'm sure if he could go back he would make a different decision, but in saying that, he's still a great player, he's got a few more years ahead of him, and you wish him nothing but the best."

Nonetheless, the Bruins felt slighted.

"We kind of took it that way, in that sense that when a guy chooses another team over your team, it kind of does light a little bit of a fire underneath you," Lucic admitted. "Fortunately, we were able to turn it into a positive more than a negative."

Said a far less cryptic David Krejci, a native Czech: "We may not have the biggest stars in the world. We may not have the best players in the world. But we may have the best team in the world."

As for Iginla, a highly respected player, his actions, too, spoke louder than his words. The defeat once again left him within only viewing distance of a Stanley Cup. He managed just five shots on goal in the entire series and spent more time in the penalty box (two minutes) than on the score sheet. Iginla said he was "very fortunate to get the chance to come to [Pittsburgh]," that he was seeking to win a championship, that the Penguins "had that chance." He was grateful for the opportunity to play with Crosby and cast no shade whatsoever on the Bruins.

"The Bruins, they played very well, they're a very good team," he said. "I was fortunate to have that choice."

As a pending free agent, Iginla would soon have another choice: the right to pick a new team again for the next phase of his career in his never-ending pursuit of a championship. And this time he chose Boston. But before that would happen, the Bruins moved on with the hopes of winning another Stanley Cup—their second in three years—without him.

* * *

Whether Jarome Iginla would have made a difference in the 2013 Stanley Cup finals is debatable and largely pointless, but it is entirely reasonable to wonder. For the second time in three years, after all, the Bruins would meet a team from the Western Conference that was indisputably the best in hockey during the regular season and that dominated opponents at both ends of the ice. The difference was that the Chicago Blackhawks were smack dab in the middle of a virtual dynasty.

And unlike the high-powered Pittsburgh Penguins, the Blackhawks were dominant in all facets of play, ranking second in the NHL in scoring and first in overall defense. And in the metric that defined the success of the 2011 Bruins team that won the Stanley Cup—five-on-five play—the Blackhawks ranked first in the league by a significant margin. Simply put, the Chicago Blackhawks of the early 2010s were a juggernaut from top to bottom, a team with speed and skill, not to mention a toughness and resiliency that the 2011 Vancouver Canucks had lacked.

True to form, the Blackhawks showed their grit in Game 1, overcoming a 3–1 deficit with two goals in the final twelve minutes of the third period to force overtime. The teams played deep into the night, through most of a third over-time period, before Chicago defenseman Michal Rozsival flipped an otherwise harmless wrist shot from the right point that changed direction twice—first off the stick of Blackhawks forward Dave Bolland (remember the name), then off the leg of forward Andrew Shaw—to snake its way behind goaltender Tuukka Rask, hockey's version of the magic bullet.

For Bruins fans, the defeat immediately evoked memories of the club's triple-overtime loss to the Edmonton Oilers in Game 1 of the 1990 Stanley Cup finals. To their credit, the 2012–13 Bruins responded—and on Chicago's ice—even after Chicago's Patrick Sharp extended the momentum from the previous night by giving the Blackhawks a 1–0 lead midway through the first period of Game 2. The Bruins tied the score in the second on a goal by Chris Kelly before the teams again went to overtime, when a rare defensive failure by the Blackhawks—forward Brandon Bollig whiffed on a chance to clear the puck out of the Chicago zone—allowed Bruins defenseman Adam McQuaid to keep the puck in the Chicago zone and shuttle it to forward Tyler Seguin along the right-wing boards. Seguin swiftly advanced the puck toward the center of the ice and teammate Daniel Paille, who whipped a labeled wrister past the glove of goaltender Corey Crawford and into the top corner, giving the Bruins a 2–1 victory and locking the series at 1.

The Bruins and the Blackhawks had played the equivalent of more than three games in two nights—slightly more than nine periods—and were dead even in games, 1-1, and goals, 5-5.

When the series returned to Boston, the Bruins picked up right where they left off, Rask continuing to play at a high level in a 2–0 Boston victory during which the Bruins scored twice in the second period. Two years after Tim Thomas did the proverbial handstands and backflips to carry the Bruins to the championship over Vancouver, Rask was in the midst of an otherworldly stretch during which he was virtually unbeatable. Beginning with Boston's clinching Game 5 victory in its second-round series against the New York Rangers, Rask had gone 7-1 over an eight-game stretch against some of the best offenses in hockey, stopping an incredible 282 of 290 shots for a save percentage of .972. His only defeat had come in the triple-overtime Game 1 loss, when Chicago's game-winning goal bounced and ricocheted as if negotiating its way down a Plinko board. The Game 1 loss, after all, had been the equivalent of *two* games in length, helping to put Rask's goals against average during the stretch at a microscopic 0.83.

Asked if his goalie's play was at all comparable to the performance of Thomas only two years earlier, Julien did not hesitate. "I think it's just as good. No doubt. Tim has been a great goaltender for us. When you lose a guy like that, there's always that fear that you're not going to be able to replace him," Julien said of Thomas, who had chosen to sit out the 2012–13 season to spend time with his family. "Tuukka's done an outstanding job. To me, he's been as much of a contributor to our team as Tim was two years ago."

Beginning in Game 4, Rask's play began to slip some, though much of that had to do with the resolve and fortitude of the Blackhawks. Built around the nucleus of center Jonathan Toews, winger Patrick Kane, and defensemen Duncan Keith and Brent Seabrook, the Blackhawks over their championship years proved capable of rubbing out opponents—to borrow a phrase from the film *Secretariat*—with the closing speed and power of a freight train. Peculiarly, the team had a rather poor history in Game 3s, having lost the third game in all four of their 2013 playoff series. While Chicago coach Joel Quenneville had been asked about the odd pattern prior to his team's Game 3 loss to Boston, there was little attention placed on the resilient, dominating fashion in which Chicago had responded to those defeats.

Faced with the prospect of a 3–1 series deficit, the Blackhawks never trailed in Game 4, putting a half dozen pucks past Rask in a pivotal 6–5 victory that sent the Finals back to Chicago all square at two games apiece. The final goal of Game 4 once again came in overtime, defenseman Seabrook blasting a slapper along the ice, just past Rask's right pad and inside the right post, after an elusive puck bounced around the Boston zone. In Chicago, the Bruins once again played without ever holding a lead, Chicago taking a 2–0 edge into the third period. The Bruins closed to 2–1 on a goal by Zdeno Chara before Bolland scored an empty-net goal with a pulled Rask watching from the bench, giving Chicago a 3–1 victory that also swung the series advantage back to Chicago, three games to two.

For the Bruins, there was little or no shame in having the series flip. But the regrets would come in the final seconds of Game 6.

In the final game of the schedule-shortened 2012–13 NHL season, the Bruins almost never trailed. The Bruins held leads of 1–0 and 2–1, the latter coming courtesy of Milan Lucic, who hammered a puck past Corey Crawford with 7:49 to go in the third period. The Bruins held the lead into the final two minutes, of a seemingly destined for a winner-take-all Game 7 in Chicago when the Blackhawks did precisely what the Bruins had done weeks earlier against Toronto, pulling their goalie in a last-gasp attempt to avoid defeat.

With 1:16 left, the Blackhawks won a battle along the boards to the right of Rask, Toews ultimate feeding Bryan Bickell directly in front of the Boston goal, from where Bickell pushed a puck between the legs of a sliding Rask to tie the game at 2. And then, incredibly, just seventeen seconds later and with the Bruins seemingly deflated, Bolland—there's that name again—collected a loose rebound to Rask's right, between Bruins defensemen Ference and Johnny Boychuk, and snapped another puck past the Boston goalie for a 3–2 Chicago lead with 58.3 seconds left in the game.

For the first time all night, the Bruins trailed, and the Blackhawks did what they did best: they closed. In the final 58.3 seconds, the Bruins failed to manage even a shot on goal. Chicago's 3–2 victory handed the Blackhawks their second Stanley Cup during a run that ultimately produced three championships in six seasons, validating their place as the preeminent team in the sport. A shortened regular season had done nothing to tarnish Lord Stanley's cherished Cup. The Blackhawks, in fact, had started the forty-eight-game schedule with the greatest start in NHL history going 21-0-3 in their first twenty-four games, their only three defeats coming in overtime—a positively mind-numbing accomplishment in a game played on a contained sheet of ice, inside boards, with sticks and a rubber puck. They finished the forty-eight-game regular season schedule with just seven losses in regulation. During the postseason, when the stakes were highest, Chicago had gone an eye-popping 10-1 in Games 4 to 7 of their four series, going 6-0 in elimination games. Simply put, the 2012–13 Blackhawks were one of the great teams of all time, an insanely talented collection of tough, talented players in the primes of their careers, at the top of their game.

But the abrupt end was just one of many reasons the Bruins felt unfulfilled.

"Although we needed to focus on our team and doing what was going to be the best thing for our team to win a Stanley Cup, in the back of our minds we wanted to do it for those kind of reasons: the City of Boston," said Julien. "[The Marathon bombings] hit close to home, and the best way we felt we could try and cheer [up] the area was to win a Stanley Cup. I think that's what's hard right now for the players. We had more reasons than just ourselves to win a Cup."

Nonetheless, in some ways, the Bruins had accomplished what they had set out to do. They had been the first team to return to the arena in the wake of the attacks. Over the next ten weeks they had captivated the region with the kind of selfless run that might have produced a championship against a team less dominant than the Blackhawks. They executed a miraculous comeback against the Maple Leafs and dismantled the Rangers. They had avenged the jilting by Iginla. They had made the necessary physical sacrifices to win, from Gregory Campbell's broken leg in Game 3 of the Pittsburgh series to the news that cornerstone Bergeron, after leaving Game 5 with an early injury, had played Game 6 with, among other things, a broken rib, torn cartilage, a separated shoulder, and a small hole in his lung.

"You've got to give credit to Chicago. They played a great series, but that's the last thing you want to say," Bergeron said. "It hurts to see them hoisting the Cup. There's not many words that can be said right now. It's definitely tough to lose, especially at this time after everything we've been through. There's not many words. It's tough."

Even then, for the Bruins and for Boston both, there was reason for optimism. In three years, the Bruins had been to two Stanley Cup finals and won a championship with a roster that seemed poised for a long run. Forward Tyler Seguin and defenseman Dougie Hamilton, acquired with two high draft picks in the blockbuster deal that had sent the enigmatic Phil Kessel to Toronto, were budding stars. Rask was one of the best young goalies in hockey. The Bruins seemed positioned for the kind of extended run that would almost certainly produce more chances at titles for a city that was collecting them en masse.

But then, for lots of reasons, 2013 had proven to be, to put it mildly, unpredictable. Soon after the loss to the Blackhawks, the Bruins made a series of stunning decisions that significantly altered their course.

The good news?

Boston had something else far more immediate and exhilarating to focus on—and that was yet another run at a championship.

CHAPTER 10

BOSTON RISES

"I loved playing baseball. I'm more of a participant as opposed to a
spectator—and with good reason. When I was playing [for the Bruins],
I wouldn't mind going to a few [Red Sox] games a year—afternoon
games—and stay for about four innings. And that was good enough for
me. [Laughs.] I just love the atmosphere of an afternoon game."
—Cam Neely, former Bruins player and current team president

THE ORIGINAL GOAL FOR THE 2013 Red Sox was to be respectable
again, to regain some dignity, to simply get back on their feet. After the
chicken-and-beer debacle that defined the end of the 2011 season, the 2012
campaign rapidly deteriorated under the watch of egomaniacal manager Bobby
Valentine, whose hiring prompted former Red Sox pitcher Curt Schilling, on
the *first day* of that season, to liken the team to the *Titanic*. The prediction
was shared by many—and made Red Sox ownership and management look out
of touch and downright foolish when the club was forced to sell off pieces and
deconstruct the roster when things went sideways.

During the off-season between 2012 and 2013, metaphorically speaking,
the Red Sox effectively entered rehab. They stopped drinking and lost weight.
They cleaned up their act. They got a job and went to work, putting in place
building blocks for a simple but rewarding existence. Then they hit the lottery.

Whether the Red Sox deserved it was a question of perspective, with strong
arguments to be made on both sides. On the one hand, during an eighty-six-year
drought without a World Series championship, the Red Sox had paid their dues,
endured some crushing failures and bad luck; in their four World Series trips
between 1918 and 2004—1946, 1967, 1975, and 1986—the Sox had gone to a

seventh game before losing. On the other hand, from 2011 to 2012, the entire organization had what felt like a psychotic break, everyone from ownership to the players, even the fans, engaging in seemingly self-destructive behavior while completely losing touch with reality.

The hiring of Bobby Valentine was the culmination of that period, a decision that Lucchino at least partly regrets. A former major-league player who had risen to prominence as a manager, Valentine was a bright and skilled game manager who had a reputation of playing head games. Listed generously at five-foot-ten, he also had a Napoleon complex. Valentine craved attention and got plenty while taking the New York Mets to the 2000 World Series against the New York Yankees, but he had all but vanished from baseball for a decade when Lucchino, with whom he had developed a relationship over the years, came calling between the 2011 and 2012 seasons.

Amid the turmoil of the Red Sox collapse in 2011, the idea was flawed on multiple levels. With the departures of both manager Terry Francona and general manager Theo Epstein, the Red Sox needed stability. Ownership's choice to replace Epstein was an internal candidate, the likable and understated Ben Cherington, who actually preceded even Epstein in the organization as a hire of former Red Sox GM Dan Duquette. One of Cherington's first tasks was to find a manager, and he had seemingly settled on former Red Sox coach Dale Sveum, a former Francona assistant who had been wildly popular with players and all but revered for his baseball acumen.

What Sveum lacked was a dynamic personality that would translate with fans and media, something of great concern to ownership and upper management, particularly following the departure of the personable Francona. Sveum ended up with the Chicago Cubs—Epstein hired him—and the Red Sox turned to Valentine, whose showmanship was a horrible match for a team and city that had recently experienced far too much drama.

"We didn't hire him until December 2011, as I remember, because we were . . . things were a little—what's the right word?—askew," club president Lucchino said years later. "There was a lot of change, a lot of transition. And we had looked at a number of other managers as well. I think what happened to Bobby is that—this is my personal opinion—is that some people spoiled the well before he got there. Some people told the players that he was the wrong guy, had the wrong attitude and all of that—and he might have been, I don't know. As it turned out, it was only a one-year experiment."

As such, the 2012 Red Sox pretty much died in the lab.

Roughly a week after Valentine's hiring, according to Lucchino, the Red Sox held their annual Christmas party, an event at which Valentine served as a bartender. If the move seemed gimmicky, it further exacerbated the notion that Valentine was a used-car salesman, however truly bright he was. Valentine's tenure with the Mets had generally been a success, after all, but every major-league organization effectively steered clear of him in the aftermath, unwilling to take on the challenges that came with him. To call Valentine's reputation "toxic" would have been far too strong, but he was generally perceived as a know-it-all whose arrogance was a divisive force.

Less than two weeks into the schedule, when Valentine offered criticism of Sox struggling star Kevin Youkilis—"I don't think he's as physically or emotionally into the game as he has been in the past for some reason"—the comment caused an immediate crisis. Sox second baseman Dustin Pedroia immediately came to Youkilis's defense—"I don't know what Bobby's trying to do, but that's not how we go about our stuff here," said the respected second baseman—and immediately exposed the chasm that existed between Valentine and the roster. Whatever fractures that existed in 2011 had only grown wider, it seemed, with Red Sox players demanding that their new manager adapt to them rather than the other way around.

While the Red Sox played better for a short time—they went 18-12 over a thirty-game stretch after starting the season 4-10—Valentine and the 2012 Red Sox never really had a chance. Valentine was still taking jabs at Youkilis weeks after the initial incident—"I don't think he ever wanted to get over it"—and the Red Sox played much of the year as if in a catatonic state, hovering near .500 through the July 31 non-waiver trading deadline. The team subsequently went 6-15 over the next twenty-one games to begin a season-ending spiral that left them at 69-93, going a miserable 16-42 over the final fifty-eight games to finish in last place, a whopping twenty-three games out of first place for a roster that, again, Boston had only a year earlier billed as arguably the greatest team in club history. The *Titanic* had sunk, doomed from the start.

"I just wish he had had a better and longer chance to prove himself," Lucchino said of Valentine many years later, in 2021, before repeating, "Maybe he wasn't the right guy at that time."

For Lucchino and the Red Sox there were two silver linings, the first of which was a blockbuster trade with the Los Angeles Dodgers on August 25 that allowed the Red Sox to shed some massive contracts, most notably in the form of pitcher Josh Beckett, outfielder Carl Crawford, and first baseman Adrian

Gonzalez, the last of whom was the Dodgers' true focus in the deal. While the Red Sox had received a pair of minor-league pitchers in the deal—Allen Webster and Rubby De La Rosa, though neither amounted to anything—the club miraculously shed more than a quarter-*billion* dollars in salary commitments through 2018, effectively clearing the way for a reconstruction of a roster and franchise that had completely imploded. In the trade with the Dodgers—a move for which Lucchino was largely credited—they had found a lifeboat.

And for the first time in a long time at Fenway Park, the skies were at least clear.

* * *

This time, instead of Bobby Valentine, the Red Sox chose someone far more familiar and appealing to the entire operation: John Farrell, a former pitching coach and trusted friend of Terry Francona who had gone on to manage the Toronto Blue Jays. Because Farrell was under contract with Toronto, the Red Sox orchestrated a trade to effectively negotiate Farrell out of his agreement with the Jays. The negotiation understandably angered many Torontonians, who felt like Farrell had been carrying on an affair with an old girlfriend almost immediately after proposing marriage. But in Boston, John Farrell and the Red Sox were both celebrating a rebirth.

The Red Sox made a succession of free-agent signings that included outfielder Shane Victorino, first baseman Mike Napoli, outfielder Jonny Gomes, and shortstop Stephen Drew, a collection of blue-collar players who, while lacking superstar-level talent, would show up for work, take their jobs seriously, and grind out their share of wins. Altogether, the 2013 Red Sox were a promise to *try*, the first step in winning back the public trust.

By the end of the season, they would become the rarest of Boston baseball clubs, a group that would match even a respected hockey team for its grit, togetherness, resiliency, and resolve. In the wake of the Marathon Bombings, even more than the black-and-gold Bruins, the 2013 Red Sox would become the symbol of Boston's recovery, a team with tough, competitive players who, over the course of their playing careers, had shown an ability to persist through inevitable black-and-blues.

Plain and simple, the 2013 Red Sox were fighters.

Nonetheless, there was question about the Red Sox ability to sustain such a workmanlike approach over a 162-game season with no real breaks. As much as the Red Sox inspired their fan base with dugout tributes and David Ortiz's vocabulary, there was serious question as to whether they could last an entire season that was often likened to . . . well, a marathon. Boston surged to a 20-8 record during April and early May then promptly lost six of seven and nine of eleven during what seemed like water inevitably finding its level.

But even then, in retrospect, the Red Sox demonstrated a steadfastness that would serve them well. In that 2-9 streak, the Red Sox never lost more than three straight. Those two victories, while seemingly insignificant in the big picture, allowed the Red Sox to at least temporarily catch their collective breath before ducking below the surface again, like a skilled swimmer seeking to tread water while trying to collect himself. Beyond that, it was a sign of their persistence: the Red Sox were the only major-league team that would not lose more than three consecutive games all year.

For that, the Red Sox had some star power to thank, most notably in the form of pitchers Jon Lester and John Lackey, two of the identified culprits from the chicken-and-beer bunch of 2011. But with former staff ace Josh Beckett now in Los Angeles, Lester, in particular, blossomed into the staff ace and leader the Red Sox had long envisioned. The same was true of Lackey, who had missed the entire 2012 debacle recovering from Tommy John surgery, after which he posted a 3.52 ERA in 189.1 innings covering twenty-nine starts, easily his best year as a member of the Red Sox. The two backboned a Red Sox staff that finished a respectable sixth in the American League in pitching and an even better fourth in ERA among starting pitchers.

And so, as May turned to June, then July and beyond, a curious thing happened: the Red Sox remained in contention. While some ever-cynical Bostonians waited for the team's demise . . . a real downturn never came. Less than a year after the fire sale, general manager Ben Cherington added pitching help at the trading deadline in the form of right-hander Jake Peavy, a veteran whose skills were diminishing but whose mentality and grit made him a perfect fit for the 2013 club.

After having fallen out of first place in the American League just briefly before the trade deadline, the Red Sox never again lost at least a share of the top spot in the American League East. Tied for the division lead on the morning of August 24, the Red Sox sprinted from the field, going 17-4 over a twenty-one-game stretch to open up a whopping nine-and-a-half-game lead over the second-place Tampa Bay Rays with just eleven games to play. Less than a week later, the Red Sox posted a 6–3 victory over the Toronto Blue Jays—the team Farrell left in the lurch—to clinch the division title and earn the team's first playoff appearance in four years.

For both an organization that needed rehabilitating and a city that needed rescuing, the Red Sox had accomplished a great deal.

"It's a great night," said left-hander Jon Lester, the appropriate starter and winner for the division clincher. "All the guys that have been here the last three years have been through a lot of ups and downs and downs and ups. I hope those guys really let this soak in, sit back and enjoy it."

Said newcomer Gomes, aware that a large segment of a still-skeptical Red Sox fan base was reluctant to believe what it was witnessing: "There is room on the bandwagon if people want to jump on."

Slightly more than a week later, the Red Sox wrapped up the regular season with a 97-65 record, tied with the St. Louis Cardinals for the best in baseball. Boston would have home field advantage over the Tampa Bay Rays in the first-round American League Division Series.

In Boston, the 2013 baseball season was about to morph from a marathon into a sprint. And regardless of whether there were still empty seats, the bandwagon was rolling, full steam ahead.

* * *

From the very beginning, October 2013 belonged to David Americo Ortiz, the Reggie Jackson of his era, Señor Octobre. As much as the 2013 Red Sox were a collection of blue-collar, workmanlike players who rebuilt their careers, a franchise, and the self-esteem of their city, October belonged to their single biggest superstar. If something good happened for Boston in October, Ortiz was almost certainly in the middle of it.

Facing the Tampa Bay Rays in the Division Series, Boston opened the playoffs with a resounding 12–2 victory in Game 1 at Fenway Park, scoring eight runs in successive fourth- and fifth-inning rallies against Tampa lefty Matt Moore, behind whom the Rays had gone a sparkling 21-6 in his twenty-seven starts during the regular season. Game 2 essentially produced more of the same, the Red Sox piercing Tampa lefty David Price for seven runs and two homers in a 7-4 Boston victory that immediately pushed the Rays to the edge of elimination.

Both Boston home runs in the game were hit by—who else?—Ortiz, who stuck Price with solo shots in the first and eighth innings, effectively serving as bookends to the Boston victory. The second chased Price from the game and made him 0-4 with a 5.81 ERA in four career postseason starts, forging a reputation that the reigning AL Cy Young Award winner was a man who shrunk in the biggest moments.

After the game, Price took particular exception with the second home run, a towering blast down the right-field line that curved around the right-field foul pole at Fenway Park. Sensitive to a fault, Price believed that Ortiz spent an inordinate amount of time watching the home run, a violation of what he perceived to be baseball etiquette.

"He steps in the bucket and he hits a homer, and he stares at it to see if it's fair or foul—I'm sure that's what he'd say," a perturbed Price sneered after the game. "But as soon as he hit it and I saw it, I knew it was fair. Run."

To make matters worse, Price subsequently went on a diatribe on social media, calling out postgame television analysts Dirk Hayhurst and Tom Verducci, the former a onetime major league pitcher, the latter one of the most respected reporters in baseball. While the criticisms of Price were mild at best—Hayhurst, for one, indicated Price should have been out of the game by the time Ortiz hit his second home run, as the Red Sox had already scored six runs—Price erupted on Twitter, telling the world that Hayhurst "couldn't hack it" as a major-league pitcher and that Verducci "wasn't even a water boy in high school," lamenting that both were still allowed to "bash a player." Price's conclusion? "SAVE IT NERDS," he tweeted in all caps.

By the time the series shifted to Tampa for Games 3 and 4, Price has issued an apology on Twitter and spoken to Ortiz, who was nothing if not gracious. Ortiz said that he and Price "straightened things out" and maintained that he had "a lot of respect" for the pitcher, emphasizing that he was "not going to make a big deal out of this." The matter was hardly dead forever—Price hit Ortiz with a pitch the first time he faced him the following spring, prompting the benches for both teams to empty, and an irate Ortiz to tell reporters, "Next time he hits me he better bring the [boxing] gloves"—but in the 2013 playoffs, as it was, the two would not square off again. While Tampa won Game 3, the Red Sox closed out the series with a 3–1 victory in Game 4. Despite a good outing by newcomer Peavy, the Red Sox trailed 1–0 entering the seventh when they scraped together a pair of runs on a wild pitch and a groundout. The Red Sox then added a run in the ninth before closer Koji Uehara set down the Rays in order, delivering Boston to the ALCS for the first time in five years.

Said Peavy after the victory, "When I got here, I just saw a fight that I've never seen in a team. I saw a willingness to prepare and a willingness to absolutely, no matter what the situation, to never quit."

And so the journey to redemption continued, the refrain as clear as ever. *Boston Strong.*

Despite those intangibles, and despite winning more games in the regular season than their opponents, the Detroit Tigers, the Red Sox were seen as underdogs in the second round. The Tigers were in their third straight ALCS, and they'd gone to the World Series the previous year—though they had been swept by a San Francisco Giants that would win three championships over the span of five seasons.

The general feeling in baseball was that the Tigers were the class of the league—and there really was no arguing it. The Tigers had absolutely dominant starting pitching built around the trio of Justin Verlander, Max Scherzer, and Anibal Sanchez, three hard-throwing right-handers who had led all American League rotations in a range of key categories ranging from ERA to innings to strikeouts, and the lineup featured the mountainous Miguel Cabrera, who won the prestigious Triple Crown in 2012 and whose 2013 season was even better.

There was, in short, nothing overly fancy about the Tigers. Their horses were just bigger than yours, and manager Jim Leyland rode their studs from the start of the ALCS, winning Game 1 by a 1–0 score on a night when Detroit pitchers combined for a remarkable seventeen strikeouts. The Red Sox did not manage a single hit until Daniel Nava singled against closer Joaquín Benoit with one out in the ninth inning. It was a series-opening statement that immediately put the Red Sox on their heels. Boston had led the American League in runs scored, after all, and had opened the ALDS by pounding the Tampa Bay Rays mercilessly. But against the Tigers, the Red Sox were completely neutered and hardly managed a whimper.

"Whether it was Sanchez or whoever they brought out of the bullpen, it was power stuff," said a blunt John Farrell, the Red Sox manager.

And in Game 2, the Tigers brought more of it. Picking up precisely where Sanchez and his bullpen left off, right-hander Max Scherzer began Game 2 for Detroit by striking out a pair of Red Sox in the first inning, two more in the second, three in the third. The Red Sox did not manage a hit against him until the sixth inning, when a two-out single by Shane Victorino and an ensuing double by Dustin Pedroia—two of Boston's grittiest hitters—plated their first run of the series. Even so, the one-two punch served as little more than an aberrant flurry in a fight during which the Red Sox were getting manhandled, the Tigers having already built a 5–0 lead. Immediately after Pedroia's double made it 5–1, Scherzer struck out the imposing Ortiz on four pitches to end the threat, then opened the seventh with whiffs of Mike Carp and Jonny Gomes. Jarrod Saltalamacchia followed with a groundout, at which point Scherzer walked off the Fenway Park mound with a 5–1 lead and Detroit with a mountain of evidence to suggest that the Red Sox simply did not have the firepower to fend off Detroit's relentless pitching staff.

To that point of the series, the Red Sox had sent sixty batters to the plate over the span of sixteen innings and had managed just three hits and one run. Incredibly, they had struck out an astonishing thirty times, an average of nearly twice per inning, a pace that was incredibly rare at the major-league level: those were Little League or video game numbers, not what you'd expect in October. But Detroit was doing so in assembly-line fashion, with Tigers pitchers cutting down the Red Sox as if simply passing a sickle from one pitcher to the next.

Facing the prospect of a 2–0 series deficit with Games 3, 4, and 5 scheduled in Detroit, Boston's fortunes suddenly looked bleak. The Red Sox, like the Bruins earlier that year, might have simply run into a better team.

* * *

Comebacks in sports are relatively common, which is to say that every team, in every sport, has them at some point of every season. The deficits can be small or large, the games meaningful or ultimately inconsequential. But rare is the comeback that alters the course of history, in the short term or the long, and that can spin an entire storyline with little warning or foreshadowing.

The Bruins had one in Game 7 against the Maples Leafs, trailing by three goals halfway through the final period in what had otherwise been a lifeless performance; they nearly used that game as a springboard to a Stanley Cup championship. In the 2008 NBA Finals, the Celtics' comeback in Game 4 at Los Angeles changed the series entirely, a championship inevitable with two of the remaining three games in Boston. And during the extraordinary twenty-year run that made Boston the center of the professional sports universe, the Patriots, too, would soon have their own historic comeback. The Red Sox, for their part, had the 2004 American League Championship Series to point to, facing a 3–0 series deficit while simultaneously trailing Game 4 by a 4–3 score in the eighth inning at Fenway Park when the scales tipped ever so slightly in their favor and delivered them their first World Series championship in eighty-six years.

But if one were to measure comebacks in terms of sheer unpredictability, down to a singular instant—the swiftness and impact of a single play—few compare to one swing of David Ortiz's bat in Game 2 of the 2013 ALCS.

For all the talent on the pitching staff of the 2013 Detroit Tigers, there was one obvious problem: the Tigers were disproportionately top-heavy. Before the series began, even Jim Leyland acknowledged that Detroit's strength was in its starting rotation and that the Red Sox "might have a little more depth" in the bullpen, which was a tactful of way of saying that the Tigers didn't need as deep a relief corps because the team's collection of elite starters handled such a massive workload.

Translation: *They're better at the back, but we're better at the front.*

In Game 2—and beyond—Detroit's back-end weakness would prove fatal. And as much as Leyland talked about bullpen "depth," the real problem was the absence of a true frontline closer, a dominant pitcher who could handle the pressure in the final innings of a playoff game, particularly in road games.

Replacing Scherzer, right-hander José Veras retired the first batter he faced, Stephen Drew, then allowed a double to Will Middlebrooks. Leyland quickly called upon left-hander Drew Smyly to face the left-handed-hitting Jacoby Ellsbury, who promptly drew a walk. Leyland then turned to the right-handed Al Alburquerque, who struck out Victorino for the second out before facing Dustin Pedroia. As the inning unfolded, Ortiz all but hovered over the entire series of events while watching from afar, waiting for his chance.

For Red Sox manager John Farrell, the goal was simple: *Give Ortiz a chance to hit.* For Leyland, it was the opposite: *End this before Ortiz even gets a chance.*

Pedroia singled to load the bases. And so, with two outs, a four-run lead, and the bases loaded, Leyland summoned closer Benoit, a right-hander who spent much of his career pitching in the seventh and eighth innings. He was the closer largely by default—a good option, but not a great one. Benoit had enjoyed one of the best seasons of his career, recording twenty-four saves in twenty-six opportunities, the large majority of them in the final two months of the season, when the Tigers played relatively low-pressure games thanks to their sizable lead in the playoff race.

Still, Benoit was a skilled reliever, a right-hander who could retire both right-handed batters and left-handers with equal efficiency, making him ideal for the late innings. During the season, in fact, he had held lefties to just a .194 average—righties had hit only .202 against him—while allowing just one home run to a left-handed batter, way back in April.

Now facing David Ortiz with a chance to close out Game 2 of the ALCS in a series the Tigers had thus far dominated, Benoit came to a set, began his delivery, and threw one of his best pitches—a split fastball that acted as a changeup—believing that Ortiz would be expecting a first-pitch fastball. Given the circumstances, most any other hitter indeed would have been expecting a fastball the way Joaquín Benoit thought he might. But David Ortiz was looking for a changeup.

"I know they [are] not going to let me beat them with a fastball in that situation," Ortiz, speaking in his second language, told a media assembly after the game. "Plus, I know that my boy, Benoit, he [has] a good splitter. And I take my chances in that situation. But that pitch was pretty much hittable. It was on the plate. And [I] put a good swing on it."

Indeed, for all of Ortiz's accomplishments and heroics during an extraordinary career with the Red Sox, the most critical part of his success was often overlooked: his intellect. In the batter's box, particularly with the game on the line, he had a capacity that most players do not: the ability to slow down the situation, think it out, strategize. Ortiz had faced Benoit, a fellow native of the Dominican Republic, twenty-seven times during regular-season games, collecting seven hits to go along with four walks and one home run. He knew Benoit's general strategy. He knew the weapons at the pitcher's disposal. He recognized the situation. He thought he knew what Benoit would throw, and—as was often the case—he was right.

From the moment Ortiz made contact, there was really just one question: *Was it high enough?* The bullpens at Fenway Park are 380 feet from home plate, framing one of the bigger right fields in baseball. Reaching them from home plate typically requires a trajectory that is, in a word, parabolic. Anything launched on a more acute angle—like the flight of a 1-iron in golf—typically ends up either in the right fielder's glove or, less likely, over his outstretched glove before caroming off the base of the bullpen wall.

Playing in right field for the Tigers was Torii Hunter, one of the more gifted defensive players of his era, a five-time All-Star and nine-time Gold Glove Award winner who had played the large majority of his career as a center fielder for the Minnesota Twins. Hunter was uniquely qualified to play the spacious right field at Fenway Park. He broke at the crack of the bat and chased Ortiz's drive toward the gap in right center, his angle of approach suggesting that he believed the ball would stay in the field of play. But as the ball continued to soar, Hunter turned his body awkwardly as he approached the bullpen, reached back in hopes of making the catch, then collided with the outfield wall and flipped over it as if attempting a handstand, his legs pointed straight into the air.

Both he and the ball instantly disappeared.

When Hunter regained his feet, Ortiz was circling the bases as the home crowd bordered on delirium, the end result a historic and most improbable grand slam that had tied the game at 5.

"It was all or nothing," Hunter later said. "Can't believe that happened."

He wasn't alone. Red Sox radio voice Dave O'Brien erupted with a Boston fan base that had been launched into a state of ecstasy.

Swing and high deep drive into right field . . . that one's scalded to right . . . Hunter on the move . . . racing back it's over his head . . . it's gone! . . . it's into the bullpen! . . . this game is tied! this game is tied . . . David Ortiz! David Ortiz! David Ortiz!

The reaction in the Tigers dugout, undoubtedly, was similar, albeit different:

David Ortiz. Fuck.

Though Benoit subsequently struck out Mike Napoli to end the inning, the damage was done. Sox closer Koji Uehara entered the game in the top of the ninth and, unlike Benoit, cruised through the Detroit lineup, recording three outs on nine pitches, including a strikeout. With the Tigers now wounded and glassy-eyed like a rubber-legged boxer, Leyland summoned right-hander Rick Porcello. The right-hander allowed an infield single to Jonny Gomes, who also advanced to second on a throwing error by José Iglesias, a player whom the Sox had traded away in the deal for Jake Peavy. (For Boston, everything was coming together.) Porcello then threw a wild pitch that advanced Gomes to third before catcher Jarrod Saltalamacchia sliced a game-winning single to left field through a drawn-in infield, giving the Red Sox an incredibly dramatic 6–5 victory.

Before the eighth inning of Game 2, the Red Sox were lifeless. Trailing by a 5–1 score, they were on the verge of a 2-0 series deficit. And then, in the span of seventeen pitches from the Tigers, a chain reaction of events produced a 6–5 victory that effectively erased everything that had happened before it. *Grand slam . . . inning-ending strikeout . . . single . . . throwing error . . . wild pitch . . . single.* Ball game. Series tied.

"Looked like we had one in hand and we let one get away," Tigers manager Leyland said in a postgame press conference that was stunningly brief. "There's no question about it."

At that instant, Leyland was talking about the game more than the series. But he could have been talking about both.

* * *

There is an old saying in baseball that goes like this: "Momentum is only as good as today's starting pitcher." It was often used to warn against over-confidence, a reminder that a dramatic win on any given night would not necessarily carry over to the next day. But if that was true for the Red Sox entering Game 3 of the ALCS, it was also true for the Detroit Tigers, who handed the ball to standout Justin Verlander, a thirty-year-old who, during his career, had already won a Rookie of the Year Award, a Cy Young Award, and an MVP Award.

For the second time in three games, the Red Sox and Tigers dueled to a 1–0 outcome, the edge this time going to Boston. Verlander allowed only a solo home run to Red Sox first baseman Mike Napoli in the seventh inning of what was, at the time, a scoreless game, striking out ten in another dominant performance. The problem was that Red Sox starter John Lackey was a whisker better, recording eight strikeouts while allowing just four hits and no walks in six and two-thirds innings. The Red Sox also got two and a third scoreless innings from their bullpen, the final four outs from the machinelike Uehara, claiming a 1–0 victory that gave Boston a 2–1 series advantage and ensured that the series would return to Fenway Park.

To that point, through three games in the series, Tigers starters Sanchez, Scherzer, and Verlander had pitched a combined twenty-one innings, allowing just six hits and two runs while amassing a ridiculous thirty-five strikeouts—and yet the Tigers were behind.

"This is what it's about in postseason," Leyland said, "good pitching. Their bullpen came out and did a great job. Our bullpen did a good job today. It's just terrific pitching and pitch making. I thought Lackey changed speeds, made pitches all day long. He was terrific, actually. And so was Verlander. But I credit this one certainly and most of this series to really good pitching."

Game 4 was the exception, the Tigers swarming Jake Peavy from the start. Detroit scored five runs in the second inning and two more in the fourth, grasping an early 7–0 lead and coasting to a 7–3 victory. Detroit's win evened the series at two games each, placing even more meaning on the improbable Red Sox win in Game 2. For the majority of the series, the Tigers had been the better team, and Games 2 and 4 could have and should have been Detroit victories were it not for the vulnerability of the Detroit bullpen and the heroics of David Ortiz. As it turned out, the Tigers' frustrations would only mount.

With the series now square after four games, the Tigers seemed well-positioned, with the trio of Sanchez, Scherzer, and Verlander lined up to pitch the final three games. This was precisely how the Tigers had been built to win, particularly against good competition, particularly in October. The longer a series went, the less chance an opponent had of matching up with Detroit's rotation.

After a brilliant Game 1, Sanchez wasn't quite as good the second time around, allowing nine hits and four runs as the Red Sox built a 4–0 lead in the first three innings. Detroit rallied for single runs in the fifth, sixth, and seventh to make the score 4–3, at which point the Red Sox did in Game 5 what the Tigers could not do in Game 2: close. With one out and the bases empty after left-hander Craig Breslow retired Victor Martinez to start the eighth, Sox manager Farrell made the aggressive decision to go to his closer, Uehara, who subsequently retired the final five Detroit batters of the game in succession. With an efficiency that has become his trademark, Uehara struck out two and did not allow a base runner, throwing nineteen of twenty-seven pitches for strikes as the Red Sox claimed a 3-2 series lead as the clubs headed back to Boston for Game 6 and, if necessary, Game 7.

"Their guys are very good . . . we know that," Leyland said of the Red Sox relief corps, anchored by Uehara. "And I tip my cap to them."

For the Tigers, Game 6 only provided greater frustration and was another game the Tigers might have (should have?) won. For the fourth time in six games, Detroit had the lead entering the final stages. Scherzer took the mound for the bottom of the seventh with a 2–1 advantage, then allowed a double and a walk to two of the first three batters he faced. The Red Sox, as a result, had runners at first and second with one out as the left-handed-hitting Jacoby Ellsbury prepared to hit. Like Sanchez before him, Scherzer wasn't quite as sharp the second time around and had thrown 110 pitches in the outing—and Ellsbury had plated Boston's only run of the night with a single against him two innings earlier. Leyland made the decision to go to his bullpen, summoning left-hander Drew Smyly to face Ellsbury.

The result? A ground ball up the middle that bounced over the bag, then into—and out of—the glove of the defensively gifted Iglesias for what should have been at least the second out. Instead, the play was ruled Iglesias's second error of the series, loading the bases with one out.

With the right-handed-hitting Shane Victorino due up, Leyland called upon right-hander José Veras, who had dominated right-handed batters during the regular season, holding them to a paltry .165 average. Veras's first two pitches were big breaking curveballs, the first for a called strike, the second that a lunging Victorino dribbled foul for strike two. The third was another looping curve that hung more in the middle of the plate—and Victorino lofted it to left field, where it dropped into the first rows of seats just above Boston's fabled left-field wall for a home run.

For the second time in two games at Fenway Park, possessing a lead and nearing a victory that would have moved them a step closer to the World Series, the Tigers had allowed a grand slam.

Though the Tigers actually managed a base runner in the ninth this time—outfielder Austin Jackson reached on an infield single—Uehara began and ended the inning with strikeouts, the latter against Iglesias. For the series, the back end of Boston's bullpen—Uehara, left-hander Breslow, and right-hander Junichi Tazawa—had pitched twelve innings, allowing just one run. The bulk of that work had been done by Uehara, who had pitched in five of the six games, allowing four hits, no runs, and no walks while striking out nine en route to being named the MVP of the series. In the six games, while being outscored by just one run (19–18), the Tigers had posted a better batting average than the Red Sox (.254 to .202) a better OPS (.659 to .609) and better team ERA (2.77 to 3.06)—and had still lost the series. Boston's grand slams were the difference and came from two batters—Ortiz (two for twenty-two) and Victorino (three for twenty-four with nine strikeouts)—who had otherwise been three for forty-four in the six games, a wretched .068 batting average.

For the bulk of the series, simply put, the Tigers had played better.

But as was the case throughout 2013, the timing of the Red Sox was impeccable.

* * *

Other than the New York Yankees, the St. Louis Cardinals have been the most successful team in baseball, having won eleven World Series championships. As such, they are the premier franchise team in the National League. In 2013, the Cardinals won ninety-seven games, tied with Boston for the most in baseball, and appeared in their third straight National League Championship Series. They defeated the Los Angeles Dodgers by the same margin the Red Sox had defeated the Tigers, four games to two, and there were many who believed the Cardinals were on the verge of winning their twelfth championship, their second in three years.

The Red Sox proved a notable obstruction—and in more ways than one.

After the teams split Games 1 and 2 in Boston—the Red Sox claimed Game 1 by a lopsided 8–1 score behind the surging Jon Lester before the Cardinals answered behind Michael Wacha in Game 2—Boston and St. Louis traveled to St. Louis for pivotal game 3, an affair that ultimately was decided by one of the more controversial plays in World Series history. After the Red Sox overcame two-run deficits in the first and eighth innings, the game was tied at 4 entering the bottom of the ninth, when the Cardinals rallied against the Boston bullpen. Right-hander Brandon Workman allowed a one-out single to Yadier Molina before Allen Craig greeted Uehara with a double to left field, placing runners at second and third bases with one out.

Needing to prevent Molina from scoring, the Red Sox pulled their infield in. On an ensuing 0-1 pitch, outfielder John Jay hit what might have been a game-winning single were it not for the brilliance of second baseman Dustin Pedroia, who made a sensational sprawling stop to his right. With Molina lumbering toward the plate, Pedroia hopped to his feet and threw a strike to catcher Jason Saltalamacchia, who then tagged Molina for the second out.

As it turned out, the play was really just beginning.

Craig was attempting to move from second to third, but Saltalamacchia's throw sliced slightly away from third baseman Will Middlebrooks. In hopes of nonetheless securing the throw and tagging Craig, Middlebrooks lunged toward his left, but the ball deflected off his glove and into foul territory in left field as Middlebrooks fell to his stomach on the infield dirt. Craig rose to his feet and tried to step over Middlebrooks right as the third baseman bent his knees and lifted his feet, which caused Craig to stumble and fall. When he got up a second time and again tried to dash home for the winning run, he was thrown out at the plate by Daniel Nava, who had been backing up the play behind Middlebrooks.

Except the home plate umpire called him safe and pointed to third base. Confused? So were the Red Sox, especially when the team was informed that third-base umpire Jim Joyce had called Middlebrooks for obstruction, granting Craig home plate, a decision that also gave St. Louis a 5–4 victory in Game 3 and a 2-1 Series lead.

Not long after the decision, Farrell called the sequence "a tough way to have a game end, particularly of this significance," and "a tough pill to swallow." A day later, in a media briefing before Game 4, he acknowledged that he "didn't have a normal night of sleep" but also supported the umpires and said "[the] call was made as it should have been."

Regardless of the debate that dominated the baseball world between Games 3 and 4, the end result was that the Red Sox faced a 2-1 series deficit on the heels of a highly debatable call, the kind that could tilt a close series between two good teams with a championship at stake. Instead, the Red Sox did on the field what Boston had done off it for the entirety of the year. They rebounded in inspiring fashion.

Despite falling behind yet again in Game 4—there was a twenty-three-inning stretch from Games 2 to 4 in which the Red Sox held a lead for a grand total of roughly a half inning—the Red Sox tied the game at 1-1 in the fifth, when David Ortiz (who else?) started a Boston rally with a leadoff double against Cardinals right-hander Lance Lynn. After television cameras caught Ortiz delivering a spirited pep talk to teammates in the dugout between innings—"Our guys look up to him," Farrell would say later—Boston's big-game monster shouted *"¡Vamonos!"* to his teammates while standing on second base, his actions every bit as driving as his words.

Let's go!

After a sacrifice fly by Stephen Drew scored Ortiz and tied the game at 1 later in the inning, the Red Sox took command in the sixth. The game was still knotted at a 1-1 with two outs and the bases empty when Dustin Pedroia singled and Ortiz walked, prompting Cardinals manager Mike Matheny to pull Lynn in favor of Seth Maness, who worked to a 2-2 count on the ensuing batter, Jonny Gomes. On the fifth and final pitch of the at-bat, Gomes unloaded on a Maness fastball and blasted it into the Red Sox bullpen for a three-run home run, a blow that propelled the Red Sox to a 4-2 victory and erased any emotional trauma from the previous night's obstruction.

The series was tied at 2. Boston's heart was beating again, the 2013 baseball season had been whittled down to a best of three.

"We've seen it many times," Farrell said of his player's resiliency. "Tonight's not the first. Granted, the stage might be bigger, but this is consistent with the way we've responded to a tough night . . . and we came in today fully expecting a very good game to be put together. That's just who these guys are, and they've shown it many times over."

A night later, having fully embraced his role as team ace after the 2012 departure of Beckett, left-hander Lester sparkled again, going seven and two-thirds innings in a 3-1 victory during which the Red Sox trailed. Farrell used just two pitchers in the game—Lester and Uehara, the bookends and anchors of his staff. The two recorded twenty-seven outs on just 106 pitches combined, striking out nine, allowing only four hits, issuing no walks, and retiring seventeen of the final eighteen St. Louis hitters of the night. Once again, the team demonstrated an uncanny ability to rise to the occasion, the whole of their operation exceeding the sum of their parts.

Now possessing a 3–2 series lead, the Red Sox found themselves in a most favorable position, needing just one win in the final two games of the series—both scheduled for Fenway Park—to win a most improbable World Series a year after finishing last during such a demoralizing season, the ownership and upper management sold off dysfunctional parts. They did not need two tries. With two out and the bases loaded in the bottom of the third inning, Victorino again took aim at the left-field wall with a three-run double that broke open a scoreless tie and the Red Sox never looked back, rumbling to a 6–1 victory. Counting the regular season, it was the final Red Sox win, their 108th of the season, their eleventh of the playoffs, and their fourth of the World Series. Once defined by their historic collapses in the late season and playoffs, the Red Sox were now winning championships that no one ever expected them to.

But make no mistake: In the wake of the April tragedy that marred the Boston Marathon, this was a championship that Boston needed, that in some ways meant more to a city that wanted to believe in itself again.

"In a time of need, In response to a tragedy, you know, I go back to our players understanding their place in this city," said a poignant Farrell. "They kind of, for lack of a better way to describe it, they get it. They get that there's, I think, a civil responsibility that we have wearing this uniform, particularly here in Boston. And it became a connection initially, the way our guys reached out to individuals or to hospital visits. And it continued to build throughout the course of the season. I think our fans, they got to a point where they appreciated the way we played the game, how they cared for one another. And in return they gave these guys an incredible amount of energy to thrive on in this ballpark."

Concluded the manager: "I'm sure that everybody in our uniform, whether they are here going forward or elsewhere, they'll look back on the events that took place and the way things unfolded as a special year. There's no way we can say it any other way."

* * *

Fenway Park is almost exactly one mile from the finish line of the Boston Marathon, about a twenty-minute walk from Ipswich Street to Boylston Street, across Massachusetts Avenue. On the night of Game 6, the Red Sox clinched the World Series at home for the first time in ninety-five years, a celebration the city had not seen since the championship in 1918. The final wins in 2004 and 2007 had been won on the road—in St. Louis and in Denver—and a clinching victory on the field at Fenway Park was an indication not merely that things had returned to normal but that things might actually be getting better.

Six months earlier—just *six months*—Boston's historic Back Bay had been the site of one of the worst tragedies in Boston's history. Now, in the same neighborhood, Bostonians were celebrating in a way they had not experienced in generations. *This is our city.* In the months since the bombings, Boston had returned to celebrating the Fourth of July on the Esplanade, slowly reclaimed its most vibrant streets, once again obsessed over the things that were most important to them—like sports, for instance—and immersed themselves in their routines. The 2013 Red Sox were as worthy of Boston's time as any edition in franchise history, a collection of players who were similarly rehabilitating.

Jon Lester, lost in the shadow of Josh Beckett, went 4-1 with a 1.56 ERA in five October starts and established himself as a big-game pitcher, his only playoff loss the 1–0 decision to Detroit in Game 1 of the ALCS; John Lackey, in his last full season in Boston, started the championship-clinching Game 6 after having pitched in relief just two nights earlier, no questions asked; Shane Victorino, in a five-for-thirty-seven slump in the final two rounds of the postseason, made two of his hits haymakers—the grand slam against Detroit and the three-run double against St. Louis, both in clinching games; Koji Uehara, who became the closer only after the failures of Joel Hanrahan and Andrew Bailey, took the job and ran with it, the anchor man in a season-long race who ultimately brought Boston across the finish line. The list went on.

"This was [bigger than] us as a group," said catcher David Ross. "This was bigger than a baseball team, an organization. The city brought passion, character. This was bigger than just the Boston Red Sox and the guys on the field. This is a great win for the city of Boston."

Said left fielder Jonny Gomes: "I don't think a win-loss record sums up how much we care about this city. I'll tell you what, I don't think we put Boston on our back. I think we jumped on [its] back."

In truth, of course, they carried each other. There was no *mine* or *yours.* There was only *ours.*

CHAPTER 11

DARKNESS AND DEFEAT

"It's definitely their team. They definitely feel like they're a part. Look I get it, I don't think I understood this twenty-five years ago, but I get it. I know what a fan is. . . . We can hear it from them when we're not doing well but I think that all comes from the right place. . . . I understand the good comes with the bad and the bad comes with the good. That's just part of the territory when you're in pro sports, especially in a place like this."
—former Patriots offensive coordinator Josh McDaniels, April 2021

FOR THE NEW ENGLAND PATRIOTS, the transitions during the new millennium were relatively subtle, proverbial first-class problems in a city where some of the other teams oscillated between extremes. From 2011 to 2015, for instance, the Red Sox suffered a historic collapse, then finished last, then won a World Series, then finished last two years in a row. The Celtics won a championship by agreeing to what was essentially a Faustian bargain, the hope of the longer term exchanged for the immediate fix. For both franchises, the bad both preceded and succeeded the good.

The Patriots, by contrast, lived with considerably less volatility. For more than ten years, they had the best coach and quarterback of their eras, in tandem, a dream team at the center of their operation. No matter what else happened, the Patriots went into most every season as a viable threat to win the Super Bowl largely due to their presence. From Bangor to Baja, any discussion about Super Bowl contenders inevitably began at the same place—the coach and the quarterback, the quarterback and the coach—and the Patriots did not have merely the best of both. They had two of the best *ever*.

And yet, there was this: After the 2004 Patriots won New England's third Super Bowl in four years, the Patriots entered the 2013 season having gone eight years without a title. During that same span, the Patriots had won more combined regular- and postseason games than any franchise in the NFL—and by a sizable margin—yet they had no championships to show for it. And while New England had twice reached the Super Bowl, both appearances resulted in a loss to the New York Giants, the most recent a 21–17 defeat to the same coach and quarterback (Tom Coughlin and Eli Manning) who had ended the Patriots' attempt at an undefeated season just four years prior.

In many places, even without a championship, an eight-year run like the Patriots experienced from 2005 to 2012 would be considered a golden age, but not in Boston, not during the start to this millennium, and certainly not in a Patriots organization where the head coach routinely changed the name of his boat to reflect the number of championships he had won. (In 2013, Belichick's boat was still named *Five Rings*, reflecting his two titles as defensive coordinator of the Giants along with his three as head coach of the Patriots.) In Boston, Belichick, Brady, and owner Robert Kraft were at the forefront of a city taking the term "championship-driven" to an entirely new level, one title seemingly fueling the next in what felt like an insatiable thirst for titles.

"Well, I mean, coming from Ohio, there's a passion for obviously the Browns and the Indians. . . . They have an affinity for those teams obviously and they want to win and they're hungry for all that stuff," Patriots offensive coordinator Josh McDaniels said in 2021. "I would say the difference to me is there's just a year-round intensity here and focus on it because of the fact that we have four sports teams, the fact that all four have in some way shaped or formed [the sports environment] and have been very successful in the last 20 years now. I can't speak obviously to before 2001 [and] the fan base is obviously intense, but there's been a lot of celebration and there's been a lot of success that they've witnessed and that they've been thankful for. . . . I mean, some may like one sport more than the other, but I think that the passion they have for everybody and for winning—it's just a little different to me. It's a little different. It's very intense and I really love the appreciation that they show when there's a job well done."

The flip side, particularly during the early 2000s? The winning was intoxicating, potentially hurtful, something demonstrated by the self-destruction of the Red Sox. The good news for the Patriots was that the Boston-area football team was run far differently, had far fewer cooks in the kitchen, and operated largely based on the desires and decisions of the uber-disciplined Belichick, who always had Brady to fall back on. Consequently, the Patriots' "bad" years were still very, very good ones, the team stacking winning seasons like dinner plates in the kitchen cupboard, always there to feed a fan base that was, at its peak, interminably hungry.

Born in Barberton, Ohio, McDaniels was the son of a renowned high school coach and attended high school in Canton, home of the Pro Football Hall of Fame. Football was built into his DNA. A high school quarterback, he played wide receiver at John Carroll in University Heights, Ohio, where he caught passes from Nick Caserio, the man who beat him out for the QB position and alongside whom McDaniels later worked in New England. McDaniels spent a brief time coaching as a graduate assistant at Michigan State before joining the New England coaching staff in 2001, beginning on the defensive side of the ball. He ultimately became the quarterbacks' coach in 2004 and was promoted to offensive coordinator following the 2005 season, remaining in that position through the 2008 campaign. He worked between Belichick and Brady, in some ways the synapse that connected the neurons in the brain of the Patriots' football operations, in other ways a neuron unto himself.

With the Patriots, McDaniels was a part of three Super Bowl winners and oversaw the historic 2007 Patriots offense that came within one win of a perfect season. A year later, after Brady was injured in the season opener and with seventh-round pick Matt Cassel as his quarterback—Cassel had never started a game in *college*, let alone the NFL—McDaniel developed a Patriots offense that finished eighth in the league in scoring, a phenomenal accomplishment under the circumstances. By season's end, the Patriots were 11-5 and had effectively overcome the loss of Brady. In the final thirteen weeks of the season, once McDaniels and Cassel started to become acclimated to one another, the Patriots scored more points than any team in the NFL, an achievement that drew natural attention to their offensive coordinator, who became one of the hottest head coaching candidates in professional football.

Denver hired him to be head coach of the Broncos, where he won his first six games before a 2-8 finish that left the team with a .500 record. The Broncos were 3-9 the next season when a videotaping scandal drew immediate comparisons to the third rail that was the Patriots' Spygate scandal of 2007, resulting in his firing. McDaniels then spent one season as the offensive coordinator of the St. Louis Rams, another failure in an industry littered with them. He returned to the Patriots in 2012 and spent the next ten years as Belichick's chief offensive coach, eight of them with Brady.

Recognizing that his next head coaching opportunity might be his last—Belichick, too, had failed during his first stint as a head coach—McDaniels chose his job interviews carefully over the years, turned down offers, once even backing out of an agreement to coach the Indianapolis Colts. Until finally agreeing to become head coach of the Las Vegas Raiders in January 2022, he had remained in Boston, where he and his wife, Laura, raised four children. He long considered himself an adopted Bostonian, someone who adapted to his environment and who learned the ways and methods of a region that is, frankly, often ill-adjusted when it comes to sports:

> For me, even though I grew up and my wife grew up in Ohio, my kids haven't lived one day of their life in Ohio. They truly are from Boston. They don't have an accent or slang to their speech, but I mean, literally, this is home. There is no other thing that they could confuse with being home other than being from Boston because they don't remember Denver and they don't remember St. Louis. They're basically all born and raised here. That is the norm for us now. Like when I say we've acclimated, we've really acclimated to [the people and lifestyle] as well. My wife and I have talked about that [and] there are really a couple of examples we've used.
>
> One: when you go back home to Ohio and you drive on the highway, if you drive faster than 55 or 60 miles an hour, you're the only person on the highway driving at that speed and everybody else is driving right at the speed limit. If you drive 60 miles an hour here on Route 1, you're going to get passed on both sides including the curb lane. You know what I mean? Laura and I—it took us a little while to get adjusted to it. It was like, 'Look, these people are going somewhere like there's urgency,' and it is not just about one topic or another; it's like, literally, *life*. Everything is moving faster. They are serious about it.
>
> "We kind of joke about the coffee shops, too. On my way to work from [home], I'm going to pass seven Dunkin' Donuts and we always say, 'It's because these people need so much caffeine to keep up the pace that they go at,' that, like, 'They *have* to have these many Dunkin' Donuts.'
>
> The other thing my wife always remarks about is, when you go to the supermarket here and you're checking out, they're flying your stuff through the [checkout]. They're not small talking and they don't even look up at you.

You know what I mean? I always tell my wife, my 14-year-old could go buy alcohol at Roche Brothers because the person checking her out isn't going to look up. In Ohio, the freaking line at the grocery store takes forever because the lady behind the counter wants to have a 10-minute conversation with each customer and that is *not* happening here.

Indeed, Bostonians were not about to needlessly wait for groceries. And they certainly weren't going to wait for their championships.

Relatively quickly, after learning a way of life in middle America, Josh McDaniels determined quickly that he would have to adapt to Boston because Boston wasn't going to adapt for him.

* * *

During the first decade of the Patriots dynasty, Patriots fans adopted certain catchphrases and terms, most of them directly from the lips of head coach Bill Belichick. He was known to repeatedly say things like "It is what it is" and "Ignore the noise" or "Do your job," messages designed to eliminate the distractions and dramas that often detracted from a person's (or team's) focus. And along the way, Patriots fans once again adopted an even simpler, more comprehensive philosophy: *In Bill We Trust.*

Through it all, Belichick nonetheless proved human, though he often operated with a cold, calculating manner that sometimes seemed to defy logic. During his time as coach, the Patriots continued to cast off key players and contributors: safety Lawyer Milloy; kicker Adam Vinatieri; wide receiver Deion Branch; defensive lineman Richard Seymour. Some of the moves worked and some of them did not—though, to his credit, Belichick usually responded to the failures with relative swiftness. After Seymour's departure contributed to a 2009 season during which the Patriots demonstrated poor leadership and a suspect defense—the Patriots were trounced *at home* in the playoffs, 33–14, by a Baltimore Ravens team that ran for 234 yards against them—Belichick went about the business of rebuilding the Patriots on the defensive side of the ball, albeit over a series of drafts that delivered safety Devin McCourty, defensive end Chandler Jones, and linebacker Dont'a Hightower to New England.

Yes, contrary to popular opinion, Belichick made mistakes. He just did not often make them twice.

The 2010 Patriots, for their part, were an overachieving team, a fact attributable largely to the play of Brady, who had fully recovered from his 2008 knee injury and returned to elite form. In winning his second MVP Award, Brady threw thirty-six touchdown passes and just four interceptions, an astonishing level of efficiency that produced a shiny, overall quarterback rating of 111.0, second-best of his career. The additions of rookie tight ends Rob Gronkowski (a team-leading ten touchdown receptions) and Aaron Hernandez fortified a revamped Patriots offense—a grumbling Randy Moss was traded early in the season and replaced with Branch, whom Belichick brought back—and undrafted running back BenJarvus Green-Ellis ran for more than 1,000 yards while scoring a team-best thirteen touchdowns. The season peaked with a 45–3 dismantling of the upstart New York Jets and coach Rex Ryan in Week 13, part of a season-ending eight-game winning streak that established the Pats as the top seed in the AFC.

"A nice way to end the season," said Belichick, whose team had actually secured the top seed before the regular season finale. Added second-year line-backer Jerod Mayo, one of the new centerpieces of the defense: "Now we're 0-0. Time for the playoffs."

What ensued was one of the more disappointing defeats of the Belichick era, Super Bowl or otherwise.

Six weeks after embarrassing the Jets and coming off the playoff bye they had earned, the Patriots began their playoff season by hosting New York in the divisional round of the playoffs. For New England, the game was a lesson in frustration. Typically a coach who preached brawn and bravado, Ryan delivered one of his best game plans as coach of the Jets, a less attacking, more patient approach that repeatedly foiled the Patriots. On New England's first posses-sion of the game, Brady threw his first interception in months, a touch pass intended for Green-Ellis that was intercepted by linebacker David Harris and set the tone for the day. While the Jets did not score on the possession—kicker Nick Folk missed a short field goal—the message from Ryan and the Jets was indisputable in the wake of their 45–3 defeat slightly more than a month prior.

You're not going to embarrass us this time.

By the time it was over, Brady had been sacked five times and the Jets, despite being sizable underdogs by 9.5 points at kickoff, had secured a 28–21 victory that abruptly ended New England's season. For the Patriots defense, too, the entire game was a harsh reality check. Second-year Jets quarterback Mark Sanchez outplayed Brady, completing sixteen of twenty-five passes for 194 yards, three touchdowns, and no interceptions for a quarterback rating of 127.3. He was not sacked even once. In the process, the Jets were simultaneously able to stifle the Patriots offense and expose an overrated New England defense, all on a day when the typically brash Ryan outwitted a blindsided Belichick.

"Anybody can be beat," Jets linebacker Bart Scott screamed as he walked off the field at Gillette Stadium during a memorable interview with ESPN reporter Sal Paolantonio.

For the second straight year, the Jets were headed to the AFC title game, which the Patriots hadn't reached for three years, though any reference to a "drought" in New England was obviously relative. Still, if the Belichick-Brady era ever had what qualified as a dark age, the team was smack dab in the middle of it. With the pick they had acquired in the trade that sent Richard Seymour to the Oakland Raiders, the Patriots selected left tackle Nate Solder in the 2011 draft, but the team the Patriots returned to the field was otherwise largely the same—and with the same flaws. Gronkowski (17 touchdowns), Hernandez (955 yards from scrimmage) and Wes Welker (122 receptions) gave Brady one of the best collections of pass catchers he had ever possessed, but the defense again lacked playmakers, particularly against good competition, and the Patriots were a relatively modest 5-3 after consecutive losses to the Pittsburgh Steelers and New York Giants in consecutive weeks, the latter on their home field in Foxboro.

Once again—and in what had become their custom during the Belichick era—the team rallied in the second half of the season, closing out the schedule with eight straight wins, including a 37–16 rout of the Jets in New York. Once again, the Patriots won the AFC East Division championship and earned a bye in the first round of the playoffs, where this time they faced a far more favorable opponent, the Denver Broncos and quarterback Tim Tebow, in a divisional round home game that longtime *Boston Globe* columnist Dan Shaughnessy would ultimately dub the annual "Tomato Can Game" for its repeated lack of a quality opponent.

After obliterating the Broncos by a 45–10 score—Brady threw a comical six touchdown passes and Tebow was sacked five times—the Patriots faced a real opponent, the Baltimore Ravens, who possessed an elite defense that regularly flummoxed Brady. With Brady playing one of the worst postseason games of his career—"I sucked pretty bad today," he would tell a packed stadium in an on-field interview after the game—Baltimore seemed headed for a victory in the final seconds, when the Ravens quite literally gave the game away.

Trailing 23–20 with just over twenty seconds left, Ravens wide receiver Lee Evans first failed to secure a touchdown pass from Joe Flacco that would have given the Ravens a win; then, when the Ravens lined up for an easy, thirty-two-yard game-tying field goal with fifteen seconds left, Ravens kicker Billy Cundiff lined up on the *right* hash mark and snap-hooked the kick wide *left*, a virtually impossible miss that sent the Patriots back to the Super Bowl for the first time in four years.

"I think we can keep things simple: It's a kick I've made a thousand times in my career," a somber Cundiff plainly admitted. "I just went out there and didn't convert. There's really no excuse for it."

Simply put, the Patriots got lucky. But then, as any Bostonian might have acknowledged over the start of the new millennium, luck was a part of winning, too.

That said, the Patriots' luck ran dry in the Super Bowl when, once again, Belichick and Brady encountered Coughlin and Manning, the Giants tandem that had become a rather sizable thorn in New England's side. And while Brady ultimately played better in Super Bowl XLVI than he had in their previous meetings, he also was called for an intentional grounding penalty from his own end zone on New England's first offensive play of the game, a blunder that awarded the Giants 2 points for a safety and required the Patriots to kick the ball right back to New York.

The Giants, naturally, seized the opportunity and drove for a touchdown to take a 9–0 lead. By the time Brady touched the ball again, New York had run twenty-one offensive plays to the Patriots' one—the safety that the *Giants* had scored on—and held the ball for 12:28 of the 12:36 that had elapsed off the game clock.

To their credit—and playing with a badly wounded Gronkowski, who had suffered a severe ankle sprain in the Baltimore game—the Patriots rallied to a 17–9 lead before the Giants scored the final 12 points of the game, the final 6 coming on an Ahmad Bradshaw touchdown run with fifty-seven seconds left in the game that gave New York a 21–17 edge. Along the way, the Patriots missed opportunities to seize control of the game and execute at the most critical times, something they had done with regularity at the start of the Brady-Belichick era. Still the possessors of a 17–15 lead almost midway through the fourth quarter, the Patriots encountered a second-and-11 at the Giants' 44-yard line with 4:06 to play, when twisting receiver Welker dropped what would have been a 20-yard gain between New York's 20- and 25-yard lines. Brady's throw had hardly been perfect, but that, too, spoke volumes. The Patriots needed one of the two to make a play—and neither succeeded.

With the ball—and game—now in their hands—the Giants drove 88 yards in nine plays, beginning with a precise 38-yard strike from Manning to wide receiver Mario Manningham just beyond two defenders on the left sideline. The throw and catch were perfect, a juxtaposition that was impossible to ignore in the wake of the miss by Brady and Welker. Incredibly, the Giants never even faced a third down on the entire possession, which ended with Bradshaw's touchdown run when the Patriots had no choice but to let the Giants score. That gave the Patriots one final chance, and Brady advanced the team to midfield before heaving a Hail Mary pass into the end zone that harmlessly fell to the ground, making Belichick and Brady a stunning 0-3 against the Giants over a stretch that included two Super Bowls.

In the immediate aftermath, Brady's wife, Gisele Bündchen, was caught on video boarding an elevator in the concourse at Indianapolis's Lucas Oil Stadium, where she certainly seemed to be heaping blame on Welker.

"He didn't even catch the ball when he was supposed to catch the ball," Bündchen said. "My husband cannot fucking throw the ball and catch the ball at the same time."

* * *

Sent back to the drawing board after yet another failure—and convinced that his offense had been reconstructed around the magical tight-end tandem of Gronkowski and Hernandez—Belichick went about the business of rebuilding his defense during the off-season between the 2011 and 2012 seasons. Of the Patriots' seven picks in the annual draft, six were on defense, including a pair of selections in the first round: defensive end Chandler Jones and linebacker Dont'a Hightower. A few months later, during training camp, the club then signed Gronkowski and Hernandez to sizable contract extensions, cementing the pass-catching core around Brady. If Belichick could get the defense to jell by the end of the season, the Pats seemed poised to make another run at the Super Bowl.

Once again, after a somewhat shaky 3-3 start had ended with a defensive miscue by rookie draftee Tavon Wilson against the Seattle Seahawks and rookie quarterback Russell Wilson in Week 6, the Patriots hit their stride. New England won seven straight and nine of ten to end the regular season, once against earning a first-round bye and the right to host the Houston Texans in the now-annual Tomato Can Game. One month after arriving in New England for a regular-season game (and eventual 10–3 loss) wearing lettermen jackets that made them look like a high school team, the Texans showed up for the playoffs . . . and played like one. The Patriots had built a 38–13 lead by early in the fourth quarter, ultimately finishing with a 41–28 victory that gave them the right to host the AFC Championship at Gillette Stadium.

Their opponent, unfortunately, would be Tom Brady's other nemesis, the Baltimore Ravens.

Inspired by the pending retirement of future Hall of Fame linebacker and team leader Ray Lewis, the Ravens had defeated the Indianapolis Colts in the first round of the playoffs and then upset the heavily favored Denver Broncos in the divisional round. After trailing 13–7 at halftime at Foxboro, the Ravens outscored the Patriots by a 21–0 score in the second half to claim a 28–13 win. Once again, Brady (one touchdown, two interceptions, and a poor 62.3 rating) had been held in check. Baltimore subsequently went on to win the Super Bowl to fittingly close out Lewis's storied career, though the Patriots certainly entered 2013 with even greater promise, thanks to the presence of young players on both sides of the ball—Gronkowski, Hernandez, Jones, and Hightower—who seemed capable of taking the team back to championship heights.

Though nobody in Foxboro was particularly interested in acknowledging it at the time, the Patriots' future looked bright. And then things got very, very dark.

* * *

As much as Bill Belichick demanded his players' focus, instructing them to "do your job" and to "control the things you can control," there is some noise that even he could not possibly ignore.

On June 26, 2013, after the Marathon bombings and the Bruins' loss to the Chicago Blackhawks but before the glorious Red Sox run to redemption, Patriots tight end Aaron Hernandez was arrested and charged with the murder of Odin Lloyd, a twenty-seven-year-old semiprofessional football player who had been dating the sister of Hernandez's fiancée. With live television cameras stationed outside of his home in North Attleborough, Hernandez was escorted out the front door wearing red shorts and black sneakers, his arms behind his back and tucked inside a white shirt that had been pulled over his torso after he had been handcuffed.

The image was nothing if not chilling. So, too, were the details, which ultimately uncovered a web of deceitful and destructive behavior—toward both Hernandez and his victims. In the early morning hours on June 17, 2013, according to police, Hernandez and two accomplices had driven Lloyd into an industrial park in North Attleborough, roughly a mile from Hernandez's home. There, Hernandez killed his twenty-seven-year-old "friend," shooting him multiple times in the back and chest. A day later, police searched his home. A day after that, Hernandez reportedly told the Patriots' owner and coach, Kraft and Belichick, that he had nothing to do with the shooting. Nine days later, he was arrested and charged with first-degree murder as well as five gun-related charges, only the first of many allegations.

Less than two hours after Aaron Hernandez emerged from his home in handcuffs, the Patriots cut ties with him, releasing him from the organization and thereby beginning the process of reclaiming some of the money they had invested in him in the form of a $12.5 million signing bonus.

The Patriots believed Hernandez would be a central figure on the team for years to come, and in the immediate aftermath of the charges a crestfallen Robert Kraft told the media he felt as if both he and the Patriots had been "duped."

In the weeks that followed, details emerged regarding a succession of incidents in which Hernandez had been (or may have been) involved: a fight at a bar in Gainesville, Florida, in 2007, when Hernandez was a student athlete at the University of Florida; a shooting at a Gainesville traffic light several months later; a fight outside Hernandez's town house in Plainville, Massachusetts, in 2011, after he had been drafted by the Patriots; a double homicide, not unlike the Gainesville shooting, in Boston in 2012; the 2013 shooting of Alexander Bradley, Hernandez's friend at the time, who alleged that Hernandez shot him in the face and blinded him in one eye; then the murder of Lloyd.

In 2015 Hernandez was found guilty of the first-degree murder of Lloyd and sentenced to life with no chance for parole. In 2017, while in prison, he was tried—but acquitted—for the double shooting in Boston in 2012. Within days of that verdict, Hernandez was found dead in his cell in what was officially deemed a suicide, ending a long and sordid tale that uncovered details of a troubled upbringing, an abusive father, an estranged mother, sexual abuse, gang involvement, closeted homosexuality. In the midst of it all, Hernandez was a gifted athlete, a rare combination of size and speed that made him the ideal candidate for someone like Belichick—because, on the football field, Aaron Hernandez was the consummate mismatch. He was bigger than the fast guys and faster than the big guys, making him virtually impossible to contain.

For the Patriots, from a pure football standpoint, the Hernandez fallout was complex and understandably prompted them to question their methods. The sheer nature of football (in general) and the NFL (in particular) had long since required that teams face the game's ugly realities: drugs, guns, and violence chief among them. But the issues were quite real. Many often rationalized the behaviors of NFL players as a tradeoff for what was often euphemized as a modern form of gladiatorial combat. But the NFL had a long history of legal issues as they pertained to the behavior of their players or former players, none more infamous than the unforgettable O. J. Simpson murder case. But there were others. Lots of them. Domestic violence. Possession of drugs and firearms. Child abuse. Even murder.

Not long before the start of training camp in 2013, Belichick conducted his first press conference in the wake of the Hernandez arrest. Gone was the typical standoffishness that had characterized many of his media briefings during his time as Patriots coach. While Belichick repeatedly cited legal reasons for being unable to answer many questions, he accepted them all with unusual patience. As the son of a highly regarded scout, Belichick had grown up in a world almost entirely built around football. But no one needed to tell him that a professional football career and real life were two entirely different things.

Said the coach in an unusually long statement:

As the coach of the team, I'm primarily responsible for the people that we bring into the football operation. . . .

Overall, I'm proud of the hundreds of players that have come through this program but I'm personally disappointed and hurt in a situation like this. As far as the whole process goes, I can tell you that we look at every player's history from the moment we start discussing it, going back to his family, where he grew up, what his lifestyle was like, high school, college experiences. . . .

Obviously, this process is far from perfect, but it's one that we've used from 2000 until today. Unfortunately, this most recent situation with the charges [that] are involved is not a good one on that record. . . .

Personally, I'm challenged by decisions that affect the team on a daily basis and I'm not perfect on that either but I always try to do what I think is best for the football team. . . . We stress high character and we stress making good decisions. We'll continue to do this and we'll work to do a better job of it as we go forward. We'll learn from this terrible experience that we've had. We'll become a better team from the lessons that we've learned.

. . . I know that there are a lot of questions, fair questions, about this
subject and related subjects. I'm not trying to make the story disappear but
I respect the judicial process and been advised not to comment on on-going
legal proceedings. I'm advising our players to do the same thing.

Asked if he had discussed the matter with friends and family because it
went beyond football, Belichick replied: "Well, it certainly goes way beyond
being a football issue, there's no question about that. This is real life, so it's a substantial issue. I don't know how it could be any more substantial or any bigger."

Not long after, the Patriots began preparations for the 2013 season. Many
in or around the organization seemed eager to return to the mindlessness that
came with the football schedule. Once again, in Boston, there was some measure
of comfort in the routine.

With regard to football, there was very little—if any—mention of Aaron
Hernandez.

* * *

During his tenure as head coach of the Patriots, Bill Belichick built his success
and reputation on one principle above all others: preparation. More than anything else, on the field or off, no matter what it was, Belichick always seemed
ready for it. For as gruff as he could be, even to the ownership family for whom
he worked, Belichick's flaws were always easier to ignore because, as the Kraft
family often stated—as if Belichick were another executive at one of their many
endeavors—he was an excellent "manager."

But as most everyone knows, there are many things that you simply cannot
be prepared for. The 2013 season, essentially in its entirety, was one of them.

With Hernandez erased from the roster, the Patriots also began the season
without wide receiver Wes Welker, a Brady crutch who had left the team via free
agency. Welker's replacement was Danny Amendola, a younger, injury-prone
knockoff who had worked with offensive coordinator Josh McDaniels during
his year in St. Louis, but the comings and goings had an understandably unsettling effect. The Patriots were going through a transition again, one that became
even more tumultuous when Amendola was injured in the very first game of
the season, a 23–21 Patriots win at Buffalo in which he had ten catches on a
team-high fourteen targets for 104 yards.

Further compounding matters was the absence of Gronkowski, the other
half of a two-tight-end attack around whom the Patriots had built their offense.

Gronk had undergone a succession of surgeries during the off-season for a broken arm and a back injury. Unsurprisingly, the Patriots' offense spun its wheels in the early part of the year, though the team's first defeat did not come until Week 5, when New England dropped a rain-soaked 13–6 decision to the downtrodden Cincinnati Bengals. The 6-point output was Brady's worst over the past seven years.

"We need to improve all the way across the board," said Belichick.

Said Brady: "It's very disappointing as an offense when you come out of the game with six points. None of us expect that."

The return of Gronkowski in the second half of the season helped, and the team seemed to be hitting their stride. They were 7-3 entering Week 12, at home against the Denver Broncos, who had signed Welker as a free agent during the off-season. Fearing that his team would be unable to keep up with quarterback Peyton Manning and Denver's explosive offense, Belichick devised a game plan that enticed quarterback Peyton manning to hand the ball off to his running backs, which Manning happily did. But though he completed only eight passes for 61 yards in the first half, the Broncos had a whopping 24–0 lead, helped by three New England fumbles.

Facing an enormous deficit against a Denver team favored to win the AFC and the Super Bowl, the Patriots staged one of the more memorable comebacks of the Belichick era. In the third quarter, the Patriots scored three touchdowns, two on passes to Edelman and Gronkowski, to close the gap to 24–21. Another Edelman touchdown reception in the fourth quarter gave the Patriots their first lead of the game, 28–24, before a Stephen Gostkowski field goal extended the advantage to 31–24. Denver then responded with a touchdown pass from Manning to Demaryius Thomas with 3:10 remaining in the game to tie the score at 31–31 and force overtime.

When the Patriots won the subsequent coin toss, on a night when the game-time temperature was twenty-two degrees and a twenty-two-mile-per-hour wind had made it difficult to travel into the north end of the field, Belichick made a curious choice: he chose to give Denver the ball first. The teams exchanged possessions twice, but on the Patriots' second punt, after the ball left the foot of punter Ryan Allen, an indecisive Welker started in, then backed off, allowing it to bounce. The kick struck teammate Tony Carter, resulting in a fumble that the Patriots recovered at the Denver 13-yard line. The wind was at their backs, plenty close for a field goal attempt. Brady ran two quarterback sneaks to take the clock to the two-minute warning before

Gostkowski converted an easy 31-yard field goal attempt, giving the Patriots a 34–31 victory.

For Belichick, the outcome validated both his decisions to kick the ball away in overtime and maybe even to cut ties with Welker, with whom he and the Patriots had an acrimonious breakup. On that night, Belichick was a football mastermind and chief meteorologist all wrapped into one.

"I just felt like the wind would be an advantage if we could keep them out of the end zone on that first drive. We were able to do that," the coach said when asked about his decision to kick off in the extra period. "The wind was significant in the game, it was definitely significant."

Said an accountable Welker: "I've got to do a better job of getting up [the field] and getting guys away from the ball so it doesn't hit them."

Presumably, underneath his grumpy exterior, Belichick was laughing hysterically on the inside.

A week later the Patriots defeated the Texans in Houston 34–31. They were now 9-3. Gronkowski had six catches for 127 yards and four touchdowns—his fourth straight game with a touchdown reception as he neared full strength. The Patriots appeared to be doing exactly what Belichick's team often did—peak—as the schedule turned to its final stages. And then things started going sideways again.

On December 8 at Gillette Stadium, in the team's forty-first offensive play and with Cleveland holding a surprising 12–0 lead, Gronkowski broke from the line as Brady took the snap and ran around linebacker D'Qwell Jackson, up the field along the numbers. Brady lofted a perfect pass over the head of Jackson and into Gronkowski's massive hands, an in-stride Gronkowski securing the ball with open field in front of him. But as he was running, five-foot-ten Cleveland safety T. J. Ward came barreling in from Gronkowski's right, diving at his legs to take him down.

Gronkowski's knee, unsurprisingly, caved in. He was carted off the field and did not return, lost to a knee injury that ended his—and perhaps the Patriots'—season.

"He means so much to the football team," said Matthew Slater, a Patriots receiver and special teams captain who was a stellar coverage man on punts and kicks. "It's like you're in a bad dream and you're hoping to wake up and it wasn't really happening."

Indeed, going all the way back to Hernandez, the Patriots were getting hit on all sides. Injuries had mounted on defense, too, most notably to linebacker

Jerod Mayo and standout nose tackle Vince Wilfork, both of whom were cornerstones in Belichick's defense. Entering Week 15, Brady was now without Hernandez, Welker, and Gronkowski, his best three pass catchers from the previous season. And while Edelman had blossomed, the absence of other viable threats—Amendola returned from his Game 1 injury but was never quite the same—teams could key on Edelman and limit his effectiveness.

Though the Patriots came back to defeat the Browns, they lost a week later, at Miami, to drop to 10-4. They subsequently rallied with wins at Baltimore and Buffalo to finish the season at 12-4, but the Miami defeat meant that they would play at Denver (13-3) if the teams were to meet in the AFC Championship Game. Once again possessing a first-round bye, the Patriots blistered the Indianapolis Colts in the seemingly annual Tomato Can Game by a 43–22 score to earn a rematch with this Broncos, this time on the latter's home field.

By the time the Patriots got to Denver, their receiving corps was decidedly thin, especially at tight end, where, instead of Gronkowski and Hernandez, Brady had Michael Hoomanawanui and Matt Mulligan. Austin Collie, who had been claimed off the scrap heap, was Brady's third option at wide receiver, behind Edelman and the compromised Amendola, who was still dealing with his season-long injury. To make matters worse, the Patriots suffered another costly injury early in the second quarter, with the score just 3-0, when cornerback Aqib Talib was knocked out of the game in a collision with Welker. It was a crushing blow to an already-wounded Patriots team that really had just one chance to win the game: on defense.

On the first play after Talib's injury, Denver completed a third-and-9 from its own 19-yard line for a first down. On a subsequent third-and-1 at the Denver 42-yard line, the Patriots committed a coverage penalty that extended Denver's possession. Five plays later, on third-and-10 at the Patriots' 39, Knowshon Moreno *ran* for 28 yards to the New England 11, further adding to a fifteen-play, 93-yard touchdown drive that ended with a touchdown pass to tight end Jacob Tamme, giving the Broncos a 10–0 lead.

Though the Patriots closed to 10-3, the Broncos kicked a field goal to make it 13-3 at halftime, then opened the second half with another touchdown drive to make it 20-3. The lead swelled to 20 points on a Matt Prater field goal, a margin Denver rode to a 26–16 victory. The Patriots never got closer than 10 points in the second and trailed 26–10 when Brady scored on a five-yard run with just over three minutes left, but any real chance at a miraculous comeback went *poof* when running back Shane Vereen was stopped on the subsequent 2-point conversion.

Given the number of personnel losses the Patriots had suffered long *after* Hernandez's crime—Gronkowski, Wilfork, Mayo, Talib, and effectively Amendola, among others—there was hardly any shame in the defeat. But that didn't stop Belichick from calling out Welker a day *after* the game, an unflattering act that poorly disguised the coach's real frustrations.

First, he and the Patriots had experienced a typically bad breakup with Welker, who was now going to the Super Bowl. Second, Belichick was a control freak of the highest order, and the 2013 season was a succession of events—on the field and off—in which he felt he had little or no control. And so, before he even took a question from reporters in his customary postmortem press conference that took place on Mondays, a typically tight-lipped Belichick immediately and uncharacteristically launched into the Welker play, crying foul.

"I was asked about the hit on Talib, and I feel badly for Aqib," Belichick told reporters. "The way that play turned out, I went back and watched it, which I didn't have a chance to do [before speaking with reporters after the game on Sunday]. It was a deliberate play by the receiver to take out Aqib, no attempt to get open. And I'll let the league handle the discipline on that play. It's not for me to decide, but it's one of the worst plays I've seen. That's all I'll say about that."

While much of the football-watching world chuckled, the NFL similarly dismissed the coach. Welker incurred no discipline, though Belichick and the Patriots certainly gained a measure of satisfaction when the Seattle Seahawks absolutely blistered the Broncos to win the Super Bowl by a score of 40–8.

Held without a championship for a ninth straight season, Belichick went back to the drawing board. When Talib departed for free agency—and to Denver, no less—Belichick answered with a well-orchestrated acquisition of Darrelle Revis, who had been released by the Tampa Bay Buccaneers. He then added to the defensive backfield by acquiring the beastly Brandon Browner, a thumper who had contributed to the Seattle defense that blasted Denver in the Super Bowl. And to augment the receiving corps, Belichick signed free agent Brandon LaFell, a big-bodied receiver from Cincinnati, to augment the group that still included Gronkowski, Edelman, and Amendola, among others.

In the short term, those were the primary changes to a Patriots roster that, when healthy, rivaled the best groups in the NFL. In the long term, Belichick braced for another, much bigger change that would have ramifications for years.

He brought in another quarterback.

CHAPTER 12

THE EMPIRE STRIKES BACK

"We know what Tom's age and contract situation is. I don't think you want to have one quarterback on your team. I don't think that's responsible to the entire team or the organization."

—Bill Belichick, May 9, 2014

TRUTH BE TOLD, FOR THE most part, Bill Belichick tried to hide his intentions. And so, while his remarks after selecting quarterback Jimmy Garoppolo sounded like a direct commentary on the play of aging franchise quarterback Tom Brady—and they were—Belichick also understood the magnitude of the matter. He tried to disguise the fact that Brady had seemingly started to slip, that he himself was planning for the long term, and so he tried to shape the discussion about his three-time Super Bowl–winning quarterback into an assessment of the Patriots' quarterback position as a whole, even going so far as to include backup quarterback Ryan Mallett in his analysis.

But nobody was really buying it.

On May 9, after all, the NFL had congregated at Radio City Music Hall in New York City for the second *and* third rounds on Day 2 of a three-day draft event. The Patriots ended up selecting just one player that day, announced to the world by former Patriots lineman Willie McGinest, who was booed by New York fans as he announced the sixty-second overall selection in the draft for "your New England and my New England Patriots . . . Jimmy Garoppolo, quarterback, Eastern Illinois." The team subsequently traded out of the third round, after which Belichick began his post–Day 2 media briefing trying to treat the selection of Tom Brady's would-be successor as if he had just chosen an anonymous right guard from the University of Iowa.

"Late night tonight, past curfew," Belichick mused to reporters. "So let's see, second round: so we took Jimmy Garoppolo. We spent a little time with him this spring. He's got a lot of qualities that we admire in a quarterback. . . . With the situation we have at quarterback, I think that we felt as an organization that we needed to address that to some degree in the future, so we'll see how all that works out. But I think you're better off being early than late at that position." Belichick then moved on, citing a trade of picks with the Jacksonville Jaguars, then shifting his commentary to the final four rounds of the draft, to be conducted on Saturday.

Nobody really cared about the trade of picks in the third round, let alone the coming choices in Rounds 4 to 7. Garoppolo, after all, was *the* story—at least as it pertained to the future of the great Tom Brady.

In the typical Q & A that followed, Belichick lapsed into obfuscation and was at times evasive, even snippy. (None of these were unusual for him.) As such, his ongoing exchange with the media only drew more attention to the most important question facing the Patriots amid the greatest stretch in their history: Who would be the next quarterback of the team?

As usual, Belichick's actions spoke louder—and much more honestly—than his words.

Garoppolo was the one.

"I don't have any control over how anything is going to unfurl," Belichick said when asked how much time Garoppolo might need to develop. "We put the players out there—and they compete and we evaluate them. I can't control that."

Translation: *We'll see what happens. Jimmy's going to need some time to learn. Tom is getting older. Maybe it will sort itself out.*

For Brady, of course, the drafting of Garoppolo struck an obvious nerve. Belichick had a long history of moving on from players, including Drew Bledsoe, whom Brady had replaced.

For 2014, at least, Brady seemed in no immediate danger, though Belichick's timeline was unclear. "I don't think any rookie player is ready to come in and play in the National Football League at any position," Belichick had said, but did that mean months or years? Brady himself was in his second year when he became the starter, something that was not terribly unusual in the NFL, especially at quarterback. But what the numbers showed, at least upon further inspection in the wake of the Garoppolo acquisition, was that Tom Brady's performance had diminished in the three years prior to the drafting of Belichick's shiny new toy.

After winning the MVP Award in 2010, Brady threw an early interception in a frustrating first-round playoff loss to the Jets. A year later he took a safety when called for intentional grounding while throwing from the end zone during the earliest stages of the Super Bowl loss to the Giants. And in 2012 he and the Patriots were eliminated by Brady's nemesis, the Baltimore Ravens, the Patriots' third straight home defeat in the playoffs.

If there had been any drop at all in Brady's game in 2011 and 2012, the variation was slight. But in 2013, while Brady's completion percentage and quarterback rating both decreased for a *third* straight season, the drop was more acute; both measures were at their lowest since 2003, when he was still more of an up-and-coming quarterback than one of the greatest winners in sports history. Whether that was the result of Brady's age or the abundance of personnel issues that had undermined the 2013 Patriots season, Brady was thirty-six years old and the arrow was more sharply pointing down. Altogether, those elements meant one thing and one thing only—like the others before him, Tom Brady was on notice, on the proverbial clock.

But as Brady would prove yet again during a career in which he most distinguished himself in the final minutes and seconds of any competition, he did not easily rattle. Tom Brady had always been at his very best when fighting against time.

* * *

Just before the start of the 2014 season, Bill Belichick put the entire Patriots roster on notice, firing a shot across the bow that caught the attention of Tom Brady and everyone else who lined up with him daily on the practice field. On August 26, less than two weeks before the season opener, Belichick traded standout left guard Logan Mankins to the Tampa Buccaneers for backup tight end Tim Wright and a fourth-round pick in the 2015 draft, a modest return for a player who had been an anchor on New England's offensive line, one of Brady's chief protectors over the years. The move was reminiscent of Belichick's decision to cut safety Lawyer Milloy just before the start of the 2003 season— and it hardly seemed a coincidence now that Milloy, like Mankins, was one of Brady's better friends on the team.

If Belichick was looking to get the attention of his entire roster, he was especially getting the attention of his quarterback.

A weekly guest on Boston radio station WEEI during much of his career with the Patriots, Brady addressed the Mankins deal for the very first time less than a week after the trade, telling hosts Gerry Callahan and John Dennis that Mankins "was a great friend of mine." His remarks did nothing to dispel reports that he was angry about the trade, which, of course, was precisely the reaction Belichick was hoping to get from his quarterback and team.

"I haven't really spoken to anybody about it," Brady told the hosts. "I have my own personal feelings that obviously are very personal to me. Whatever those are, I just want our team to be the best it can be for this year. I love Logan. . . . Nobody stood for Patriot football more than him. But he's moved on. I hope he's happy. We'll keep in touch. . . . I don't think [the departure of a close teammate] has ever gotten easier for me. And I don't think [it] ever will. But you've got to come to grips with it also and learn to deal with things in a mature way."

In the end, he didn't have a choice.

Nonetheless, as was the case following the Milloy release in 2003, the Patriots got off to a poor start, losing the season opener (a 33–20 defeat at Miami). After a pair of wins against Minnesota and Oakland, Week 4 handed the Patriots a Monday night game against the Chiefs in Kansas City, where the Patriots got utterly and uncharacteristically annihilated in a 41–14 rout that was never close. Brady fumbled twice and threw two interceptions in the game, the first of which was a lazy throw after a miscommunication with his receiver, the second of which was returned for a touchdown. It was arguably the worst performance of his career.

After the second interception, Belichick had seen enough, pulling Brady from the game with 10:28 to play in the fourth quarter and turning the offense over to Garoppolo, who promptly took the Patriots down the field and threw a touchdown pass to Gronkowski. Brady gave half-hearted congratulations to many of the New Englanders players coming off the field after the relatively meaningless score, albeit with one notable exception: Garoppolo, whom he seemingly refused to recognize as if he were a toddler ignoring a newborn baby brother.

In the aftermath of the defeat, the tension in the Patriots locker room and organization was quite real. Asked if he would "evaluate" the quarterback position, an evil-eyed Belichick all but shot lasers at a reporter. Admitting that "you never expect these things," Brady redirected his anger and frustration at someone other than his coach, citing public "negativity" and the inevitable reality that "everyone is going to tell us how terrible we are." Fifth-year defensive back Devin McCourty called the defeat "probably the most embarrassing game I've been part of."

Two days after the defeat, with his team in a short week because of the Monday night game, Belichick did his first media briefing of the week, a session intended to focus on the team's next opponent, the Cincinnati Bengals, and repeatedly refused to answer any questions from multiple reporters about the Chiefs debacle during an exchange that became, well, legendary.

Reporter: "How difficult is it to react to the adversity of Monday night and get back on track?"

Belichick: "We're on to Cincinnati."

Reporter: "You mentioned Tom's age at the draft ..."

Belichick: "We're on to Cincinnati."

Reporter: "But do you think having a 37-year-old ..."

Belichick: "We're on to Cincinnati ... it's nothing about the past. It's nothing about the future. Right now, we're preparing for Cincinnati."

Reporter: "OK, do you feel the talent here is good enough?"

Belichick: "We're getting ready for Cincinnati."

Reporter: "I'm just asking, do you think you've done enough to help Tom Brady?"

Belichick: "We're getting ready for Cincinnati. That's what we're doing."

So was born the new rallying cry of Patriots loyalists: *We're on to Cincinnati.*

Nonetheless, media speculation intensified, and respected NFL insiders reported on the tension in the locker room following both the selection of Garoppolo and the removal of the respected, bearded Mankins. (Brady had even grown a beard as a show of solidarity for his former teammate.) On the morning of Sunday, October 5, with the Patriots due to finally play Cincinnati that night, ESPN's Chris Mortensen reported with certainty that Garoppolo had been drafted as Brady's successor—and that the change could happen "sooner than later" if the team's poor play continued. The story essentially coincided with team president Jonathan Kraft's weekly appearance on the pregame show of the team's radio rightsholder, 98.5 The Sports Hub, where he acknowledged a "type of unhappiness, an internal frustration" over the team's poor play to that point in the season.

Things had reached a breaking point, it seemed, and, with the vultures circling, the Patriots did what they did best during the Brady-Belichick marriage: They circled the wagons and rallied. And then they went on a historic run.

With Brady leading the way, the Patriots obliterated the Bengals by a 43–17 score, then moved on to Buffalo and beat up on the Bills 37–22. Over the next five weeks, the Patriots piled up wins over the Jets, Bears, Broncos, Colts, and Lions, improving to 9-2 during a stretch that cemented them as a favorite in the AFC. While Brady was stellar during the seven-game winning streak—he threw twenty-two touchdown passes against four interceptions while compiling a quarterback rating of 111.7—the team was also fortified by the encouraging play of its defense, which had been shutting down some of the best passing offenses in the league. Over the final four weeks of the streak, after Browner had returned to the lineup following a season-opening suspension for violating the NFL's substance-abuse policy, the Patriots held opposing quarterbacks Jay Cutler, Peyton Manning, Andrew Luck, and Matthew Stafford to a combined seven touchdowns while recording four interceptions and seven sacks.

After the Chiefs embarrassment, in fact, the only meaningful game New England would lose for the balance of the regular season occurred in Week 13, when Aaron Rodgers and the Green Bay Packers defeated the Patriots 26–21 at Lambeau Field in what many believed might be a Super Bowl preview. The Patriots followed with wins against the Chargers, the Dolphins, and the Jets to secure the top seed in the AFC and improve to 12-3—11-1 since the Kansas City game.

In the last regular season game, against the downtrodden Bills, Garoppolo took the bulk of the snaps in what amounted to an exhibition game. By that point, nobody was talking about quarterback controversies. Most everyone was talking about something far more familiar to Bostonians of all ages: another championship.

"We've been able to score points against a lot of good teams, a lot of good defenses," said Brady, his team finishing fourth in the league in scoring offense and eighth in scoring defense despite a horrific start. "[But] nothing that we've done this past season is going to help in two weeks from now."

The comment, while relatively innocuous, was nonetheless noteworthy.

Tom Brady wasn't looking back anymore—be it at Garoppolo or Mankins or anyone else.

He was looking squarely ahead—at the opponents who stood between him, the Patriots, and a fourth Super Bowl title.

* * *

In the twenty years that Tom Brady and Bill Belichick worked together, the New England Patriots played in forty-one postseason games, including fourteen AFC Championship games and nine Super Bowls, winning six titles. Those extraordinary realities put the Patriots in the enviable and unusual position of being able to rate their seasons and accomplishments, all of which had different values. The 2004 team, for instance, was likely the Patriots' best. The 2001 season? The most important. And the 2007 edition was the most heartbreaking.

The 2014 postseason was, by many measures, the most eventful.

Blessed with a roster possessing astonishing star power—Brady, Revis, and Gronkowski all ranked among the greatest ever at their respective positions—the Patriots began their 2014 championship run at home against the Baltimore Ravens, otherwise known as Tom Brady's Kryptonite. The 2014 Ravens were a wild card team, but they possessed championship DNA. They had won the Super Bowl only two years earlier. And they were among the few teams who seemed unafraid of the Patriots. From the start, Baltimore had New England on its heels.

On the first possession of the game, the Ravens ran just five plays—four passes—to score the game's first touchdown, a 19-yard strike from quarterback Joe Flacco to wide receiver Kamar Aiken. Baltimore subsequently forced an immediate punt and went on another scoring drive, this one a longer, eleven-play, 79-yard trek that produced a 9-yard scoring strike from Flacco to Steve Smith, making it 14-0. Slightly more than ten minutes into the game, Baltimore had run sixteen offensive plays to the Patriots' four, and New England was rather suddenly in desperation mode.

Their defense reeling, the Patriots offense responded, Brady completing a relatively swift eight-play, 78-yard touchdown drive with a 4-yard rush by, of all people, the QB himself. After the defense finally awoke to stop the Ravens on two consecutive possessions, the Pats went down the field again, this time scoring on a pass from Brady to Danny Amendola, tying the game at 14-14 and erasing what had been a horrific start.

The euphoria didn't last long. With 1:03 left in the half and after a Brady interception—his eighth in three and a half career postseason games against the Ravens to that point—Flacco again effortlessly carved his way through the Patriots vaunted (possibly overrated) pass defense, completing five of seven passes over a mere fifty-three seconds to produce a 21-14 Baltimore lead at halftime. When the Patriots punted to start the second half, the Baltimore quarterback picked up right where he left off, overseeing another touchdown drive, this one culminating with a 16-yard strike to running back Justin Forsett, giving Baltimore its second 14-point lead of the day, 28-14, just five minutes into the second half. In slightly more than two quarters, a Baltimore passing attack that ranked a mediocre fourteenth in the NFL in efficiency was slicing up the Patriots like deli meat.

For the second time, the Patriots went into desperation mode, though this occasion made the prior one look like a rather simple test of the emergency broadcast system.

In NFL history, after all, no team ever had overcome two 14-point deficits in a playoff game.

Having driven into Baltimore territory, New England faced a second-and-6 at the Baltimore 24-yard line when the Patriots lined up in an unconventional formation featuring just four down linemen instead of five, a violation of NFL rules—or so it seemed. Confused, the Ravens failed to cover tight end Michael Hoomanawanui, who secured a 14-yard pass from Brady to the Ravens' 10-yard line. An irate John Harbaugh, the Ravens coach, subsequently ran onto the field to express his displeasure with the officials and was called for an unsports-manlike penalty, advancing the ball an additional 5 yards to the Baltimore 5. After one incomplete pass, Brady hit Gronkowski for a score to make it 28–21, shifting the game's momentum yet again and triggering a second incarnation of the Patriots dynasty that would consistently feature one theme.

The comeback.

After the game, Harbaugh openly and publicly complained about the rul-ing on the field, accusing the Patriots of "deception," a no-no in the rule book. Brady, as a retort, suggested Harbaugh "learn the rules." In the ensuing debate that lasted for days, the NFL ultimately sided with the Patriots, saying their formations and plays were entirely legal—no small victory for New Englanders given the cheating accusations and penalties that had resulted from Spygate only seven years earlier.

Still, the Ravens led by a touchdown when their offense returned to the field, but Baltimore's possession lasted all of fifty-eight seconds before punter Sam Koch kicked the ball away from his own 22-yard line and hit a 48-yard punt that went out of bounds at the New England 30. The Patriots wasted no time going right back on the offensive—and into their bag of tricks. Operating out of the no-huddle offense, Brady threw a 9-yard completion to Julian Edelman and a 10-yard completion to running back Shane Vereen. And then, with Brady now back under center, the quarterback took a quick snap and threw a backward out to the left sideline, where former college quarterback Edelman had settled. Edelman, in turn, fired a 51-yard touchdown strike to a wide-open Amendola, who scurried into the end zone to tie game at 28–28 and send Gillette Stadium into a state of bedlam.

On this play, Harbaugh had nothing to complain about. From the time the Patriots lined up with four offensive linemen to the time Edelman fired a perfect strike to Amendola, a mere three minutes had come off the clock. *Three minutes.* In less time than it took to soft boil an egg, the Ravens had lost a second 14-point lead as if they were coughing up breakfast after a long night out.

"Josh [McDaniels, the offensive coordinator] called it at the perfect time. We actually got the perfect look . . . ," Brady said after the game. "They bit up, obviously to try to go tackle Jules and Danny slipped behind them and Jules threw a dime. Pretty sweet play. We needed it. We needed a lot of plays. . . . A lot of guys fought through—a lot of mental toughness and I'm glad we pulled it out."

The Ravens, to their credit, actually pushed ahead yet again, albeit this time with a field goal. Brady returned to the field with 10:10 to play and the likelihood of at least two New England possessions before the end of regulation—but he needed only one. The drive was vintage Brady. On a ten-play, 74-yard masterpiece that consumed roughly half the game's remaining time, he completed eight of nine passes for 72 yards, his only incompletion coming on a deliberate throwaway to avoid a loss of yardage. He connected with six receivers, including Edelman, Vereen, Gronkowski, Amendola, Hoomanawanui, and Brandon LaFell, the last of whom caught both the drive starter (for 7 yards) and ender (23 yards and a touchdown) to give the Patriots their first lead of a hectic game, 35–31.

Needing a touchdown to go ahead, the Ravens took possession at their own 11 with 5:13 left. Flacco drove them to the New England 36 before throwing an interception in the end zone. The Patriots killed much of the remaining game clock before Baltimore had one final chance at a Hail Mary, which fell incomplete. The Patriots were headed to the AFC Championship Game for a fourth straight year, an affair that would prove this year's version of the Tomato Can Game after the back-and-forth struggle with the Ravens.

On this occasion, the Indianapolis Colts would serve as the opponent. And while the Colts would have little in common with the Ravens on the field of play—they were obliterated—they shared a common belief with Baltimore.

Specifically, they thought the Patriots were cheating again.

* * *

In retrospect, the only play that mattered in the game that crowned the 2014 AFC champion occurred just before the midpoint of the second quarter, when the Patriots already had a 14–0 lead. With the Patriots driving against the Colts for a third touchdown that would have the score 20–0 pending an extra point, Tom Brady dropped back on first-and-10 from the Indianapolis 26-yard line and targeted Rob Gronkowski near the goal line. Colts linebacker D'Qwell Jackson had excellent coverage of the play and intercepted the pass before being tackled at the 7-yard line, though the play ultimately did little to prevent the Colts from getting vaporized in a 45–7 Patriots victory.

As it was, Jackson returned to the sideline and handed the ball to a Colts staffer, triggering the scandal that would forever become known as "Deflategate."

For the Patriots, the ramifications would be considerable, but the greatest damage may have come in the relationship between Brady and Bill Belichick, the two men who stood at the nucleus of the Patriots operation.

At the time, particularly in the wake of the Patriots' trick-play victory over the Ravens, Deflategate took on a life of its own. Going on ten years without a championship, the Patriots in general—and Belichick in particular—were seen more and more as pathological cheaters, a team and coach who so desperately wanted to win that they would stop at nothing to do so and now had what amounted to a rap sheet: the clandestine videotaping of opponents; loophole formations that deceived the opposition; tampering with game balls. Were they all crimes against the league? No. But they all added to the perception that the Patriots were *shady*, the kind of organization that would pull the plug on an opposing team's headsets during a game.

And, of course, there was the trump card: *They had drafted a murderer, for goodness' sake.*

From the start, the Patriots organization seemed to make a concerted effort to protect Belichick from the matter, distancing him from any wrongdoing. They really had no choice. Following Spygate, believing that Belichick might still face a suspension, the Patriots hired former Carolina Panthers head coach Dom Capers to their staff as a secondary coach and special assistant—Capers was overqualified for the position—presumably to safeguard them if Belichick were disciplined by the league. Any transgression subsequent to Spygate might have necessitated worse, resulting in a firing or long-term suspension of arguably the greatest coach in football history.

In his first media briefing after the story first broke, Belichick pleaded ignorance—an impossible defense to accept given his acute attention to detail.

When the Patriots were preparing for Super Bowl XLVI against the Giants in Indianapolis, for instance, Madonna was scheduled to provide the entertainment at halftime. To accustom his team to the unusually long break that took place in the big game, Belichick halted practice for the same length of time as the halftime show and had Patriots staffers play songs by Madonna over speakers.

And yet, there Belichick was, in the immediate aftermath of the Patriots' dismantling of Indianapolis by a 45–7 score in the AFC Championship, claiming he generally knew nothing about the state of the footballs from game to game, let alone the idea that the Patriots would deliberately deflate them below league specifications to gain a competitive advantage.

"My overall knowledge of football specification and what happens on game day with the football is limited," he said. "During the course of the game, I have never touched a game ball. It's not something I have any familiarity with. I was completely and totally unaware of any of this that we're talking about in the last couple days until Monday morning." Added the coach: "In my entire coaching career I have never talked to any player [or] staff member about football air pressure. That is not a subject that I have ever brought up. To me the footballs are approved by the league and game officials pregame, and we play with what's out there."

Publicly, the media scoffed. Privately, Patriots players told stories of how Belichick would let the air out of footballs at practice when the team was preparing for games in extremely cold weather, knowing the drop in the temperature would affect the feeling and flight of kicks, in particular.

But of all the things Belichick said on Thursday, January 22—four days after the game—one comment stuck out the most.

"Tom's preference on the footballs is something he can talk about more in detail," Belichick said.

The message was clear: *Don't ask me. Go talk to Tom.*

And so what, exactly, were the Patriots thinking at the time? Only heaven knows. Maybe the Patriots thought the incident was nothing more than a brushfire. Maybe they believed Brady would get nothing more than a small fine, a relative slap on the wrist and nothing more. But they were mistaken. Many NFL owners felt the Patriots got off lightly in Spygate, that commissioner Roger Goodell had protected New England owner Robert Kraft, his supporter. In that instance, the league had admitted to destroying evidence. Now the Patriots were up to something again, leaving Goodell with little choice but to proceed (and prosecute?) aggressively, albeit after the Super Bowl.

Whatever the politics, Brady was now caught squarely in the middle of it, something his most trusted and loyal aides emphasized to him.

"Belichick has really dropped this in your lap right now," Brady's personal assistant, Will McDonough, wrote to the quarterback on January 22 in an email that later became public. "Don't take this lightly."

Not long after Belichick met with the media, Brady similarly spoke for the first time, looking and sounding unsettled and uneasy. Asked directly if he was a cheater, Brady said, rather boyishly, "I don't believe so." By the weekend between the conference championship games and the scheduled Super Bowl that would feature the Patriots and reigning champion Seattle Seahawks, an avalanche of reports and speculation had outlined the particulars. According to league rules, game balls were to be inflated to between 12.5 and 13.5 PSI for every game. Some of the Patriots game balls were below that number. ESPN'S Chris Mortensen initially reported that "11 of the New England Patriots' 12 game balls were inflated significantly below the NFL requirements," a report that eventually proved inaccurate but nonetheless triggered a firestorm. Before the end of the week following the AFC Championship Game, NFL commissioner Roger Goodell announced that he would commission an independent investigation into the Patriots' activities.

Along the way, perhaps sensing that the team had now dropped a ticking bomb into Brady's lap, Belichick, in particular, seemed to reverse course, delivering an unusual, out-of-character press conference in which he detailed the process by which the Patriots prepared game balls before handing them over to referees before the game. The coach acknowledged that Brady liked the balls on the low end of the allowed range—a PSI of 12.5—then introduced an array of variables—including the ideal gas law—that may or may not have contributed to the alleged drop in air pressure.

And then Belichick delivered the most memorable line of the entire extended briefing, citing a movie character that won actress Marisa Tomei an Academy Award in the hit film *My Cousin Vinny.*

"I just want to share with you what I've learned over the past week. I'm embarrassed to talk about the amount of time that I put into this relative to the other important challenge in front of us," said the coach, who was obviously busy trying to prepare his team for the Super Bowl. "I'm not a scientist. I'm not an expert in footballs. I'm not an expert in football measurements. I'm just telling you what I know. I would not say that I'm [the] Mona Lisa Vito of the football world, as she was in the car expertise area, alright?"

Just like that, Bill Belichick's unforgettable press briefing had its name: *The Mona Lisa Vito Press Conference.*

In the days that immediately followed, Deflategate became something less of a distraction, at least to the Patriots and Seahawks. The media, naturally, focused on it for much of the two weeks leading into the game. The Patriots' owner, Robert Kraft, addressed the matter himself upon arriving at the Super Bowl on January 26, 2015, proclaiming his team's innocence, said he would expect an apology from the league, and then vowed to speak no further about the matter as the Patriots, the Seahawks, and the NFL approached the biggest annual event on the sports calendar.

Little did anyone know that roughly a year and a half would pass before Deflategate would play out in its entirety—and that Brady and the team both would suffer significant penalties. Three months after the Super Bowl, investigator Ted Wells released the findings of his report, stating that it was "more probable than not [that] Tom Brady was at least generally aware" of a plan to deflate the footballs, a scheme that involved Patriots equipment man John Jastremski and game-day staffer Jim McNally, the latter of whom delivered the balls to and from the officials' locker room. The report included detailed text messages to and from Brady, Jastremski, and McNally—and the damning information that Brady had destroyed his cell phone, presumably to prevent the retrieval of additional communications. (Brady claimed this was something he did routinely.)

Five days after the Wells report was released, Goodell handed down the penalties: a $1 million fine and the loss of draft picks (a first- and fourth-rounder this time) for the Patriots, and a four-game suspension for Brady. On the same day the punishments were announced—May 11, 2015—Kraft said Goodell's verdict "far exceeds any reasonable expectation"; eight days later, the owner said the club would "reluctantly" accept the commissioner's decree because he did "not want to continue the rhetoric." In between, the Patriots launched their own rather embarrassing website, The Wells Report in Context, written by team lawyers, attempting to debunk the findings of Wells. Among the assertions: that McNally referred to himself as "the deflator" in text messages not because he was up to anything devious with the footballs but because he was trying to lose weight. Outside of blindly loyal Patriots fans, nobody was buying it.

Amid it all, on May 14, Brady formally appealed his suspension with the league, a hearing that took place with Goodell as arbiter in late June. On June 28, Goodell announced his decision and upheld Brady's four-game suspension. Brady appealed his case in July and, in August, went before New York–based judge Richard Berman, who tried to broker a settlement before ruling in Brady's favor in early September. As Brady prepared to play the full sixteen-game 2015 season, the NFL returned serve and appealed Berman's decision, placing the matter, incredibly, in the hands of a United States appeals court.

In April 2016, after the entire 2015 NFL season, the appeals court ruled in favor of the NFL, a victory that validated the power of the commissioner as outlined in the collective bargaining agreement between NFL owners and players. By July, Brady faced the choice of appealing the matter to the Supreme Court or accepting the penalty and putting the entire issue to rest; he mercifully chose the latter on July 15, 2016—precisely 544 days after the 2014 AFC Championship Game against the Colts.

During the eighteen months of muck: Equipment man Jastremski and staffer McNally were fired from the Patriots organization and never heard from, a fate similar to that of former Patriots aide Matt Walsh, a key source in Spygate; the Patriots and Brady restructured Brady's contract, lowering his base salary in 2016 so as to minimize any salary lost by the player during his suspension; Jimmy Garoppolo started at quarterback for the Patriots to begin the 2016 season, driving a wedge further between Brady and Belichick.

* * *

Lest anyone forget, at the very beginning of it all, the Patriots and Seattle Seahawks played one of the truly great and memorable Super Bowls in NFL history—perhaps the greatest. From the start of the 2013 NFL season and through three rounds of the 2014 playoffs, the Seahawks had established themselves as the most fearsome team in football. Including the playoffs, Seattle posted thirty wins in thirty-seven games, going 5-0 in the postseason. They had scored the third-most points in football while allowing the fewest, the latter of which was the result of a fast, physical, and downright ferocious defense known as the "Legion of Boom." And in the Super Bowl that concluded the 2013 NFL season, the Seahawks bullied and battered the Denver Broncos from the start, thundering their way to a dominating 43–8 victory over Peyton Manning and a Denver offense that had set an NFL scoring record.

The Seahawks were a force. But the Patriots were a vastly different team than they had been the previous season, for one reason above all others: health. Brady had a full complement of weapons at his disposal, from Gronkowski to

Edelman to LaFell and Amendola, and he would need them all against Seattle's intimidating pass defense. The Seahawks played a bruising style on both sides of the ball—running back Marshawn Lynch, known as "Beast Mode," was the central figure in their offense—and they had a young, athletic, accurate, and poised quarterback, Russell Wilson, who managed the game smartly.

And then there was this: For the Patriots, the game would be played at University of Phoenix Stadium in Glendale, Arizona, site of the team's Super Bowl XLII defeat to the New York Giants that ended New England's undefeated season and, it seemed, the team's stranglehold on the Vince Lombardi Trophy. If the Patriots were to resurrect themselves, they would have to do so in the graveyard where their perfect season had died.

"It's the matchup I wanted," said Patriots defensive back Brandon Browner, who played on the Seattle team that defeated the Broncos. "Them my boys. Them my brothers. One of the brothers is going to have bragging rights for the whole offseason. I'm trying to be the one. I've been thinking about this for months. . . . It's Ali-Frazier if that's what you want to call it. May the best team win."

And then, for one of the relatively rare times in history, the teams played a game that exceeded the hype.

With the game scoreless early in the first quarter, the Patriots were driving on their second possession of the game when they faced a third-and-10 at the Seattle 10-yard line. Working out of the shotgun, Brady took the snap and surveyed the field, unable to find an open receiver. He bounced on his feet and patted the ball with his left hand, then threw a careless, errant pass into the middle of the field that defensive back Jeremy Lane easily intercepted. Lane turned to his right and started scampering upfield near the right sideline when a relentless Edelman barreled into his left leg, an airborne Lane attempting to break his fall with his left arm as he landed to the turf at the Seahawks 14-yard line.

Lane broke his left wrist on the play. He was done for the night. And so, with less than a quarter gone in a Super Bowl featuring two of the most intense and competitive teams in all of sports, the message was clear: *Play at your own risk.*

When the Patriots got the ball back the next time, they finished the job. After Brady kept the drive alive with a 23-yard completion to Edelman on third-and-9 at the Seattle 35-yard line, the Patriots faced a second-and-9 at the Seattle 11. Again Brady lined up in the shotgun with Brandon LaFell lined up wide to his left across from Tharold Simon, who had replaced Lane in the game. A far more decisive Brady accepted the snap and rifled a quick pass to LaFell, who had broken inward toward the hash marks, Simon off his left hip. The ball zipped through a brief opening between Simon and highly regarded safety Earl Thomas, LaFell securing the pass and slipping into the end zone as the Seattle defenders collided, giving the Patriots a 7–0 advantage.

The margin for error on the play was slim, the message again clear: *You'd better be damned near perfect.*

After the teams exchanged quick possessions, the Seahawks, too, found their rhythm—and through an unlikely source. After the Patriots possessed the ball for more than fifteen of the game's first twenty minutes, Seattle put together an eight-play, 70-yard scoring drive highlighted by a 44-yard pass from Wilson to relatively unknown receiver Chris Matthews, who took the ball to the Patriots 11-yard line. The Seahawks then gave the ball on three straight plays to battering ram Lynch—remember this—who pounded his way into the end zone to tie the game at 7.

Almost instantly, a first quarter that generally highlighted the defenses turned offensive, with the teams trading punches. Less than two minutes after the Seahawks' score, Brady lobbed an easy 22-yard touchdown pass to Gronkowski, who had drawn single coverage from linebacker K. J. Wright—an enormous mismatch in favor of the Patriots. The strike came with just thirty-one seconds remaining in the quarter and seemed certain to give the Patriots a lead into halftime, though Seattle still had a chance at a field goal with thirty-one seconds and three time-outs remaining before intermission.

The Seahawks, in fact, initially seemed content to go into halftime with the score as it was, then gained 19 yards on a draw play to running back Robert Turbin, whose gain out to the 39-yard line immediately prompted Seattle to call the first of its three time-outs. With just twenty-four seconds remaining on the clock, Seattle ultimately ran four plays, beginning with a scramble by Wilson, who scurried 17 yards before stepping out of bounds at the Patriots' 44-yard line with seventeen seconds to go. After an incomplete pass, Wilson completed a 23-yard strike to receiver Ricardo Lockette, who caught the pass after escaping a face-masking penalty by Patriots defensive back Kyle Arrington. The additional yardage from the penalty moved the ball to the Patriots' 11-yard line with six seconds left, when Seattle coach Pete Carroll decided to make at least one attempt at a touchdown.

After a Seattle time-out and working from the shotgun, Wilson took the snap and fired quickly at the six-foot-five Matthews, who was given a spongy cushion by Pats defensive back Logan Ryan. Fearing a pass over his head in much the same way that Gronkowski had exposed Wright on the game's previous touchdown, Ryan instead allowed the bigger Matthews to box him out while securing a pass just inside the goal line, tying the game at 14 with two seconds to play in the half.

Incredibly, Seattle had traveled 80 yards in twenty-nine seconds on just five plays—including an incompletion.

When the game resumed—and because they had the ball to start the second half—the Seahawks began imposing their will. Seattle again advanced with little resistance, going 63 yards in three plays, concluding with another long strike to Matthews, this one for 45 yards. Once again lined up to Wilson's left, Matthews this time easily outjumped the much shorter Arrington down the sideline, placing Seattle at the New England 17-yard line less than two minutes into the half. When Lynch followed with a 7-yard run, the Seahawks had a second-and-3 at the New England 10-yard line and seemed destined again to breeze into the endzone.

Though the Patriots defense stiffened, stopping Lynch on third-and-1 at the New England 8 to force a field goal, the Seahawks held their first lead of the game, 17–14, when Brady threw another interception. This one, however, came on the New England side of the field and proved much more costly than the first.

The Seahawks breezed down the field and into the end zone, this time on an easy 3-yard toss from Wilson to a wide-open Doug Baldwin after Revis, who was covering on the play, collided with an official in the middle of the end zone. Shortly after a frustrated Revis tossed his hands in the air back at the official, television cameras caught Seattle counterpart Richard Sherman on the sideline, holding up two fingers and then four—the number (24) worn by Revis—mouthing the player's name while pointing to the replay on the scoreboard.

In a game that featured two of the game's best cover corners, Sherman now had the edge. And so did the Seahawks, 24–14.

Now blessed with a 10-point lead and the best defense in football, Seattle had New England precisely where they wanted them. The teams traded possessions until early in the fourth quarter, when the Seattle lead was still at 10, and just twelve minutes and ten seconds remained on the game clock.

At that instant, the Seattle Seahawks were just one of the obstacles facing the Patriots in the sixth Super Bowl of Tom Brady's career. The other was time.

* * *

Roughly nine months after the Patriots selected Jimmy Garoppolo and less than two weeks after Bill Belichick saddled him with Deflategate, Tom Brady trotted onto the field at University of Phoenix Stadium and reclaimed his place atop the NFL with the best fourth quarter of his career.

After a short completion to LaFell on second down, Brady stepped up in the pocket on third-and-14, firing a 21-yard strike to Edelman, who held on to the ball despite a hellacious hit from safety Kam Chancellor. Four plays later, on third-and-8, Brady and Edelman connected again, Edelman this time landing in a soft spot of the Seattle zone defense before catching the pass and squirting forward to the Seattle 4-yard line. On the very next play, Edelman lined up to Brady's left against Jeremy Lane's replacement, Tharold Simon, and darted in toward the middle of the field. Just before Brady started to throw, Edelman sharply planted and reversed direction and Simon skidded, leaving Edelman wide-open for a touchdown. But Brady overthrew him slightly, the ball deflecting off the tip of Edelman's right hand for an incompletion.

On the next play, lined up in the slot to Brady's left, Amendola slid into the middle of Seattle's zone, turned his body, and caught a Brady laser for the Patriots' third touchdown of the game, making the score 24–21 with just over four minutes to play.

For the third straight series after taking a 24–14 lead, the Seattle Seahawks went three plays and out, taking a mere 1:03 off the game clock and giving Tom Brady the ball back with 6:52 to play. That was a mistake.

Beginning what would be the Patriots' final drive of Super XLIX, Brady guided the Patriots on a ten-play, 64-yard touchdown drive that was downright surgical and, from his standpoint, perfect. The Patriots actually snapped the ball eleven times on the drive, but one play was negated by an offensive interference penalty against Amendola, negating what would have been a 6-yard completion to running back Shane Vereen. Two of the other ten snaps were runs garnering nine yards. Seven of the final remaining eight were passes—all completions—to Vereen (8 yards), Vereen again (5 yards), Edelman (9 yards), Gronkowski (20 yards), Vereen (no gain), Gronkowski (13 yards), and LaFell (7 yards).

The remaining play was the same one the Patriots had called on the prior drive—Edelman, out left, defended by Simon—with Edelman to the inside, then back out toward the sideline. Once again Edelman was wide-open. And this time Brady didn't miss.

All in all on the drive, counting the play negated by the Amendola penalty, Brady was nine for nine for 71 yards and a touchdown. Combined with the previous drive, with the Patriots' season on the line, Brady had gone fourteen for sixteen for 130 yards and two touchdowns against the best and most intimidating defense in the NFL to give the Patriots a 28–24 lead with slightly more than two minutes to play.

But, incredibly, the game wasn't even close to being decided.

After a touchback on the ensuing kickoff, Seattle immediately attacked. On first down and with Wilson in the shotgun formation with an empty backfield, bulldozer Lynch lined up to the far left, like a wide receiver, then shuffled his feet at the snap, acting as if he were a decoy. Lynch then burst past linebacker Jamie Collins, who was in coverage, and hauled in a 31-yard strike down the left sideline that brought the Seahawks all the way to the New England 49-yard line, the clock stopping immediately as the teams reached the two-minute warning.

With precisely 1:55 remaining on the clock, the teams had just begun one of the most astonishing sequences that would end with one of the most extraordinary finishes in sports history—football or otherwise.

After two incompletions, Wilson faced a third-and-10 from the New England 49 with 1:41 to play when he connected with receiver Lockette, who caught a hitch just before the first down marker before turning upfield for an additional three yards, eleven in all. First down. On the next snap, with the clock still running . . . *1:12* . . . *1:11* . . . *1:10* . . . Wilson lofted a ball down the right sideline for receiver Jermaine Kearse, who had a step on backup and relatively unknown cornerback Malcolm Butler to the outside. (Butler had entered the game as replacement for Arrington, who had played poorly.) As the ball approach the 12-yard line, both men jumped, the pass deflecting off their hands as both fell to the turf. As they landed together, the ball followed, glancing off both of Kearse's legs and then back into the air. Both players now *on their backs*, the ball drifted toward the goal line—over Kearse's head and just beyond his outstretched arms—when Kearse rolled backward toward his left shoulder and miraculously secured the pass. He then stood up before Butler forced him out of bounds at the New England 5-yard line.

In real time, as referees marked the ball at the 5, millions watched in amazement, uncertain of what had just taken place. *What the* . . . *?* Replays ultimately confirmed that the play was indeed a catch—no ifs, ands, or buts—drawing immediate and inevitable comparisons to David Tyree's circus catch for the New York Giants seven years earlier.

On the sideline, Brady shook his head in disbelief as he watched a replay of Kearse's catch on the scoreboard.

The Seahawks then called time-out, their second. They had one remaining. After conferring on the sideline, Wilson returned to the field with 1:06 to play. The Seahawks broke the huddle and Wilson handed to Lynch, who bulled his way through the right side of the Patriots defense, prevented from scoring by linebacker Dont'a Hightower, who sufficiently shed his block to get Lynch to the ground with what amounted to one arm. It was second-and-goal from the 1-yard line. Seeking to drain as much of the clock as possible to prevent Brady from getting another chance to score, the Seahawks did not call a time-out. Belichick curiously did the same, letting time dwindle as the Seahawks approached the line of scrimmage for second down, seemingly on the verge of a second consecutive Super Bowl title with a simple handoff to the human tank known as Beast Mode, who had led the NFL in rushing touchdowns (thirteen) during the regular season and whose forty-eight touchdowns over a four-year span far outdistanced any running back in the NFL.

Unbelievably, Seattle did not give him the ball.

With Lynch to his left and just twenty-five seconds remaining in the game, Wilson operated from the shotgun and took the snap. He took one step back and immediately snapped a pass for Lockette, who converged with the football and Butler in the middle of the field. In the final, violent collision of a game filled with them, an airborne Lockette ricocheted toward the 2-yard line while Butler bounced backward toward the end zone, the football in his hands. Interception, Patriots. Heartbreak, Seahawks. And another championship for Boston.

Brady watched it all from the New England sideline like a fan, euphorically jumping up and down as if he had just sprung from his sofa.

"Unbelievable play by Malcolm," he said later. "We didn't call a timeout and the clock was winding down, and we realized, you know, this is basically it if we stopped them. I saw the interception and couldn't believe it. It was just an incredible play. You know, what a play. A championship play."

Said exasperated Seattle coach Pete Carroll, whose decision to pass—and bypass Lynch—would go down as one of the great blunders and what-if moments in sports history: "It's a miraculous play the kid made to get in front of that route. It's a play that really tries to keep him from getting in front. I told those guys, 'It's my fault,' because everyone was like, 'Why don't we just run it?' That's a real good thought, but we had plenty of time to win the game, and we would have in our minds done it on third or fourth down, and that's how we were playing—for third or fourth down—give them no time and it would have been just right. But it didn't work out that way."

No, it didn't.

Following the New England victory, the fallout was considerable for both franchises on and off the field. Though the Seahawks remained one of the better teams in the NFL during the union of coach Carroll and quarterback Wilson, they never again reached the Super Bowl, destroyed by a combination of regret, finger-pointing, and frustration; in fact, they never again reached the conference championship game. The Legion of Boom defense was dismantled over a succession of years, never again reaching elite status. Lynch played just one more season for Seattle, limited to just seven games because of injury, and sat out the 2016 season before resuming his career with the Oakland Raiders. What might have been a Seahawks dynasty seemingly disintegrated with the most basic offensive decision: *Should we run or should we pass?*

For the Patriots, after nine seasons without a championship, the win triggered a new phase in their dominance, a second bookend to perfectly frame their dynasty. But this win was largely about Brady, whose sixth Super Bowl appearance and fourth championship raised him to immortal status. A year after being devoid of pass catchers in the loss at Denver, Brady finished with four touchdown passes—one each to LaFell, Gronkowski, Amendola, and Edelman—and tied his boyhood idol Joe Montana for the most Super Bowl wins in history (four). Just as importantly, he had reversed the downward trajectory that had produced decreases in completion percentage and passer rating for three straight years that led the team to draft Garoppolo.

Asked immediately after the game whether a fourth Super Bowl title prompted him to ponder his legacy, Brady shook his head.

"No," he said. "I've got a lot of football left."

His answer went on for a bit, Brady outlining the challenges of winning in a game like football, in a league like the NFL. But the essence of it was in those seven words. *I've got a lot of football left.*

As it turned out, nobody could have possibly imagined how much.

CHAPTER 13

THE C'S RISE . . . THEN FALL

"That's the way I felt when we moved here—a small town . . . with lots of traffic."

—Celtics coach Brad Stevens, July 2020

BRAD STEVENS WAS BORN, BRED, and built in Indiana, where basketball is taken seriously. In that way, Boston made all the sense in the world for him. Stevens was born and went to high school in Zionsville, attended DePauw University in Greencastle, and became a coach just outside Indianapolis at Butler University, home to fewer than 5,000 undergraduate students and one of the ten NCAA Division 1 basketball programs in the state of Indiana. In his third and fourth seasons of what proved to be a six-year career with the Bulldogs, Stevens took Butler to consecutive NCAA Championship games, nearly upsetting Duke in the 2010 title game when a final, half-court shot by then Butler player Gordon Hayward bounced off both the backboard and the rim.

In the end, Butler lost both title games—but Stevens earned a reputation as a basketball prodigy, precisely the kind of young, ambitious coach around whom Celtics chief basketball executive Danny Ainge wanted to build Boston's next basketball championship team with sustainability in mind.

For Brad Stevens, in retrospect, Butler was basketball boot camp.

"I've said this many times to my friends: I don't know if it was intrinsic or if it really was the outside expectations and pressure of coaching in your hometown and making a couple of Final Fours, then continuing on after that for a couple of years, [but it] was as much as internal pressure as I've ever felt," Stevens said of his Butler years in July 2020, during his seventh season as coach of the Celtics. "Basketball matters so much in Indianapolis that I felt really responsible for having a good team."

And Boston?

"It's funny," Stevens continued. "In 2018, the Bruins are in the Stanley Cup and my kids would be like, 'Dad, you blew it, you guys are the only ones who didn't win this year—the Red Sox, the Patriots won.' And they're killing me. They're just killing me. And I'm just like, 'One of these days, you'll probably live someplace or you'll be someplace where it's okay to win a lot of games and put your best foot forward and give it your best shot.' But you live in Boston. And so you've got to understand that just comes with it if you're coaching or playing. A lot of times, the way you're viewed is very simple. It's either: did you win it all or didn't you win it all? And [that's] the way your tenure is viewed. But I don't think that that's the way that any of us that are inside of it view it."

Not long after Stevens arrived in Boston, he received a text from Bill Belichick. Though they'd never met, Belichick got his number and sent him a message as if delivering a warm batch of chocolate chip cookies to a new neighbor. Not long after, Stevens had lunch with Josh McDaniels, who had grown up in Ohio. They were roughly the same age and had come from the same part of the country. They both had families and were in the same profession. The two forged a friendship that has grown and strengthened over the years, outsiders who penetrated the city walls and become part of a thriving sports empire.

"When he got the job, I just reached out to him because I knew [Stevens and his wife, Tracy] were a very similar age to my wife [Laura] and I, and I knew they were from the Midwest," McDaniels recalled. "So I extended an invitation just to say, 'Hey, if there's anything we can do to help you . . . we came from Ohio, I know you guys are coming from Indiana. We'd love to help in any way that we can—the transition to the East Coast, to Boston, schools, etc.' He returned my call, basically, immediately, and took us up on the offer and we started talking about different things in this area. He moved to Wellesley, we live in Westwood, so, we're not very far away from one another. Basically, the friendship has grown since then. We've been to dinner with him and his wife multiple times and been to a lot of Celtics games. He's brought his son, Brady, to a Patriots playoff game. He's been over here to see us practice now numerous times in the spring and in training camp. We talk about the sports that we're involved in, but we've also been able to talk about other things outside of that. We're both obviously fathers, with kids in high school and middle school, and it's been interesting to kind of see the process and the maturation of our families as we've kind of now grown up here in Boston."

Over the years, Stevens has made trips to Foxborough to explore the inner workings of the Patriots operation, to exchange coaching philosophies and methods, to pick the brains of those who have succeeded as much as any coaches in history, probably more, albeit in a different sport. On occasion, Stevens has brought Celtics players with him, including Jayson Tatum, the player who would become the cornerstone of the Celtics' quest for an eighteenth championship, the nucleus for their run at *sustainability*. McDaniels similarly attended Celtics sessions, sometimes with Nick Caserio, the Patriots' personnel director and a former college teammate of McDaniels. The roads from Foxborough to Boston were two-way streets, thoughts and ideas flowing both ways.

In the quest for sustainability, of course, the Patriots, in particular, were an invaluable resource. No one was better equipped to discuss it than Belichick, who would go on to have a whopping nineteen straight winning seasons in New England, seventeen in a row with at least ten wins. When Stevens arrived in 2013, Belichick had taken his team to five Super Bowls and won three; and he was about to go to a sixth that would produce a fourth title. Belichick had become to football what longtime Celtics great Red Auerbach had been to basketball.

So what did Stevens learn? That coaches—at least the good ones—all have a something in common, no matter how obvious: a belief in fundamentals, a demand for them. An unbending insistence. He saw this in Belichick, who during his time in New England repeatedly coached disciplined teams that played mistake-free. They protected the football. They did not commit penalties. They generally blocked well and tackled well. They were usually where they were supposed to be. To win consistently, you always had to start there.

"I think you learn a lot from going over there," Stevens said.

And you know what—and I'm sure this isn't top secret stuff, maybe Bill will be mad at me, but whatever—every time he's been over here . . . every time we've been over there he's said, "You can't win 'til you keep from losing." I just think there's truth in that, and how many times have the Patriots just won because they didn't beat themselves and the other team shot themselves in the foot? It's basically—I always talk about how every one of us has a margin for error. Our margin for error isn't probably what the Lakers' or the Bucks' is, so we have to manage our margin for error better than they do. And that's what the Patriots do, they manage that margin of error. And the other thing I'll never forget Bill Belichick telling me was when I asked him, "What do you think about this year's team?"

It was one of the years they went on to win the Super Bowl and he said, "We have enough." A lot of coaches might say, "Well, I'm a little concerned about our . . . whatever . . . *this, this or that, this.*" But now it's just about finding the right button to push and those types of things. I thought that was great. He's as good as advertised. When you are coaching a complex game like football or a game that moves at the speed of ours, but you're trying to get in a ton of different things to get ready for the game or run a ton of different plays or have done different coverages where the case may be, if you can simplify everything to the best degree so that people can play fast, free and to do so with great purpose, that's a coach's job. It's to simplify the message and to have a plan of attack that makes sense and that can be easily executed with the right amount of work. I'm not sure I've ever seen anybody in coaching who seems less . . . who seems to be distracted less by anything else that doesn't matter. I just think we all live our daily lives, we all have so much going on in our minds, I just . . . I get the impression when I'm there that Belichick just has the ultimate focus of, "This is what our team needs to do to get better today so we can beat the next team we're playing." That's the way I feel when I'm around him. There is no sense of distraction.

This was the world Brad Stevens walked into when he arrived in Boston in 2013. He walked into a place where Belichick was a royal, where he had met Red Sox manager John Farrell through a mutual friend, where he had encountered Bruins coach Claude Julien in the TD Garden, the arena the teams shared. And he entered a world where all four sports were treated the way basketball was treated in Indiana, and where everyone seemed to know everyone and your business was their business.

Brad Stevens's first instincts about Boston, in short, were correct. Small town. Lots of traffic.

* * *

Danny Ainge had played in Boston long before he had worked there, so he knew what to expect. He also knew that Stevens would fit. As Ainge began deconstructing the Celtics roster in 2013, he knew that a new coach would be part of the process—that Doc Rivers had no particular interest in coaching a young and inexperienced team, not after the years with Kevin Garnett, Paul Pierce, and Ray Allen.

The off-season between the 2012–13 and 2013–14 seasons was the perfect time to take it all apart. The Celtics were going from buyers to sellers, and the Clippers and Nets—both longtime, losing franchises—were eager to deal. In the span of a week, Ainge dealt Rivers to the Clippers for a first-round pick in the 2015 draft, Pierce and Garnett (in tandem) to Brooklyn for a complex collection of players and draft picks that ultimately landed Boston first round picks in 2014, 2016, and 2018—plus the right to swap picks with Brooklyn in 2017. Altogether, Ainge effectively acquired five unprotected first-round selections for his coach and two best players, pieces that he hoped would allow him to draft or trade for the players who would join Stevens at the center of the Celtics' next era.

In the NBA, more than any other league, such trades were common, often an indication that a franchise was preparing to lose deliberately to increase the value of its own draft picks and the odds of finding the most valuable commodity in the game: the franchise player. History had shown that NBA championships were almost always built around superstars. Ainge knew this, but he also knew that Boston was hardly the kind of place where deliberately losing would be mocked.

"We are not tanking," Ainge told reporters. "That's ridiculous. This is the Boston Celtics."

For him, the Brooklyn trade allowed the best of both worlds. He could focus on building his roster—with an astute, fundamentally driven coach—and deliver his city an honest product. And he could wait for the Nets' short window to expire, then let the Nets tank for him.

The plan, at least at the outset, pretty much worked to perfection. Stripped bare in the wake of the Brooklyn trade, the Celtics went 25-57 in 2013–14, their roster built around mercurial point guard Rajon Rondo, a rookie on the championship team of 2008 and a perfect illustration of how the NBA worked. With Garnett, Pierce, and Allen, Rondo went to two finals, played in four All-Star Games and twice led the league in assists. But when those players departed, he proved incapable of leading a good team. None of that was an indictment on Rondo so much as it was a reality of the superstar-driven NBA.

As such, despite rampant speculation about making Rondo a centerpiece of the new Celtics—a popular rumor had Ainge building the Celtics around Rondo and power forward Kevin Love, who was similarly stuck in Minnesota—Rondo lasted only slightly more than a year in Boston without the big three.

Using their own pick in the 2014 draft, the Celtics selected point guard Marcus Smart from Oklahoma State with the No. 6 selection, then used the first of their Brooklyn selections (No. 17) of forward James Young of Kentucky. That December, Ainge traded Rondo to the Dallas Mavericks in a move that delivered, among others, forward Jae Crowder to Boston. Two months after that, Ainge executed a multiple team trade that also brought undervalued point guard Isaiah Thomas to the Celtics, all while Stevens guided the team to a surprising 40-42 record that landed the Celtics in the playoffs, where they were swiftly dismissed by the Cleveland Cavaliers, elevated overnight back to contender status thanks to the return of LeBron James.

In the aftermath of the Celtics' exit, James gave his stamp of approval to the Celtics' growth, no small endorsement given his standing and power in the league.

"I highly respect their coaching staff and especially their head coach—a very well coached team," James said. "He put those guys out there every night and put them in position to win the game, and I think Brad Stevens is a very good young coach in our league."

And so it went, the Celtics building upon themselves with a collection of draft picks, a studious coach, and some smaller subtle moves that would ultimately lead to bigger ones.

After the series loss to Cleveland, the Celtics selected Terry Rozier with the draft's sixteenth overall pick. The subsequent season, they won forty-eight games, nearly double the total from Stevens's first year, though they were again bounced in the first round of the playoffs, this time by the Atlanta Hawks in six games. Under Stevens, the Celtics had become young, scrappy, and likable—and yet they still fell significantly short of the standard required to be an NBA champion. Their defeat to the Hawks spoke volumes, because Atlanta, like Boston, had finished 48-34. And after defeating the Celtics in six games—the Celtics lost pivotal Game 5 of a 2-2 series in Atlanta by 27 points, indicating the gap between the clubs—the Hawks were then walloped by LeBron James and the Cleveland Cavaliers in a four-game sweep.

The moral of the story: In the NBA, youth and pluck might work during the regular season but were useless in the playoffs. When the star players like James were focused and committed, the Celtics simply did not measure up.

Ainge, of course, knew this as well as anyone, having spent a lifetime in basketball, many of those years alongside Larry Bird in the Celtics' glory years of the 1980s. He also knew that the chances of landing a superstar in any draft were relatively slim. So as Ainge amassed assets, he at least partly did so with the idea of replicating the trade that had delivered Kevin Garnett to Boston during the summer of 2007, albeit with one significant difference. He wanted someone younger, someone around whom the Celtics could possess a longer championship window.

During the summer of 2016, Ainge had a specific target in mind: Kevin Durant. And when the Celtics made their pitch to the player, Ainge summoned a secret weapon: Tom Brady.

Under normal circumstances and at a normal time, the idea of recruiting a basketball player with a football player might have seemed far-fetched, ridiculous, entirely self-serving. And while it was still all of those things, it was simultaneously the single greatest example, on the field or in the arena, of one Boston team trying to help another during the city's reign as a North American sports empire. Certainly, the players and coaches had interacted over the years, but this was Ainge, of the *Celtics*, bringing Brady, of the *Patriots*, on a recruiting trip to the Hamptons to secure one of the greatest free agents in sports history—and a player with whom Ainge had something of an obsession.

Back in 2007, while most NBA types looked to big man Greg Oden as the No. 1 selection, Ainge had his eye on Durant, rumors persisting when Ainge was seen at a Texas game sitting next to Durant's mother during a conference tournament, a no-no that drew the Celtics a small fine.

Oden, of course, went to the Portland Trailblazers with the No. 1 selection but had injury problems early in his career and proved a bust. Durant went No. 2 to the Seattle Supersonics (who quickly moved to Oklahoma City and became the Thunder), then went on to have one of the most prolific careers in NBA history.

Boston basketball fans took note: *Danny was right.*

So, in 2016, Ainge brought out the big guns. "He's a huge Tom Brady fan," Ainge told the *Boston Herald* of Durant. "They talked for a minute or two and then we sat down as a group."

Said Durant to the *Herald* months after the meeting: "I was ready to just say, 'All right, let's go, I'm ready to go,' seeing Tom Brady there. Just seeing someone so successful at his craft and just a great ambassador for the game of football and the city of Boston, it was just great to be in the presence of greatness. But, at the same time, I knew I couldn't let that distract me. But he was great. It was great to see him."

Of course, Brady wasn't enough. Durant took the most direct path to his first championship and signed with the Golden State Warriors to join both Stephen Curry and Klay Thompson, giving Golden State arguably the greatest shooting trio of teammates in NBA history, an unstoppable collection of talent that effectively sealed any and all discussions about league dominance so long as the three were healthy and playing together.

During Durant's first year in Golden State, the Warriors went 67-15 during the regular season and a preposterous 16-1 in the playoffs, their only loss coming in Game 4 of the NBA Finals at Cleveland, when they had already built a 3-0 series lead. (They won the championship on their home floor in Game 5.) The Warriors had gone an insane 31-2 over their final thirty-three games, at a time of year when, in theory, the competition mattered most. No one else was even close, including the Celtics.

Having lost out on Durant, the Celtics instead signed center and power forward Al Horford, a would-be five-time NBA All-Star who was a perfect fit for Stevens. Though he was not an elite NBA athlete, Horford was smart and skilled, the perfect complement to a superstar. The ongoing problem, of course, was that the Celtics didn't possess the latter. In 2016–17, Boston ultimately won fifty-three games during the regular season and won its first two playoff series under Stevens, advancing to the conference finals. Once there, they were unceremoniously dismantled by James and the Cavaliers in five games, their four defeats coming by an average of 27 points. Cleveland then got obliterated by the Warriors, a sobering reminder of how the NBA was structured.

The championship teams were *here*. The Celtics, like most everyone else, were *there*. In between was an entire galaxy.

"We were all disappointed in the way we ended this season, but we were able to take a lot of positives away," Celtics guard Avery Bradley told reporters. "Out of all the teams in the NBA, we're one of the [four] teams left at this time of the year and that was one of our goals. Obviously our main goal was to make it to the championship and win it, but for us to be in the Eastern Conference finals after the first year of this team really being together, adding additions like Al Horford . . . I can go down the list of guys that we needed to learn to play with. And for us to talk about where we wanted to be and actually make it, it's a big-time accomplishment."

In the short term, for certain, there was some cause for optimism. The Celtics were still young. They were still getting better. In addition to Horford, the Celtics also had selected young forward Jaylen Brown, from the University of California, with the No. 3 overall selection of the draft—a pick they had acquired from the Brooklyn Nets, who had deteriorated rapidly into nothingness. Boston now had good, developing young players, a stabilizing presence in Horford, money to spend on the free-agent market. More high draft picks from Brooklyn were assuredly coming. Boston was positioning itself to become a potential force in the league, on the verge of something successful and *sustainable*, with optimism about the team's future continuing to mount.

And yet, simultaneously, the challenge of playing in the NBA was very much akin to the challenge of playing in Boston, something coach Brad Stevens would eventually learn if he had not learned it already.

A lot of times, the way you're viewed is very simple. It's either: Did you win it all or didn't you win it all? And that's the way your tenure is viewed.

The Celtics hadn't won anything yet.

* * *

During the 2016–17 season, the Brooklyn Nets had finished with the worst record in the NBA and had dismantled a team they never should have built in the first place, giving the Nets the best odds of securing the No. 1 pick in the annual NBA Draft. Of course, when the Nets subsequently won the annual NBA draft lottery, the pick went to Boston.

For Ainge, all of this was an extraordinary coup, particularly because the Celtics had simultaneously positioned themselves to be players in NBA free agency for a second straight summer. And so, one year after acquiring the respected Horford, Ainge set his sights one of Stevens's former star players at Butler University: Gordon Hayward. The reunion of Hayward and Stevens seemed a foregone conclusion from the very beginning—a bag job, really—as if the Celtics had an inside track to the player all along, which, of course, they did.

"You know, I always had a dream to play in the NBA, but he was the first person that I think made me realize I could maybe get there one day," Hayward would say of Stevens weeks later during his introductory press conference in Boston. "And so to be back and reunited with him again, I'm just beyond excited and can't wait to get to work."

Hayward's arrival alone would have been cause for celebration in Boston. But on the day he made that remark, he was largely a supporting actor because of who was seated next to him: Kyrie Irving.

How that all came to be is a novel unto itself, but the short story was this: In what amounted to slightly more than a calendar year, through a succession of moves in the draft and free agency, Ainge had built the Celtics into one of the better teams in the NBA. In a deal that ruffled feathers, he had traded popular point guard Thomas and a host of other pieces, including one of the remaining Brooklyn picks to the Cleveland Cavaliers for Irving, who had grown disgruntled being a pawn in the world of LeBron James; he had signed Horford and Hayward; he had selected Jaylen Brown with the No. 3 pick in the 2016 draft; and in 2017, after winning the draft lottery, Ainge had negotiated a trade with the Philadelphia 76ers in which he traded the pick (which Philadelphia used to draft point guard Markelle Fultz) for a future first-rounder and the No. 3 overall selection, which he then used to obtain Duke forward Jayson Tatum.

Piled all together, the haul seemed like Boston's basketball version of *The Brink's Job*: Irving, Horford, Hayward, Tatum, and Brown, the first three of whom already had been NBA All-Stars and the final two of whom would be.

The Celtics weren't quite on the level of Golden State yet—who was?—but they were getting close to adding a championship banner to the ones that hovered above the courts of both their game and practice facilities.

"We all know in Boston what we're shooting for. You know, that's a given, right? That's what you're playing under, both in this facility and at the practice facility," Stevens said on the day Irving and Hayward were both formally introduced. "But ultimately the path is . . . are you getting better? And so the good news about our opportunity is that we've got a chance to go to work. We should be excited about our opportunities ahead. We've got a lot of good players in the room, and we're all going to have to find out what role we can play in order to help us get better."

Six weeks later, the season began. And it all started to unravel, sometimes in gruesome fashion.

Less than six minutes into their first game together, on a night the new-and-reloaded Celtics opened their season against James, Crowder, and the revamped Cavaliers, Irving lobbed a pass to Hayward, who ran and jumped toward the rim. As James and Crowder converged to challenge and ultimately deflect the pass, Hayward fell to the ground, simultaneously breaking his left fibula and dislocating his left ankle. The injury so damaged Hayward's lower leg that the toes on his left foot were pointed to nine o'clock, a grotesque image literally that had players wincing, gasping, and turning away.

For Hayward, the injury was merely the beginning of a cursed existence in Boston. And, simultaneously, it triggered a series of events that ultimately undermined, for Ainge, what might have been a brilliantly executed plan.

On paper, the 2017–18 Celtics season was largely regarded as a success, the team finishing with a 55-27 record—the fourth straight in which Stevens increased his win total—en route to the second seed in the Eastern Conference, behind only the Toronto Raptors. Late in the season, the team also lost the services of Irving, who needed surgery to remove hardware from his left knee in the wake of surgery he had required earlier in his career. (The Celtics knew this was likely when they had acquired him, but the timing was nonetheless poor.) The team subsequently relied heavily on the play of youngsters like Rozier, Brown, and Tatum, a trio that had produced a combined 40 points per game during the regular season.

Incredibly, the Celtics went on a run. Stabilized by a veteran group that still included Horford and newcomer Marcus Morris, the Celtics defeated the Milwaukee Bucks in seven games in their first-round playoff series, then wiped out the Philadelphia 76ers in five. The Celtics then held a 3-2 series lead against James and the Cavaliers—yes, them again—before dropping Games 6 and 7. The final defeat took place in Boston, beneath the championship banners that Stevens himself had cited, though the truth is that—minus Irving and Hayward—the young Celtics weren't ready. And the more experienced Celtics weren't good enough.

But given the Celtics' place as Boston and NBA blue bloods, the emphasis was on what was to come.

"When you play for the Boston Celtics you're always thinking [of] winning a championship," the dignified Horford told reporters in the aftermath. "That's why I came here—to be in the position to play in those types of games. Kyrie and Gordon know that, and it's something we're all looking forward to. . . . Kyrie is an unbelievable player. You can't think about what could have been, but when he's with our team we're at another level. That's just the reality. We didn't have Kyrie now, but we can count on him moving forward."

Or so everyone thought. As it turned out, the decline of the Celtics felt as swift and steep as their ascension. Internally, at the start of the 2017–18 season, the Celtics' expectations had been higher than some had realized. While most regarded the Warriors as an NBA juggernaut—and the Warriors would ultimately repeat as champions, this time sweeping James and the Cavaliers—Ainge believed in his roster. When the additions of Irving and Hayward kicked the

Celtics up another level, one onlooker suggested to Ainge that the Celtics were now ready to overtake LeBron James and Cleveland—that the Celtics might have the best team in the East. Ainge's reply? "We might have the best team in the *league*," he steadfastly answered—a statement that spoke volumes.

Had Hayward not suffered a freakish injury and Irving remained healthy enough to play in their first year together, there is no telling what might have happened. The Celtics probably would have secured home court throughout the NBA playoffs and highly touted draft picks Tatum and Brown would have developed at a far more deliberate pace.

Instead, Hayward effectively needed two years to return to form while a gap grew between Irving and the younger future stars of the Celtics who had reached the conference finals without him. Brown, Tatum, Rozier, and Smart all started to believe they were better than they actually were—at least at that stage of their respective careers. Irving felt just as he had in Cleveland, where he lived in James's shadow, a spoke in someone else's wheel. Lost in it all were the on-court frustrations of Hayward, who similarly had come to Boston to be a centerpiece in a Stevens-run team only to find himself in a cluttered operation where talented youngsters like Tatum and Brown were stealing his playing time. It all got very, very messy—and very, very quickly.

At the start of the 2018–19 season, the Celtics had the fourth-best championship odds in basketball, behind only Golden State, the Houston Rockets, and the Philadelphia 76ers. Of those teams, only the Warriors were truly in another class. In early October, during a question and answer session with season ticket holders at the TD Garden and sounding like a young man making a marriage proposal, Irving unexpectedly professed a desire to remain with the Celtics beyond the end of his existing contract, which was due to expire at year's end. "I shared it with some of my teammates as well as the organization and everyone else in Boston," he said famously over the public address system, microphone in hand. "If you guys will have me back, I plan on re-signing here next year."

If you guys will have me back.

The crowd roared with approval. Before long, though, those words seemed filled with both false modesty and false intentions. And while Irving may have believed what he said at the time, his behavior and attitude turned so moody and sour that the Celtics privately wondered whether he had a personality disorder. While Irving's first season in Boston had been a relatively happy one, there was one incident in October when, as the Celtics walked under the stands and back to the locker room after a win in Philadelphia, a fan taunted Irving with the memory of James.

"Kyrie, where's LeBron?" the fan shouted in a video caught on cell phone.

Replied Irving, without breaking stride, "Suck my dick."

Well, then.

A year later, Irving's attitude got worse. While Hayward was easing his way back from an injury that was truly traumatic, the Celtics spun their wheels early. Through their first twenty games, they were an inexcusably mediocre 10-10. In late November, when a reporter wished Irving a Happy Thanksgiving, the player's reply was surly and downright disturbing. "Fuck Thanksgiving," he said. The Celtics played well at times—they won eight in a row at one stage of the season, ten of eleven during another—but their play was as inconsistent as Irving's mood. In January, during the final seconds of a loss at Orlando, Irving openly chastised Horford after a pass to Jayson Tatum that resulted in a missed shot at the buzzer, believing instead that Horford should have passed the ball to him.

When the Celtics returned home four nights later against Toronto, the Celtics and Raptors were tied at 106–106 when Irving made an eighteen-foot jump shot to give Boston a 108–106 lead. After a Toronto miss, Irving kept the ball in his hands and ignored the direction of Stevens, launching a thirty-one-footer in the face of Raptors star Kawhi Leonard—a two-time NBA Defensive Player of the Year—that hit nothing but net. As the crowd erupted, Irving began tugging at his jersey and shouting at his audience, proclaiming his own greatness.

But as great as he was, Irving's behavior amplified what was at the core of the Celtics' problems: a power struggle for the spotlight between Irving and his teammates, Irving and his coach, Irving and everyone. For all that Irving had grown to resent James in Cleveland, he desired the same kind of superstar deference in Boston. There was, of course, one problem: Irving wasn't James. He wasn't as big, which made him something of a liability on the defensive end of the floor, and he simply wasn't as good. That seemed apparent to everyone but him.

"I had to call 'Bron and tell him I apologize for being that young player that wanted everything at his fingertips," Irving said after his Raptors heroics. "I wanted to be the guy that led us to a championship. I wanted to be the leader. I wanted to be all that." Added the complex point guard: "I did a poor job of setting an example for these young guys what it's like to get something out of your teammates. Going forward, I want to test these young guys, but I can't do it publicly. That was a learning experience for me, realizing the magnitude of my voice and what I mean to these guys. . . . The responsibility of being the best in the world and leading your team is something that is not meant for many people. . . . Only few are meant for it, or chosen for it, and I feel like the best person to call was him."

Even in issuing an apology, Irving couldn't help but inflate himself and demean those around him.

Unsurprisingly, then, the fractures in the Celtics deepened. By the NBA All-Star break, only four months after pledging his love for Boston and the Celtics, Irving was sneaking around behind their backs, wooing others. He and Kevin Durant, one of his best friends in the league, effectively had a tryst in Charlotte, site of the All-Star Game. A cell phone video captured them presumably plotting to sign with the New York Knicks: "Two max slots," Irving said, according to lip-readers, referring to the Knicks' ability to sign two elite free agents. Caught with his hand in the proverbial cookie jar, Irving did what most every scoundrel does. He lied.

Asked by longtime *Herald* reporter Steve Bulpett if he might want to quell speculation about the conversation between him and Durant, Irving bristled.

"This is the stuff that just doesn't make the league fun," Irving said. "Nobody helps promote the league even more by doing shit like that—putting things [in public] on what we're talking about. . . . It's two people talking, having a conversation. If this was the real world, would it be anybody else's business. I don't get it."

When Bulpett responded—rightly—that the fans were understandably interested in the matter, Irving dug himself deeper.

"The *fans*? You brought up the *fans*? C'mon man. You do it for the likes and clicks. Everybody does. Everybody wants to hear me talk like this. Everybody wants every athlete to talk about shit like this. . . . It's not real life. It's not real."

Of course, the truth was precisely the opposite. It *was* real. In fact, it was very real. And it was so real that Irving could not cope with the reality that he had been exposed.

While Durant himself would eventually admit the meeting was precisely what it appeared to be, that acknowledgment would not come until years later. And according to basketball sources, the Celtics had been planning for a similar scenario.

"The plan [for the Celtics] was always to have Kyrie bring in Durant or Anthony Davis," said one NBA evaluator.

The Irving-Durant liaison—and Irving's subsequent handling of it—further doomed the Celtics, who certainly did not need the additional help falling apart. They were already broken beyond repair. And while the club finished the regular season with six wins in its final eight games, the Celtics' win total under Brad Stevens decreased for the first time in five seasons. Internally, the Celtics were far less concerned about Irving teaming with Durant on the Knicks than on the other New York team: "I'm worried about *Brooklyn*," said one voice in the organization. Irving had grown up in New Jersey rooting for the Nets and wanted to go play for his hometown team.

After all that—the trade with the Nets, the wheeling and dealing that brought and sent Isaiah Thomas, the courting of Durant with Tom Brady, the signings of Horford and Hayward, and the trade that brought Kyrie to Boston with one of the Brooklyn draft picks Ainge had secured from the Nets—Brooklyn was going to get Kyrie and Durant. And the Celtics would be left splintered.

Appropriately, Irving's final days with the Celtics came over the span of nine postseason games that perfectly illustrated the mercurial nature of both the entire Boston basketball season and the star player. The Celtics won the first five, sweeping the Indiana Pacers in the first round of the playoffs and then posting an impressive, eye-opening 22-point win over the favored Milwaukee Bucks in Game 1 of the Eastern Conference semifinals. The Celtics looked like world beaters. But once the Bucks hit back and claimed Game 2 by 21 points, the Celtics wilted. They ate themselves from within. Milwaukee won the next three games by 7, 12, and 25 points, bouncing what Ainge had believed *might be the best team in the league* by an average of more than 16 points.

Generally someone who made himself accessible and accountable—qualities that made him popular with the media—Ainge was spared the indignity of answering for his team, though hardly under desirable circumstances. In May, during the postseason, he had suffered a mild heart attack, the second of his career. The stress of the season had taken its toll on him, too. Celtics players generally said the right things after the season and declined to point fingers, but the team was among the most talented (in any sport) during Boston's extraordinary twenty-year reign, but the Celtics would ultimately go down with the 2011 Red Sox as one of the most unlikable and underachieving groups.

"I just remember walking in the first day and we had open gym playing 5-on-5, and I'm like damn, we have a lot of guys, it's gonna be a lot of fun this year," said guard Terry Rozier. "Then you put all of those guys together—guys who have a lot of money, All-Stars, guys trying to make a lot of money, and then we just tried to figure it out. But it's tough. We never did [mesh] the whole year."

As Rozier departed, he declined to answer questions about his future. Many other Celtics similarly avoided speculating. Irving, of course, did not return, signing with Brooklyn, as the Celtics had feared. Durant left Golden State and went with him. Al Horford signed with Philadelphia. Left to scramble, the Celtics included departing free agent Rozier in a sign-and-trade for Charlotte guard Kemba Walker, a far more likable but significantly less talented version of Irving, in an exchange that proved to be a mistake. And as the Celtics broke apart and tried to salvage whatever they could from a chance at sustainable excellence, Rozier's words hovered.

You put all of those guys together . . . guys who have a lot of money . . . guys trying to make a lot of money . . .

There it was: the cause of the Celtics' demise.

Selfishness.

CHAPTER 14

SAME OLD BRUINS

"You know, that's the fear I have about being a playoff team. I mean, that's not the goal. Obviously, you have to get to the playoffs to get to the ultimate goal of winning the Stanley Cup. If you look at what we call our core players and you look at where they're at in their careers—and, you know, you could all have your opinions on how many years they have left—we look at that and then we say, 'Okay it's our job to supplement those guys with players that are going to help us win a Stanley Cup.'"

—Cam Neely, June 2019

THE PROBLEM WITH WINNING, IF such a thing can be said, is the intoxicating nature of it, particularly in Boston, especially during the start of the twenty-first century. At times, winning quite literally became everything and the only thing, the credo fashioned by longtime Green Bay Packers football coach Vince Lombardi. The Packers won three NFL Championships and two Super Bowls during seven seasons under Lombardi from 1961 through 1967, all of them with Bart Starr at quarterback during a romanticized era that established Green Bay as *Titletown*. As soon as Lombardi and Starr split, nearly three decades passed before the Packers won again.

The point? The challenge everywhere was the same, in Green Bay or in Boston, pre–salary cap or post-. Sustainability.

Unlike the Celtics, the Bruins elected to keep their core together, a logical decision given the age of their nucleus. The 2009 trade that sent Phil Kessel to Toronto had turned into one of the great steals of general manager Peter Chiarelli's tenure with the Bruins, delivering Boston two high picks that had produced forward Tyler Seguin (No. 2 overall in 2010) and defenseman Dougie

Hamilton (No. 9 overall in 2011), both regarded as cornerstones of the team's future. When the Bruins won the Stanley Cup in 2011, their present and future seemed as bright of that as the 2007 Red Sox, who had just won their second World Series under Theo Epstein with a younger, newer roster. The 2013 Bruins, in fact, had returned to the finals two years later, only to lose to a Blackhawks team that was indisputably the league measuring stick.

Nonetheless, the feeling in Boston remained the same. *We'll be back.*

Still, the Bruins grappled with difficult decisions following the defeat to Chicago, something they were clearly eager to share with fans with the release of their home-produced series, *Behind the B*. The NHL was the only of the four major sports leagues with a hard salary cap, which is to say that it prohibited some of the creative accounting that the NFL and NBA allowed to accommodate player contracts. Football deals could be structured and restructured to minimize the implications of payroll restrictions. In basketball, the NBA allowed for "exceptions" to a complex matrix of league rules that required what became known as "capologists." By those standards, the NHL was relatively simple. If the league-wide salary cap was $70 million per team, that was it. As such, drafting and player development became critical for the long-term success of any franchise.

And in the early part of the 2010s, the Bruins had it. Seguin, in particular, was seen as something of a phenom, blessed with speed and skill. What he lacked was toughness and maturity, the latter of which was entirely understandable given that he was drafted at eighteen. His second year—and first real season in the NHL—had produced twenty-nine goals and 67 points in eighty-one games, excellent output for a player who spent much of the season playing at age nineteen. The NHL work stoppage of 2018–19 seemed to retard Seguin's progress, however, and he failed to score a goal in the finals loss to the Blackhawks.

Along the way, given Seguin's ability and potential, the team had signed him to a six-year, $34.5 million contract that had begun in the 2012–13 season. He had five years remaining at a reasonable average annual salary of $5.75 million when the Bruins made the surprising move of trading him to the Dallas Stars, a deal that seemingly flew in the face of salary cap logic.

"I just think there's too many red flags with him," Bruins director of player personnel Scott Bradley said during a meeting headed by Chiarelli and chronicled by the Bruins' in-house video team. "He has a lot talent—we know that—he should be scoring. I'm disappointed when [another Bruins official] brings up [Chicago forward Patrick] Kane [as a comparison and contrast]. If he gives us half of Kane, we win the Stanley Cup. You know, I don't like the way his game is going. He hasn't proven that's he's tough enough or plays our style of game. I don't know if a leopard ever changes his spots, but he's going to have to or else we're going to be sitting here next year doing the same thing."

That the Bruins were having such a discussion about Seguin was hardly surprising: organizations routinely had conversations about players throughout the league, in and out of their organization. The job required it. The surprise was the Bruins' disclosure of the talks, particularly after losing the Stanley Cup to the Blackhawks in a six-game series during which Kane, playing a speed-and-skill game akin to that of Seguin, had led all Chicago scorers with three goals and 5 points. Of course, by the time Bruins fans had seen the video, the decision had already been made. Tyler Seguin was already gone, traded to Dallas along with winger Rich Peverley for a smattering of players that included veteran forward Loui Eriksson; prospects Reilly Smith and Matt Fraser, both forwards; and defenseman Joe Morrow.

Said Chiarelli of Seguin at the time: "He's got to commit his mind and focus on the one task at hand. He's got to become more of a professional. And you know what? I can say that about a lot of 21-year-olds. I know he got criticized for playing on the periphery and all that stuff. He did. He's got to commit to being a professional and focusing on the game."

At best, as it turned out, the Seguin deal was a draw for the Bruins, if only for the fact that Seguin never fully blossomed in Dallas, despite some productive years; at worst, it was a lost opportunity that had a crippling effect over time, on multiple levels. The decision to trade him at all was certainly one thing, at least partially an indictment on the Bruins' inability to integrate a talented young player into their *culture*, which typically frowned on finesse. But getting back four smaller parts for Seguin—ponies for a horse, as it was often described in sports—did little to help a Bruins team that was starting to slide in the wrong direction.

By the time the Bruins had reached the spring of 2015 two years later, they were in something of a financial crisis. While re-signing veteran players like Milan Lucic and Chris Kelly to sizable contracts, the Bruins had drafted relatively poorly and traded away a cluster of players who were young, talented, and cheap. They missed the playoffs for the first time under coach Claude Julien, who had just concluded his eighth season in Boston. General manager Chiarelli was fired and replaced by Don Sweeney, a onetime Bruins defenseman who had started his post-playing career as the Bruins director of player development, at the core of the drafting and player development system that was the lifeblood of any franchise.

The message from Sweeney was simple: *I'm going to build the Bruins from the inside out. And we're going to be patient.*

"[When] we've done it well, when we've developed players . . . generally we've allowed them the proper time it takes to develop into an NHL player," Sweeney told the assembled media upon his introduction.

"But they're not ready-made players when they get here. It's not a plug-and-play system. That's where the impatience comes in at times, and we've made some mistakes and allowed some players to leave this organization that we might regret.

"But going forward, I'd like to allow us the opportunity to not have the impatience in the integration peaks, and to work with them and allow them the proper time at the NHL level to get acclimated. You can't trade anything in this league for experience."

The indictment of the drafting and player development operation was, of course, only part of the issue. While Charlie Jacobs, the CEO of the Bruins' parent company, Delaware North, spoke of a "new era" in Bruins history, Sweeney spoke of the "difference between [salary] cap compliance and cap management," adding, "I think we need to make sure that we're very cognizant of the latter rather than the former." The comment was a direct criticism of Chiarelli's payroll management, which was, again, tied to the drafting and player development system. In the end, it all came back to the same thing: In a league with a hard player payroll budget, the Bruins had failed to find, develop, and integrate young talent that would ensure a successful future.

As such, Sweeney immediately went about the business of planting the seeds, most everyone understanding that it was a process requiring years, not months or weeks—though at the outset it felt as if Sweeney set off to rebuild the Bruins in a day. On June 26, the first day of the annual NHL draft, the Bruins traded veteran winger Milan Lucic to the Los Angeles Kings for a first-round selection, goaltender Martin Jones, and promising young defenseman Colin Miller; just prior, he had already dealt the unhappy Dougie Hamilton to the Calgary Flames for another first-rounder in 2015 and two second-round selections. Four days after both trades, Sweeney then dealt Jones—the goalie acquired in the Lucic trade on the twenty-sixth—to the San Jose Sharks for a first-round selection in 2016.

In the end, the Bruins ended up with three sequential picks in the first round of the 2015 NHL draft—Nos. 13, 14, and 15—in addition to future picks (including the first-rounder from San Jose) in 2016, a strategy similar to the one that Danny Ainge had employed with the Celtics.

While many saw the Hamilton deal as hypocrisy on the part of Sweeney—*Didn't he just say he was going to be patient with young players?*—any comparison to Seguin, in Sweeney's defense, was imperfect. While with the Bruins, Seguin had signed a second contract and had been secured for the longer term; Hamilton, by contrast, was unhappy in Boston and wanted out. With the risk of eventually losing him to free agency in a year, Sweeney took the preemptive measure of dealing Hamilton immediately. And had the draft turned out differently, nobody would have given it all a second thought.

For the Bruins, at least at the outset, the plan was to take pick Nos. 13 to 15 and use them as collateral to trade up to No. 5, where the team wanted to draft six-foot-three, 215-pound defenseman Noah Hanifin of Boston College. But the deal blew up. In the aftermath—a scramble that, years later, Sweeney would call a "steep learning curve"—the Bruins chose three questionable prospects, including defenseman Jakub Zboril, left-winger Jake DeBrusk, and right-winger Zach Senyshyn, the last of whom, in particular, was regarded as a major stretch. Across the NHL, the selections were almost immediately greeted with befuddlement—*What the fuck are they doing?* was a common refrain—and many hockey insiders throughout the NHL believed the Bruins had taken Lucic and Hamilton and effectively given them away for next to nothing.

In the short term, of course, Sweeney had time on his side. Nobody knew yet what Zboril, DeBrusk, and Senyshyn would become. In Sweeney's first season, the Bruins missed the playoffs for a second straight year. In the third, they fired their coach, Julien, largely because the team's playing style had become both stagnant and stale. The Bruins subsequently rallied under new coach Bruce Cassidy to make the playoffs in the 2016–17 season before being bounced in the first round by the Ottawa Senators, but there were signs of progress that masked some of the problems building in the organization.

Entering the fourth and fifth years of Sweeney's tenure, the Bruins were starting to rise again, their core group still intact. And it would not be long before they were again knocking on the door of a championship.

* * *

For all of the changes that took place in Boston over the start of the new millennium, the transformation of the Boston Bruins was, in some ways, among the most visually shocking. During their existence, the Bruins generally had possessed the same identity, which is to say they were tough, hardworking, blue-collar—traits that the game and their city demanded. They were rarely, if ever, flashy. The Big, Bad Bruins of the early 1970s had forged that image; the Cam Neely Bruins of the 1980s had fortified it. But by the time Claude Julien was fired as coach during the 2016–17 season, the Bruins were playing a methodical, plodding style in a league and world where physical play was being legislated thanks to heightened concerns over concussions. The NHL was getting smaller and faster. And at the behest of Sweeney and under Cassidy, the Bruins would do something they had been unwilling to do for nearly their entire existence. Adapt.

During Bruce Cassidy's first full year as head coach, the Bruins finished sixth in the league in scoring (based on goals per game), while finishing fourth in goals against—which is to say the sacrifice from the Julien principles were little or nonexistent. Their power play—at best average during their peak years under Julien, at worst a laughingstock—became frighteningly potent, finishing fourth-best in the league in efficiency. If the final years under traditionalist Julien had again lapsed into something far too conservative—"It's not about trying to win 0–0," Neely had famously said on a radio interview with longtime Boston host Greg Hill way back in 2011—the new years under Cassidy were a blast of spring air through a Bruins philosophy that had grown rather staid.

"The core group, the veteran leadership, they gave me an opportunity to go in and earn their respect," said Cassidy, whose only previous stint as a head coach, with the Washington Capitals from 2002 to 2004, had been an epic disaster. "They bought into what we were selling for the most part. Not for the most part—100 percent. One hundred percent, the veteran guys afforded me that opportunity and I can't thank them enough. We've got some Stanley Cup champions in that room and it showed. We're trying to build something together now. That's the process going forward."

And as for the Bruins' playing style?

"We implemented a couple of things and off we went," he went on. "We talked right away about being a team that would play—and the term 'play fast' is getting thrown around a lot out there—but we were going to upgrade our transition game. We were going to move the puck quicker and attack. I guess that was our description of playing fast. I think it worked. It got our [defense] involved, so you start scoring and, obviously, that helped. People get excited about that—scoring goals and getting on offense. And I don't think we lost a lot on the defensive side of things. As we went along, we tried to maintain that balance. So that was the message right away. Players bought in and we had success, and that obviously helps. Winning solves a lot of problems and puts a lot of smiles on people's faces."

Still, while the 2017–18 season was a step in the right direction, the Bruins again fell short of their ultimate goal. After finishing the regular season with the fourth-best record in hockey, they defeated the Toronto Maple Leafs in seven games to win their first-round playoff series. The victory propelled Boston into a matchup with the Tampa Bay Lightning in the second round, where the gap in talent showed. After Boston won the series opener by a stunning 6–2 score, Tampa responded with victories of 4–2, 4–1, 4–3, and 3–1. Cassidy's tweaks and changes—as effective as they were—were nowhere near enough to overcome a Tampa team that, as a division rival, was an obstacle on virtually any path to another championship. And the Bruins knew it.

While Patrice Bergeron expressed disappointment at the lopsided nature of the season-ending defeat—"We believed we had a better team," he said plainly—Cassidy praised the Lightning and, in the process, identified an issue that would prove critical going forward.

"You've got to give them credit," Cassidy said. "We're a team that scored all year with different players in and out of the lineup, we scored against Toronto. But it's not like after 89 games we forgot how to score. . . . To get inside [and in front of the net], you really had to work, and I felt like they did a good job with us not allowing us to get inside."

For Sweeney, the impact of his philosophy was nonetheless starting to have an impact, at least partly the result of Cassidy's willingness to promote and engage young players, some of whom were starting to flourish. Forward David Pastrnak, who had been drafted under Chiarelli and was growing into an elite scorer, partnered with Bergeron and Brad Marchand on what was coming to be known as the "Perfection Line." Defenseman Charlie McAvoy, drafted in the first round of the 2016 draft under Sweeney, already had broken into the lineup and was being identified as the heir to captain Zdeno Chara's role as No. 1 defenseman. DeBrusk, who had been the Bruins' second selection (No. 14 overall) in Sweeney's inaugural 2015 draft, had produced an encouraging 43 points in seventy games during the regular season and shone in the first-round series against Toronto, scoring five goals in the seven games, including a pair in decisive Game 7.

Inside the Bruins operation, the team was encouraged by the progress being made by forwards Anders Bjork, Ryan Donato, Jakob Forsbacka Karlsson, and Trent Frederic and defensemen Brandon Carlo, Jeremy Lauzon, and Urho Vakannainen. Asked to do what many believed to be a professional sports impossibility—contend and rebuild at the same time—Sweeney seemed to be executing a tightrope act that had the Bruins back in the discussion as one of the best teams in hockey while simultaneously putting in place the pieces for a promising future.

"This is a process, but the future is bright," owner Jeremy Jacobs would say months later as the Bruins prepared to embark on the 2018–19 season. "Given how the farm system has been replenished, the number of kids that are ready or almost ready to play for the Boston Bruins, I feel that Donnie has done an excellent job."

While Sweeney's tenure had hardly been perfect, that was generally true. And thanks to a little luck, things were about to get a good deal better.

* * *

Beginning with the 2007–2008 season that began the reissuance of Bruins hockey, the Bruins entered the 2018–2019 season as one of the most successful franchises in hockey, appearing in two Stanley Cup finals with one championship and nine playoff appearances. Including postseason, Boston had played in more games than all but three franchises—Pittsburgh, Chicago, and Washington—and won more games than all but four. (San Jose, along with the aforementioned three, was also ahead of Boston.) And yet, while the Bruins had every right to place themselves among the league's best, the indisputable truth was that Chicago and Pittsburgh were the elite of the elite, franchises that had won multiple championships.

Still, for all that the Blackhawks were during a nine-year run that had established them as arguably the best team in hockey for essentially a decade, the subsequent dip in their play was precipitous. After beating the Bruins in the 2013 finals, Chicago had not won a single playoff series and had missed the 2017–2018 postseason altogether. That streak would extend into the 2020s, by which point the Blackhawks were all but dismantled, only Jonathan Toews and Patrick Kane remaining from a dynasty that had become nothing more than a shell of itself.

For the Bruins, the realities in 2018–2019 were not quite as daunting, but they were realities nonetheless. By the end of play on January 31, 2018, the Bruins rested in fifth place in the Atlantic Division of the NHL Eastern Conference, behind both the rival Montreal Canadiens and Buffalo Sabres, a whisker out of the playoffs. Teams like Tampa Bay and Washington seemed far, far superior. But as the Bruins prepared for the annual Winter Classic on January 1, 2019, at Notre Dame Stadium against the Blackhawks, the team had so restocked their feeder system that there was still the hope of another championship run.

Unlike previous seasons, when Sweeney had to carefully navigate the trade market, the Bruins were now in position to add, to fortify their roster in hopes of making another stretch run.

"I wouldn't be out of context to share that we've had the discussions that we have this window with Patrice [Bergeron] and with David [Krejci] and the centers and players that we have—and it's not going to last forever," Charlie Jacobs told the team's radio rightsholder, 98.5 The Sports Hub, before the New Year's Day affair with Chicago. "We have a number of young kids that are coming up. I've gotten reports from the world juniors in Western Canada, and we've got a player on just about every national team that is doing quite well. So I think there's an opportunity there." Translation: *We have prospects to deal.*

Said owner Jeremy Jacobs of Bergeron and Krejci, career Bruins who, as centers, served as the spinal cord for the Bruins' roster: "They're part of our history, part of today's game. They're not part of tomorrow's game necessarily."

Added Charlie Jacobs: "We're coming up on 1,000 games with Patrice. We don't have another 1,000—we know that."

While such an approach seemed like a long shot, it wasn't—at least, not in hockey, even with the dominance of the Lightning, who were en route to one of the most historically dominant regular seasons in history. Particularly in the NHL, the playoffs were an entirely different matter. The eighth and final seed still felt they had a chance to win the tournament; as naïve and idealistic as they may have sounded, it had happened in 2012 with the Los Angeles Kings. By 2018–19, the Bruins had a long-established veteran core that viewed the regular season as nothing more than a qualifying heat. Once the real race started, there were too many variables and pitfalls to bank on anything, even if a team had gone 82-0-0.

Having lived through the 2001 Patriots and the 2007 Patriots, the 2004 Red Sox and the 2013 Red Sox—and everything else along the way—Bostonians knew it, too.

At the same time, of course, Boston knew a winner when it saw one—but hockey was hard to handicap. Before the 2011 Bruins won the Stanley Cup, after all, players like Bergeron and Krejci had to learn to pace themselves. By 2019 they knew the drill. Possessors of a 20-14-4 record on January 1, the Bruins defeated the Blackhawks 4–2 for a second consecutive victory. They subsequently extended the streak to five. The next six games produced five losses as the calendar turned to February, a month of the hockey season that almost always includes the annual trading deadline, a point by which most every team in every sport had to answer a question that most every young man inevitably faces with a longtime girlfriend or partner:

So what's it going to be? In or out?

As much as any team during the team's renaissance, the 2018–19 Bruins knew this. As such, they answered the question in emphatic fashion:

Are you serious? We're in. You bet your ass we're in.

In the three weeks preceding the February 25 trading deadline, the Bruins played their best hockey of the season. Beginning with a 1–0 victory over the defending champion Washington Capitals on February 2, the Bruins won eight of nine through a 6–5 victory over the San Jose Sharks on February 18. Two days later, Sweeney traded prospect Ryan Donato to the Minnesota Wild for Charlie Coyle, filling a need at third-line center. The Bruins then won at Las Vegas before losing in a shootout at St. Louis, after which Sweeney made a second deal, this one to acquire skilled winger Marcus Johansson from the New Jersey Devils for second- and fourth-round picks, respectively, in the 2019 and 2020 drafts. The Bruins then won another six in a row. The back-and-forth played out like a Pavlovian experiment between an experienced team and a former Bruins player now serving as GM—*You win, I add*—and by March 9 the Bruins were no longer on the NHL playoff bubble. They were a threat.

All told, beginning on January 29 and extending through March 9, the Bruins played nineteen games—nearly 25 percent of their season schedule—and did not lose a single game in regulation. Not one. The team's 15-0-4 record produced 34 of a possible 38 points in the standings, moving them into second place in the division, behind only Tampa Bay and in comfortable possession of a playoff spot. By the time the regular season ended, the Bruins were the possessors of a 49-24-9 record, a 107-point output that was second only to the record-setting total of 128 (!) posted by Tampa Bay, which had posted an eye-popping 62-16-4 record that had tied an NHL record for wins in a single season.

"I feel terrific," Cassidy said upon completion of the regular season. "I'm an optimist. I like our team. We play hard. We're one of the better teams from start to finish, I think, in the National Hockey League, specifically the second half of the year. We've played well at the right times. We've earned our way."

Indeed, there was little reason to debate the Bruins' presence in the play-offs. They belonged. But with Tampa Bay looming in the second round—and, potentially, Washington in the third—the NHL Eastern Conference looked like a minefield. In the four meetings with Tampa during the regular season, the Bruins had lost three. The 1–0 defeat against Washington in February had been the Bruins' first against the Capitals in a stunning fifteen games over five years dating back to 2014, but the Bruins had lost the other two meetings during the regular season. The records hardly inspired fan confidence for the playoffs.

Just the same, everyone knew the postseason was different. To start, the Bruins would have to face—yet again—the Toronto Maple Leafs. If the Bruins could win that series, there was always the chance that Tampa might suffer a key injury, that the Lightning would be overconfident, that the Lightning would succumb to the pressure that came along with being a historically good team. There was also the small chance the Lightning could lose.

* * *

As much as any postseason in Boston sports history, the 2018–19 hockey playoffs proved to be a life lesson: *You just never know. See what happens. Play it out.*

As one of the NHL's Original Six franchises, the Toronto Maple Leafs are among North America's richest in tradition in history and Canada's most valuable hockey franchise, ahead of even the Montreal Canadiens. And yet, the Leafs are now regarded as the Cleveland Browns of hockey or the Los Angeles Clippers of the NBA, something Red Sox and Chicago Cubs fans knew quite well before their respective teams ended long droughts and won championships in the 2000s. A standard for futility.

Having lost to the Bruins in seven games in the first round of the NHL playoffs in both 2013 and 2018—the former in a historic Game 7 collapse—the Leafs faced the Bruins again in 2019 and immediately undermined themselves yet again, proving the strength of the self-fulfilling prophecy. One year after being suspended for three games of the seven-game first-round series following a dirty boarding hit on Bruins forward Tommy Wingels, recidivist Leafs forward Nazem Kadri again dealt himself and his team a fatal blow, this time courtesy of a cross-check to the face of Bruins winger Jake DeBrusk in Game 2. The hit came in retaliation of a DeBrusk hard check on Leafs veteran forward Patrick Marleau, drawing Kadri the fifth suspension of his career—for the balance of the series this time, a span covering five games—thereby stripping the Leafs of one of their better two-way players.

Though the Leafs were already trailing Game 2 by a 3–1 score, Kadri's absence proved costly in the long run, particularly given Toronto's weakness on defense. The Leafs, in fact, took Game 3 in Toronto before the Bruins won Game 4, then won Game 5 in Boston. Having yet to face a series deficit, the Leafs returned home for Game 6 with a chance to clinch the series, then claimed an early lead in Game 1 when defenseman Morgan Rielly beat Bruins goaltender Tuukka Rask to give Toronto a 1–0 advantage 9:42 into the game. Little did the Leafs know it would be their final lead of the season.

Before the end of the first, the Bruins scored a pair of power play goals—one by Marchand, the other by defenseman Torey Krug—to take a 2–1 advantage. By the end of the second the lead was 3–1 courtesy of a goal by DeBrusk. The Leafs closed to 3–2 before an empty-net goal by Marchand secured Boston's victory, forcing the series back to Boston for a decisive seventh game—the third time in seven seasons that the Leafs and Bruins would square off in a seventh game on the TD Garden ice.

Like the first two, Toronto would lose. With Rask outplaying counterpart Frederik Andersen, the Bruins rolled to a 5–1 victory that included two empty-net goals but nonetheless highlighted the difference between the teams: the goalies. On Boston's first goal, Andersen failed to seal the left post, allowing an otherwise harmless shot by Joakim Nordstrom to inexcusably dribble into the net. Goals by the Bruins' Johansson and the Leafs' John Tavares left the score at 2–1 entering the third, when Bruins forward Sean Kuraly wristed a shot that somehow beat Andersen from the face-off circle on a night when Rask had all but sealed the Boston goal with plastic wrap, further frustrating the Leafs.

For Sweeney, the series victory privately offered some measure of satisfaction following a failed pursuit of Tavares, who signed with the hometown Leafs as a free agent after spurning Boston's offers. For the Leafs, the series loss was the third incarnation of a horror movie that always ended with the Leafs wondering how they lost a series they could have and probably should have won.

Said Toronto winger Mitch Marner after the defeat: "It's the same shitty feeling."

For the Bruins, however, another Toronto failure was only half of the reason for celebration. The other was the incredible collapse of the Tampa

Bay Lightning, who were defeated by the Columbus Blue Jackets *in four games* of their first-round playoff series in one of the great upsets in NHL history. Adhering to the suffocating style preached by their militant coach, John Tortorella, the Blue Jackets won Game 1 by a 4–3 score. The ensuing Columbus victories came by scores of 5–1, 3–1, and 7–3, a thorough dismantling of the Tampa team that had led the NHL with a whopping 325 goals during the regular season. Columbus outscored Tampa by a 19-8 margin in the series while exposing Tampa's mettle, offense, and goaltender Andrei Vasilevskiy, the last of whom finished the series with a putrid save percentage of just .856.

Tampa coach Jon Cooper had nowhere to hide—and didn't.

"When you have the amount of points we had, it's a blessing and a curse, in a way," Cooper said. "You don't play any meaningful hockey for a long time. Then, all of a sudden, you have to ramp it up. It's not an excuse. It's reality. That's how it goes: You have a historic regular season—and we had a historic playoff."

Just like that, Tampa's season was over. And a door opened for the Bruins.

For Sweeney and Cassidy, the Columbus victory was a twofold benefit. First and most obviously, the Bruins had a more favorable matchup. Second, the demise of the Lightning made for an easy message to the players: *Do not take this Blue Jackets team lightly.* Tortorella had won a Stanley Cup as a head coach, ironically as the head coach of the Lightning in 2004. He had a reputation of getting the most out of his talent, at least in the short term, with a defensive, grinding style that was miserable to watch but that produced results. Tortorella's teams typically blocked a truckload of shots, contested every puck, waited for the opposition to lose patience and flounder. And then they pounced, just as they had on Tampa Bay.

And then, for the Bruins, there was also this: While Tampa was being blindsided by the Blue Jackets, Washington was similarly losing to the Carolina Hurricanes, dropping Game 7, at home, in double overtime. Just like that, the playoff favorites and the defending champions had both been eliminated by seemingly inferior opponents, clearing the Bruins' path to the Stanley Cup finals as if guided by a police escort. Incredibly, the Bruins were already the top remaining seed in the East.

Nonetheless, and despite winning Game 1 in overtime, the Bruins found themselves precisely where they did after three games against the Leafs: trailing the series two games to one, mostly thanks to Columbus goaltender Sergei Bobrovsky, an elite talent who was playing at the top of his game.

Noted Bruins defenseman Brandon Carlo of the opposing goalie in the wake of Game 3: "The secondary saves he is making are very impressive, but he's definitely going to crack at some point. I have a lot of faith we'll put pucks past him here pretty soon. We've had some great opportunities today throughout all three periods to put pucks behind him. Credit to him today, but I don't think it's going to last."

Just like that, the goaltending flipped, and the series turned with it, though that was hardly a coincidence. Playing with a purpose in Game 4, the Bruins jumped to a 1-0 lead and endured a potentially series-altering officiating mistake that tied the game in the first period. The Jackets were pressing Rask when a deflected puck went airborne and struck the protective netting above the glass behind the Bruins goal, clearly out of play. Somehow the officials missed the carom and allowed play to continue, whereupon Jackets sniper Artemi Panarin tied the game at 1. Based on league rules, the play was not reviewable on replay, a stunning reality in an age when nearly everything is reviewed to excruciating detail in an absurd, unrealistic, and often needless pursuit of perfection.

While Bruins coach Bruce Cassidy praised his team for playing on—"You have to play through it at the end of the day," said the coach—the mishap proved to be the only goal Columbus would score on the night. thanks to the brilliance of Rask, who outplayed Bobrovsky in a pivotal 4-1 win.

"This day and age, I think it's crazy," said the Bruins goaltender. "If the ref didn't see it, why can't the league call? They're watching the game, right? What if that's in overtime? It didn't cost us, but I just think it's funny they can look at a lot of other goals and call them back in the league offices but not that."

Just the same, the Bruins did what any coach would have demanded in an age before replay, when teams were expected to overcome and look past officiating mistakes instead of whining about them. They endured.

With Bobrovsky now pierced, the Bruins never again trailed in the series, their loss in Game 3 marking the final time they trailed on the scoreboard. In Game 5, the Bruins took a 1-0 lead into what would be a frantic third period, then doubled the advantage to 2-0 on a strike by Marchand. The teams traded goals—2-1, then 3-1—before Columbus struck twice past the midway point of the final period, tying the game at 3 with precisely 6:02 left to play. Slightly more than four minutes later, young winger Pastrnak flipped a slick feed from Marchand past the left pad of the acrobatic Bobrovsky for a 4-3 Bruins lead, an advantage that held up when a sprawling Rask somehow kept the puck out of the net with his right pad as time expired.

Two nights later, the Bruins went to Columbus and shut out the Jackets to end their season, Rask turning away all thirty-nine Columbus shots in a 3–0 victory that sent the Bruins to the conference finals. Rask had completely turned the tables on Bobrovsky in the final three games of the series, stopping 111 of 115 Columbus shots for a remarkable .965 save percentage—and one of the Columbus goals had been on the controversial play that should have been blown dead.

"You need your goalie to deliver, and I think that's stating the obvious. He looks real composed and they were bumping him," Cassidy said of his goalie. "They hit him pretty hard tonight and they got called for it, but he kept his composure. I think there was some gamesmanship that most teams go through to try and get a goalie off his game, and it seems he was able to play through that as well."

Said Rask: "It's the playoffs and it's mind games, always. It's entertaining. It's the entertainment industry, I guess. That's what the fans and media want. When I'm playing, I don't read it. But if I'm a spectator, I like to read it because it's entertaining."

Having reached the league semifinals for the third time in nine years, the Bruins found an opponent waiting for them—a young and budding Carolina team that had just swept the New York Islanders in their second-round series. Among the Carolina youngsters was defenseman Dougie Hamilton, an offense-first player who had subsequently been traded away by Calgary, who had happily acquired him when Hamilton had been unwilling to resign with Boston. After signing Hamilton to a six-year, $34.5 million contract, the sides had made it halfway through the deal before Calgary had sent Hamilton to Carolina in a package for, of all people, Noah Hanifin—the same player the Bruins had been hoping to acquire when they traded Hamilton to Calgary in the first place.

While there was obvious concern of a letdown in the Carolina series, the Bruins never really experienced one. Carolina took a 2–1 lead into the third period of Game 1 before the Bruins erupted for four goals, the final two empty-netters to secure a 5–2 win. By then, the Bruins were getting consistent production throughout their lineup, mostly notably from Coyle and Johansson, the two forwards Sweeney had acquired at the deadline. Coyle and Johansson each scored in Game 1, giving them a combined nine goals in the postseason to that point, a huge boon to the Bruins offense.

As it turned out, Carolina's 2–1 lead in Game 1 lasted precisely thirteen minutes and eight seconds and was their only lead of the series. The Bruins blistered the Hurricanes in Game 2, racing to a 6–0 lead en route to a 6–2 victory. Carolina's best chance for a win came in Game 3, at home, when Rask turned away thirty-five of thirty-six shots to preserve a 2–0 advantage built on goals by Chris Wagner and Brad Marchand. The Hurricanes were then shut out in Game 4, the Bruins "Perfection Line" of Bergeron, Marchand and Pastrnak combining for all four Bruins scores to close out a lopsided series in which the Bruins outscored Carolina by the chasmic margin of 17–5.

In the wake of the lopsided series against the younger 'Canes, the words from Sweeney's inaugural press conference echoed throughout the minds of anyone who cared to remember them: *You can't trade anything in this league for experience.*

"You need everybody to be a part of it and contribute. It's been that way—that's the only way you can really advance," Bruins center Bergeron said after the Carolina series, citing the need for a full, complementary roster containing youth, experience, skill, and brawn. "There's a lot of work in front of us, but it's a special feeling."

Five days later, having earned some rest thanks to the rapid series sweep, the Bruins learned of their opponent in the Stanley Cup finals. They would face the St. Louis Blues, who had defeated an extremely talented San Jose Sharks club that had a history of failing in the postseason. San Jose had posted the second-highest point total in the Western Conference during the regular season and had twice beaten the Bruins during the regular season. But, like Tampa Bay and Washington, the Sharks were now nothing more than roadkill.

In Boston, it certainly felt as if the path to the Stanley Cup was clear. Of course, it wasn't.

* * *

The 2019 Stanley Cup finals will be remembered as a paradox of styles, eras, and social classes that bordered on Dickensian. With their third trip to the finals in nine seasons, the Bruins were one of the NHL's crown jewels of the 2010s, a team amid one of the great eras in its history. The St. Louis Blues were plumbers, part of the league's masses, a middling organization that ranked fourteenth of thirty-two NHL franchises in winning percentage since joining the league as an expansion franchise in 1967. Remarkably, the Blues went to the Stanley Cup finals in their first three seasons but were swept each time, the last one when a certain Bruins defenseman clinched the city's first championship in decades with one of the most memorable goals in the league's history. And the Blues hadn't been back to the finals since. Simply put, St. Louis was due.

Of course, such rationalizations are based on nothing more than math, though the Blues presented a different and realer kind of challenge, too. They were big. They were physical. They were hungry. They were, in short, precisely what the Bruins were when Boston upended Vancouver to win the Stanley Cup eight years earlier. Further, following a 2–1 home loss to the New York Rangers on December 31, 2018, the Blues were 15-18-4, possessors of a league-low 34 points that quite literally made them the worst team in the league. Their goaltending was poor. They had already fired their coach, Mike Yeo, and replaced him with the hard-nosed Craig Berube, a former NHL enforcer who accumulated more than 3,000 penalty minutes during a career that had labeled him as one of the tougher and more intimidating players in league history.

In their final forty-five games of the regular season, the Blues had lost just ten times in regulation, going 30-10-5. In the postseason they had trailed both the Dallas Stars, three games to two, and the Sharks, two games to one. They had come back to win both times. And in the San Jose series, the Blues had withstood a horrendous officiating call that allowed the Sharks a game-winning goal in overtime of Game 3 that granted San Jose a 2-1 series lead. St. Louis responded by winning the next three games. The St. Louis Blues were hard to kill.

"Well, they are bigger than us in the back end, but I think both teams move the puck well, I think both teams create problems for the other to get inside," Cassidy said before the start of the series. "I think that's why we're still playing, because this time of the year it's tougher to score. Both teams have goaltenders on top of their games, so it's kind of like, 'Let the best man win now.' And we're looking forward to it."

Said Berube: "Our team identity is our team. We play a team game and nobody's bigger than the team. That's really the bottom line. We demand a lot from our players and the team has to come first. That's our identity."

If Bostonians were listening and watching closely enough, they would have heard and seen characteristics that were present—and heralded—during their very own championship years.

From the start, the 2019 Stanley Cup finals were a war of attrition, bodies flying and colliding everywhere. As they tended to do, particularly after a layoff, the Bruins showed rust in the early going of Game 1, falling behind by a 2–0 score early in the second period. The Bruins responded with the next four goals of the game, including one with St. Louis goaltender Jordan Binnington pulled in the final minutes to secure a 4–2 victory on Boston's home ice at TD Garden. The signature moment of the game came midway through the third period when, after losing his helmet—or "bucket," as players were wont to call it—in a tussle with St. Louis forward David Perron in front of his own goal, spunky Bruins defenseman Torey Krug skated the length of the ice, locks flowing, to deliver a massive, bone-rattling check on St. Louis's Robert Thomas, both players sent airborne as a bloodthirsty Boston crowd boiled over.

The message from the Bruins was clear: *We're not afraid of you.*

Said Bruins center and former Blues captain David Backes, "That gave me goosebumps."

It also gave the Bruins a 1-0 series lead and set the parameters for a rock 'em, sock 'em series in which the teams traded games like punches.

After St. Louis responded with an overtime win in Game 2—the victory made the Blues a revealing 6-1 in the postseason following a loss—the teams traveled to St. Louis for Game 3, where the Bruins blasted away at Binnington in a lopsided 7–2 victory. And then, in the middle stages of Game 4, the resilient Blues had a 2–1 advantage when, just over three minutes into the second period, center Brayden Schenn snapped a shot that Bruins defenseman Zdeno Chara deflected by extending his stick, the puck shooting upward and striking Chara squarely in the face. The Bruins captain hunched over on all fours, blood leaking from his mouth, before being escorted off the ice and into the Bruins locker room for evaluation.

Though Chara returned to the bench, he did not play for the balance of the game. The series tied at 2 and headed back to Boston, the Bruins had the good fortune of an extra travel day between games, a respite the club badly needed.

Chara had broken his jaw. During the two days between games, he underwent a procedure to stabilize the area and wire his mouth shut—and then did what hockey players often do in the final stages of the playoffs, with a championship at stake, much as Patrice Bergeron had done against the Chicago Blackhawks years earlier when he played with broken ribs and a hole in his lung. Chara played.

By then, the rough-and-tumble (black and) Blues had long begun doing what they had done to every opponent throughout the playoffs: wear down the opponent. In the first three rounds of the playoffs against Winnipeg, Dallas, and San Jose, the Blues had gone a combined 7–1 in Games 5 to 7 of their series, which was hardly a coincidence. St. Louis was bigger than most every opponent. The Blues were stronger. St. Louis opponents had combined for just ten goals in those eight games, as sure a sign as any that opposing forwards had been beaten down, unable and perhaps unwilling to navigate through what Cassidy often called "the dirty areas," most notably in front of the St. Louis net. Led by the six-foot-six Colton Parayko, the Blues defensemen seemed as if from the Land of Giants, ranging in size from six-foot-two to six-foot-four and between 200 and 230 pounds.

While the return of Chara certainly gave the Bruins some lift, the Blues won Game 5 in Boston by a 2–1 score. The Bruins, to their credit, responded with a resounding 5–1 victory in St. Louis in Game 6, forcing a seventh game on the TD Garden ice that would serve as the final game of the 2018–19 NHL season, one way or another.

By that point in the series, Rask was still playing perhaps the best hockey of his career, his save percentage at a sterling .944 beginning with Game 7 of the first round series against Toronto. But in Game 7 against Binnington and the relentless Blues, he had arguably the worst game of his postseason career, allowing four goals on just twenty shots. Rask certainly had plenty of help in the downfall, the second St. Louis goal coming when Bruins forward Marchand lazily allowed Blues defenseman Alex Pietrangelo entry into the Bruins zone to score St. Louis's second goal of the game on just the team's fourth shot.

In the end, the final score of Game 7 was 4–1, and the consequences for the Bruins were severe. In three trips to the finals with the core built around Bergeron and Krejci, they had lost twice. For all the winning Boston had done over the years, the Bruins had only one Stanley Cup to show for it.

"It's an empty feeling," said Cassidy. "It's a long year. Someone had to win and someone had to lose, and we came out on the wrong side of it. It's not the way you picture it. It's as simple as that."

Admitted Rask: "It was a nightmare for me, obviously. Barely didn't make a save in the first. And you know we tried to create, we had good chances, and [Binnington] made the saves when they needed."

In the resulting rubble from Boston's defeat, the Bruins faced some obvious and difficult choices, the words of their owner and CEO still hanging in the air. They were getting older. Bergeron had played his one-thousandth game months earlier and, as Charlie Jacobs had noted, "We don't have another 1,000—we know that." He and Krejci, while part of "today's game," as Jeremy Jacobs had said, were probably "not part of tomorrow's."

Change was coming again. But this time it felt more lasting—and it wasn't necessarily for the better, either.

CHAPTER 15

COSTLY MISTAKES

"Boston has a history and that history . . . listen, it's just like a player's reputation. It's hard to get rid of. It really is. And you can do things over and over and over the right way, but your history still follows you a little bit."
—former Celtics coach Doc Rivers, July 2021

TO MANY BOSTONIANS, THE SUBJECT of racism exposes the rawest of nerves and is a charge for which the city has no answer—and never really will. The worst scars, after all, never truly heal. They serve as reminders of mistakes made with the hope that those transgressions will never be made again, though expecting as much is undoubtedly naïve and unrealistic. The monsters exist, as the saying goes, and there will always be a responsibility to fight them.

In the words of philosopher George Santayana: "Those who forget history are condemned to repeat it."

More than any other team in Boston's history—and with good reason—the Red Sox have been the recipient of accusations of racism dating back decades, mostly the result of actions by Thomas A. Yawkey, the team's owner beginning in 1933 and for forty-three years until his death from leukemia in 1976. During Yawkey's ownership, the Red Sox became the last team to integrate, in 1959, when infielder Pumpsie Green became the first African American player to appear in a game for Boston. Green's debut came a disturbing twelve years after the major-league arrival of barrier-breaking Brooklyn Dodgers infielder and Hall of Famer Jackie Robinson, who had previously tried out for the Red Sox and was dismissed by Yawkey, whom Robinson later referred to as "probably the most bigoted man in baseball."

In the decades since, Boston as a whole has worn that label like a scarlet letter, rightly or wrongly, among a complex history that has ranged from sad and troubling to, on occasion, encouraging and progressive. Busing riots triggered by racial desegregation in the 1970s further emblazoned the wound on the city's chest that cannot—and will not—be erased. The simple fact is that many Americans view Boston as racist, and that is something Bostonians simply have to accept.

"Historically, that has been a perception," said Dan Lebowitz, executive director of the acclaimed Center for the Study of Sport in Society at Northeastern University.

> But if you think about certain realities, Boston, in terms of the Celtics, was probably the first [NBA] team ever to put five African-Americans on the floor at the same time, the first ever to have an African-American player coach [in Bill Russell]. So sometimes perceptions die hard around sports teams because they are being tied to some of the things that happened in the city. Has Boston, in terms of a northern city, had a reputation around racism and specific to racism that might be deserved? That's true. Have the Boston sports teams always been part of that? I would say that we have an awful lot of history that shows that many of those sports teams have embraced social change and absolutely have been the leaders of creating that social change. And so, I think, you can never look at sports teams as just defining a community. Sometimes they're the ones that are actually leading it to a better place. And I would say that in many respects . . . the Celtics in our city and the Patriots are the two teams that probably most embrace that. In some respects, there have been so few African-Americans in hockey, you can't say the Bruins haven't been engaged—[and former Bruins winger] Willie O'Ree was the first [African American] ever to play in the league. And so, I think as a whole, the city has tried to embrace social change. There's obviously been some history with the Red Sox that's been painful that people talk about relative to their owner for a long period of time, but I think that particularly with the Celtics in that space, you see how they became the leaders of social change in the city.

In the case of the Red Sox, change has been decidedly slow, though any progress was often obscured by the team's past. African American first baseman Mo Vaughn became the team's centerpiece in the mid-1990s before departing via free agency, for instance, and remains one of the more popular players in team history to this day. The Red Sox championship teams of the early 2000s were built around Manny Ramirez and David Ortiz, both people of color, the latter arguably now the most beloved player in the history of the franchise. And by the mid-2010s, Boston had a core of young players that included Aruban-born Xander Bogaerts as well as African Americans Jackie Bradley and Mookie Betts, all respected for both their talents and their professionalism.

But the truth, even after the change in ownership that occurred when John Henry and his partners bought the Red Sox from the Yawkey Trust in early 2002, is that the damage of the Yawkey Years persisted. And that Boston often made things worse for itself.

Prior to the start of the 2017 season, after a 2016 campaign that was merely the beginning of a Red Sox career defined by extremes, pitcher David Price was the subject of a story written by reporter Peter Abraham in the *Boston Globe* during which he expressed frustrations over what was a largely transitional year. Signed to a seven-year, $217 million contract by general manager Dave Dombrowski to lead Boston back to championship status, Price went a respectable 17-9 with 3.99 ERA in 230 innings covering thirty-five starts, totals that nonetheless failed to meet expectations. His greatest failure, however, came in October, where he was pounded in a 6–0 loss to Corey Kluber and the Cleveland Indians in Game 2 of the Indians' eventual 3–0 sweep in the American League Division Series. Signed precisely to win games of those magnitude in support of a young, talented Boston lineup, Price instead self-destructed, fueling theories that his sensitive and temperamental nature was not suited for the intensity of the Boston market.

Speaking with Abraham, Price said his intention was to win over the fans of Boston, to prove that he could handle the pressure that came along with a big contract in Boston. And in the process, he introduced an issue that hurt the city to the bone and triggered a firestorm.

"It got pretty rough," Price said in the story, published on January 13, 2017. "If you don't like it, pitch better. That's all it is. Mike Brenly, our bullpen catcher, he stood up for me multiple times. The Fenway guards, too, [and] the bullpen cop."

Were any of the taunts racial?

"I got it all," Price said. "It's all right. I don't care about that. My mom is white and my dad is black. I've heard that since I've been in school. There's nothing you can say to me that I haven't heard before. Your ignorance is not going to affect what I'm trying to do. But I feel sad it's still out there."

Naturally, a certain segment of the Boston population erupted. *What did he say?!* Perceived as a $200 million baby trying to deflect accountability, Price was effectively shouted down, called a liar. Some took his comments to heart, while others believed Price made the whole thing up. To put it kindly, Boston has had finer moments.

In actuality, Price took a great deal of responsibility in his conversation with Abraham, much of the criticism directed at himself. When he arrived in Boston, Price was an unsightly 0-7 in his career as a postseason starter. The implosion against Cleveland as a member of the Red Sox had made him 0-8. That was a reality he, too, had to accept. "I'm not trying to prove anybody wrong. I want to prove myself right," he told Abraham. "I know I can handle Boston. I know I can be successful in Boston. I've been successful my entire career. Going to Boston ain't going to change that." Added the pitcher: "I can't make excuses. I need to go out there and dominate and not leave it in anybody else's hands."

But the disclosure of racial taunts resulted in the rest of his remarks being ignored. Within weeks, Price seemed to soften the remarks, tried to downplay their significance. During an annual promotional event known as the Red Sox "Winter Carnival," Price was among a team contingent to appear at the Foxwoods Resort Casino in Ledyard, Connecticut. The last thing the team wanted or needed during the quest for another championship was to have its highest-paid player feuding with a vocal segment of its fan base—or the media—over racial issues that might never be solved.

Asked about his comments to Abraham during an interview on WEEI, the Red Sox radio rightsholder, Price said his comments were "taken a little bit out of context" and attempted to emphasize baseball over all else.

"It can be a tough place to play," said Price, who had been recently married and was an expectant father. "I've experienced it on the other side, sitting in the third-base dugout. They love this team. I like that. I really do like that. People can have a little bit too much fun sometimes, whether it's having too much to drink or whatever it is. To me, I don't worry about it. I'm having my child in Boston. I'm going to raise him for however long I'm in Boston. That's where he's going to be. I love the city of Boston. I like the people here. Everything. I don't think [the incident] speaks for the entire city."

Had that been the end of it, the matter might have subsided. But before long Price wasn't alone. On May 1, 2017, during a game between the Red Sox and Baltimore Orioles, visiting outfielder Adam Jones was berated by fans at Fenway Park who assailed him with racial taunts, one going so far as to throw a bag of peanuts at the talented center fielder. Like Price, Jones spoke openly with reporters after the game—"I was called the N-word a handful of times tonight. Thanks. Pretty awesome," he said—and acknowledged, like others, that Boston was often an uncomfortable and unpleasant place to play for African Americans. In Boston, there was now a pattern of racist behavior—again.

"It's different. Very unfortunate," Jones said. "I heard there was 59 or 60 ejections tonight in the ballpark [that related to a variety of incidents, a total the Red Sox later contended was roughly half Jones's estimate]. It is what it is, right. I just go out and play baseball. It's unfortunate that people need to resort to those type of epithets to degrade another human being. I'm trying to make a living for myself and for my family.

"It's unfortunate. The best thing about myself is that I continue to move on, and still play the game hard. Let people be who they are. Let them show their true colors."

In the wake of the incident, many sensitive Bostonians again bristled, including some sports radio talk show hosts who wanted evidence of the verbal abuse Jones was alleging. Other Bostonians simply hung their heads in shame. While the Red Sox issued an apology to Jones and vowed to make Fenway safer and friendlier, Yankees pitcher CC Sabathia spoke for the sixty-two active African American players in the major leagues at the time, telling *Newsday*: "We know. There's sixty-two of us. We all know. When you go to Boston, expect it." Meanwhile Red Sox outfielder Betts posted a message on Twitter that read: "Fact: I'm Black too. Literally stand up for @SimplyAJ10 (Jones) tonight and say no to racism. We as @RedSox and @MLB fans are better than this."

That night, May 2, Jones prepared to step into the batter's box and was largely cheered by Fenway Park fans, many of them standing. Red Sox pitcher Chris Sale stepped off the mound to allow fans their say—and to give Jones the chance to acknowledge them, which he did with a tip of the cap. Betts, playing right field, similarly removed his cap and applauded, slapping his bare right hand against the side of his glove.

In the short term, the aftershocks of the incident simmered; the games resumed. In the longer term, it was always there, softly bubbling beneath the surface.

* * *

Between the World Series championship of 2013 and the latter part of the 2010s, the Red Sox were in a seemingly constant state of upheaval, oscillating from one extreme to the other with dizzying speed. In 2014, just months after an improbable World Series title, they plummeted back to last place, trading off, among others: pitcher John Lackey, whom they sent to the St. Louis Cardinals; shortstop Stephen Drew, whom the club had rashly signed amid defensive concerns about the developing Bogaerts; and left-handed reliever Andrew Miller, who went to Baltimore in exchange for left-handed pitching prospect Eduardo Rodriguez. But the most alarming transaction was the departure of left-hander Jon Lester, a homegrown ace, whom the club sent to Oakland with outfielder Jonny Gomes after having alienated Lester in preseason contract talks with a four-year, $70 million offer the player deemed laughable.

And so, less than a year after winning back their fans with a World Series, the Red Sox were back sleeping on the couch again, a reality that then prompted an excessive reaction in the *opposite* direction.

Having lowballed Lester and overplayed their hand in the wake of their unlikely 2013 World Series win—the Sox did virtually nothing to augment their roster during the 2013–14 off-season—Boston went on a spending spree between the 2014 and 2015 seasons, spending money as if on some drug-induced binge. General manager Ben Cherington signed third baseman Pablo Sandoval and outfielder Hanley Ramirez to contracts for $95 million (over five years) and $88 million (over four years), respectively, all while flipping assets from the Lester deal to the Detroit Tigers for right-handed starter Rick Porcello, whom they subsequently signed to a four-contract worth an additional $82.5 million.

In all, the Red Sox agreed to more than a quarter billion in long-term contracts on players with a spotty reputation (Ramirez), a shaky work ethic (the overweight Sandoval), and middle-of-the-rotation talent (Porcello)—all basically within one year of espousing the benefits of fiscal responsibility in the wake of the 2013 championship. The result? Another last-place finish in 2015 and one that triggered (in the middle of the season) the dismissal of Cherington, who was replaced with deposed Detroit general manager Dave Dombrowski, who had similarly been dismissed by the Tigers.

Got all that? No? Well, let's put it this way: The Red Sox were a mess.

"Boston's a big market," Dombrowski said upon being hired, when he was officially announced as the club's president of baseball operations. "It's a great sports town. Look at the coverage you get at this press conference. It's passionate. . . . I think that's part of the fun of it, in many ways. You know when you're a general manager, or club president—people are not going to agree with your decisions all the time. Hopefully more of them will work than don't. That should be the case. But once in a while something's not going to work and you take what's attached to that. But, no, I don't think I'll have any problem whatsoever. I look forward to it."

Of course, under the circumstances, Dombrowski knew precisely what he was getting into. As a young executive, Dombrowski first became a general manager with the Montreal Expos, where he had helped build an organization that was threatening for a World Series championship in 1994 when a work stoppage brought an end to the season. By then, Dombrowski already had been hired to construct the expansion Florida Marlins, who began play in 1993 and, four years later, engaged in a massive spending spree at the behest of team owner and Blockbuster Video king Wayne Huizenga, building the 1997 Marlins team that won the World Series.

One of the Marlins minority owners at the time? John Henry, the future owner of the Red Sox.

Four years after their World Series title, of course, the Marlins had been completely dismantled, again at the order of Huizenga, whose team naturally suffered in the standings as a result. Understandably, Dombrowski wanted out. And by 2002, the then forty-five-year-old executive signed on with owner Mike Ilitch as general manager of the Detroit Tigers, a move that began and shaped his thinking as a baseball executive over what would be the balance of his career.

After serving as general manager of small-market teams in Montreal and Florida—excluding the free-spending year in 1997—Dave Dombrowski had come to a conclusion derived by many middle-aged men as they reached their peak professional years: He liked money. Even more so, he liked to spend someone else's when it came to building a baseball team.

From 2006 to 2014, under Dombrowski's watch, the Tigers won 790 games, an average of 88 per season that ranked fourth-best in baseball, one place ahead of the Red Sox. They made the playoffs five times and won two league championships, twice reaching the World Series. During those years, Detroit also had one of the highest payrolls in the game, something that was about to change when the Tigers fired Dombrowski in the middle of the 2015 campaign, not long after both the annual major-league draft and the July 31 trading deadline. With his own team in disarray—and with Dombrowski now on the market—Henry pounced.

"Today is about the future of the Boston Red Sox," Henry said in a prepared statement at Dombrowski's introduction in Boston. "We have a history of success over the past 14 years, characterized by a certain boldness of purpose. That's very much alive here today."

For Cherington, who would soon be elsewhere, and Lucchino, who had just announced his decision to "step down" after the season, the writing wasn't merely on the wall; it was etched into the famed brick face at the team's historic main entrance near the junction of Brookline Avenue and Yawkey Way.

There's a new sheriff in town.

Through it all, in the final months of a 2015 season marked by organizational cataclysm, the Red Sox on the field began to turn a corner. As Bogaerts, Betts, and Bradley became part of the team's everyday lineup, the Red Sox went 28-16 over a 44-game stretch near the end of the season, a pace that would produce 103 victories over the course of a 162-game schedule. And while such extrapolations could be dangerous in baseball given the nature of the sport, all the shortcomings of the Red Sox really could be addressed with a large purchase or two, which was just the way Dave Dombrowski liked it.

And so, with John Henry's credit card in hand, Dave Dombrowski happily entered his first off-season as the chief Red Sox decision-maker thinking big—and with the freedom to spend big.

* * *

For all of the maneuvering and shuffling the Red Sox did between 2011 and 2016, on the field and off, the one question was impossible to ignore: What if John Henry had chosen differently and had decided to keep Theo Epstein and jettison most everyone else? What if the Red Sox had committed to Epstein and his willingness to endure *bridge years*?

By the baseball off-season of 2015–16, after all, any comparisons and contrasts between Dombrowski's Red Sox and Epstein's Cubs were impossible to ignore. While Epstein had built the Chicago Cubs largely from the inside out, he had begun augmenting the roster with impact free-agent signings with precisely the kind of blended philosophy he had preached in Boston. In 2015, after doing what the Red Sox would not—signing Jon Lester to a big contract—the Cubs won ninety-seven games to qualify for the postseason, whereupon they advanced to the National League Championship Series before being swept by the New York Mets. By Epstein's assessment, the Cubs had arrived "a year early" in the five-year plan he had envisioned to bring them to championship caliber, but there was no longer any point in debating Chicago's viability. The signing of Lester to a free-agent contract worth $155 million over six years had seemed exorbitant at the time, but it was a price Epstein was willing to pay as the Cubs filled in around a talented young core leading into the 2015 season.

The Red Sox, of course, had eschewed that principle, believing that multimillion-dollar, multiyear investments in thirtysomething pitchers were anything but smart business. But a year after the Lester signing in Chicago, Dombrowski knocked over a thirty-year-old David Price with a seven-year, $217 million contract that made the Lester deal look like a bargain.

For Dombrowski, the Price acquisition was the biggest domino in an off-season during which the Red Sox also traded four prospects to the San Diego Padres for closer Craig Kimbrel, providing bookends to a Boston pitching staff that had lacked elite talent. Reliever Carson Smith was also acquired in a trade with the Seattle Mariners, completing a three-week splurge.

And so, on December 8, 2015, the Red Sox introduced Price to Boston, Dombrowski calling the left-hander "one of the best pitchers in baseball" and "a true No. 1," a title Price would hold with the Red Sox for the entirety of one season.

In retrospect, the 2016 season in Boston was remembered more for the departure of David Ortiz than for the arrival of Price, whose season to got off to a hellish beginning from which he never completely recovered. By June, Price still had an ERA above or hovering near an unsightly 5.00. And while the team was still very much in playoff contention, the club's standing had much more to do with the performance of right-hander Rick Porcello, the right-hander whom Dombrowski had traded to Boston from Detroit only to re-inherit a pitcher he did not want.

But, as was often the case in sports, it was better to be lucky than good.

By the time the playoffs arrived, in fact, Red Sox manager John Farrell had settled on Porcello—and not Price—as the team's starter for Game 1 against Terry Francona's Cleveland squad, a decision that proved costly when Porcello allowed five runs in four and one-third innings of an eventual 5–4 Red Sox defeat. Price was then hammered in the Game 2 loss, sending the series to Boston with Cleveland holding a decisive 2-0 series edge. Even then, the Red Sox still had a chance when they took a 2–1 lead into the sixth inning of Game 3 when left-hander Drew Pomeranz—whom Dombrowski had acquired at the trade deadline—surrendered a two-run homer to former Red Sox outfielder Coco Crisp that propelled the Indians to a 4–3 win and 3-0 series sweep.

The end proved terribly anticlimactic for Ortiz, who went just one for nine in a series during which the Red Sox batted an anemic .214 as a team. His final at-bat in a major-league uniform was an eighth-inning walk that helped produce the final run of the Red Sox season, after which Ortiz remained on the field to pay tribute to the Red Sox and their fans.

"I'm happy, not just for me, not just how my career went down, but for the organization, the step that we took, from going from last place to win the division this year—even if things didn't end up the way we were looking for," he said. "But I believe that in baseball—it's a big step. . . . And I told my teammates, I want them to feel happy and proud about themselves and [to] do what I did back in the day—reflect [on] that in the following year and come back and fight. I told them, 'Listen, we only played three games these playoffs, but you guys saw the intensity. You guys saw the emotions. You guys saw the best of the best playing. You guys take a little bit of that. Make sure that carries over for the following year.'"

With regard to Dombrowski, many of his efforts and investments in the 2016 Red Sox generally proved ineffective. Kimbrel made the All-Star team and converted thirty-one of thirty-three saves, but he walked a whopping 5.1 batters per nine innings and finished with a mediocre 3.40 ERA that was the highest of his career; Price was good, not great, and failed in the playoffs; Smith, who had a delivery that begged for arm issues, got hurt and appeared in just three games; Pomeranz, acquired as a starter, ended up in the bullpen and blew the final game of the playoffs. In the end, for all the money that Dombrowski threw at the roster, the Red Sox didn't win a single playoff game.

So, during the winter of 2016–17—after the Chicago Cubs won the World Series for the first time in 108 years and Theo Epstein had ended another curse—Dombrowski did exactly what he did the first time. He threw more resources at it, albeit in the form of prospects instead of dollars.

On the same day, December 6, 2016, Dombrowski executed a pair of trades in which the Red Sox sent a total of eight minor leaguers, four each to the Chicago White Sox and the Milwaukee Brewers. In the first deal, Boston acquired left-hander Chris Sale, who immediately supplanted Price at the front of the Red Sox rotation; in the second, he acquired right-handed reliever Tyler Thornburg with the idea of displacing Carson Smith as the setup man to Kimbrel. The chief sacrifices made by the Red Sox in the deal were talented infielder Yoán Moncada, pitching prospect Michael Kopech, corner infielder

Travis Shaw, and shortstop Mauricio Dubon, varying degrees of prospects who had been acquired under Epstein and Cherington.

As was often the case when teams changed executives in sports, Dombrowski was getting rid of *their guys* and bringing in *his guys*.

While Dombrowski told reporters that he was interested in only truly elite talent to augment the Boston pitching staff—"It was pretty much Sale or nothing," he said—New York Yankees general manager Brian Cashman was all too happy to put all the pressure on the Red Sox and Dombrowski, whose decision to sacrifice elite talent for Sale amounted to an all-in, go-for-broke mentality.

"Boston is the Golden State Warriors of baseball now," said Cashman, making an analogy that resonated with Bostonians for obvious reasons. "They've got their Durant and Green and Thompson and Curry."

Acknowledged Dombrowski: "It's a situation where if you have a chance to win, you want to give yourself every opportunity to do so. We're thrilled."

Of course, for all the praise the Red Sox were getting—and heaping on themselves—there was an obvious element to the story that could not be overlooked. One year into the mountain that was David Price's seven-year contract, the Sox clearly had doubts about his ability to win in October. There was no real way to minimize that. While manager John Farrell tried to spin the Sale pursuit a different way—"In light of David Ortiz's retirement, how were we going to improve our team? We wanted to upgrade our pitching," Farrell said—the truth was that the Red Sox were still trying to replace Jon Lester, who had been an integral part of Chicago's championship run while Price was melting in the autumn chill.

After going 19-5 with a 2.44 ERA to finish second in the National Cy Young Award balloting during the 2016 regular season, Lester went 3-1 with a 2.02 ERA in the postseason, earning honors as MVP of the National League Championship Series. It was the kind of performance that a team would expect from . . . well, an ace.

Just the same, the Sale acquisition had its desired effect—at least during the summer. With Sale en route to a 17-8 record, a 2.90 ERA, 308 strikeouts, and a second-place finish in the American League Cy Young Award balloting, the Red Sox overtook the Yankees atop the American League East in late June, then effectively remained at the top of the division for the balance of the season. Dombrowski made a pair of notable pickups at the trade deadline, acquiring infielder Eduardo Núñez and reliever Addison Reed, the latter necessary because Thornburg, like Smith, had similarly been derailed by injury.

Over the final two months of the season, beginning on the annual July 31 trading deadline, the Red Sox went 36-20 in their final fifty-six games, a .643 pace that would translate into 104 wins over a 162-game schedule. Though they weren't quite the Golden State Warriors, Boston went 93-69 and won the American League East, earning the right to face the Houston Astros in the American League Division Series.

For Farrell, the division title was his third in five seasons as manager beginning in 2013, making him the first Sox skipper in history to win three division titles.

"I think he's done a great job," said Dombrowski. "It's a tough job. Managing is a tough job, period. I think it's a tougher job here than maybe anywhere else [with] the scrutiny you receive. Being in the game as long as I've been in the game, I'm amazed somewhat by the scrutiny aspect of it."

Indeed, for all that Farrell had endured during his time with the Red Sox—two last-place finishes, a change in general managers, a cancer diagnosis that sidelined him at the end of the 2015 season, even a rumored relationship with a journalist who covered the team—the division title earned him a unique place in Sox history. In the process, he joined Terry Francona as the only Sox managers in seventy years to manage five full seasons with the club.

As it turned out, he barely made it. Two weeks after praising Farrell in the wake of a division-clinching win over the Houston Astros, Dombrowski fired the manager after yet another disappointing playoff performance.

Having been swept by the Cleveland Indians in 2016, the Red Sox this time fell in four games to the Astros. Making his first career postseason start, Sale was tattooed in an 8-2 Game 1 loss during which he allowed nine hits, seven earned runs, and three homers in just five innings. In just two innings of Game 2, Pomeranz (five hits, four earned runs, two homers) was similarly bludgeoned. Sidelined by an arm injury for much of the season, Price actually pitched quite well in four innings of relief in Game 3—a resounding 10-3 Sox win—before Porcello labored in Game 4, lasting just three innings in a 5-4 defeat that ended the season.

Instead of looking like the Golden State Warriors, the Red Sox looked more like the Celtics of the Kyrie Irving era—expensive, underperforming, incapable of handling adversity. Dombrowski's players were failing everywhere. The stringy Sale, who had a history of fading in Chicago, was mismanaged down the stretch and posted a 4.64 ERA after the All-Star break. Price, Carson Smith, and Tyler Thornburg all suffered injuries. Pomeranz had failed in October. Meanwhile, Boston's lineup managed just fifteen runs in six postseason losses over two seasons.

Two days after the final loss to Houston, a cryptic Dombrowski was vague in detailing his final meeting with Farrell and was circumspect in outlining the reasons for Farrell's dismissal.

"That's really something I'm going to keep to myself," Dombrowski said. "I'm not going to get into anything beyond that other than there were a lot of different factors. . . . I'm not one of these guys that thinks it's a flip of a coin when you get to the playoffs, but there's also much more left to chance when you have a shortened series. I can't tell you that postseason [failure] is a driving force." The Red Sox chief baseball executive concluded: "A new manager coming in will provide just an overall different dynamic, a change. And we'll see what happens in that regard."

And so, having used the currency of both cash and prospects to augment the Boston roster during an unsuccessful tenure to that point as the Red Sox chief baseball decision-maker, Dave Dombrowski set out in the off-season to find a new manager for his team, too.

And, of course, he threw a little more money at the problem, too.

* * *

If there was truly a rivalry between professional Boston sports teams in the twenty-first century, if the titles inspired a game of one-upmanship, the 2018 Red Sox were either a beneficiary or a casualty—or both. But, regardless, they were proof.

In retrospect, from the moment Dave Dombrowski was hired to run the baseball operation, Red Sox owner John Henry was in so deep that there was simply no turning back. Over a span of three off-seasons, the Red Sox stopped at nothing. They signed premium free agents, they traded away prospects, they fired the manager. And after John Farrell paid the price—rightly or wrongly—Henry and Dombrowski (in that order) settled on a former Red Sox player to take on the responsibility on winning a championship.

Alex Cora would prove the right man for the job, in large part because he knew precisely what he was getting into.

"Something about this place pushes you," the native Puerto Rican said upon his introduction on November 6, 2017. "Boston, for a lot of people, is a challenge. For me it's not. This is a city that I understand. They live baseball

24/7, but you know what? I come from a country [where] we live baseball 24/7. In my family, for breakfast, we talk baseball. For lunch, we talk baseball, and for dinner, too. My dad was the founder of the Little League chapter in Caguas, where I'm from. He passed away in 1998, and that's what he preached . . . school and baseball. My mom, if you talk to her, she'll be around during the season. She'll talk baseball with you guys. This is going to be fun." He added: "I think I understand what the process is, what I need to be successful, what the team needs to be successful, and it starts with the people around you. We put in a great staff around me, the analytic department is going to be involved. I don't want this to be [separated by] analytics, coaches, players. We have to be connected, because that's information that I need for them to be better. And if they're better, I'll be fine."

They would be better. A lot better.

Though he had no major-league managerial experience, Cora spent parts of four years, from 2005 to 2008, playing for the Red Sox as a utility infielder, winning a championship on the team managed by Terry Francona in 2007. Often on the bench during games, he was an astute observer. He was someone teammates relied upon for critique and advice. He was the kind of player who could make others better purely through his presence and his smarts, and he was a baseball junkie. Cora had served as bench coach for the Houston Astros team that had dismantled the Red Sox in the 2017 playoffs and gone on to win the World Series, and he was so sure of himself that Henry once suggested that Cora was "almost *too* confident." And while the Red Sox tried to pass him off as a hiring by Dombrowski, the facts suggested otherwise. Dombrowski, after all, had no prior experience working with Cora—no relationship, no real knowledge. The owners and the baseball people knew much more about Cora than Dombrowski ever could.

While much was made of the fact that Cora, a native of Puerto Rico, was the first person of color to manage the Red Sox in their nearly 120-year history, the far more relevant color in his hiring was green—as in money. The Red Sox had invested a king's ransom in their roster, and, under Farrell, many of Boston's younger players had stagnated and, in some cases—Bogaerts, for example—clashed with the former manager. Cora's job was to tap into their talent, to get everyone pointed in the right direction, to fix the cracks and keep the team together over the very long season.

From the start and repeatedly throughout the year, Cora gave them essentially the same message, over and over again.

You guys really don't know how good you are. When I was coaching with Houston, we looked across the field and saw all your talent. We feared you. You are capable of great things. You can achieve them.

Offensively, Cora pounded the Red Sox with what became a team catch-phrase: *Do damage.*

In 2017, in Farrell's final season, Boston's offense was often anemic. The Red Sox finished ninth in the league in batting average and fifth in on-base percentage, but their slugging percentage was a dreadful fourteenth among the fifteen major-league clubs. To help fill the void created by Ortiz's retirement, the Red Sox signed J. D. Martinez to a five-year contract worth up to $110 million, one of the biggest contracts to someone who would largely serve as a designated hitter. But that was only part of the problem. The rest of the issue was not necessarily something that Dombrowski could throw any more money at, namely the underperformance of someone like Bogaerts, who was six-foot-two and 220 but often swung the bat like a man half his size. Under Cora, that would change.

When the starting gun sounded, the Red Sox steamrolled opponents with such force—and regularity—that there was little doubt they would be playing in October. After a 6–4 loss to the Tampa Bay Rays on Opening Day, the Sox won nine in a row. Then came a loss to the Yankees. Then eight more wins to improve their record to an incredible 17-2. They never really hit any kind of slump. By June 14, after a win at Seattle, the Red Sox were 48-22, on a 111-win pace. Roughly two weeks later, they were 55-27, still coasting right along, but—somewhat incredibly—a mere one game ahead of the Yankees, who were playing at a similarly scalding pace. The Red Sox arrived at Yankee Stadium and lost two of three, the finale an 11–1 defeat that completed a series in which all three games were decided by at least seven runs, leaving the teams tied atop the AL East with eighty-five games in the book and seventy-seven to play.

"It's going to be a dogfight," Cora said of the division race. "We have a good team, they have a good team."

Countered Yankees manager Aaron Boone, with whom Cora had developed a friendship when both were working as baseball analysts for ESPN: "I'm sure it's going to be a fun few months."

It was over in a few weeks.

After leaving New York, the Red Sox won ten in a row, then dropped a 13-7 decision to Toronto, then won three more. They suddenly had a five-and-a-half-game lead. The Sox then won seven of the next eleven, extending their run to 19-5, after which they still held a spongy five-game lead over the Yankees entering the teams' next meeting, a four-game series from August 2 to 5 at Fenway Park. By that point Dombrowski had long since added right-handed pitcher Nathan Eovaldi and right-handed-hitting first baseman–designated hitter Steve Pearce to the Boston lineup to address potential situational short-comings, giving Cora roster flexibility. The Red Sox won the first game 15–7. Then the second 4–1. Then the third, again by a 4–1 score. The teams then played the nationally televised series finale Sunday night on ESPN, when the Yankees were three outs from a 4–1 victory that would have left the Red Sox with a seven-game lead in the division.

Instead, the lead ballooned to nine. Against erratic Yankees closer Aroldis Chapman, the Red Sox rallied for three runs in the ninth inning, giving the Red Sox a 5–4 win and a whopping nine-game lead in the division with forty-nine games to play, effectively ending the division race.

"A tough way to obviously end a tough weekend, but we can't let this define what has been a great season," Boone said.

Incredibly, the Red Sox weren't done. They won nine of their next eleven games to improve their record to a gaudy 90-39, a .698 winning percentage that had them on a historic 113-win pace. Since losing two of three at New York, they had gone 32-7 to leave the Yankees and everyone else in their dust. Following a 7–0 win against Cleveland on August 23, the Red Sox had an expansive ten-and-a-half-game lead over the Yankees and established themselves as the best team in baseball.

When asked about the team's play, Cora said, "The whole thing about this is, we talk about this [game], we talk about this series. And tomorrow when we get to Tampa, it's the same mindset."

The message to the players was clear. *Keep your eye on the ball. Don't look ahead.* And they clearly took it to heart. Over the seven months from the start of spring training, Boston was never really knocked off their stride, maintaining a pace never before seen by a Red Sox team. Their 108 victories broke the record of 104 set by a 1946 club that had played eight fewer games, but few were quibbling over details at this stage. Far more relevant was what had happened to the '46 Red Sox after that season: They failed to win the World Series. For the 2018 team, that was all that mattered now.

* * *

As dominant as the Red Sox were during the 2018 regular season, their stam-
pede through the American League was not entirely devoid of drama. Slightly
more than halfway through the season, ace left-hander Chris Sale was shut
down with a shoulder issue. Sale sat out more than two weeks, came back to
pitch against Baltimore on August 12, then missed another month. He pitched
just twelve innings over four starts during the month of September, posting
a 5.63 ERA in two season-ending outings in which the velocity of his fastball
had noticeably dipped. While both Sale and the Red Sox proclaimed him fit
for the postseason, one obvious question persisted: In the postseason, against
the best of the best, could the Red Sox still win without him—or with him at
something less than full throttle?

"If I take the mound, I expect to win," said Sale, whom Cora named to
be the Red Sox Game 1 starter in a best-of-five division series against the New
York Yankees. "I don't care what I have on a given day, I should be able to find
a way with whatever I have."

Sale lasted just five and one-third innings in Game 1 against the Yankees
but as promised, he was good enough. The Red Sox raced to a 5–0 lead against
Yankees starter J. A. Happ and held on to win the game 5–4 despite a rally
against Boston closer Kimbrel in the ninth. But in Game 2 the October troubles
of David Price returned in full force, with Price allowing three hits, three runs,
two walks, and two home runs while failing to make it through the second
inning. The Yankees never trailed and won by a lopsided 6–2 score, after which
the Yankees walked from the visiting clubhouse to their team bus right past
the Red Sox clubhouse. On the way, Yankees outfielder Aaron Judge reportedly blasted his boom box to the tune of "New York, New York," the song they
customarily played at Yankee Stadium following a New York victory.

Given the October failures of the Red Sox in 2016 and 2017, many
viewed Judge's display as taunting. The player denied it. Regardless, New
York was feeling good about themselves, and Bostonians couldn't help but
wonder if the Red Sox were headed for another hollow postseason. *Here we
go again. Dead October.*

"Coming into the playoffs, we knew we had to win series," an even-keeled
Cora said during the travel day between Games 2 and 3. "I think we did an
outstanding job throughout the season just staying in the moment. . . . Nothing
changes. Like today, regular off day. Some guys showed up. They took some
hacks. They got treatment, had a good dinner in New York City—and [they
will] come tomorrow and play the way we can play."

If the Red Sox had any self-doubt, they did not show it. And then they came out in full force. Behind right-hander and deadline acquisition Nathan Eovaldi, the Red Sox relentlessly pounded the Yankees, taking a 3–0 lead into the third inning against New York starter Luis Severino and then exploding for seven more runs. Things got so bad for the Yankees that New York used bench player Austin Romine *to pitch* in the ninth inning, when he allowed a two-run home run to utility man Brock Holt that completed a four-hit night in which Holt batted for the cycle.

One night later, albeit with Kimbrel again wobbling, the Red Sox took a 4–1 lead into the ninth and held on for a 4–3 victory, eliminating the Yankees from the playoffs and winning their first playoff series without David Ortiz in nineteen years.

In the visiting clubhouse at Yankee Stadium following Boston's series victory, music blared: "New York, New York."

"A lot of people gave up on us after losing Game 2 and we showed up yesterday, and we did an outstanding job. And tonight we had our plan mapped out," Cora said. "[The players] stay in the moment. They play the right way, run the bases well, play good defense. . . . We have a great team. We're very versatile. We count on everybody, and it was a great team victory."

For their efforts, the Red Sox earned a rematch with Cora's old team, the defending world champion Astros, the second Boston opponent to have reached at least one hundred wins during the regular season in what was rapidly becoming a murderers' row schedule. Sale labored through five innings but allowed only two runs, and the Astros took a 3–2 lead into the final inning when they erupted for four runs and a 7–2 victory.

Though the Red Sox rebounded to win Game 2 despite a poor outing from Price—the final score was 7–5—the Red Sox appeared to be teetering on both ends of the pitching staff. With the Red Sox holding a 6–4 lead entering the eighth, Cora took the aggressive measure of using starter Rick Porcello as a reliever in the eighth inning, something he had similarly done with success in Game 1 against New York. Once again, the message to the clubhouse was clear: *We will use anyone and everyone at any time to win these games. Anything is possible. So be ready.*

When the series switched to Houston for Games 3, 4 and 5, the task of the Red Sox seemed simple. Winning two of three was a reasonable, realistic goal against the Astros, who had been the best team in baseball over the span of two seasons. Boston held a 3–2 lead entering the eighth inning when Bradley

highlighted a five-run Red Sox rally with a grand slam against Houston closer
Roberto Osuna to key an 8–2 Red Sox win. The victory gave Cora's team a
2-1 series edge entering Game 4, which proved to be one of the more wildly
entertaining games in postseason history. Frankly, like many of the affairs
involving Boston teams from 2001 through early 2019, it could have been a
book unto itself.

With the Red Sox leading 2–0 in the bottom of the first, Houston's Jose
Altuve appeared to hit a game-tying two-run homer—only to have it reversed
thanks to the brilliant athleticism of would-be American League MVP Betts,
who leapt and reached into the stands, where it was rightly deemed that fans
interfered with him. Houston nonetheless inched ahead in the middle innings,
holding leads of 4–3 and 5–4 before a two-run home run by Bradley pushed the
Red Sox back in front, 6–5. The Red Sox added individual runs in the seventh
and eighth innings before Boston's athleticism once again flashed, this time in
a pair of breathtaking outfield plays that highlighted the versatility that Cora
had referred to.

Leading off the eighth, Houston speedster Tony Kemp yanked a hit down
the right field and into the corner for a seemingly certain double. A speeding
Betts cut the ball off, wheeled, and fired a strike to second base to cut down
the batter, helping to limit the Astros to just one run in an inning that might
have produced many more.

And then, in the ninth—and after Astros right fielder Josh Reddick made
a diving catch to end the inning and leave the bases loaded—Houston loaded
the bases in the bottom, whereupon all-world third baseman Alex Bregman hit
a two-out liner to left field. With the game on the line, Sox left fielder Andrew
Benintendi charged the ball and made an all-or-nothing dive, extending his
right arm outward to record the final out of the game and preserve an 8–6
Boston victory filled with heart-stopping moments.

The game lasted a ridiculous four hours and thirty-three minutes—and
was one of the few occasions in modern baseball history where the investment
was entirely worth it.

"We do feel that we have the best outfield in the big leagues," Cora said, following Bradley's two-run homer and the slick defense of Betts and Benintendi.
"The effort by Mookie on the ball at the wall, the effort on the Tony Kemp ball
down the line and then Beni taking a chance there. Those three guys, when
they're together, they're pretty special."

A night later, for the first time in twelve career postseason starts, David Price finally recorded a win. In six spectacular innings, Price struck out nine while walking none and allowing just three hits, two of them singles. He left with a 4–0 lead. Cora turned to Eovaldi for a scoreless one and one-third innings of relief that included a strikeout of the cocky Bregman with a blistering fastball that registered 102 miles per hour on the stadium radar gun.

"They have the most wins in the league for a reason," Astros manager A. J. Hinch said after the game. "They're as complete a team as we are, and their at-bats are really exceptional. And that's not taking away from their pitching. They pitched well. Their bullpen stepped up when they needed to. They have tremendous balance. They put pressure on you from the very beginning. They don't concede any at-bats. . . . They do it right. And that's why it's hard to get 27 outs against them. When the season started, there was a great unknown of how they were going to adapt to a lot of the changes that were made. The talent was there. But they had to go out and play and prove it. And then when people doubted them, you know, it seemed like they got better. And they never stopped. They never stopped coming at you. They're a relentless group."

Incredibly, the Red Sox were now 5-0 on the road in the postseason against the only two other American League teams to have won at least one hundred games. There were no arguments to be made. Boston had the best team in the American League. And the Red Sox were going back to the World Series.

* * *

For all the winning the Red Sox did in 2018, arguably the team's most memorable moment came in defeat, an epic 3-2 loss in World Series Game 3 that lasted a historic seven hours and twenty minutes and required eighteen innings. Boston trailed by a 1–0 score entering the eighth, when a Bradley homer against Dodgers closer Kenley Jansen tied the score. The teams then traded runs in the thirteenth to knot the game at 2 as they played deep into the California night. By then, working out of the bullpen, Eovaldi was making his sixth appearance (four in relief) in twelve postseason games, a workload unheard-of for any pitcher, let alone a starter. His ninety-seventh and final pitch of the game was a cut fastball clocked at 90 miles per hour that Dodgers infielder Max Muncy hit for a game-winning solo home run, a Los Angeles victory that trimmed the Red Sox series to 2-1 but further galvanized the Boston clubhouse.

"Effort-wise, I don't know . . . that was one of the best performances probably in the history of the World Series," said Cora of the right-hander, whom
Red Sox players treated like a hero.

As was the case in the Houston series, Game 4 once again proved the
Red Sox mettle, this time with a captivating comeback that seemingly came
out of nowhere. Mesmerized by crafty left-hander Rich Hill through the
first six innings, the Red Sox drew the ire of pitcher Sale, who delivered an
in-game pep talk similar to the one Dave Ortiz had issued in St. Louis five
years earlier. After Dodgers manager Dave Roberts—yes, the same man who
stole second in the 2004 Red Sox ALCS win over the Yankees—curiously
removed Hill from the game, Red Sox first baseman Mitch Moreland nearly
erased the entirety of a 4–0 deficit with a three-home run that changed the
tenor of the game. After Steve Pearce tied the game with a solo homer in the
eighth, the Red Sox erupted for five runs in the ninth and won going away,
a shaky Kimbrel finishing a 9–5 victory that moved the Red Sox within one
win of a championship.

Just as he had done in Houston, Cora then handed the ball to Price in
the series clincher, where a reborn Price basked in the moment. Staked to an
early 2–0 lead in the first, Price allowed a solo home run to leadoff man David
Freese, then surrendered just two more hits over seven innings. The Red Sox
closed out a 5–1 victory with Sale pitching the final inning in relief, a fitting
end to a series and year that validated Dombrowski's avalanche of expensive
signings and acquisitions.

Eovaldi, after all, had been acquired by Dombrowski at the trade deadline,
when the GM had endured much criticism; Pearce, who had been picked up by
trade earlier, was named the World Series MVP; and the wounded Sale closed
out the third consecutive postseason win by Price, who had posted a combined
1.42 ERA in Game 5 of the ALCS and Games 2 and 5 of the World Series.

"It was tough, absolutely," Price said when asked about having to deal
with incessant questions about his October failures. "To answer that question
in spring training day [after] day . . . and over and over and over and over . . .
anytime it got to September, playoffs—I hold all the cards now. And that feels
so good. That feels so good. I can't tell you how good it feels to hold that trump
card. And you guys have had it for a long time. You've played that card extremely
well. But you don't have it anymore, none of you do, and that feels really good."

After a 108-54 regular season, the Red Sox went 11-3 against the Yankees,
Astros, and Dodgers, leaving them with an incredible 119 victories in 176 games.

Said owner Henry of manager Cora: "I give him all the credit in the world. We have a unity that was unlike any I've ever seen. And it was Alex. Alex brought that. He did everything right, on every level."

Indeed he did.

At least for a while.

* * *

With the exception of the 2007 team that reached Game 7 of the ALCS the following year, the Boston teams that won World Series all had one disturbing trait: none of them won even a single playoff game the following season. The 2004 Red Sox, still hungover from a party that was eighty-six years in the making, qualified for the postseason but were swept by the eventual world champion Chicago White Sox in the first round in 2005. And the overachieving 2013 Red Sox predictably came crashing back to earth, partly due to the law of averages, partly because Red Sox ownership and upper management, as the saying goes, started to believe their own bullshit.

But nothing can compare to the demise and deconstruction of the historic 2018 team, which came apart in far less time than it took to assemble.

After a lethargic spring training in which it often felt like the Red Sox were clinging to 2018—"Do we really want to turn the page?" Alex Cora asked during spring training, suggesting the Red Sox were content to merely continue what they had achieved—the Sox started the season losing eight of ten and were a dreadful 6-13 after a two-game sweep at the hands of the Yankees. The feeling around the team was never the same, from the start, and after re-signing Eovaldi (four years, $68 million) and extending Chris Sale (five years, $145 million) before the season began, Dombrowski had little room to maneuver. At about the time the Red Sox were losing eight in a row and nine of ten straddling the major-league trading deadline, the only pitcher the club added was right-hander Andrew Cashner, who had a most dubious distinction. Of the eighty-nine major-league pitchers from 2010 to 2019 who had pitched at least 1,000 innings in the major league, Cashner ranked dead last with a winning percentage of .396.

On the field and in the front office, it seemed, the Red Sox were in perfect sync. They were giving up. Things unraveled so quickly that it was hard to remember what the 2018 Red Sox ever looked like.

Unbeknownst to many, after the 2018 championship, Dombrowski and Henry met just as they had in the middle of the summer in 2015, when

Dombrowski had been hired. This time the meeting did not go so well. As Dombrowski approached the final year of his contract and eyed an extension, Henry came to the conclusion that he and his chief baseball decision-maker were no longer in alignment. Dombrowski wanted to keep adding, keep spending; Henry meanwhile, was understandably concerned about the toll Dombrowski's roster building had taken on the Red Sox both financially and in the farm system. In building the 2018 team, Dombrowski had burned through so many resources that the Red Sox left a carbon footprint as big as the Atlantic.

By early December, and without the contract extension he coveted, Dombrowski confronted ownership and was fired. For a time, the Red Sox operated with an interim management team while beginning the search for its next general manager, all at a time when the team faced major roster questions. Price, Eovaldi, and Sale all had been injured during the season—the last of the three almost certainly facing elbow surgery that would wipe out the 2020 season, which was to be the first on his new five-year deal. Meanwhile, multitalented outfielder Mookie Betts was approaching the final year of his career in Boston, with free agency looming for the player at the end of 2020.

Though the Red Sox had attempted to sign Betts to the biggest contract in team history, he had resisted the team's efforts, insisting he wanted to get to free agency. While Bogaerts, for instance, eagerly signed a six-year, $120 million contract before the 2019 season to remain in Boston—"It's a very special place to play, man," he said—Betts and the Red Sox never got particularly close to an agreement, as the Red Sox lagged behind the market while Betts simultaneously kept stringing them along.

By the spring of 2019, when the Red Sox offered Betts a reported deal worth roughly $300 million over ten years, the going rate for comparable players was approaching $400 million. Again Betts said no. And Boston being Boston, fans landed on one side or the other, blasting the Red Sox for being foolish with their expenditures while others wondered why Betts was not choosing to remain with the organization that had drafted him—the organization with which he won both an MVP Award and a World Series—in a city where winning had become everything.

In February 2020, with the superstar tied to the Red Sox for one more year, just before the start of spring training, the Red Sox traded Betts and David Price to the Los Angeles Dodgers in a blockbuster deal that brought outfielder

Alex Verdugo, infield prospect Jeter Downs, and minor-league catcher Connor Wong to Boston. Boston also had to pay half of the remaining salary of Price's overpriced contract. Boston's new, young general manager—Chaim Bloom, who had been given the title of chief baseball officer—was taking apart the team built by his predecessor, Dombrowski, piece by piece. The Red Sox were simultaneously shedding talent and salary, sliding back into the middle class of Major League Baseball.

Introduced by the Dodgers after the trade, Price and Betts were noticeably happy, smiling, laughing. Not long after, the Dodgers signed Betts to a whopping twelve-year, $365 million contract extension that raised a multitude of questions, none of which Betts really cared to answer.

Hadn't Betts said that he intended to go to free agency? What changed? And what if the Red Sox had given him precisely the same deal the Dodgers had?

"Um, I think that's a very valid question," Betts answered. "You know, I think I just want to stick with [that fact that] I'm here, in LA, for 12, 13 years. I'm super excited about this opportunity. Like I said, the goal is to bring back some rings over this period of time and that's what I'm going to be here and work for." Added the player of the Red Sox: "They didn't owe me anything, I didn't owe them anything. The city didn't owe me anything, I didn't owe the city anything. We did what we were supposed to do. And at that point, it's a business."

As it was, Betts's departure and subsequent committal to the Dodgers was just the final blow during one of the most hellish off-seasons in baseball history. Only a month earlier, after all, the Red Sox had parted ways with Cora in the wake of an MLB investigation into the Astros, who were discovered to have executed a massive sign-stealing operation during their championship season of 2017. Using a video camera and dugout monitor, the Astros would watch the signs relayed from the opposing catcher to the pitcher, then pound on trash cans as if they were Paul Revere hanging lanterns in the Old North Church: *One if for fastball, two if for curve.* Astros players were granted immunity in exchange for information provided to investigators from Major League Baseball, who subsequently exposed the alleged chief architect of the operation: Alex Cora, the onetime Astros bench coach who had become manager of the champion 2018 Red Sox.

The Astros, of course, suffered the steepest penalties, including an organizational fine and the dismissal of both general manager Jeff Luhnow and manager A. J. Hinch. But the cost for the Sox was great also. Cora and the Red Sox "mutually agreed to part ways," according to a club statement, another haymaker in an off-season filled with them. In the span of just a few months, the Red Sox had lost Sale to a season-ending elbow injury that would require major surgery, fired the general manager, traded away their best player, then split with their manager because he had been involved in one of the game's worst-ever cheating scandals.

Presumably, at that stage, the Red Sox had nowhere to go but up. Little did they know that the entire world was about to be derailed by something greater than cheating scandals or contractual matters. But as a pandemic enveloped the globe, the Red Sox would have far different things on their minds.

CHAPTER 16

OUT WITH A BANG

"There's no quarterback I'd rather have than Tom Brady."

—Bill Belichick, said repeatedly during his career
with the New England Patriots

AS DESPERATE AS THINGS COULD become in Boston, even during the good times, there was always a fail-safe. Like the coach of their football team, Patriots fans could always turn to Tom Brady, the impeccable quarterback with the supermodel wife and a penchant for the dramatic. Along with Bill Belichick, Brady was the rock on which Boston's sports superiority was built: Mr. Everything, the kind of talent that came around once in a generation—no, once in a *lifetime*—and continued to find solutions when there appeared to be none.

When the Bruins, Celtics, and Red Sox faltered, as they did, there was always Brady.

After the comeback win against the Seattle Seahawks in Super Bowl XLIX, the Patriots had a curious following season, starting 10-0 before a loss to an aged Peyton Manning and the Broncos on November 29. A week later, for whatever reason, Belichick tried an onside "mortar" kick with special teamer Nate Ebner against the Philadelphia Eagles, triggering a Philadelphia comeback at Gillette Stadium that led to a shocking second consecutive defeat. The Patriots rallied for a pair of wins before a loss to the New York Jets in which another Belichick decision blew up in the coach's face, this one when he chose to kick off with the wind in overtime only to see the Jets march right down the field and score a game-winning touchdown.

Asked to explain the logic for his decision after the game, the ever-defiant Belichick promptly donned his invisibility cloak and disappeared into his favorite abyss: coach's discretion.

"I thought that was the best thing to do," Belichick said of his decision. "There wasn't any confusion."

Nor was there any confusion a week later when, needing a victory to secure home field throughout the AFC playoffs, the Pats lost again, 20–10, this time against the woebegone Miami Dolphins. Apparently intent on improving a Patriots running game that had been anemic for much of the season, Belichick let Brady throw just twice on the game's first seventeen plays, by which point a Dolphins team that had nothing to play for came to the realization that it had a chance to win the season finale.

For a man who often stated that he loved having Tom Brady as his quarterback, Belichick certainly didn't use Brady much, pulling him at the end of the game after New England blew home field advantage.

"Everybody felt like we were confident in the game plan," observed receiver Danny Amendola. "Everybody knew what we wanted to do. We just couldn't get it done." And it cost them.

For all of the things Belichick has accomplished during his accomplished and peerless coaching career, his management of the Patriots at the end of the 2015 season was a bungling of epic proportion. After defeating the Kansas City Chiefs in the AFC divisional round, the Patriots traveled to Denver for the second time and promptly lost the final meeting between Brady and Manning, who would retire weeks later after, thanks to Denver's ferocious defense, he won the second Super Bowl title of his career. The deciding factor of the championship game at Denver was, unquestionably, the venue, particularly when the Patriots repeatedly had communication issues along the offensive line amid the deafening noise at Mile High. And while Brady already had four Super Bowl titles to what would soon be Manning's two, all five times the two had met in the postseason, which included four AFC Championship games, the home quarterback had emerged victorious.

"They played better," Patriots veteran safety Devin McCourty said when asked how much of a difference home field might have meant. "I don't care where we're at, Denver or New England—anywhere [else] you want to name across the country. They just played better football."

Nonetheless, many wondered: What in the name of Vince Lombardi was Bill Belichick trying to prove?

In the end, all of this served as prelude to the 2016 season, a year in which Brady's never-ending battle with the league over Deflategate came to its merciful conclusion and the gap would widen between the greatest tandem of coach and quarterback in NFL history. Having stood down against commissioner Roger Goodell and accepted his four-game suspension from the league, Brady sat for the first four games of 2016 while Belichick opened the year with his favorite student, Jimmy Garoppolo. While many theorized that Brady could be better off physically in the long run after taking a beating at the end of the 2015 campaign, the appearance of Garoppolo in games of consequence offered New Englanders their first glimpse of Life After Tom, which undoubtedly played a role in the years going forward. Belichick, after all, got to see it, too. And he liked what he saw.

Underdogs for Week 1 against an Arizona team that had finished 13-3 a year earlier before losing in the conference championship, the Patriots pulled out a 23–21 victory thanks in no small part to the play of their third-year quarterback. Garoppolo completed twenty-four of thirty-three passes, including a 37-yard strike to Chris Hogan for the game's first touchdown. And in the fourth quarter, with the Patriots trailing 21-20, he led the club on a thirteen-play, 61-yard scoring drive that included a 32-yard completion to Amendola, all of which proved critical when Stephen Gostkowski converted a 32-yard field goal for the game's final points.

A week later at home, Garoppolo went eighteen for twenty-six for 232 yards and three touchdowns while the Patriots built a 24–0 first-half lead against Miami, though his outing was abruptly cut short when he dislocated his right shoulder while being sacked by Miami linebacker Kiki Alonso. Even so, Garoppolo's totals over his first two NFL games were beyond encouraging: while going 2-0, he completed more than 71 percent of his passes for 496 yards, four touchdowns, no interceptions, and a whopping passer rating of 119, the last of which exceeded even the 117.2 Brady had posted in his record-breaking 2007 season, albeit in a very small sample.

The conclusion for everyone—including Belichick—was the same: *Jimmy can play.*

Nonetheless, even at an early stage, the injury to Garoppolo was concerning. During his entire tenure as quarterback of the Patriots, Brady had rarely missed a game to anything other than a season-ending injury (2007) or suspension. His consistency and reliability were among his greatest assets, even including his heroics in the final minutes of so many games. Brady was always there.

He was always driven. He rarely lost focus. Garoppolo's absence, even for a week or two, amplified the attributes for which teammates respected Brady the most: namely, his toughness, commitment, willing to sacrifice himself—physically, mentally, and even financially—for the greater good.

Garoppolo missed the next game, on Thursday night, which was understandable. Third-round draft pick Jacoby Brissett started and led New England to a 27–0 victory at home over Houston. But the following week against Buffalo, Brissett and the Patriots were shut out, and many took note.

"Bro, we lost two games [all season]," then Patriots tight end Martellus Bennett said in 2021 on a podcast by, of all people, twin brothers Devin and Jason McCourty, both of whom ended up playing for the Patriots, with the former also playing alongside Garoppolo.

"One of them was because Jimmy Garoppolo was being a bitch. He decided not to play right before the game. Jacoby [Brissett] came out and played with a fucked-up thumb and played his heart out, but Jimmy was just being a bitch about it all. That's why he—you can't win with a bitch for a quarterback, first of all. That was the whole thing with him: He didn't want to come out and do anything because his agent was trying to protect his body or some shit like that, which, I can't fault him for that. But like, you should have made that decision on Thursday. Now it's Sunday. So anyways, he's not going out there, so now Jacoby straps up and we lost to the Buffalo Bills. We shouldn't have lost. It was just last-minute, trying to make adjustments for what Jacoby could do."

For the Patriots, at least, it wouldn't matter. Garoppolo never ended up taking another meaningful snap in New England.

When Brady returned from his suspension, predictably, he played some of the best football of his career, continuing to reverse the disturbing slide in his efficiency that had taken hold just before Garoppolo's arrival. For the third straight season, now at age thirty-nine, Brady's completion percentage and passer rating both increased, the latter to 112.0, its highest since his record-breaking 2007 season, which had taken place *nine years earlier*. His interception rate was the lowest of his career. The Patriots went 11-1 during Brady's twelve games, dropping only a 31–24 decision to the Seahawks at Gillette Stadium in another epic between the teams that had met in Super Bowl XLIX. New England's greater loss from the game proved the loss of tight end Rob Gronkowski, who took a vicious hit from Seattle safety Earl Thomas that ultimately sidelined him for the balance of the season.

All in all, through twelve regular season games and two conference playoff affairs, Brady threw thirty-three touchdown passes against four interceptions, including a thirty-two-for-forty-two performance for 384 yards and three touchdowns in the AFC Championship at Foxboro. The Patriots easily defeated the Pittsburgh Steelers by a 36–17 score to return to the Super Bowl for the seventh time, and Brady's four-game suspension—as well as any threat posed by Garoppolo—had long since vanished.

"It was a good day. We're going back to Super Bowl, man," Brady said. "We've got to be happy now."

But in New England, of course, simply playing in the Super Bowl was hardly ever—or never—enough. In Super Bowl LI, the Patriots faced an Atlanta Falcons team that was operating like a buzz saw in the final weeks of the season, primarily thanks to an offense under the watch of coordinator Kyle Shanahan that seemed impossible to stop. While scoring the most points in the NFL during the regular season, the Falcons peaked at the end of the year, winning their final four regular-season games and two playoff affairs in light-show fashion, averaging a mind-numbing 39 points. And against the Patriots, they seemed headed for another blowout win.

After a scoreless first quarter, Atlanta scored three touchdowns with astonishing speed. After a fumble by Patriots running back LeGarrette Blount, Atlanta went 71 yards in five plays and under two minutes to score the game's first touchdown on a run by Devonta Freeman. The Patriots went three and out on their next possession before Atlanta again snapped with the wrath of a cobra, going 62 yards in five plays covering one minute and forty-nine seconds. The Patriots then succeeded in slowing the game down on their next possession before Brady threw an ill-advised pass intended for Amendola that was intercepted by Falcons defensive back Robert Alford, who scampered 82 yards for another touchdown that gave Atlanta a gaping 21–0 lead.

As Alford began sprinting down the field, a helpless Brady—looking very slow and very old—lunged at him in attempt to make a tackle. He didn't come close.

Counting the play on which Alford intercepted Brady, Atlanta had handled the ball for eleven plays covering less than four minutes, and they had scored 21 points. The Patriots, meanwhile, had snapped the ball nineteen times over a span of 7:48 and had scored zero.

After the Patriots managed a field goal at the end of the first half, the teams exchanged possessions to start the third quarter before Atlanta took over again, this time on its 15-yard line. In eight plays covering 85 yards, the Falcons had gains of 17, 5, 35, 13, 9, and 6 yards, the final distance coming on a touchdown run by Tevin Coleman. After kicker Matt Bryant converted the extra point and executed a touchback on the ensuing kickoff, the Patriots took the field facing a 28–3 deficit with precisely twenty-three minutes and thirty-one seconds remaining in the game.

If New England was to somehow get back in the game, the Patriots would have to outscore the high-powered Falcons by more than a point per minute over the final quarter and a half. Their outlook was, to put in kindly, bleak.

"A lot of teams, when they got down to those guys, they folded," Patriots cornerback Logan Ryan said of the Falcons. "Green Bay folded. Seattle folded. We had a bunch of guys who weren't afraid to get knocked down."

Maybe so. But what the Patriots really had was Brady.

As is almost always the case in sporting events featuring an extreme swing of momentum, the losers were complicit in their demise, something Belichick often relied upon. The St. Louis Rams might have won the Super Bowl that ended the 2001 season if they had just committed to running with Marshall Faulk, but head coach Mike Martz had bought into the hype surrounding his "Greatest Show on Turf" and wanted to throw; the Seahawks could have ended the 2014 season with a championship if they had just handed the ball to Marshawn Lynch at the goal line, but they got needlessly cute with their play calling and the game clock. Always, there was something the other guys brought upon themselves.

On New England's final possession of the third quarter, the Patriots went 75 yards in thirteen plays to make the score 28–9, but kicker Stephen Gostkowski missed the extra point. After Atlanta went three and out, the Patriots began the fourth quarter with a twelve-play, 72-yard drive that featured eleven Brady drop backs and ten passes, the final pass play resulting in a sack. Faced with a fourth-and-goal from the Atlanta 15-yard line instead of a fourth-and-10—and needing three scoring possessions to at least tie the game—Belichick sent Gostkowski out to kick a 33-yard field goal, which made the score 28–12.

Atlanta resumed possession with 9:40 to play and a 16-point lead, most every factor in its favor. After two runs, the Falcons faced a third down at their own 36-yard line, needing just one yard to collect a first down and kill at least an additional two minutes off the game clock. Incredibly, Ryan lined up in the shotgun, running back Freeman offset to his right. He took the snap and looked *deep* down the left sideline, completely oblivious to an onrushing Dont'a Hightower, whom Freeman had failed to block. The result was a sack and fumble recovered by Patriots defensive lineman Alan Branch at the Atlanta 25-yard line, giving the Patriots a chance for a quick touchdown after a long drive that had failed to produce one. Five plays later, Brady threw a touchdown pass to Amendola, and James White converted a two-point rush, making the score 28–20 with just under six minutes to play.

Said Brady later: "The strip sack was huge. That got us right back in it."

Atlanta got the ball back on their own 10-yard line with 5:53 to play. Falcons quarterback Matt Ryan promptly moved them right down the field on a pass play for 39 yards, a 2-yard run, and another pass for 27 yards. Just like that, Atlanta had advanced all the way to the New England 22-yard line, covering 68 yards in sixty-six seconds to put themselves in scoring position.

And then, needing just a field goal to extend its lead to 10 points—two offensive possessions for the Patriots—the Falcons got greedy and, frankly, stupid. Rather than just run the ball on three plays, burning up the game clock or forcing the Patriots to use time-outs (which New England did after the first down play), on second-and-11 at the New England 23-yard line with 3:56 left, Ryan, incredibly, went back to pass and was sacked by defensive lineman Trey Flowers for a significant 12-yard loss that placed the ball at the New England 35-yard line. The Patriots called time-out. Atlanta kicker Matt Bryant was now looking at something like a 53-yard kick, so on the next play Ryan completed a short pass to Mohamed Sanu that effectively negated the sack and put the Falcons back in line for a more makeable 44-yard field goal. Only there was one small problem on the play: Atlanta's left tackle, Jake Matthews, had wrapped his left arm around the neck of Patriots pass rusher Chris Long, resulting in a holding penalty that moved the Falcons back another 10 yards.

As quickly as the Falcons had moved down the field, they had just gone backward 22 yards and consumed a mere fifty-six seconds off the game clock, a brain fart so massive that it shook the ground throughout football history. Now facing a third-and-33 from near midfield—third-and-33!—Ryan threw incomplete, stopping the clock and forcing the Falcons to punt.

Just like that, what might have been Atlanta's first-ever Super Bowl championship had turned into one of the great choke jobs of all time.

Having foolishly given another opportunity to the Patriots and the great Tom Brady, the Falcons paid dearly. Beginning at his own 9-yard line with 3:30 to play, Brady took the Patriots 91 yards in ten plays, culminating in a 1-yard run by running back White. The drive included a 23-yard pass on first-and-10 from Brady to Edelman, who made an incredible, circus-like catch, preventing the ball from hitting the ground with the very tips of his fingers. Brady completed a 2-point conversion pass to Amendola to tie the game at 28–28, leaving just fifty-seven seconds on the clock.

Even then, the Falcons compounded their problems. The team having already burned all of its time-outs, Falcons return man Eric Weems fielded the kickoff one step inside his own goal line and foolishly attempted a return only to get tackled at the 11-yard line, costing his team 14 yards and five seconds. Atlanta only got as far as the 27 before being forced to punt, allowing the Patriots just one play before time expired.

Atlanta never got the ball again.

Of course, New England won the coin toss in overtime, elected to receive, and traveled 75 yards in eight plays, the final one a 2-yard touchdown run by White that gave the Patriots a 34–28 win and made Brady and Belichick the first quarterback and coach in history with five Super Bowl championships. Brady finished the game with a prolific 466 yards on sixty-two attempts, including two touchdowns and one interception, his performance in the final moments as certain as a morning sunrise.

Patriots defensive back Ryan said to reporters after the victory: "When it got to overtime, I basically untied my cleats and watched Brady like you guys did."

As for the Falcons, they never truly recovered. The defeat broke their spirit. Offensive coordinator Shanahan left the team immediately after the season to become the head coach of the San Francisco 49ers, and the franchise quickly melted back into oblivion. Years after the egregious decision to pass on second-and-11 from the Patriots' 23 in the closing minutes, Shanahan accepted responsibility for the blunder.

"But it comes down to one play. That's what I've always said, like yeah, I wish I called a different call on that one play," Shanahan said on a podcast with host Peter Schrager. "I don't want to go to the final everything . . . but like, that one right there—I think it would have been different."

* * *

Before the 2017 season even began, for the first time in the Brady-Belichick era, the single greatest question surrounding the Patriots on the football field did not necessarily concern their chances of winning another championship.

New England had five Lombardi Trophies to go along with five championship rings, the latest of which had 283 diamonds to commemorate the team's 28–3 deficit in Super Bowl LI. The team's Hall of Fame at Patriot Place might as well have been a jewelry store akin to Tiffany's or Barmakian Brothers, the latter a longtime New England institution that had produced glitter for more than a century.

Still, if the winning wasn't getting old, the quarterback was.

With Jimmy Garoppolo entering the final year of his contract and Tom Brady about to turn forty, Bill Belichick operated curiously, executing a number of trades that looked like they prepared the Patriots for the seemingly inevitable change at quarterback. Most notably, the Patriots traded their first-round selection in the 2017 draft for New Orleans Saints wide receiver Brandin Cooks, a speedy big-play receiver who seemed more suited to the talents of Garoppolo than Brady. Given the nature in which Belichick had greased the skids for many accomplished Patriots players over the years—and the list was long and distinguished—one couldn't help but wonder.

Holy shit. Is Bill getting ready to pull the plug on Tom?

In the months that preceded the season, Garoppolo's future—and thus Brady's fate—were the primary focus, particularly amid reports from credible media sources that Belichick had no intention of trading away Garoppolo. ESPN insider Adam Schefter, for one, said prior to the NFL draft that the Patriots wouldn't accept an offer including as many as four first first-round picks for Garoppolo, a stunning statement that made Belichick's preference for Garoppolo indisputably clear.

"The facts are the facts," said Schefter, who made a series of reports and radio appearances reaffirming his information, once going so far as to ask two talk show hosts, "Are we clear on that?"

Sure, enough, come the opening week of the 2017 NFL season, Jimmy Garoppolo was on the Patriots roster, albeit still as the backup.

Brady, for his part, was still antsy—and with good reason. He had seen a succession of valuable teammates and friends jettisoned from New England over the years, and a career that had established him as the greatest quarterback of all-time did not make him invulnerable to the insecurities that exist in any human being. *If he did it to those guys*, Brady reasoned, *he'll do it to me.* And in Brady's mind Bill Belichick had a new favorite son in Jimmy Garoppolo.

If it seemed far-fetched to some, others didn't doubt it. Brady's father, Tom Sr., had long since made public comments acknowledging that his son's career with the Patriots would almost certainly end badly. Along the way, Belichick privately told at least one member of the media that Brady would succumb to ego as his list of accomplishments grew. "Tom's going to be a problem at the end," Belichick reportedly said, referring to the one thing hated in players above all else: entitlement.

To that end, the 2017 season often felt like a tug-of-war between the coach and the quarterback, Belichick at one point going so far as to prohibit Brady's personal trainer, Alex Guerrero, from access to team facilities. The decision greatly angered Brady, who was maniacal about his training and preparation—especially after Garoppolo arrived—and believed he had earned some latitude. But Guerrero also started working with other Patriots players, thereby undermining the efforts of the Patriots' medical and training staff, which had been preaching its own method.

Most notable among those caught in the crossfire: tight end Rob Gronkowski, whose injury in 2016 had forced him to miss the balance of the season, including the Super Bowl. When he returned, Gronkowski adopted Guerrero's methods and began using Brady buzzwords like "pliability," forgoing some of the mass and muscle building that Belichick deemed an essential part of Gronkowski's game.

Having beaten most everybody else over the course of their seventeen years together, maybe it was only natural that Brady and Belichick began competing with one another.

Though the Patriots got off to a bit of a rocky start in 2017—they were just 2-2 after four games—they had righted the ship to improve to 6-2 following Week 8 of the NFL season, when Belichick was confronted by a pair of realities. First, owner Robert Kraft was not going to let Brady go anywhere—at least at that time. Second, Belichick was unable to extend the contract of Garoppolo. In a complicated potential conflict of interest, Garoppolo was represented by agent Don Yee, who also repped Brady. The agent reportedly had rejected a four-year offer for Garoppolo said to be in the range of $17 million per year. Only one of the quarterbacks could be guaranteed the starting spot.

So, on October 31—the date of the trading deadline—Belichick traded Garoppolo to the San Francisco 49ers for a second-round draft pick in the 2018 draft. And while Belichick insisted that the trading deadline forced his hand with the player, the truth is that the coach could have extended the matter into the spring, as he did with backup Matt Cassel in 2008, and gotten a better return in the trade. Belichick's unwillingness to do so—or Kraft's insistence that he act immediately—ultimately resulted getting a poor return on the trade.

Meanwhile, after having offered little or nothing beyond a prepared statement when asked about previous players he had traded away over the years, Belichick offered extensive, unsolicited praise of Garoppolo when addressing the deal, delivering a 450-word monologue that not so subtly carried an important message: *I did not want to do this.*

For the Patriots, conveniently, the trading deadline coincided with the team's bye week, allowing matters to more fully settle before the team returned to the field. The Patriots subsequently picked up where they left off, going 7-1 over the second half of the season to finish with a 13-3 record and a first-round bye and home field advantage.

As it turned out, the Patriots needed every bit of it.

After walloping quarterback Marcus Mariota and the Tennessee Titans in the Tomato Can game, the Pats hosted the AFC Championship and the Jacksonville Jaguars, who had upset the Steelers in Pittsburgh. With Belichick nemesis and Jags president Tom Coughlin watching from above, an inferior Jacksonville team held a 20–10 lead halfway through the fourth quarter when Brady worked his usual magic. With less than nine minutes to play, he threw *two* touchdown passes to Danny Amendola, who also contributed a critical 20-yard punt return to send the Patriots back to the Super Bowl for the third time in four years, and the eighth time overall under Belichick.

Amendola's performance was essential in the absence of tight end Gronkowski, who had left the game after suffering a concussion on a hit from Jaguars safety Barry Church that drew a 15-yard penalty. Brady, meanwhile, played the game with a gash on his left hand that required twelve stitches, the result of a fluky handoff during practice in the days leading up to the game.

While teammates deemed Brady's efforts typically heroic—"He's the G.O.A.T., man," said safety Duron Harmon—comments from both Brady and Belichick after the game further highlighted the tension between the two, Brady making sure to cite the contributions of his personal trainer, Guerrero, among others.

"I thought out of all the plays, my season can't end on a handoff in practice. We didn't come this far to end on a handoff. It's just one of those things," Brady said. "Everyone did a great job kind of getting me ready and the training staff and the doctors and Alex. It was a great team effort. Without that, I definitely wouldn't be playing."

A dismissive Belichick countered: "Tom did a great job. He's a tough guy—we all know that. But we're not talking about open-heart surgery here."

The Patriots opened Super Bowl LII as a favorite against the Eagles, who reached the game despite having lost starting quarterback Carson Wentz to a season-ending knee injury in Week 14. The Eagles had subsequently struggled over the final few weeks of the regular season while scoring just 34 points over three games, but they tweaked the offense around backup quarterback Nick Foles, who had played brilliantly while posting a 141.1 rating over the Minnesota Vikings in the NFC Championship.

Still, most dismissed the Eagles as undermanned and inexperienced, including, perhaps, Belichick, who immediately made himself a focal point when he benched cornerback Malcolm Butler for the game.

Like Brady, Butler had been in a contract dispute with the team for some time, unwilling to accept a multiyear offer that he believed was well below market. (He was ultimately proven right.) As was the case with Welker, whom Belichick had all but rescued from irrelevancy via a trade with the Miami Dolphins, Belichick seemed to take the matter personally. Prior to the season, Belichick had signed free-agent cornerback Stephon Gilmore to a blockbuster contract, swiping him from the Buffalo Bills to simultaneously safeguard the team from Butler's likely departure and strengthen his leverage.

Now, with Butler in tears on the Patriots' sideline at the start of the Super Bowl—the same stage where the undrafted Butler had made one of the great plays in Super Bowl history three years prior—Belichick was seemingly delivering the same message he had dealt Welker.

While many media members often cited this flaw in Belichick as hubris—or arrogance—Belichick's actions were far more consistent with someone possessing a god complex. He has disregarded league directives in Spygate. He was the only NFL coach who eschewed the coaches' association. (This prevented him from being portrayed in products like NFL video games.) And despite repeatedly justifying questionable actions by saying he was merely doing what was "best for the team," he often acted as if he were carrying out personal grudges.

As such, in a game the Patriots would eventually lose by a shocking 41–33 score, Butler spent the entire game on the sideline and played just one snap—on special teams. He never took part in the defense. In a game where Brady (following a regular season in which he was named MVP for the third time in his career) passed for a record 505 yards, and three Patriots pass catchers eclipsed 100 yards—Amendola (152), Chris Hogan (128), and Gronkowski (116)— the Patriots defense allowed the Eagles to go ten of sixteen on third down and two of two on fourth down while amassing 538 yards of offense. The game was still in doubt when Brady was strip-sacked at his own 33-yard line with just over two minutes left, after which the Eagles burned much of the game clock—and New England's final time-out—before a field goal that gave them an 8-point lead.

Butler's benching was so controversial and mystifying that, among others, former Red Sox executive and native Bostonian Theo Epstein texted members of the media from his home in Chicago (where he was still running the Cubs) with the same question everyone else had: *Why didn't Butler play?*

"You have to ask Coach," Harmon had said after the game. "Coach makes all the personnel decisions and I just play football."

Of course, *Coach* wasn't sharing.

"I respect Malcolm's competitiveness and I'm sure he felt he could've helped," Belichick said. "I'm sure other players felt the same way. In the end, we have to make the decisions we feel are best for the football team. That's what I did. That's really all I can say about it."

When he was asked if he considered using Butler at any stage of a game in which the Eagles punted only once, Belichick all but scoffed. "I just covered that," he said, a comment that proved quite fitting. On the entire night, after all, the Patriots didn't cover much of anything.

Butler, for his part, was still distraught after the game, telling ESPN reporter Mike Reiss on his way out of the stadium: "They gave up on me. Fuck it. It is what it is."

A day after the game, amid rampant rumors and speculation that Butler was benched for health and disciplinary reasons, the player posted a message on Instagram that denied any such wrongdoing and effectively served as a fare-well to New England. Numerous players offered their support on the message, including Brady, which only added to the perception that the Patriots had turned on their coach. In the immediate aftermath of the game, Gronkowski had even hinted at retirement, concluding a season which, in retrospect, often seemed as if Belichick grew more and more intent on demonstrating his power—from the banning of Brady's trainer, Guerrero, to the benching of Butler, who had played virtually every defensive snap of the season to that point.

Before leaving the team via free agency, receiver Amendola became merely the latest to publicly question the Butler decision and Belichick's methods.

"In hindsight, it's like, really, 'What agenda are we on?'" Amendola said in a podcast with Kayce Smith, then of NBC Sports. "It's something I'll probably never understand."

Through it all, Belichick's unwillingness to grant a contract to another Patriots player may have been the at the root of it all. Despite his wishes, Brady still had not received a new contract from the team—even after the trading of Garoppolo—which ultimately drove the quarterback to act. As detailed by author Jeff Benedict in *The Dynasty*, Brady subsequently visited with owner Robert Kraft with a simple but stunning request—one that would ultimately play out like a stormy Hollywood romance.

Tom Brady wanted out.

* * *

In the days before Super Bowl LII, Patriots owner Robert Kraft and his son, team president Jonathan Kraft, conducted a handful of interviews, ranging from a local visit with the team's radio partner, 98.5 The Sports Hub in Boston, to a visit with longtime NFL reporter Andrea Kremer. The Krafts were asked about the future of Tom Brady and how his end in New England might come, and they gave revealing answers.

"I think that Tom Brady's earned the right to have that be a decision he makes when wants to make it," Jonathan Kraft said.

For an organization like the Patriots, who had been praised for making the kind of tough decisions that many believed factored into the long-term success of the franchise, that was a stunning admission. And it was a public acknowledgment that Bill Belichick had been and would be overruled. For years, Belichick had operated with a mantra when it came to turning over personnel, one he even uttered on the day he drafted Garoppolo: *Better too early than too late*. But now, after the team had traded Garoppolo, the Patriots had gotten to the most important position on the field and thrown that philosophy out the window. Instead, Tom Brady would make that call.

For the first time in the nearly two decades that Belichick and Brady had been together, the dynamic seemed untenable. The chain of command had been complicated, and one of them seemed destined for the door.

"Dysfunction is when people take energy and use it to think about how to undermine other people," Jonathan Kraft told Kremer. "That does not happen. If it happens in this organization, I haven't seen it."

Of course, trainer Alex Guerrero was precisely such a case. By recruiting teammates to work with Guerrero, Brady was undermining the training staff and his coach, who had put a stop to it. And on the matter of Garoppolo, Brady had expressed his displeasure to Kraft, who then intervened.

There was more undermining than the Patriots wanted to admit. After the loss to the Eagles, according to Benedict, Kraft met with Brady and his wife, Giselle Bündchen, at the owner's home. Bündchen expressed displeasure that the coach treated Brady like "fucking Johnny Foxboro," a term Belichick had negatively used to describe Brady's play during one team film session.

Brady had two years remaining on his contract but asked to be let out of his deal—according to the Krafts, remember, Brady "had earned that right"—but Kraft wasn't about to let Brady walk just months after trading Garoppolo, at least in part to appease his veteran quarterback.

On some level, Brady's audacity had to perturb the owner. Brady had wanted no part of Garoppolo from the moment his anointed successor had entered the picture—and, eventually, the Patriots traded Garoppolo away. And yet, here was Brady, still wanting out even after the Patriots had granted his wish. Again, it reeked of dysfunction.

And then, in the wake of it all, there was this: During the same off-season, Belichick had tried to trade tight end Gronkowski to the Detroit Lions for a first-round draft pick, potentially as part of a plan to move up in the 2018 draft and draft another quarterback, perhaps Baker Mayfield. The teams had essentially agreed to the trade. But the deal was nixed, possibly due to the intervention of Kraft or Brady. For his part, Gronkowski had threatened to retire if traded.

"Yeah, it happened," Gronkowski admitted shortly after New England lost to the Detroit Lions in Week 3. "Brady's my quarterback, that's all. Wasn't going anywhere without Brady."

The day after the game, asked about Gronkowski's remarks on his weekly appearance on Boston sports station WEEI, Brady told the station he felt "as strongly about him as he does about me. I love the guy. He's had a big impact on my career—personally and professionally. Like I said, I'm very lucky to play with him and we're going to keep fighting."

Amid all that undermining and, yes, dysfunction, the most extraordinary development of all may have been this: The Patriots found a way to keep winning. With a record of just 1-2 after the Week 3 loss to the Lions, New England rallied to win six straight, including a 43–40 win over blossoming second-year quarterback Patrick Mahomes and the Kansas City Chiefs. The Patriots entered their bye week at 7-3 but then lost three times over the next five games, including defeats at Tennessee and Pittsburgh in which the offense scored a combined total of 27 points. In between, the Patriots blew a game at Miami when the Dolphins scored a 69-yard touchdown on the final play of the game, an intermediate pass from quarterback Ryan Tannehill to receiver Kenny Stills, who then lateraled the ball to teammate DeVante Parker, who then lateraled the ball to teammate Kenyan Drake. A running back, Drake turned the corner and then sprinted by Gronkowski, who had been put on the field to defend against a potential Hail Mary pass.

The blunder was one of many that included Brady uncharacteristically taking a sack with no time-outs at the end of the first half when the Patriots should have had at least a field goal. The final score of the defeat was 34–33.

"There's a lot of things we could have done better," said Belichick. "It came down to one play, but there were a lot of things besides that."

Said Gronkowski of the game-ending sequence: "I mean, it sucked. I've never really been a part of anything like that. I feel like it's going to test our character big time, how we bounce back from something like that. And, just, gotta make that tackle."

Frustrated by his team's inability to consistently pass the ball during the regular season, Belichick and offensive coordinator Josh McDaniels convened near the end of the regular season and, according to Belichick in a team video production released after the year, asked themselves a simple question: *What do we do well?* The coach and coordinator decided New England's best chance was to run the ball in power sets that utilized Gronkowski's excellent blocking skills and, often, an extra offensive lineman. By that point in the NFL, many teams had faster, undersized defenses to counter a league that had become ridiculously pass heavy and offense oriented, so the Patriots did the opposite.

In the final two weeks of the regular season, with an entirely new philosophy, the Patriots posted one-sided wins over both the Buffalo Bills (24—12) and the New York Jets (38—3) while rushing for a combined 404 yards, including 244 in the season finale. But the quality of the competition (or lack thereof) was impossible to overlook. Combined, the Bills and Jets had won ten games. The Patriots finished 11-5 and managed a first-round bye thanks to the ineptitude of most other teams in the conference, but there was no way of knowing whether the Patriots would be able to ride their new offense at all in the postseason.

Somewhere along the line, after all, the Patriots would need to pass efficiently to win the Super Bowl, particularly if they were to travel to Kansas City, where the high-powered Chiefs had finished as the top seed in the AFC.

When the Patriots and Chiefs both won easily in the divisional round, the matchup for the AFC Championship was set. It was the fourteenth as a tandem for Brady and Belichick, who would face Mahomes, coach Andy Reid, and the explosive, trendy, flavor-of-the-month Chiefs.

At the time, no one could have imagined that the game would feature the final dramatics of Tom Brady's career as a Patriot, a performance that would further cement his place as perhaps the greatest winner in the history of American sports.

* * *

Under normal circumstances, with a far more typical aging player, the 2018 AFC Championship would have been a changing of the guard, a transference of power from Tom Brady to his successor. But Tom Brady hadn't acquiesced to Jimmy Garoppolo, and he wasn't about to acquiesce to Patrick Mahomes.

Backed by a power running game that held the ball for more than twenty-one minutes in the first half alone, the Patriots built a 14-0 lead over the Chiefs in the first half at Arrowhead Stadium, amassing 245 yards of offense to Kansas City's 32. New England ran forty-two offensive plays to the Chiefs' thirteen and, frankly, would have held a 21-0 lead at intermission were it not for the interception of a Brady pass intended for Rob Gronkowski early in the second quarter. The Patriots went a perfect eight of eight on third down, a trend that would ultimately prove decisive.

All of that served as a mere prequel for what would be one of the great halves in NFL postseason history. After the break, the Chiefs erupted for 31 points *in the second half,* a testament to quarterback Mahomes and coach Andy Reid given that it came against Bill Belichick, who knew he could contain the Chiefs for only so long. Kansas City opened the third quarter with a four-play, 74-yard touchdown drive that took all of 2:04 off the game clock and included a 54-yard strike to wide receiver Sammy Watkins before Mahomes hit tight end Travis Kelce in the end zone from 12 yards out. Just like that, what might have been a Patriots' 21-point lead was a 14-7 game, and all bets were off.

After a New England field goal late in the third quarter extended the Patriots' advantage to 17-7, Mahomes and Brady exchanged haymakers over the next twenty to twenty-five minutes before a winner was ultimately decided by what amounted to the flip of a coin.

Exploiting the Patriots' inability to match up with running back Damien Williams on two drives midway through, Mahomes completed four passes for 61 yards and two fourth-quarter touchdowns to Williams—the latter after a costly interception by Brady—to give the Chiefs their first lead, 21–17, with just 7:45 left in the game. The Patriots responded with a ten-play, 75-yard touchdown drive concluding with a 10-yard run by Sony Michel before the Chiefs again struck swiftly, this time on a two-yard run by Williams that had followed a 38-yard strike from Mahomes to Watkins. Kansas City led 28–24 when Brady trotted onto the field at his own 35-yard line with 1:57 left. Shortly thereafter, the Chiefs made a colossal mental blunder and Brady, as usual, pounced on the opportunity.

On third-and-10 from the Kansas City 34-yard line with 1:01 to play, Brady took a shotgun snap and turned to his right, where he spotted an open Gronkowski still stationed on the line of scrimmage. Brady zipped a pass that was a little high and deflected off the tops of Gronkowski's hands before popping forward and into the hands of defensive back Charvarius Ward for what felt like a game-sealing interception. As Ward began to run, he fumbled the ball out of bounds . . . just as a penalty flag appeared on the field.

Incredibly, Chiefs pass rusher Dee Ford had lined up offside on the play, negating what would have been Brady's third interception. Brady got another chance—now on third-and-5—and completed a 25-yard strike to Gronkowski before running back Rex Burkhead scored on a 4-yard touchdown run, giving the Patriots a 31–28 lead with thirty-nine seconds left. Yet again, a New England opponent had been complicit in its own demise.

With thirty-two seconds remaining and just one time-out, Mahomes took possession on his own 31-yard line, eluded pressure, and scrambled to his right, completing a 21-yard throw to a diving Spencer Ware, a Chiefs running back. Kansas City called time-out. Now with twenty-three seconds remaining—as New England defensive lineman Trey Flowers jumped offside this time—Mahomes completed a 27-yard strike to Chiefs wideout Demarcus Robinson, advancing the ball all the way to the New England 21. Because of the penalty, the clock stopped with sixteen seconds left. The Patriots had six defenders lined up near the goal line when Mahomes threw the next pass out of the end zone, at which point Reid sent out kicker Harrison Butker, who took the field with eleven seconds left and drilled a 39-yard field goal—dead center—to send the game to overtime locked at 31–31.

As the teams convened at midfield, referee Clete Blakeman explained the sudden-death overtime rules to the team captains, then asked Patriots veteran special teamer Matt Slater to call the coin toss.

"Heads," said Slater just before Blakeman flipped the coin.

The coin landed.

"It is heads," Blakeman said. "Do you—"

"We want the ball," Slater interrupted, with an eagerness that caused television announcer Jim Nantz to chuckle.

Over the next four minutes and fifty-two seconds, the Patriots ran thirteen plays, the first nine of which included eight passes. Brady completed only four of them, just three of them after a drive-starting, 10-yard completion to Chris Hogan. But the other three all came on third downs—all on third-and-10, to be exact—and highlighted, once more, Brady's uncanny knack for making the biggest throws at the biggest moments. All in all, Brady had gone five for five on third downs in the fourth quarter and overtime, the only blemish the interception from Gronkowski's hands that had been negated by penalty.

Three plays after Brady's final throw of the day—a 15-yard completion to Gronkowski—the Patriots had a first-and-10 at the Kansas City 15-yard line. Burkhead ran three times for gains of 10, 3, and 2 yards, bulling his way through a sizable hole for a touchdown that gave the Patriots a 37–31 victory.

Brady ran off the field, took off his helmet, and jumped into the arms of ecstatic teammates.

"The odds were stacked against us. It hasn't been that way for us in a while, and it certainly was this year," Brady said. "We started off so slow. Like I said, the last four games have been our best games. We ran it great in Buffalo. We threw it pretty well in the Jets [game]. We were really balanced. The defense was playing really well. We played great against the Chargers last week. . . . Offensively, we did a good job. We had a couple of little screw ups but pretty good for the most part. Defensively, they hung on and played their butts off—shut them out in the first half, which was pretty spectacular. You are not going to shut this team out for four quarters, certainly not at home. It was a great team win."

Said Chiefs quarterback Mahomes about the importance of New England winning the coin toss: "I thought if we got the chance we'd score." And he was probably right.

Two weeks later, in a game that did not come close to matching the drama of the AFC title game, the Patriots appeared in their third straight Super Bowl and fourth in five years, defeating the St. Louis Rams 13–3. In a game generally dominated by both defenses, Brady and Gronkowski teamed up a final time on the game's only touchdown drive, when Brady completed both of his pass attempts to the all-world tight end whom Belichick wanted to trade at the beginning of the season. Used primarily as a blocker at the end of his Patriots tenure, Gronkowski caught twelve passes for 166 yards in his final two games, including six for 87 yards (his jersey number) in the win over the Rams. His final catch as a Patriot was a pretty 29-yard throw-and-catch on second-and-3 that placed the ball at the St. Louis 2-yard line midway through the fourth quarter of what was then a 3–3 game, setting up a Sony Michel run that produced the only touchdown of the game.

"He knows to trust in me and throw the ball," Gronkowski said after the game. "And I'm going to grab it."

Together, Bill Belichick and Tom Brady had won a sixth Super Bowl, lapping the field in the race through NFL history. Boston had yet another trophy, the city's twelfth during an unprecedented era of widespread team success.

But at Gillette Stadium, the epicenter of Boston's reign, the trust was now gone.

* * *

As silly as it now seems, Tom Brady's final long-term contract with the Patriots was agreed upon in 2013 when owner Robert Kraft stated that he believed Brady would be a Patriot for life. But after Brady fought off Jimmy Garoppolo and became MVP of the 2017 NFL season, Brady began pushing for another long-term deal. The team resisted. After the 2013 deal, Brady's contracts with the team were essentially restructures or short-term agreements of just one or two years, which frustrated the quarterback. Brady had clearly had enough of Belichick comparing him to *Fucking Johnny Foxboro* and, consequently, had long since begun skipping optional off-season workouts. By the time training camp arrived in 2019, entering the final year of his time in New England, Brady and Kraft had agreed that New England would not retain Brady's rights through a collectively bargained league mechanism known as the franchise tag, clearing the way for Brady to hit free agency and leave New England altogether.

Everybody knew the score.

This time there would be no dramatic finish that led to a celebration. "It's a unique situation I'm in," Brady told reporters. "I'm in my 20th year with the same team. I'm 42 years old, so pretty much uncharted territory I think for everybody."

Again, incredibly, the Patriots kept winning, a testament to their ability to compartmentalize even amid organizational strife. Minus Gronkowski, who had retired rather than deal with the coach, the Patriots began the year 8-0 despite Brady's obvious unhappiness, most outwardly with the team's shortage of pass catchers. To appease him, the team signed troubled free-agent wide receiver Antonio Brown, who played one game for the Patriots in Week 2—a 43-0 New England win—before the club released him due to allegations of sexual assault. Belichick later traded a second-round draft pick for wide receiver Mohamed Sanu, who showed some initial promise before an injury; he, too, ended up being a bust. The Patriots' first loss was a 37–20 defeat at Baltimore in Week 9 that effectively triggered a collapse in the second half of the season, the team suffering consecutive losses in Weeks 13 and 14 against Houston and Kansas City, the latter defeat at home.

Despite it all, the Patriots took a 12-3 record into the final week of the regular season, needing only a home victory against the Miami Dolphins to earn a first-round bye. With 3:53 to play in the game and New England trailing 20–17, Brady threw a 13-yard touchdown pass to running back James White to give the team a 24–20 lead, the Patriots needing only to stop Miami on the game's final possession to secure the victory.

As Brady watched from the sideline, Miami quarterback Ryan Fitzpatrick drove the Dolphins down the field and threw a touchdown pass to tight end Mike Gesicki to give Miami a 27–24 lead and, ultimately, victory, forcing the Patriots to play on wild card weekend for the first time in nine years. By that point New England had gone 4-4 over its final eight games of the season and was fading, both in the short term and, with Brady's departure imminent, the long.

On January 4, 2020, Brady played his final game as a member of the Patriots, a 20-13 loss to former teammate and now head coach Mike Vrabel and the Tennessee Titans. With the Patriots trailing 14–13, a deteriorating Edelman dropped an easy pass on second-and-4 from the New England 37-yard line on the team's final drive of the game, necessitating a Patriots punt. By the time New England got the ball back at its own 1-yard line, there were just fifteen seconds remaining in the game.

Brady dropped back into his end zone and threw a pass intended for Sanu that popped into the air and into the arms of former teammate Logan Ryan, who traipsed into the end zone to seal the Tennessee victory. Following the game, Brady was asked about the prospect of retiring but seemed to dismiss the idea.

"I would say it's pretty unlikely," he said. "I love playing football. I don't know what it looks like moving forward."

Roughly ten weeks later, after the cancellation of America's first professional sporting event due to COVID-19, Tom Brady signed a two-year contract with the Tampa Bay Buccaneers. In nineteen years with the Patriots representing Boston, he had gone 219-64 during the regular season and 30-11 in the playoffs. He had led the Patriots to thirteen AFC Championship game appearances and nine Super Bowls, winning an unprecedented six. He had passed for more than 74,000 yards and thrown 541 touchdown passes, leading the way on a dynastic run for Boston unlike that in the history of any other North American city.

Brady had changed history. And now history, it seemed, was finally changing back.

CHAPTER 17

STARTING OVER

"I would say the duck boats. A lot of great food and restaurants, but those duck boats are famously awesome."

—former Patriots tight end Rob Gronkowski, to ESPN reporter
Mike Reiss, when asked what he missed most about Boston
before Tom Brady and the Tampa Bay Buccaneers played at
Gillette Stadium in 2021

BY THE SPRING OF 2020, when Tom Brady left for the Tampa Bay Buccaneers, many Bostonians could recount their four teams' accomplishments in the twenty-first century as if singing "The Twelve Days of Christmas": twenty-nine trips to the semifinal rounds, eighteen appearances in the championship game or series, twelve champions . . . *and a pahtridge in a peah tree.* Many might have attributed the seeming end to the departure of Brady. Others, or more combative Bostonians, might have told you that it took a global pandemic.

And even then, there was no guarantee it was over.

When professional sports in America shut down in the spring of 2020 as a result of COVID-19, no Boston team might have sacrificed more than the Bruins, who had the best record in hockey. Through seventy games—when the season was interrupted—the Bruins were the possessors of an incredible 44-14-12 record, the only NHL team to have recorded 100 points. And goaltender Tuukka Rask was playing perhaps the best hockey of his career.

When the NHL resumed play in August in competitive "bubbles" in Toronto and Edmonton, the circumstances were obviously much, much different. The league effectively operated in isolation, in arenas devoid of fans, removed from families and friends in a time of great anxiety. Players had gone five months between stints. The Bruins then played three relatively lackluster warm-up games to determine playoff seeding and lost all three, something they had not done since January during the normal flow of the schedule. When the playoffs started, Rask looked substandard, the Bruins splitting Games 1 and 2 of their opening-round series against the Carolina Hurricanes when the season took a turn head-on into a brick wall.

Between Games 2 and 3 of the Carolina series, the Bruins announced that goaltender Rask had opted out of the bubble—as players had been given the option to do—and returned home to his family. His season was over. While the Bruins supported their goaltender, public sentiment oscillated. Players spoke of the difficulty of long-term isolation from families during a time of concern—"My wife is very strong, she can handle it," winger Brad Marchand remarked at one point—and Rask later disclosed, in early 2021, that his daughter had a medical emergency requiring an ambulance to be called to the player's home.

"It was a tough decision to leave, but then again, it wasn't," Rask said. "I knew it was more important for me to be home at the time. So, that was easy to live with. On the other hand, you're home knowing you could be there, you should be there, playing hockey. So, it's tough to watch the games. Your brain is kind of spinning at that point . . . [I]t was tough for a few weeks."

Though the Bruins defeated the Hurricanes in five games behind the play of backup goaltender Jaroslav Halak, they were subsequently eliminated in five games by the Tampa Bay Lightning, the same franchise that had eliminated Boston in 2018 and that the Bruins had avoided in the 2019 postseason. Though the Bruins won Game 1, the rest of the series was decidedly one-sided. Tampa won Games 2 to 5 by a combined score of 15–7 and Game 3 by an embarrassing score of 7–1, ending the Boston hockey season and, as it turned out, the Bruins career of longtime team captain Zdeno Chara.

In the middle of the series, with the Bruins trailing three games to one, Bruins coach Bruce Cassidy spoke as if the end was imminent.

"We've said it before, we support Tuukka's decision 100 percent," said Cassidy. "But then as we get back to work, of course it's going to affect us. He's a Vezina Trophy finalist, one of the elite goaltenders in this league. [Halak], we feel if he's not the best backup in the league, then he's right up there. But now he's pushed to No. 1 duty and you've got Danny Vladar coming in at No. 2, and he just doesn't have any NHL experience.

"It does affect you mentally. It affects how you construct your lineup when you had those back-to-backs. . . . Do you believe you have all the pieces to win? You'd have to ask the players that. I always do. I'm an optimist. . . . But I think it does take a toll."

More than just missing a goalie, the mental wear-and-tear of a world in disarray took a toll on teams in both the NHL and NBA, the latter of which was also operating in a bubble. Often, when teams were on the brink of elimination, they didn't need to be pushed so much as they jumped.

Screw it, they seemed to decide. *Let's just go home.*

Thanks to the interrupted 2019–2020 NHL season, the 2020–2021 campaign began late and consisted of just fifty-six games in geographically aligned divisions that limited travel as the world continued to deal with COVID. The Bruins ended up with the Pittsburgh Penguins, New York Islanders, and Washington Capitals, the last of whom had signed Chara as a free agent. Boston subsequently defeated Washington in six games in the first round before falling to the Islanders in a disappointing Round 2, a season that further aged a core that was past its prime.

In the aftermath of that season, center David Krejci left the Bruins and returned to play in his native Czech Republic, where he wanted to raise his children. Rask underwent major hip surgery that had affected him in the series loss to the Islanders, both the player and the team leaving open the door for his return. But for really the first time in more than a decade, the Bruins began a new season—this one a full campaign in 2021–2022 that had the promise of being played in fan-filled arenas under relatively normal traveling conditions—without true Stanley Cup aspirations.

With Patrice Bergeron now serving as captain and entering the final year of his contract—and with no hint of a contract extension, a situation akin to that of Brady—the long-term prognosis for the Bruins seemed relatively bleak, perhaps more so than any of Boston's four major sports franchises. Having displaced his predecessor Peter Chiarelli with a campaign platform built on drafting and player development, general manager Don Sweeney had let the proverbial well run dry, ultimately failing in both areas. While the Bruins had a smattering of success—defenseman Charlie McAvoy and goaltender Jeremy Swayman seemed like foundational pieces—the Bruins were otherwise left to fill their lineup with a series of veteran signings, many of them players near the bottom of the roster.

Meanwhile, as the Bruins slid into the NHL's middle class—or, perhaps, the *lower* middle class—the Tampa Bay Lightning had established themselves as the league's marquee franchise, winning consecutive Stanley Cup championships. After defeating Boston in the Toronto bubble in 2020, the Lightning defeated both the Islanders and Dallas Stars to effectively erase their failure from the previous season, when Tampa had lost to Columbus in an embarrassing first-round series sweep. Tampa promptly won the championship again in 2021, wiping out a surprising Montreal Canadiens team in five games of the Cup final.

In between, while Tampa's baseball team, the Rays, made a run at the World Series, the Buccaneers had been sprinkled with the magic dust of Tom Brady, who brought instant credibility to one of the most unsuccessful franchises in all of sports. At Brady's side was none other than tight end Rob Gronkowski, who had happily come out of retirement to play again with Brady as a member of the Bucs. (Belichick traded Gronkowski to Tampa Bay for a fourth-round pick.) In their new home, Brady and Gronkowski periodically filmed promotional internet videos titled *Tommy & Gronky* during which they sometimes read fan mail with their feet resting in a kiddie pool, an obvious contrast to the cold, intense environment they shared in New England.

Neither Brady nor Gronkowski extended Boston a middle finger in any of the videos, but they might as well have.

* * *

For the Celtics, the defection of Kyrie Irving created an odd opportunity and was, in some ways, addition by subtraction. Before Irving joined forces with Kevin Durant in Brooklyn, Durant had suffered a serious Achilles tendon injury in Golden State that would sideline him for the entirety of his first season in Brooklyn. Even with LeBron James having joined forces with Anthony Davis on the Los Angeles Lakers, the NBA landscape felt far more balanced that it had in ages, with teams like the Los Angeles Clippers (Kawhi Leonard and Paul George) and Houston Rockets (James Harden and Russell Westbrook) also believing they had a path to the title.

In the East, however, the absence of Durant and the departure of Leonard (who had gone to the Clippers after leading Toronto to a championship) had created a muddle neat the top of the conference. That group included the Celtics, who, when healthy, had a collection of offensive options that still placed Gordon Hayward alongside developing youngsters Jaylen Brown and Jayson Tatum as well as newcomer Kemba Walker.

But before Boston could gain any momentum, Hayward sprained his ankle late in the team's first postseason game during an eventual first-round series sweep of the Philadelphia 76ers. The injury was expected to sideline Hayward for roughly a month and was yet another setback for a player who had spent the season playing his best basketball since arriving in Boston.

"It's definitely gutting. It sucks," Hayward said. "There's nothing else to say about that. It's definitely frustrating [and] it doesn't feel great at the moment. Just try to get better as soon as I can. . . . I heard it and felt it and knew it wasn't just your casual rolled ankle. It was swollen by the time I was leaving the court, so I knew it was definitely worse than normal. As far as timeline, it's kind of up in the air. I think it's kind of just how my body responds to the rehab and all that stuff. Maybe I could use some Disney magic to help me get better."

If Hayward never really got any, his teammates did.

After burying the Sixers, the Celtics jumped to a 2-0 series lead against the Raptors, winning Game 1 by 18 points. Coupled with a run to the end of the regular season when the teams had resumed play in the bubble in late July, the Celtics had won ten of eleven and appeared destined for the Eastern Conference finals. They looked on the verge of another sweep when a weaving Walker made a brilliant bounce pass to Daniel Theis for an easy dunk to give Boston a 103–101 lead with 0.5 seconds left in Game 3, prompting Toronto to call a time-out.

Incredibly, on the subsequent inbounds play, the Celtics were late covering Toronto forward OG Anunoby, who caught an entry pass from Kyle Lowry and released a 3-pointer—all in under 0.5 seconds—that gently swirled through the basket and gave Toronto a series-turning 104–103 victory.

Though the Celtics ultimately won the series in seven games, the Anunoby bucket punctured the team's confidence, leading to a six-game series in which Boston was picked apart at the most critical moments by a tougher, more cohesive, and more experienced Miami Heat team led by Jimmy Butler. The Heat subsequently lost to LeBron James, Anthony Davis, and the Lakers in the Finals, but there was at least some reason to believe that the Celtics were again on the upswing, particularly as young franchise swingmen Brown and Tatum continued to mature.

"We're gonna lean on a couple of those guys for a long, long time that were making big plays," Celtics coach Brad Stevens said. "I think that ultimately that's the benefit."

Indeed, like the NHL, the NBA faced a condensed scheduled for the 2020–21 season, this one just seventy-two games. The off-season would be short. And as it turned out, so would the Celtics roster.

Though Hayward had returned to the floor for the end of the Miami series, he had been limited significantly by his ankle injury. His three seasons in Boston derailed by a variety of factors—injuries, the Kyrie Irving experience, insufficient playing time in a positional logjam with Tatum and Brown—he resisted the Celtics' offers to keep him and signed as a free agent with the Charlotte Hornets. Even then, Hayward's departure was clouded by reports that the Celtics were trying to work out a sign-and-trade with Hayward's preferred choice, the Indiana Pacers. When the Pacers walked away, Boston was left with nothing more than a trade exception, which Ainge eventually used on Evan Fournier, at best an off-brand version of Hayward.

Meanwhile, Kemba Walker was suffering from a degenerative knee issue that had robbed him of quickness and potency, more bad news for a Celtics organization that suddenly looked as if it were deteriorating as quickly as the 2018 Red Sox.

Buoyed by their run to Game 7 of the conference finals against LeBron James and the Cleveland Cavaliers in the 2017–18 season, Boston's talented young core believed it was better than it was. But when things didn't go the group's way, they erupted and pointed fingers at one another—as guard Marcus Smart had done in a locker room disagreement with Brown following a loss in the Miami series. The only thing the Celtics hadn't done was cheat, which might have been advisable under the circumstances.

By the time the 2021–22 season arrived, the Celtics had undergone a massive organizational overhaul, too, Ainge having departed after retiring . . . or being fired . . . or jumping from the deck of what felt like a sinking ship. Seemingly tuned out by his star players, Brad Stevens was promoted to an executive position as the head of basketball operations—replacing Danny Ainge, the man who had hired him—and then hired a new coach, former Brooklyn Nets assistant Ime Udoka. The hope was that Udoka could tap into the souls of Tatum and Brown and lead the Celtics into a new age, but while there were (very) brief flashes of individual brilliance, there was little reason to believe anything had really changed, and the team was mired in the middle again: on the bubble of playoff contention, not bad enough to get a top draft pick. Having been in Boston for going on nine years now, Stevens had long since accepted the reality of his own assessment.

It's either: Did you win it all or didn't you win it all?
During his time as coach, the Celtics did not.

* * *

From 2001 through 2019, the Patriots and Red Sox combined for ten champion-ships, six Super Bowls, and four World Series, each the most in their respective sports during the first twenty years of the new millennium. For two franchises whose prior existence had been known largely by failure, the turnaround was nothing short of shocking. The Red Sox went from a history of October collapses to winners behind one of the greatest clutch hitters in baseball history, the great David Ortiz. The Patriots went from arguably the biggest laughingstock franchise in all of sports to the most respected, celebrated, and accomplished behind the inimitable and incomparable duo of Bill Belichick and Tom Brady, the greatest coach and quarterback of their era if not all time.

In 2020, both were grounded with a resounding thud.

The good news for the Red Sox—only if there was any at all—was that they were so bad, they were never remotely relevant, particularly as Major League Baseball owners and players engaged in an embarrassing, tactless dispute over protocols during the global pandemic. Unlike the NHL and NBA, Major League Baseball had not begun its regular season when the country shut down just a few weeks before Opening Day, leaving little time to sort out issues. At a time when America needed a diversion and baseball might have had an empty stage all to itself while providing a much-needed public service, owners and players openly bickered. Fans who were not insulted should have been. The World Series between the Los Angeles Dodgers and the Tampa Bay Rays drew the event's worst television ratings ever, even though aided by a controversial ending in which the analytics-driven Rays pulled their starting pitcher, Blake Snell, in the middle of what felt like one of the more memorable postseason pitching performances in recent baseball history.

In some ways, of course, that ending was appropriate. Given the chance to provide people with positive, lasting memories, baseball instead undermined itself and proved utterly forgettable.

Nowhere was that truer than in Boston, where the Red Sox plunged to a level of irrelevance not seen since the early days of Beatlemania. With the departure of Alex Cora just before the scheduled start of spring train-ing, the Red Sox had already named Cora's bench coach, Ron Roenicke, as interim manager. Shortly after the pandemic hit, the club then announced that pitcher Chris Sale would undergo season-ending elbow surgery. Less than three months later, while players and owners were still battling over the parameters of a shortened season, pitcher Eduardo Rodriguez contracted COVID and developed myocarditis, an inflammation of the heart that ended his season. Less than two years removed from their historic 2018 season, the Red Sox had no Mookie Betts and no pitching, which left the sacrificial Roenicke with no chance.

Twenty-four games into the season, the Red Sox were 6-18. By the short season's end, they were 24-36 and possessors of the fourth-worst record in baseball, earning their highest draft pick ever in the annual amateur draft. The dreadful Red Sox pitching staff allowed 98 home runs and issued 252 walks—both the most in the major leagues—a rather disturbing tandem. Team president Sam Kennedy went so far as to call the club's play "embarrassing" near season's end. Incredibly, that was an understatement.

By that point, without fans in the stadium, the Patriots had begun life without Tom Brady, albeit after a surprisingly passive attempt (if any) to find his replacement. In a market rife with possibilities—Brady was just one among a handful of notable options who changed teams, a group that included Matthew Stafford, Carson Wentz, Teddy Bridgewater, and others—Belichick waited for the market to completely shake out before signing Cam Newton. Naturally, many football pundits immediately cited Belichick's brilliance, suggesting that the Patriots, by spending less money at quarterback than any team but the Jacksonville Jaguars, would now have more money to spend on the balance of their roster.

As it turned out, the Patriots didn't spend. And at quarterback, they got exactly what they had paid for: a has-been quarterback who was closer to the end of his career than he was willing to accept—and certainly one that was much, much closer to the end than Tom Brady.

After a reasonably promising start to the season, the Patriots were 2-1 after three games, their only loss a 35–30 defeat at Seattle in which Newton passed for 397 yards and a touchdown while rushing for another 47 yards and two scores. But then Newton contracted COVID after a relatively lackluster Week 3 win over the Las Vegas Raiders, a development that helped send the Patriots into a spin.

New England lost four straight and ultimately finished at 7-9. Two of the team's wins came over the stink-bomb New York Jets. And when the Patriots played good competition in the final weeks, they were trucked in a 24–3 defeat at the Los Angeles Rams in Week 14 and blown off the field by the Buffalo Bills at home, on national television, in a 38–9 defeat in Week 16.

After their last game, a 28–14 win at home over the Jets, Belichick declared a "positive" end to a disappointing season, but he declined to answer questions about a pregame media report that said the Patriots had not ruled out the possibility of bringing back Newton.

Long since accustomed to being part of the NFL's extended schedule in January and February, Patriots fans might have felt lost if not for what was happening down in Florida, a story that captivated them as much as any Super Bowl run by their team over the first twenty years of the millennium.

After leading the Tampa Bay Buccaneers to four straight victories over the final weeks of the regular season, Tom Brady had guided his new team into the playoffs as an NFC wild card team. At Washington, he passed for 381 yards and three touchdowns in a 31–23 victory. A week later, backed by a defense that ravaged Saints quarterback Drew Brees in the divisional round, Brady threw two more touchdown passes in the Bucs' 30-20 win. Then came three more touchdowns in a stunning 31–26 victory over Aaron Rodgers and the Packers in Green Bay, sending Brady to the tenth Super Bowl of his career against the defending champion Kansas City Chiefs and phenom Patrick Mahomes.

For those who still had questions as to whether Brady or Belichick had been the greater reason for the Patriots' success over the years, the scales had tipped—and the luck had, too. During a year in which the Bucs had to play three playoff road games—something Brady had never been required to do during his time with the Patriots—Brady did so during a pandemic, when there were few or no fans in the stadium. And when he reached the Super Bowl, he even got to play on his home field in Tampa, which had been designated the game's host city four years prior.

The indisputable conclusion: If the Patriots possessed any intangible or immeasurable forces during their winning years, they did not exist because of the uniform or the coach. They came—and went—with the quarterback.

Though the Chiefs scored first in Super Bowl LV, the game was a rout. Brady played his best game of the postseason, completing twenty-one of twenty-nine passes for 201 yards, three touchdowns, and a passer rating of 125.8. Two of his touchdown passes went to Rob Gronkowski, who had his best game since joining the Bucs. Tampa won the game 31–9, and Brady finished with more touchdown passes in the postseason—ten—than Newton had thrown during his entire stint with the Patriots.

"Tom is playing for his teammates right now," said Tampa head coach Bruce Arians in an interview with *Sports Illustrated*. "He wants those guys to experience what he's experienced six times [before]. I think personally, too, he's making a statement. You know? It wasn't all Coach Belichick."

In fact, it felt like all Brady.

In the aftermath of the Super Bowl, the Buccaneers had what was called a "boat" parade, which allowed fans to share in a socially distanced celebration of their football season. And though they weren't the duck boats that Gronkowski had told ESPN were his favorite part of Boston, they served their purpose for Tampa's new quarterback, who stepped off the Hillsborough River needing assistance.

His rubber legs had nothing to do with anything remotely close to seasickness.

"What a journey it's been," Gronkowski said. "What a story it's been."

Nonetheless, it wasn't quite over.

In the fourth week of his second season with the Tampa Bay Buccaneers, Tom Brady returned to New England for a prime-time matchup against the Patriots, though the game ended up being only a fraction of the story. Before kickoff, Patriots owner Robert Kraft waited—with a cameraman at his side—to greet Brady on the field during warm-ups. Brady never came out. After Tampa claimed a surprisingly close 19–17 victory in which Brady played rather poorly, Belichick took an entirely different and far less self-serving tack, visiting privately with his former quarterback—no television cameras in tow—presumably to clear the air over what had been a bitter breakup filled with barbs and digs, some subtle, others not so much.

After that, for the most part, the grumbling between Brady and Belichick stopped.

And the grumbling between Brady and his new coach, Bruce Arians, seemingly intensified.

While Tampa finished the season with a 13–4 record and the number-two seed in the NFC playoffs, the Bucs were in no real shape to defend their title. After passing for a career-best and league-leading 5,316 yards with 43 touchdowns during the regular season, Brady was under constant pressure in the divisional playoffs against the eventual Super Bowl champion Los Angeles Rams, who surged to a 27–3 lead in Tampa. But right on cue—and with the help of the sloppy, self-destructive Rams—Brady brought Tampa back to tie the game at 27–27 with a mere 42 seconds left in regulation, rivaling the comeback he had led for the Patriots against the Atlanta Falcons in Super Bowl LI.

As it turned out, for a relative instant, Tampa's seven-play, game-tying touchdown drive was seemingly the final act of Tom Brady's incomparable, stellar career.

Aided by breakdowns on the Tampa Bay defense, Los Angeles quarterback Matthew Stafford guided the Rams to a game-winning field goal as time expired, ending the Buccaneers' season. Roughly two weeks later, reports surfaced that the forty-four-year-old Brady was seriously considering retirement, a surprising development given both his excellent play and his previously stated commitment to play through age forty-five. And on February 1, 2022, Brady posted on Instagram that it was time to "leave the field of play to the next generation of dedicated and committed athletes." Brady never actually used the word "retirement" in his post; nor did he make any mention whatsoever of the Patriots or anyone connected to them, a glaring and seemingly deliberate omission that suggested he still harbored ill will toward owner Robert Kraft, head coach Bill Belichick, and the organization that drafted him.

As it turned out, Brady was merely engaged in another dispute with his head coach and employer, once again leveraging his talent and status in a manner that further portrayed him as an egomaniacal diva who placed his wants above those of all else.

Long gone was the boyish, All-American sixth-round draft pick who seized an opportunity and became the most celebrated player in NFL history.

Six weeks after announcing his "retirement," Brady announced his return to the Bucs, a decision that conveniently came just before the start of NFL free agency. Slightly more than two weeks later, Bucs coach Bruce Arians announced *his* retirement, ending yet another power struggle between Brady and his coach. Unlike the Patriots, however, the Buccaneers chose their quarterback over their coach, with defensive coordinator Todd Bowles replacing Arians as chief decision maker—other than Brady, of course—on the Tampa Bay sideline.

During it all, reports surfaced that Brady actually had tried to leverage his way out of Tampa entirely in hopes of joining the Miami Dolphins, where he would join head coach Sean Payton, who had recently resigned from the New Orleans Saints. When that plan went *poof,* Brady came out of retirement and returned to the Bucs after a rumored meeting (or discussion) with Buccaneers co-chairman Joel Glazer.

However it all precisely transpired, this much was clear: Tom Brady was still throwing his weight around, bullying Arians, Tampa Bay, and anyone else in such a shameless manner that the Patriots began to look like sympathetic figures.

And by then, of course, Bill Belichick and the Patriots had long since found a new leading man for their offense.

* * *

In the modern sports world, governing mechanisms make dominance difficult, mostly through the presence of salary caps, contractual restrictions, and draft rules. In the draft, the worst teams always pick earliest. Payroll restrictions can prevent the best teams from retaining good players who reach the open market. Even then, generational or once-in-a-lifetime talents ultimately cede to age.

Of the twelve championships Boston won beginning with the 2001 Patriots, after all, nine were built around Tom Brady and David Ortiz, two of the great winners in modern American sports history.

Just the same, reports of Boston's demise following the departure of Tom Brady may have been exaggerated. Not long after Brady won Tampa Bay a playoff game for the first time in eighteen years—yes, the Bucs went without a single postseason win during much of the time the Patriots were collecting Lombardi Trophies as if they were baseball caps—the Red Sox took the field in 2021 with a new outlook and familiar face: Alex Cora. With both Cora and the Red Sox having suffered greatly during the manager's one-year absence, the Red Sox signed Cora to a two-year contract and a club option for two more, all while general manager Chaim Bloom attempted to rebuild the Red Sox with one familiar Boston buzzword in mind: "sustainability."

After starting the 2021 season with three ugly losses, the Red Sox promptly won nine straight. By early July, Boston was 54-32 and possessed the second-best record in baseball, on pace for a startling 102 victories. When Bloom subsequently took an extremely conservative approach at the deadline and failed to address the team's greatest needs—a true first baseman and pitching, not necessarily in that order—the Red Sox skidded badly, falling nine games behind the Tampa Bay Rays in the American League East and in danger of missing the playoffs entirely.

Through it all, Bloom adhered to the longer-term principles that he had also preached at the trading deadline, but at the expense of 2021.

"I think the important thing is just to stay true to the goals that got us to this place where we're trying to win as many championships as we can," Bloom had said. "This year's a big part of that, so we want to do everything we can to help this year's group. You've seen it on the field. I mean, not only have we had a lot of success, but it's a group that believes in itself and is a whole heck of a lot of fun to watch. When you have that legitimate shot at a championship, you want to do everything you can to support it. . . . [But] we're also not doing our jobs if, by doing that, we make it much harder to win championships in every year that follows."

The Red Sox were up and down over the final two weeks but earned a place in the wild card play-in game against the Yankees with a come-from-behind victory in their final game of the season.

With the rival Yankees in town for a winner-take-all affair that would send the winner to the American League Division Series against Tampa Bay, Fenway Park rumbled back to life with an intensity that it had not experienced in years. Jumping to an early lead, the Red Sox defeated the Yankees 6–2.

In the ALDS, after Tampa defeated Boston by a 5–0 score in Game 1 in decisive fashion, the Red Sox responded with improbable victories in Games 2, 3, and 4, the middle victory requiring a fortuitous bounce when a potential go-ahead hit by Tampa outfielder Randy Arozarena ricocheted out of play off the body of Red Sox outfielder Hunter Renfroe, keeping the game tied at 4 in the eighth inning. The Red Sox ultimately won the game in the thirteenth inning on a home run by catcher Christian Vazquez and then eliminated the Rays a night later to advance to the American League Champion Series.

The series win over the Rays advanced Boston to its stunning thirtieth league semifinal in twenty-one years, a stretch that began with the Patriots' 2001 Super Bowl run.

"We always said we had a good baseball team that had some holes—and we still have some holes—but at the end, for how bad it looked sometimes, we're still here," Cora said. "We're still in the dance. We're still in the tournament, and we're moving on to the ALCS."

On a macro scale, if Bostonians were nodding silently, who could blame them?

Damn right. We're still here.

If Cora's story was one of atonement, perseverance, or persistence—or all of the above—it was the beginning of another theme that developed as 2021 drew to close, a new Boston buzzword also seeping into the developing story of the revamped New England Patriots: "redemption."

Pummeled on the field and off during the public-relations disaster that was the departure and continued greatness of Tom Brady, the Patriots in general—and Bill Belichick, in particular—set about the business of reinventing themselves during the off-season that followed Brady's record seventh Super Bowl title. With the fifteenth pick in the annual draft, New England selected quarterback Mac Jones from the University of Alabama, the most dominant program and what amounted to a developmental camp for many Patriots players. Under coach Nick Saban (a longtime Belichick friend), Alabama had won six national titles—the same number Belichick had won in New England—during an empire that spanned from 2008 to the present day. With Jones at quarterback, Alabama had finished the season a perfect 13-0 and was so dominant that many regarded the Crimson Tide as perhaps the greatest college football team in history.

"So, Mac was available there at our pick and he's a guy we spent a lot of time with. And [we] felt like that was the best pick at that time for us," Belichick said in typically monotonic fashion. "[We] look forward to working with him. He's a smart kid. He's been in a system that's similar to ours. We have had a lot of good conversations with him. I think he'll be able to process the offense. It's obviously going to take a lot of time. We'll see how it goes. Cam's our quarterback. Whatever position, whatever time Jarrett [Stidham, drafted in 2019] or Mac are ready to challenge and compete, then we'll see how that goes. But right now, Mac—he's just got a lot of learning in front of him."

But as many had projected, Mac was a fast learner. Just before the start of the 2021 NFL regular season, in a move that stunned many, the Patriots released Newton and named Jones their starter, though the emphasis on Jones was still over the longer term. *It's obviously going to take a lot of time.* The Patriots subsequently got off to a slow start, winning two of their first six games. But beginning with a resounding 54–13 victory over the punching-bag Jets in Week 7, New England won a stunning seven games in a row and became, for a time, the top seed in a conference that seemingly lacked a truly dominant team. New England's play bore some similarity to the early Belichick years—mistake-free quarterback play and airtight defense, particularly in the passing game—and seemed to reenergize the coach, city, and region. The possessors of a 9-4 record following a Week 13 win at windswept Buffalo in which the Patriots attempted just three passes, Belichick repeated a line he had used many times over the years, though this time the words had taken on new meaning. The Patriots, after all, were building something again.

"I'm really proud of our players," said the coach.

What happened next was hardly the stuff of fairy tales—the Patriots dropped four of their final five games, including a 47–17 defeat in a return to Buffalo, during which the Bills scored seven touchdowns on seven possessions. But the general sentiment among the fan base was that the Patriots were clearly headed in the right direction. And even as offensive coordinator Josh McDaniels finally left the organization to become the head coach of the Las Vegas Raiders, fans in New England eventually shifted their focus to arrivals rather than departures, believing fully that the Patriots had arguably the biggest piece necessary to return to dominance.

As Boston knew quite well, after all, any great comeback usually started with the quarterback.

* * *

As this book was going to print, in their first year under new head coach Ime Udoka, the Boston Celtics finally matured, almost overnight, to championship status. Possessors of an underachieving 18-21 record after losing to the New York Knicks on January 8—the Celtics led by as many as 25 points at one stage in that game—the Celtics crystallized at the snap of a finger, taking off on an improbable run as if they had boarded one of Jeff Bezos's Blue Origin rockets.

Beginning on January 8, the Celtics went 33-10 to finish the season with a record of 51-31, often overwhelming opponents with swarming defense and an avalanche of 3-point shots. They went a preposterous 22-3 over one 25-game stretch and finished as the No. 2 seed in the Eastern Conference, a transformation so rapid it felt like a remake of the 1983 hit film *Trading Places*.

"We just had a talk about how we both want to be [in Boston], we both want to figure it out," forward Jayson Tatum said of a conversation with fellow star Jaylen Brown that many believe was the axis for the change. "There aren't many players in the league like JB. The grass ain't always greener. . . . We gotta figure some things out, but I think the most important thing is we both want it extremely bad. We want to try to figure it out together."

And when they gave it their all, they nearly *won* it all.

Facing the Brooklyn Nets and the treasonous Kyrie Irving in the first round of the playoffs, the Celtics pulled out a dramatic Game 1 victory on a buzzer-beating layup by Tatum, then went on to sweep the Nets in four games.

("Their window is now," a seemingly defeated Irving said in the middle of the series.) In the second round, after blowing Game 5 against the defending champion Milwaukee Bucks at home, the Celtics responded by winning the next two games—and the series—fueled by Tatum's gargantuan 46-point performance in Game 6. The Eastern Conference Finals then featured another seven-game series victory, this one over the Miami Heat, after the Celtics similarly missed an opportunity at home in Game 6.

But every time they failed, they responded with a victory, ultimately landing in the NBA Finals against the Golden State Warriors, a team that had established itself as the league's marquee franchise while making its sixth trip to the Finals in a span of eight seasons.

"Every kid can imagine themselves being in the NBA and being in the Finals, but actually living out your dream in real time is a surreal feeling," Tatum said. "Sometimes you have to pinch yourself, right? I walk in, I see this backdrop, and it's like, 'Damn, I *am* in the Finals.'"

Nonetheless, while the matchup felt like a potential changing of the guard, someone forgot to tell the Warriors, who had similar motivations to those of the Celtics, specifically in disproving a treasonous former teammate now wearing the uniform of the Brooklyn Nets. In Kevin Durant's absence, many had left the Warriors for dead. But led by the incomparable Stephen Curry—the NBA may never see another shooter quite like him—the Warriors had returned to the Finals intent on delivering a message to anyone who believed, as Irving had noted, that the Celtics' window was now.

That may be so, the Warriors seemed to say. But ours isn't quite closed yet.

With the Warriors facing a 2–1 series deficit entering Game 4 in Boston, Curry turned in a historic 43-point performance to even the series at 2–2. The Celtics' inability to close out the game despite a five-point lead with less than seven minutes remaining was reminiscent of their late-series failures against both Milwaukee and Miami, but this time the breakdown proved fatal. Curry and Golden State went on to win both Game 5 (in San Francisco) and Game 6 (in Boston), the latter thanks to a blistering 21–0 run early in the game that left the Celtics rubber-legged.

In the aftermath of the defeat, gracious members of the Warriors embraced devastated members of the Celtics as if consoling younger siblings.

"Y'all will be back," Warriors forward Draymond Green was assuring them on the historic floor of the TD Garden.

Boston, of course, was banking on it.

ACKNOWLEDGMENTS

The simple thing is to say that this project started in early 2020, when Susan Canavan of the Waxman Literary Agency approached me and stoked an idea that had long smoldered in the considerable, empty space between my ears. But the truth is that this all really began more than twenty years ago, in the early part of the millennium, when Bill Belichick, Tom Brady, and David Ortiz headlined a cast of characters that placed Boston on center stage for the kind of run that would, as it turned out, rival *The Phantom of the Opera*.

Like many, I have only been fortunate enough to watch it, talk about it, and write about it in a place where history has always mattered and been made, good and bad, and where the residents have always been, as much as anything else, *impassioned*.

As for the title, that, too, was Canavan's idea. Sitting across from each other over lunch, we were brainstorming—mostly the result of her brain—when we started recounting Ortiz's memorable speech in the aftermath of the 2013 Boston Marathon bombings, when her eyes widened and a lightbulb all but appeared over her head.

"That's it!" she gasped. "That's the title."

This is our city.

Between then and now, a great many offered their time, interest, and support, and my fear, of course, is that someone has slipped through the cracks. Canavan and Scott Waxman found a willing and capable partner in Abrams Books, who placed me in the talented hands of Garrett McGrath and Jamison Stoltz. While the world was derailed by the COVID-19 pandemic, all the people at Abrams demonstrated extraordinary patience, which was of particular value to someone (ahem) who often possesses relatively little of it.

A special thanks, then, to Garrett and Jamison, as well as to Lisa Silverman, all of whom undoubtedly juggled numerous projects at a time when the entire world felt as if it were up in the air. They waited (and waited) for copy—and then they made it better and better. They were open-minded and detail-oriented, the latter a particularly valuable attribute given what (and whom) they were working with.

Outside of Abrams, a special thanks to Jim Louth, the assistant program director at 98.5 The Sports Hub, Boston's leading all-sports radio station, who gave his personal time to review the long list of events that marked the timeline of the last twenty-plus years. That kind of task required someone who both loved and lived Boston sports while possessing extraordinary recall. So, thanks, Louthy. You are the definition of a team player.

Thanks, too, to Michael Felger, Jim Murray, Jimmy Stewart, Billy Lanni, and Kevin Maggiore, who knowingly or unknowingly helped trigger thoughts and ideas, and all of whom tolerated a coworker's inevitable distractions. And thanks to market manager Mary Menna, program director Rick Radzik, and promotions director Kelley Anderson, all of whom embraced the idea of the project and expressed interest in it. I am grateful for your support.

Of course, thanks to the many who offered their time and insight, many of whom agreed to interviews despite no prior relationship with the author and many who simultaneously accepted the criticisms that come along with being a player, coach, or executive in a city with a rabid fan base and often obnoxious sports radio hosts. The full list is too long to mention, but thanks, especially, to: Theo Epstein, Terry Francona, and Sam Kennedy, all of or formerly of the Red Sox; Jonathan Kraft, Bill Parcells, Josh McDaniels, Tedy Bruschi, Ted Johnson, and Rob Ninkovich, all of or formerly of the Patriots; Wyc Grousbeck, Brad Stevens, and Danny Ainge, all of or formerly of the Celtics; and Cam Neely of the Bruins. None of them said the following, but they easily could have: Boston is a busy place and they had better things to do.

As for those who have worked in and around the Boston media, you may have contributed even without knowing so. The archives of the *Boston Herald* and *Boston Globe* proved an invaluable resource to an assortment of events, furthering the belief that the best collection of professional sports teams in North America has the best collection of writers, reporters, and columnists. Thanks, specifically, to longtime *Boston Globe* columnists Dan Shaughnessy and Bob Ryan, as well as longtime sports editor Joe Sullivan; and thanks to all the *Boston Herald* writers and editors with whom I worked, especially longtime sports editor Hank Hryniewicz, who has the unique distinction of having been both a friend and colleague from the time I was a teenager.

I am beholden, too, to longtime colleagues Greg Bedard and Ian O'Connor, each of whom helped open doors that otherwise might have remained closed. In that way, the entire sports media world remains its own tight-knit community.

Finally, great thanks are due my wife and two sons for their eternal patience and understanding. Any project like this requires, above all else, time, which often comes at the expense of others. So thank you, Natalie, for picking up the kids and dropping off the dog, and for keeping our home both a well-oiled machine and a place where can escape—from everyone and everything, as well as, sometimes, from each other. And thank you, Alex and Xavier, for understanding when I'm not always available, whether for a performance or a simple game of "Horse."

And thank you, too, to the people of Boston, who are the number-one reason there is no better place to do what people in our business do.

Tony Massarotti
May 2022

INDEX

Abraham, Peter, 298–99
Adams, Ernie, 38, 120
Addai, Joseph, 115
Affleck, Ben, 74
African Americans, 126–27. *See also*
    racism
Aiken, Kamar, 245
Ainge, Danny, 8, 45, 125, 126, 128,
    134, 137, 182, 184, 263–66, 268,
    269, 270–71, 274, 348
Alford, Robert, 325
Allen, Ray, 126–33, 137, 179–83,
    263, 264
Allen, Ryan, 235
Alonso, Kiki, 323
Amendola, Danny, 234, 237, 238,
    245, 246, 247, 253, 256, 257,
    259, 322, 327, 331, 333–34
Andersen, Frederik, 287
Andrews, Shawn, 114
Anthony, Carmelo, 129
Arians, Bruce, 352, 353, 354
Arozarena, Randy, 355
Arrington, Kyle, 254, 257
Arroyo, Bronson, 56, 62, 66
Auerbach, Red, 126, 262

Backes, David, 293
Bailey, Andrew, 221
Baldwin, Doug, 255
Ballard, Keith, 162
Banks, Don, 37
Bartkowski, Matt, 193, 195

Beane, Billy, 47–49, 52, 83, 86, 89
Beckett, Josh, 91–92, 95, 97–99, 172,
    174–76, 205, 207, 219, 221
Belichick, Bill, 3, 16–17, 22–29,
    32–34, 37–44, 71, 90, 94–95,
    103–5, 117, 223–27, 230,
    234–36, 238, 261, 321–22, 351,
    356–57
    assistant coaches of, 106–7
    Brady, T., and, 18–20, 22, 35, 72,
        120–23, 211, 224, 239, 248, 321,
        322, 328–32, 335, 337, 340,
        349, 353
    Deflategate and, 248–51
    Garoppolo and, 239–59, 330–31,
        334
    Hernandez, A., and, 232–34
    Kraft, R., and, 17–18, 92–93
    The Mona Lisa Vito Press Conference
        by, 250–51
    Parcells and, 76–80, 107, 117
    Spygate and, 9, 106, 108–11, 332
Bellhorn, Mark, 65
Benedict, Jeff, 334, 335
Benintendi, Andrew, 314
Benoit, Joaquín, 210, 212–14
Bergeron, Patrice, 144, 149, 152, 155,
    157, 162, 166, 167, 194, 202, 282,
    284, 285, 291, 294, 295, 345
Berman, Richard, 252
Berube, Craig, 292
Betts, Mookie, 298, 300, 314, 318,
    319, 350

Bias, Len, 13, 14
Bickell, Bryan, 200
Biekert, Greg, 30
Bieksa, Kevin, 164
Bigbie, Larry, 86
Billups, Chauncey, 134
Bird, Larry, 13, 135, 265
Bjork, Anders, 283
Blakeman, Clete, 339
Bledsoe, Drew, 16, 18–19, 20, 25,
        34–37, 93, 240
Bloody Sock Game, 65
Bloom, Chaim, 319, 354–55
Blount, LeGarrette, 325
Bobrovsky, Sergei, 288, 289–90
Bogaerts, Xander, 298, 303, 310
Bolland, Dave, 199, 200
Bollig, Brandon, 199
Boone, Aaron, 52, 54, 310, 311
Boras, Scott, 84
Borges, Ron, 15
Boss, Kevin, 121
Boucher, Brian, 154
Bourque, Raymond, 141–42, 144, 195
Bowles, Todd, 353
Boychuk, Johnny, 161, 201
Brackett, Gary, 115
Bradley, Alexander, 232
Bradley, Avery, 267
Bradley, Jackie, 298, 313–14, 315
Bradley, Scott, 277
Bradshaw, Ahmad, 229, 230
Brady, Kyle, 104
Brady, Tom, 3, 25, 26, 27, 40, 71, 76,
        93, 104, 112, 115–16, 223, 231,
        237–38, 325, 327–28, 332–33,
        337–38, 339, 340
    Belichick and, 18–20, 22, 35, 72,
        120–23, 211, 224, 239, 248, 321,
        322, 328–32, 335, 337, 340,
        349, 353
    Bledsoe injury and, 18–19
    with Buccaneers, 342, 343, 346,
        351–54

Deflategate and, 248–52, 323
    drive and heroics of, 323–24
    Durant and, 266–67, 274
    first games of, 20–22
    Garoppolo and, 239–59, 340
    Gronkowski and, 335
    Guerrero, A., and, 330, 331, 333, 335
    injury of, 224, 331
    Kraft, R., and, 330, 334, 335, 340,
        353
    Manning, P., and, 112–16
    return from injury by, 226–27
    as sixth-round draft selection, 19,
        353
    in Snow Bowl, 29–34
    suspension of, 251–52
    voluntary diminished pay by, 170
Brady, Tom, Sr., 329–30
Branch, Alan, 327
Branch, Deion, 93–94, 226
Brees, Drew, 351
Bregman, Alex, 314, 315
Brenly, Mike, 298
Breslow, Craig, 216, 217
Brewer, Eric, 157, 158
Bridgewater, Teddy, 350
bridge years, 171, 303
Brissett, Jacoby, 324
Brown, Jaylen, 268, 269, 270, 271,
        346, 348
Brown, Kris, 36
Brown, P. J., 132
Brown, Troy, 30, 35, 36, 42–43, 94
Browner, Brandon, 253
Bruce, Isaac, 23, 39
Bruins, 3, 9, 138–69. *See also specific
        individuals and topics*
    COVID-19 and, 343–45
    Dark Ages of, 143–44
    Marathon bombings and, 188–89,
        192–202
    Perfection Line of, 282
    power play of, 281
    racial integration of, 297

Bruschi, Tedy, 16, 25, 34, 110–11, 114, 115, 122–23
Bryant, Kobe, 125, 126, 135, 136
Bryant, Matt, 326, 327
Buck, Joe, 81
Buckley, Terrell, 40
Buckner, Bill, 14
Bulger, Whitey, 9, 82–83
Bulpett, Steve, 273
Bündchen, Gisele, 230, 335
Burkhead, Rex, 338
Burress, Plaxico, 118, 123
Burrows, Alexandre, 161, 162, 164
Butker, Harrison, 338–39
Butler, Jimmy, 347
Butler, Malcolm, 257, 258–59, 332, 333
Byrnes, Josh, 86

Cabrera, Miguel, 210
Cabrera, Orlando, 59
Cairo, Miguel, 66
Caldwell, Reche, 94, 95
Calipari, John, 9
Callahan, Gerry, 242
Campbell, Gregory, 197, 201
Capers, Dom, 248
Carlo, Brandon, 283, 289
Carp, Mike, 211
Carpenter, Keion, 26
Carroll, Pete, 17, 254, 258–59
Carter, Jeff, 146
Carter, Tony, 235
Caserio, Nick, 224, 262
Cashman, Brian, 306
Cashner, Andrew, 317
Cassel, Matt, 224, 330
Cassidy, Bruce, 280, 282, 286, 288–90, 292, 294, 344–45
Celtics, 3, 4, 11, 13, 124–37. *See also specific individuals and topics*
COVID-19 and, 346–49
racial integration of, 297
September 11, 2001 and, 45

windows of, 179–84
Chancellor, Kam, 256
Chandler, Chris, 21
Chapman, Aroldis, 311
Chara, Zdeno, 144, 149, 151, 159, 167, 192, 200, 282, 293, 344
Cherington, Ben, 86, 91, 204, 207, 301, 303
Chiarelli, Peter, 145–46, 148–50, 167, 195–96, 276–79
Church, Barry, 331
Clark, Tony, 63, 66
Clayton, Mark, 116
Clemens, Roger, 13–14, 98
Clements, Nate, 26
Coates, Ben, 16
Colborne, Joe, 149
Coleman, Walt, 30, 31
Collie, Austin, 237
Collier, Sean, 187
Collins, Jamie, 257
Connolly, John, 82–83
Conwell, Ernie, 24
Cooks, Brandin, 329
Cooper, Chuck, 126
Cooper, Jon, 288
Cora, Alex, 308–19, 349, 354, 355
Coughlin, Tom, 117–19, 122, 223, 229, 331
COVID-19, 342, 343–50
Coyle, Charlie, 285, 290–91
Craig, Allen, 218
Crawford, Carl, 173, 205
Crawford, Corey, 199
Crennel, Romeo "RAC," 21, 107
Crisp, Coco, 304
Crockett, Zack, 30
Crosby, Sidney, 196, 197
Crowder, Jae, 265, 269
Cruz, José, Jr.., 86
Cundiff, Billy, 229
Curry, Stephen, 267
Curse of the Bambino, 2, 69, 89, 97
Cutler, Jay, 244

Dahl, Craig, 118
Dale, Norman, 81
Daluiso, Brad, 28
Damon, Johnny, 50, 64, 67
Damon, Matt, 74
Davis, Anthony, 274, 346
DeBrusk, Jake, 280, 282, 286-87
Decision, The, 182-83
Dee, Mike, 171-72
Deflategate, 9, 248-51, 323
De La Rosa, Rubby, 206
Dennis, John, 242
DesLauriers, Rick, 187
Dillon, Corey, 79, 104
Dombrowski, Dave, 298, 301-9, 311, 316-19
Donato, Ryan, 283, 285
Downie, Steve, 157-58, 164
Downs, Jeter, 319
Drake, Kenyan, 336
Drew, J. D., 95, 99
Drew, Stephen, 206, 219, 301
Dubon, Mauricio, 306
Duquette, Dan, 46-47, 204
Durant, Kevin, 266-67, 273-74, 346
Dynasty, The (Benedict), 334

Ebner, Nate, 321
Edelman, Julian, 19, 235, 237, 238, 246, 247, 253, 256-57, 259, 328, 341
Edes, Gordon, 53, 85, 86
Edler, Alex, 161
Education of a Coach, The (Halberstam), 37-38, 78
Ellsbury, Jacoby, 95, 97, 216
Embree, Alan, 51, 52, 54-55
Eovaldi, Nathan, 311, 313, 315, 316, 317, 318
Epstein, Theo, 9, 49-54, 58-60, 81, 83-92, 95-102, 106, 171, 172, 178, 204, 277, 303, 305, 333
Eriksson, Loui, 278
Estrella, Matt, 107-8

Evans, Dwight, 14
Evans, Heath, 115
Evans, Lee, 228-29

Farrell, John, 206, 208, 216, 218-20, 263, 304, 306-10
Faulk, Kevin, 23, 40, 114
Faulk, Marshall, 23, 37-41, 326
Favre, Brett, 37
Feaster, Jay, 195, 196
Feeding the Monster (Mnookin), 89, 91
Ference, Andrew, 153, 189, 201
Fitzpatrick, Ryan, 341
Flacco, Joe, 228-29, 245
Flowers, Lee, 35
Flowers, Trey, 338
Foles, Nick, 332
Folk, Nick, 227
Football Life, A, 77
Ford, Dee, 338
Forman, Stanley, 126
Forsett, Justin, 245
Foulke, Keith, 54, 66, 68
Fox, Chad, 51
Francona, Terry, 53, 63, 87, 96, 97, 101, 175-80, 204, 206, 304, 307, 309
Franson, Cody, 193
Fraser, Matt, 278
Frederic, Trent, 283
Freeman, Devonta, 325, 326-27
Fultz, Markelle, 269

Gaffney, Jabar, 116
Gagne, Eric, 124, 125
Gagne, Simon, 146, 147
Gammons, Peter, 97
Garciaparra, Nomar, 50, 53, 56-60, 73, 89
Garnett, Kevin, 124-35, 137, 179-83, 263, 264, 266
Garoppolo, Jimmy, 239-59, 323-24, 329-31, 334, 340

Gasol, Paul, 181
Gehrig, Lou "Iron Horse," 19
George, Paul, 346
Gesicki, Mike, 341
Giambi, Jeremy, 50
Gibson, Bob, 71
Gilmore, Stephon, 332
Givens, David, 94
Gladwell, Malcolm, 61
Glazer, Joel, 353
Gomes, Jonny, 190, 206, 208, 211, 214, 219, 221, 301
Gonzalez, Adrian, 173, 174, 205–6
Goodell, Roger, 9, 108–9, 249, 251–52
Gordon, David, 117, 270
Gordon, Tom, 64
Gostkowski, Stephen, 235, 236, 323, 326
Goucher, Dave, 194
Graham, Shayne, 26
Gray, Jim, 182
Green, Jarvis, 114, 121
Green, Jeff, 125–26, 183
Green, Pumpsie, 296
Green-Ellis, BenJarvus, 227
Gronkowski, Rob, 227, 228, 230, 231, 242, 245–48, 252–56, 259, 333, 336, 337, 339–41, 343
Brady, T., and, 335
with Buccaneers, 346, 351, 352
injuries of, 229, 234–36, 238, 324, 330, 331
Grousbeck, Wyc, 4, 11
Gruden, John, 28, 30–33
Guerrero, Alex, 330, 331, 333, 335
Guerrero, Vladimir, 60

Hackman, Gene, 81
Hakim, Az-Zahir, 23, 41
Halak, Jaroslav, 344
Halberstam, David, 37–38, 40, 43, 78
Hall, John, 28
Hamill, Dorothy, 140

Hamilton, Dougie, 202, 276–77, 280, 290
Hamm, Mia, 59
Hanifin, Noah, 280, 290
Hanrahan, Joel, 221
Hansen, Jannik, 161
Happ, J. A., 312
Harbaugh, John, 246, 247
Harden, James, 346
Harmon, Duron, 331, 333
Harrington, John, 46
Harris, Antwan, 36, 40
Harris, David, 227
Harrison, Marvin, 115
Harrison, Rodney, 81, 121–22
Hayhurst, Dirk, 209
Hayward, Gordon, 260, 268–72, 274, 346, 347, 348
Hedgecock, Madison, 123
Henderson, Dave, 14
Henneberry, David, 187
Henry, John, 46, 52, 59, 68, 85, 89, 92, 102, 142, 175, 177, 298, 302–3, 308, 309, 317–18
Hernandez, Aaron, 227, 228, 230–34, 237, 238
Hernandez, Orlando, 63
Hernandez, Roberto, 99
Hightower, Dont'a, 226, 230, 231, 258, 327
Hill, Greg, 281
Hill, Rich, 316
Hinch, A. J., 315, 319
Hobbs, Ellis, 122
Hochstein, Russ, 115
Hogan, Chris, 323, 333, 339
Hohler, Bob, 175
Holovak, Mike, 15
Holt, Brock, 313
Holt, Torry, 23, 40
"Home" (Phillips), 185
Hoomanawanui, Michael, 237, 246, 247
Hoosiers, 81

Horford, Al, 267–68, 269, 272, 274
Horton, Nathan, 152, 154, 157, 159,
    163, 166, 193
House, Eddie, 128, 136
Howard, Dwight, 180–81
Hoyer, Jed, 86, 91
Huizenga, Wayne, 302
Hunter, Torii, 213–14

Iginla, Jarome, 195–98, 201
Iglesias, José, 214
Ilgauskas, Zydrunas, 132
Impossible Dream, 70
Irving, Kyrie, 268–75, 307, 346, 348
Iverson, Allen, 125
Izzo, Larry, 30

Jackson, Austin, 217
Jackson, Chad, 94, 95
Jackson, D'Qwell, 236, 248
Jackson, Edward "Pookie," 190
Jackson, Phil, 136
Jackson, Reggie, 208
Jacobs, Brandon, 121, 123
Jacobs, Charlie, 279, 284, 295
Jacobs, Jeremy, 142, 168, 283, 284,
    295
Jagr, Jaromir, 194, 196
James, Edgerrin, 72
James, LeBron, 131–32, 180, 182–83,
    265, 269–73, 346–48
James, Stacey, 74–75
Jansen, Kenley, 315
Jastremski, John, 251, 252
Jefferson, Al, 124
Jeter, Derek, 4, 53, 54, 56, 61–62, 63
Johansson, Marcus, 285, 287,
    290–91
Johnson, Magic, 135
Johnson, Randy, 54
Johnson, Rob, 21
Johnson, Ted, 21, 24, 71, 77, 79–80,
    103
Jones, Adam, 9, 300

Jones, Chandler, 226, 230, 231
Jones, Mac, 356
Jones, Martin, 279
Jones, Tebucky, 41
Jordan, Michael, 3–4, 140
Joyce, Jim, 218
Judge, Aaron, 312
Julien, Claude, 144–45, 147, 151, 152,
    154, 155, 162, 167, 189, 193, 201,
    263, 278, 280, 281

Kaberle, Tomas, 148, 149, 150
Kadri, Nazem, 192, 193, 286–87
Kane, Patrick, 200, 278, 283
Karlsson, Jakob Forsbacka, 283
Kearse, Jermaine, 257–58
Keith, Duncan, 200
Kelce, Travis, 337
Kelly, Chris, 148, 149–50, 152, 158,
    199, 278
Kemp, Tony, 314
Kennedy, Sam, 86, 350
Kerrigan, Joe, 45, 46–47
Kesler, Ryan, 161
Kessel, Phil, 144, 145–46, 193, 202,
    276
Keteyian, Armen, 29
Khokhlachev, Alex, 195
Kiam, Victor, 16
Kim, Byung-Hyun, 51
Kimbrel, Craig, 304, 305, 313, 316
Kirby, Terry, 32
Kluber, Corey, 298
Knuckler (Wakefield), 1
Koch, Sam, 246
Kopech, Michael, 305
Kosar, Bernie, 22–23, 28
Kraft, Jonathan, 334
Kraft, Robert, 16, 20, 37, 43–44, 76,
    110, 223, 243
    Belichick and, 17–18, 92–93
    Brady, T., and, 330, 334, 335, 340,
        353
    Deflategate and, 251

Hernandez, A., and, 232
Parcells and, 22, 83
Krejci, David, 144, 146, 149, 153–55,
    157, 159, 167, 193, 194, 197, 284,
    285, 294, 345
Kremer, Andrea, 334
Krug, Torey, 287, 293
Kulemin, Nikolai, 146
Kuraly, Sean, 287

Lackey, John, 172–73, 175, 176, 207,
    215, 221, 301
LaFell, Brandon, 238, 253–54, 256,
    259
Lajoie, Bill, 49, 87, 91
Landsmark, Ted, 126
Lane, Jeremy, 253, 256
Lapierre, Maxim, 164
La Russa, Tony, 50
Lauzon, Jeremy, 283
Law, Ty, 16, 24, 27, 39
Lebowitz, Dan, 297
Leonard, Kawhi, 272, 346
Lester, Jon, 95, 97, 101, 175, 207,
    208, 218–21, 301, 303, 306
Lewis, Dave, 144
Lewis, Michael, 48
Lewis, Mo, 19, 20
Lewis, Ray, 231
Leyland, Jim, 210, 212, 214, 216
Lieber, Jon, 65
Little, Grady, 47, 51, 52, 58
Lloyd, Odin, 231–32
Loaiza, Esteban, 64
Lockette, Ricardo, 254, 257, 258
Lombardi, Vince, 276, 322
Long, Chris, 327
Long, Howie, 74, 102
Long, Terrence, 52
Longoria, Evan, 175
Lou Gehrig's disease, 19
Love, Kevin, 264
Lowe, Derek, 9, 51–52, 61–63, 67, 68
Lowell, Mike, 91, 101

Lowry, Kyle, 347
Lucchino, Larry, 9, 46, 48–49, 54,
    73, 75, 171, 172, 176, 177, 303
    Epstein and, 81, 83–87, 91–92, 106
    Marathon bombings and, 186,
        190–91
    Valentine and, 205
Lucchino, Stacy, 85–86
Lucic, Milan, 144, 145, 147, 152, 154,
    161, 162–63, 193, 194, 197, 278,
    279
Luck, Andrew, 244
Lugo, Julio, 95
Luhnow, Jeff, 319
Luongo, Roberto, 160, 164–65
Lynch, Marshawn, 253, 255, 257,
    258, 326
Lynn, Lance, 219

Madden, John, 42, 43
Madison, Sam, 118
Madonna, 249
Mahomes, Patrick, 336–40, 351
Malkin, Evgeni, 196, 197
Mallett, Ryan, 239
Manchester, Tom, 3
Maness, Seth, 219
Mangini, Eric, 94, 106, 107, 108, 109
Mankins, Logan, 241–42, 243
Manning, Eli, 118, 121–23, 229, 230
Manning, Peyton, 20, 72, 94–95,
    112–16, 235, 244, 321, 322
Manningham, Mario, 230
Marathon bombings, 3, 185–202,
    206–7, 220–21
Marchand, Brad, 144, 157, 163, 166,
    194, 282, 287, 289, 291, 294, 344
Mariota, Marcus, 331
Marleau, Patrick, 287
Marner, Mitch, 287
Maroney, Laurence, 114, 118, 121
Martin, Curtis, 16
Martinez, J. D., 310
Martinez, Pedro, 52, 62, 64, 67, 92, 99

Martinez, Victor, 216
Martz, Mike, 24, 25, 38, 40, 326
Matheny, Mike, 219
Matsui, Hideki, 62
Matsuzaka, Daisuke, 95
Matthews, Chris, 254–55
Matthews, Jake, 327
Mayfield, Baker, 335
Mayo, Jerod, 227, 237, 238
McAlister, Chris, 117
McAvoy, Charlie, 345
McCourty, Devin, 226, 242, 322, 324
McCourty, Jason, 324
McDaniels, Josh, 222–26, 234, 247, 261, 262, 336, 357
McDonough, Will, 17, 83
McGinest, Willie, 16, 36, 41, 72, 239
McHale, Kevin, 124
McKenna, Sarah, 191
McLaughlin, Tommy, 190
McNally, Jim, 251, 252
McQuaid, Adam, 146, 152, 155–56, 199
Menino, Tom, 1
Menounos, Maria, 74
Meriweather, Brandon, 116
Michel, Sony, 338, 340
Middlebrooks, Will, 218
Mientkiewicz, Doug, 59–60
Millar, Kevin, 50, 57, 62–64, 67, 84
Miller, Andrew, 301
Miller, Colin, 279
Milloy, Lawyer, 71, 72, 81, 90, 93, 226, 241, 242
Mills, Brad, 176
Mirabelli, Doug, 55
Mitchell, Brandon, 36
Mitchell, Kawika, 118
Mnookin, Seth, 89, 91
Modell, Art, 23
Molina, Yadier, 218
Mona Lisa Vito Press Conference, 250–51
Moncada, Yoán, 305

Moneyball (Michael Lewis), 48
Montana, Joe, 259
Moore, Matt, 208
Moreland, Mitch, 316
Moreno, Knowshon, 237
Morgan, Bill, 64
Morris, Jack, 14
Morris, Marcus, 270
Morris, Sammy, 104
Mortensen, Chris, 243, 250
Moss, Randy, 104–7, 110, 115, 118, 122, 125, 127, 227
Moulds, Eric, 26
Mueller, Bill, 50, 63
Mulligan, Matt, 237
Muncy, Max, 315
Murton, Matt, 59
My Cousin Vinny, 250
Myers, Gary, 110

Nantz, Jim, 339
Napoli, Mike, 206, 214, 215
Nava, Daniel, 210, 218
Neely, Cam, 142–43, 148–1150
Nelson, Jeff, 50
Newton, Cam, 350–51, 356
Nicklaus, Jack, 7
Nixon, Trot, 50, 56, 64, 67
Nordstrom, Joakim, 287
Núñez, Eduardo, 306

O'Brien, Dave, 214
O'Connell, Mike, 144
Oden, Greg, 266
O'Donnell, Joe, 46
O'Hara, Shaun, 118
Okajima, Hideki, 95–96
Olczyk, Eddie, 161
Olympic Games, 196
O'Neal, Shaquille, 181
One Fund Boston, 191
Ordoñez, Magglio, 53
O'Ree, Willie, 297
Orr, Bobby, 139–41

Orthwein, James, 16
Ortiz, David, 1–4, 50, 60–62, 64, 67,
    96, 98, 99, 208–14, 217, 219,
    298, 304–6, 313, 349, 354
Marathon bombings and, 191, 207
Osuna, Roberto, 314

Pagliuca, Steve, 127
Paille, Daniel, 199
Panarin, Artemi, 289
Paolantonio, Sal, 228
Papelbon, Jonathan, 96, 175
Parayko, Colton, 294
Parcells, Bill, 5, 15–16, 18
Belichick and, 76–80, 107, 117
Kraft, R., and, 22, 83
Parker, DeVante, 336
Parker, Jack, 138, 140–41
Pastrnak, David, 282, 289, 291
Patriots, 3, 5, 11–12. See also specific
    individuals and topics
in AFL, 7
COVID-19 and, 349–50
Deflategate, 9, 248–51, 323
drug problem in, 15
name change to, 28–29
September 11, 2001 and, 20–21
Spygate, 9, 106, 108–11, 224, 246,
    248–49, 332
Patten, David, 24, 26–27, 30, 31, 35,
    36, 39
Paxton, Lonie, 33
Payton, Sean, 353
Pearce, Steve, 311
Peavy, Jake, 207, 209, 215
Peck, Danielle, 99
Pederson, Barry, 142
Pedroia, Dustin, 95, 97, 100, 205,
    210, 212, 218, 219
Perfection Line, 282
Perkins, Kendrick, 182, 183
Perron, David, 293
Peverley, Rich, 148–50, 158, 278
Phillips, Phillip, 185

Picard, Noel, 140
Pierce, Paul, 125–32, 135–37, 179–
    83, 263, 264
Pietrangelo, Alex, 294
Pioli, Scott, 107, 179
Pipp, Wally, 19
Plekanec, Thomas, 152
Pomeranz, Drew, 304, 307, 308
Porcello, Rick, 214, 301, 304, 307
Posada, Jorge, 63
Posey, James, 128, 136
Powe, Leon, 136
Prater, Matt, 237
Presidents' Trophy, 145
Price, Carey, 151, 152, 305, 315, 316
Price, David, 4, 208–9, 298–300,
    304, 306–8, 312, 318–19
Primeau, Wayne, 144
Proehl, Ricky, 23, 40, 41

Quantrill, Paul, 63
Quenneville, Joel, 200

racism, 9, 126–27, 296–300
Ramirez, Hanley, 91, 301
Ramirez, Manny, 45, 46–47, 50, 53,
    63, 64, 89, 96, 99, 298
Rask, Tuukka, 146, 147, 193, 197,
    199–202, 287, 290, 291, 294,
    343, 345
Recchi, Mark, 147, 151, 161, 163
Reddick, Josh, 314
Redmond, J. R., 32, 42
Red Sox, 1–4. See also specific
    individuals and topics
bridge years of, 171, 303
COVID-19 and, 349–50
Marathon bombings and, 186, 189–
    90, 206–7, 220–21
racial integration of, 296–98
September 11, 2001 and, 20
windows of, 170–78
Winter Carnival of, 299
Reed, Addison, 306

Reid, Andy, 337, 338–39
Reimer, James, 192–93, 194
Reimold, Nolan, 175
Reiss, Mike, 333, 343
Renfroe, Hunter, 355
Renteria, Edgar, 67–68
Revere, Paul, 3, 319
Revis, Darrelle, 238, 245, 255
Rice, Jim, 97
Richard, Martin, 185
Richards, Mike, 146
Rielly, Morgan, 287
Ripken, Cal, 4
Rivera, Mariano, 50, 61, 63, 64
Rivers, Doc, 125, 127–30, 132, 133,
    137, 179–83, 263, 264, 296
Rizzo, Anthony, 173
Roberts, Dave, 57, 60, 63, 316
Robinson, Demarcus, 338
Robinson, Jackie, 296
Rodgers, Aaron, 244, 351
Rodriguez, Alex, 53–56, 59, 61, 66,
    73, 89
Rodriguez, Eduardo, 301, 350
Roenicke, Ron, 349
Roloson, Dwayne, 159
Rome, Aaron, 163, 166
Romine, Austin, 313
Rondo, Rajon, 264
Ross, David, 221
Roy, Logan, 89
Rozier, Terry, 265, 270, 271, 274–75
Rozsival, Michal, 198–99
Russell, Bill, 126, 127, 297
Russo, Rene, 74
Ruth, Babe, 19, 58
    Curse of the Bambino and, 2, 69,
    89, 97
Ryan, Bob, 6, 7, 33, 128
Ryan, Logan, 255, 326, 328, 342
Ryan, Matt, 326–27
Ryan, Rex, 115, 116, 227, 228
Ryder, Michael, 147, 151

Saban, Nick, 356
Sabathia, CC, 172, 300
Sabol, Steve, 31
Sale, Chris, 300, 305–7, 312, 316–18,
    350
Saltalamacchia, Jarrod, 190, 211,
    214, 218
Samuel, Asante, 121
Samuelson, Ulf, 143
Sanchez, Anibal, 91, 210, 215, 216
Sanchez, Mark, 227
Sanderson, Derek, 140
Sandoval, Pablo, 301
Santayana, George, 296
Sanu, Mohamed, 327, 341, 342
Savard, Marc, 144
Schaefer Stadium, 29
Schefter, Adam, 329
Schenn, Brayden, 293
Scherzer, Max, 210–11, 215, 216
Schilling, Curt, 53, 54, 56, 61–66, 92,
    97–99, 203
Schiraldi, Calvin, 14
Scioscia, Mike, 60
Scott, Bart, 116, 228
Scott, Chad, 35
Seabrook, Brent, 200
Seau, Junior, 114
Second Wind (Russell), 127
Sedin, Daniel, 161–62
Seguin, Tyler, 149, 155, 157, 162, 195,
    199, 202, 276–78, 280
Seidenberg, Dennis, 146, 151, 153,
    159
Selig, Bud, 46, 85
Senyshyn, Zach, 280
September 11, 2001, 20–21, 26, 45
Severino, Luis, 313
Seymour, Richard, 226, 228
Shanahan, Kyle, 325, 328
Shaughnessy, Dan, 81, 85–86, 87,
    228
Shaw, Travis, 306
Sherman, Richard, 255

Shot Heard 'Round the World, 11, 29, 43

Simms, Phil, 31

Simon, Tharold, 253–54, 256

Simpson, O. J., 233

Sinden, Harry, 139, 142

Skwar, Don, 73

Slater, Matthew, 236, 339

Smart, Marcus, 265, 271, 348

Smith, Antowain, 23, 27

Smith, Carson, 304, 307–8

Smith, Kayce, 334

Smith, Otis, 26, 27, 40

Smith, Reilly, 278

Smith, Steve, 122

Smyly, Drew, 212, 216

Snell, Blake, 349

Snow Bowl, 29–34

Solder, Nate, 228

Spears, Marc, 127

Spygate, 9, 106, 108–11, 224, 246, 248–49, 332

Stafford, Matthew, 244, 350, 353

Stallworth, Donté, 104, 114

Stanley, Bob, 14, 142

Stanton, Mike, 50

Starr, Bart, 276

Steinberg, Charles, 66, 75, 190

Steinbrenner, George, 54–55, 84

Stevens, Brad, 260–70, 347, 348

Stewart, Kordell, 36

Stidham, Jarrett, 356

Stills, Kenny, 336

Strahan, Michael, 122

Stuart, Mark, 149

Sturtze, Tanyon, 56

Subban, P. K., 152

Succession, 89

Sullivan, Joe, 70, 73, 74, 75

Sveum, Dale, 204

Swayman, Jeremy, 345

Sweeney, Don, 278–80, 282, 284, 285, 287, 288, 291, 345

Tagliabue, Paul, 43–44

Talib, Aqib, 237, 238

Tamme, Jacob, 237

Tannehill, Ryan, 336

Tannenbaum, Mike, 108

Tatum, Jayson, 262, 269, 270, 271, 346, 348

Tazawa, Junichi, 217

Tebow, Tim, 228

Teixeira, Mark, 172

Tellem, Arn, 59

Testaverde, Vinny, 22–23, 28

Theis, Daniel, 347

Theodore, George, 64

Thomas, Adalius, 104, 109

Thomas, Demaryius, 235

Thomas, Earl, 254, 324

Thomas, Isaiah, 265, 274

Thomas, Robert, 293

Thomas, Tim, 146, 151–52, 154, 157–58, 160–67, 199–200

Thompson, Klay, 267

Thornburg, Tyler, 305, 308

Thornton, Joe, 144, 145, 149, 162–63, 167

Timlin, Mike, 52

Toews, Jonathan, 200

Tomato Can Game, 228, 230, 331

Tomei, Marisa, 250

Torre, Joe, 64

Torres, Raffi, 161

Tortorella, John, 288

Tsarnaev, Dzhokhar, 185–89

Tsarnaev, Tamerlan, 185–89

tuck rule, 31, 33

Turbin, Robert, 254

Tyree, David, 121–22

ubuntu, 128

Udoka, Ime, 348

Uehara, Koji, 209, 214, 216–21

Vakannainen, Urho, 283

Valentin, John, 170

Valentine, Bobby, 203, 204, 205
Varitek, Jason, 50, 56, 64, 65, 68, 97
Vaughn, Mo, 297–98
Vazquez, Christian, 355
Vazquez, Javier, 67
Veras, José, 212, 216–17
Verducci, Tom, 209
Verdugo, Alex, 319
Vereen, Shane, 246, 247, 256
Verlander, Justin, 210, 215, 216
Victorino, Shane, 210, 212, 216–17, 221
Vinatieri, Adam, 11–12, 16, 23, 26, 27, 36, 40, 42, 72, 226
Shot Heard 'Round the World by, 11, 29, 43
in Snow Bowl, 31–32, 33
Vladar, Danny, 344
Vrabel, Mike, 39, 341
Vujacic, Sasha, 136

Wacha, Michael, 218
Wade, Dwyane, 183
Wagner, Chris, 291
Wakefield, Tim, 1, 52, 62, 68
Walker, Antoine, 126
Walker, Kemba, 275, 346, 347, 348
Walker, Todd, 50
Wallace, Rasheed, 180
Walsh, Bill, 178
Walsh, Marty, 3
Walsh, Matt, 120, 252
Walter, Ken, 31
Ward, Charvarius, 338
Ward, Joel, 9, 40
Ward, T. J., 236
Ware, Spencer, 338
Warner, Kurt, 23, 24, 37, 39–41
Washburn, Jarrod, 60–61
Watkins, Sammy, 337, 338
Watson, Ben, 94, 116
Wayne, Reggie, 115
Weems, Eric, 328
Weis, Charlie, 36

Welker, Wes, 104, 115–16, 228–30, 234, 236–38
Wells, Ted, 251
Wentz, Carson, 350
Werner, Tom, 46, 68, 85
Wesley, Glen, 142
Westbrook, Russell, 346
Wheeler, Blake, 149
White, James, 327, 328, 341
Wiggins, Jermaine, 27, 30, 43
Wilfork, Vince, 237, 238
Wilkins, Jeff, 41
Williams, Bernie, 66
Williams, Damien, 338
Williams, Edgar Bennett, 85
Williams, Gregg, 27
Williams, Jimy, 45, 47
Williams, Ted, 71
Williamson, Scott, 51, 52
Wilson, Mookie, 14
Wilson, Russell, 230, 253–55, 257, 258, 259
Wilson, Tavon, 230
Winborne, Jermaine, 116
windows, 170–84
Wingels, Tommy, 286
Winter Carnival, 299
Wong, Connor, 319
Woodson, Charles, 30–31
Workman, Brandon, 218
Wormer, Dean, 175
Wright, K. J., 254
Wright, Tim, 241

Yastrzemski, Carl, 70
Yawkey, Jean, 46
Yawkey, Thomas A., 46, 126, 296, 298
Yeo, Mike, 292
Youkilis, Kevin, 205
Young, James, 265

Zboril, Jakub, 280